"Rarely has a book dealt with the psychodynamics and analytic treatment of psychotic patients with the breadth and scholarship of this comprehensive volume. I enthusiastically recommend this wonderful book."

– Lawrence J. Brown, IPA Psychoanalyst, Boston, USA;
author of *Transformational Processes in Clinical Psychoanalysis: Dreaming, Emotions, and the Present Moment* (Routledge, 2019)

"The psychoanalytic research on unrepresented (psycho-somatic, autistic or autistoid etc) and psychotic states has an increasingly and important impact of the current psychoanalysis. Reading this book is a touching experience, discovering how psychotic patients can be open to psychoanalysis, so that holding and containing processes can occur."

– Bernd Nissen, IPA Training and Supervising Analyst,
Berlin, Germany; editor of *Jahrbuch der Psychoanalyse*

Psychoanalysis of the Psychoses

Psychoanalysis of the Psychoses brings together a distinguished international set of contributors, offering a range of views and approaches, to explore the latest thinking in the psychoanalytic treatment of psychosis and related disorders.

Drawing on findings from neuroscience, theory and clinical material from many schools of psychoanalytic thought, this book offers a comprehensive guide to understanding how psychosis is conceptualised from a psychoanalytic perspective. It looks at how to work with psychotic patients, typical problems in treating psychosis and the role of pharmacology. It demonstrates the relational dimension, capable of strengthening the patient's observing Ego and facilitating the integration of the different areas of the personality. This process can identify and work through the main psychological stress factors involved in psychotic disturbances, transforming chaotic thoughts into springboards for important insights, and offering patients the precious chance to construct for the first time a creative relationship with their own existence.

Psychoanalysis of the Psychoses will be of great interest to psychoanalysts and psychoanalytic psychotherapists as well as psychiatrists wishing to draw upon psychoanalytic ideas in their work.

Riccardo Lombardi, MD, is a Psychoanalyst and Psychiatrist. He maintains a full-time private practice in Rome, Italy, and teaches at the Roman Psychoanalytic Institute of the International Psychoanalytic Association (IPA). He is also a Training and Supervising Analyst of the Italian Psychoanalytic Society.

Luigi Rinaldi is a Psychiatrist and Training Analyst, and Member of the Italian Psychoanalytic Society and IPA. He has been Head Psychiatrist and has taught in the University schools of specialization in Psychiatry and Clinical Psychology in Naples, Italy.

Sarantis Thanopulos is a Psychiatrist and Supervising and Training Analyst of the Italian Psychoanalytic Society and IPA, based in Naples, Italy.

Psychoanalytic Ideas and Applications Series

Recent titles in the Series include

The Analytical Process: Journeys and Pathways
Thierry Bokanowski

Psychotic Organisation of the Personality: Psychoanalytic Keys
Antonio Perez-Sanchez

**Psychoanalytic Perspectives on Virtual Intimacy and
Communication in Film**
Edited by Andrea Sabbadini, Ilany Kogan and Paola Golinelli

**Transformational Processes in Clinical Psychoanalysis:
Dreaming, Emotions and the Present Moment**
Lawrence J. Brown

**The Psychoanalyst and the Child: From the Consultation to
Psychoanalytic Treatment**
Michel Ody

**Psychoanalytic Studies on Dysphoria: The False Accord in the
Divine Symphony**
Marion M. Oliner

**Contemporary Perspectives on the Freudian Death Drive:
In Theory, Clinical Practice and Culture**
Edited by Victor Blüml, Liana Giorgi and Daru Huppert

**Psychoanalysis of the Psychoses: Current Developments in
Theory and Practice**
`dited by Riccardo Lombardi, Luigi Rinaldi and Sarantis Thanopulos

`ι full list of titles in this series, please visit www.routledge.com

Psychoanalysis of the Psychoses

Current Developments in
Theory and Practice

Edited by Riccardo Lombardi,
Luigi Rinaldi and
Sarantis Thanopulos

Routledge
Taylor & Francis Group

LONDON AND NEW YORK

First published 2019
by Routledge
2 Park Square, Milton Park, Abingdon, Oxon, OX14 4RN

and by Routledge
52 Vanderbilt Avenue, New York, NY 10017

Routledge is an imprint of the Taylor & Francis Group, an informa business

This book is a translation of a work previously published in Italian as
Psicoanalisi delle psicosi by Raffaello Cortina Editore, 2016.

British Library Cataloguing-in-Publication Data
A catalogue record for this book is available from the British Library

Library of Congress Cataloging-in-Publication Data
Names: Lombardi, Riccardo (Psychoanalyst) editor. | Rinaldi, Luigi
    (Psychiatrist) editor. | Thanopulos, Sarantis, editor.
Title: Psychoanalysis of the psychoses : current developments in
    theory and practice / edited by Riccardo Lombardi, Luigi Rinaldi and
    Sarantis Thanopulos.
Description: New York : Routledge, 2019. | Series: The international
    psychoanalytical association ideas and applications book series |
    Includes bibliographical references and index.
Identifiers: LCCN 2018059786 (print) | LCCN 2019008437 (ebook) |
    ISBN 9780429028748 (Master) | ISBN 9780429650147 (Adobe) |
    ISBN 9780429644863 (Mobipocket) | ISBN 9780429647505 (ePub3) |
    ISBN 9780367136833 (hardback : alk. paper) | ISBN 9780367138240
    (pbk. : alk. paper) | ISBN 9780429028748 (ebk)
Subjects: LCSH: Psychoanalysis. | Psychoses.
Classification: LCC RC504 (ebook) | LCC RC504 .P7593 2019 (print) |
    DDC 616.89/17—dc23
LC record available at https://lccn.loc.gov/2018059786

ISBN: 978-0-367-13683-3 (hbk)
ISBN: 978-0-367-13824-0 (pbk)
ISBN: 978-0-429-02874-8 (ebk)

Typeset in Palatino
by Apex CoVantage, LLC

Contents

Contributors

Editors

Riccardo Lombardi is a Training and Supervising Analyst of the Italian Psychoanalytic Society and an IPA Full Member. His books include *Formless Infinity. Clinical Explorations of Matte Blanco and Bion* (Routledge, 2015) and *Body-Mind Dissociation in Psychoanalysis: Development after Bion* (Routledge, 2017).

Luigi Rinaldi is a Training and Supervising Analyst of the Italian Psychoanalytic Society and an IPA Full Member. He co-authored the book *Le Figure del vuoto* [Figures of the Void] (Rome, 2012) and edited *Stati caotici della mente* [Chaotic States of Mind] (Milan, 2003).

Sarantis Thanopulos is a Training and Supervising Analyst of the Italian Psychoanalytic Society and an IPA Full Member. His books include *Lo spazio dell'interpretazione* [A Place for Interpretation] (Rome, 2009) and, with Olga Pozzi, as co-editor, *Ipotesi Gay* [The Gay Theory], a collection of essays by various writers about homosexuality and psychoanalysis (Rome, 2006).

Authors

Mark J. Blechner is a Training and Supervising Analyst at the William Alanson White Institute, New York, and an IPA Full Member. He is a former Editor of *Contemporary Psychoanalysis*, and his books include *The Dream Frontier* (The Analytic Press, 2001), *Sex Changes: Transformations in Society and Psychoanalysis* (Routledge, 2009), and *The MindBrain and Dreams: An Exploration of Dreaming, Thinking and Artistic Creation* (Routledge, 2018).

Stefano Calamandrei is a Member of the Italian Psychoanalytic Society. He is a Consultant in the psychoanalytic treatment of adolescent psychosis and the Institutional Supervisor of Psychiatric Services in Florence, Italy. He has published many papers on psychosis and primitive mental states.

Giuseppe Civitarese is a Training and Supervising Analyst of the Italian Psychoanalytic Society and a former Editor of *Rivista Italiana di Psicoanalisi*. His many books include *The Necessary Dream: New Theories and Techniques of Interpretation in Psychoanalysis* (Karnac, 2014) and *Truth and the Unconscious in Psychoanalysis* (Routledge, 2016).

Franco De Masi is a Training and Supervising Analyst of the Italian Psychoanalytic Society and an IPA Full Member. His many books include *Making Death Thinkable* (Karnac, 2004) and *Vulnerability to Psychosis: A Psychoanalytic Study of the Nature and Therapy of the Psychotic State* (Karnac, 2009).

Didier Houzel is a Member in Full Standing of the Association Psychanalytique de France and Professor of Child and Adolescent Psychiatry at the University of Caen, France. He has published many books on the psychoanalysis of children and on the psychoanalytic treatment of autism spectrum disorders in childhood. He won the Frances Tustin Memorial Prize in 2002.

John Kafka is a Training and Supervising Analyst at the Washington Psychoanalytic Institute and an Emeritus Professor of Psychiatry at The George Washington University. One of his many papers and books on psychosis and schizophrenia is *Multiple Realities in Clinical Practice* (Yale University Press, 1989).

Giuseppe Martini, a psychiatrist and psychoanalyst, is a Member of the Italian Psychoanalytic Society and the International Psychoanalytic Association. He is the Head of Psychiatry for the Italian National Health Service of the 17th District of Rome. Among his books are *Ermeneutica e Narrazione* [Hermeneutics and Narration] (Turin, 1998) and *La psicosi e la rappresentazione* [Psychosis and Representation] (Rome, 2011).

Michael Robbins is a Member of the Boston Psychoanalytic Society and the International Psychoanalytic Association. He was Professor of Clinical Psychiatry at Harvard University's Medical School in Boston and at the University of California, San Francisco (UCSF). He is the author of *Experiences of Schizophrenia* (Guilford Press, 1993), *The Primordial Mind in Health and Illness* (Routledge, 2013), and *Consciousness, Language and the Self* (Routledge, 2018).

Ira Steinman is a Psychiatrist and Psychoanalyst in San Francisco. He studied with Ronald Laing in London. He is a Member of the International Society for Psychological and Social Approaches to Psychosis. He is the author of *Treating the Untreatable* (Karnac, 2009) and, with David Garfield, the co-author of *Self Psychology and Psychosis* (Karnac, 2015).

Paul Williams is a Member in Full Standing of the British Psychoanalytic Society and a former Editor-in-Chief of the *International Journal of Psychoanalysis* (2001–2007). He is the author of many books on psychosis, including *A Language for Psychosis* (Whurr, 2001) and *Invasive Objects* (Routledge, 2010).

Series editor's foreword

The Publications Committee of the International Psychoanalytic Association continues, with the present volume, the series "Psychoanalytic Ideas and Applications".

The aim of this series is to focus on the work of significant authors whose works are outstanding contributions to the development of the psychoanalytic field. In doing so, this series will bring forward relevant ideas and themes, generated during the history of psychoanalysis, that deserve to be known and discussed by present day psychoanalysts.

The relationship between psychoanalytic ideas and their applications needs to be put forward from the perspective of theory, clinical practice and research in order to maintain their validity for contemporary psychoanalysis. The Publications Committee's objective is to share these ideas with the psychoanalytic community and with professionals in other related disciplines, so as to expand their knowledge and generate a productive interchange between the text and the reader.

The present volume, *Psychoanalysis of the Psychoses: Current Developments in Theory and Practice*, contributes substantially to the Publications Committee's goal, that is, to bring forward and discuss in depth a central theme in psychoanalysis, in this case, the psychoanalytic theory and the clinical approach to psychosis and its development up to today. The authors reinvigorate the exploration of the most severe forms of psychic affliction, the study of which can shed light on the deepest, most complex and most significant levels of mental functioning. This study can also shed light on psychic functioning in less severe ailments. This volume addresses as well the need to encourage psychoanalytic training institutes to promote the psychoanalytic treatment of psychosis.

The contributors from different IPA regions who participated in this volume share an interest and commitment to the practice and the study of the psychoanalytic psychotherapy of psychosis. They all underscore the important role of psychoanalysis for the understanding and treatment of psychosis.

The reader will find a remarkably rich array of topics related to psychosis, for example, psychosis in children, the question of body and mind dissociation, discussion of the long-term treatment of a schizophrenic patient as well as theoretical questions such as those related to psychotic thinking and regression. Skillfully organised in four parts, the volume first addresses general perspectives on the psychoanalytic experience with psychosis. The second part focuses on communication and empathy with the psychotic analysand. The third part studies the question of particularities of thought. The final part is about the flexible integration between psychoanalysis and pharmacology.

I have no doubt that this book is a great contribution. The authors' thorough overview of the current psychoanalytic understanding of the topic of psychosis has resulted in significant contributions from major psychoanalytic traditions. In this manner, the authors have succeeded in reawakening the theoretical and clinical interest in psychosis. I am confident that this book will be useful and of much interest not only to the psychoanalytic reader worldwide, but to anyone interested in the significant subject of psychosis. It will certainly be an important reference point for future debates and conceptual developments on the subject.

Gabriela Legorreta
Series Editor
Chair, IPA Publications Committee

Permission acknowledgements

Chapter 2 was previously published as John Kafka (2011), J Am Psychoanal Assoc. Feb; 59(1): 27–47. Reprinted with the permission of Sage Publications, Inc.

Chapter 6 is reprinted in a shortened and modified version from Robbins, M. (2012), *The successful psychoanalytic therapy of a schizophrenic woman*, Psychodynamic Psychiatry. 40: 575–608, by permission of Guilford Publications, Inc. This version of the chapter first appeared in Robbins, M. (2018) *Psychoanalysis Meets Psychosis: Attachment, Separation, and the Undifferentiated Unintegrated Mind*. Abingdon and New York: Routledge.

Introduction to the psychoanalysis of psychoses

Current developments in theory and practice

Riccardo Lombardi, Luigi Rinaldi and Sarantis Thanopulos

Elyn Saks begins her account of her personal journey through madness with the following story. Her book *The Center Cannot Hold* was a major bestseller in the United States and was chosen as one of the ten best books of the year by *Time* magazine in 2007:

> I am seven, or eight, standing in the cluttered living room of our comfortable house, looking out at a sunny day.
>
> "Dad can we go out to the cabana for a swim?"
>
> He snaps at me, "I told you, I have work to do, Elyn, and anyway it might rain. How many times do I have to tell you the same thing? Don't you ever listen?"
>
> My heart sinks at the tone of his voice: I've disappointed him.
>
> And then something odd happens. My awareness (of myself, of him, of the room, of the physical reality around and beyond us) instantly grows fuzzy. Or wobbly. I think I am dissolving. I feel – my mind feels – like a sand castle with all the sand sliding away in the receding surf. What's happening to me? This is scary, please let it be over! I think maybe if I stand very still and quiet, it will stop.
>
> This experience is much harder, and weirder, to describe than extreme fear of terror. [. . .] Consciousness gradually loses its coherence. One's center gives way. The center cannot hold. The 'me' becomes a haze, and the solid center from which one experiences reality breaks up like a bad radio signal. [. . .] Sight, sounds, thoughts, and feelings don't go together.
>
> (Saks, 2007, pp. 12–13)

For the late Oliver Sacks – the English neurologist known also for his writings, including the celebrated *Awakenings*, from which a successful and highly praised film was made – Saks' book is "the most lucid and hopeful autobiography about living with schizophrenia" that he had ever read, and he said he knew of no better corrective than *The Center Cannot Hold* to the notion that *schizophrenia* is an "ominous word", something that "we too often equate . . . with a life of misery, isolation, and psychotic torment" (Saks, 2007, backcover of the book).

The widespread appeal of Saks' book gives us an idea of the growing interest in the singular features that human experience can assume in the context of mental disorders, including the most upsetting and extreme ones. The transformation of what is generally considered simply an illness into an enriching form of human experience is catalyzed to a great extent by the light that the psychoanalytic process can throw on these areas, by making use of the participation and investigation that take place within the analytic relationship. Thus schizophrenia – and psychosis in general – can be restored to the dimension of experience, i.e., to something that can be recounted with all the richness of detail characteristic of the most meaningful experiences of one's life.

This book of ours about psychoses is based on the proposition that the sphere of psychotic experience potentially includes a wealth of what is for the most part as yet unexplored knowledge, whose exploration can be of use to anyone interested in the human condition, and particularly those whose work has to do with mental health. We are, in fact, convinced that psychoanalysis can benefit enormously from the exploration of psychoses as the basis for a renewal that further evolution requires. Unfortunately, there is ever more talk of a decline in psychoanalysis, to be imputed to the delay with which scientific updating tends to take place in our branch of science. "Although psychoanalysis began in a spirit of open-ended inquiry, with an orientation above all to be helpful to the patient, it took on a self-perpetuating guild mentality that, unhappily, has increasingly gotten away from the original scientific enterprise": thus Owen Renik – the former Editor in Chief of the august American journal of psychoanalysis *The Psychoanalytic Quarterly* and the author of the highly successful book *Practical Psychoanalysis for Therapists and Patients* (2006b) – publicly criticized our discipline in an interview in *The New York Times* (October 10, 2006a). While it would be hard to argue with Renik's knowing insider's disillusioned criticism, it does follow that there is an urgent need to bring our scientific discipline back to its clinical origins, reintroducing the exploration of the most extreme forms in which mental illness appears, i.e., those in which the deepest, most significant and most propulsive levels of mental functioning are involved.

One thing that the renewal of psychoanalysis requires is to get past the unitary mind-set that has, in the past, led to regarding psychological and pharmacological interventions as mutually exclusive choices in the treatment of serious pathologies. This false opposition has been, in some cases, dramatic, as, for example, when not assigning pharmacological therapy to a psychotic patient became the basis of a legal suit that led to the end of the historic experiment of Chestnut Lodge. John Kafka's essay in this volume bears witness to the importance of that experiment. The difficulty of translating the pharmacological containment of psychotic anxiety into plausible neurochemical hypotheses about the etiopathogenesis of schizophrenia (whose complex origins, involving biological, environmental and psychological factors, are the object of ongoing research) in no way undermines the necessary integration of psychoanalysis with pharmacotherapy. Giuseppe Martini's contribution here focuses on this very subject.

But how are we to say where the borders between the province of pharmacological treatment and that of psychoanalytic therapy are to be drawn? Once again our incisive guide in this territory is Elyn Saks, who for thirty years has benefitted from pharmacological treatment as well as psychoanalysis for her serious psychosis. As an invited participant in a debate held by the *Journal of the American Psychoanalytic Association* on the psychoanalytic treatment of psychosis, Saks acknowledged among the merits of analysis the ability to identify stress factors and also how to deal with them, helping to reinforce an observant ego, working through the narcissistic wound of suffering from a mental illness, as a result of which one needs both psychoanalysis and pharmacological treatment, the ability to offer a safe haven where one can bring one's chaotic thoughts, offering interpretations that can be the source of insight, together with the help of a kind and supportive person who is non-judgmental and can accept another human being not only with her/his good aspects, but also with the ugly and bad ones (see Saks and Evans, 2011).

These well-defined observations by Saks, which do not restrict the role of analysis to the activation of important insights or to mere relational support, seem in line with the recent tendency to regard the therapeutic effect of psychoanalysis as a complex phenomenon to which a plurality of factors contributes (Gabbard and Westen, 2003), and this is particularly true in notably complex situations such as the psychoses. All of this makes it seem quite unrealistic to maintain that the use of psychoactive drugs could invalidate or diminish the value of psychoanalysis for these conditions. The problem is instead how to encourage psychoanalysts to consider the possibility of treating the psychoses, since there do not appear to be any signs – apart from sporadic or inconsistent ones – of actual interest or encouragement from psychoanalytic societies or training institutes in promoting the treatment of psychoses.

It should, however, be noted that there are various psychoanalytic enterprises with a particular interest in psychosis, such as the Association for Psychoanalytic Psychotherapy (APP) in the National Health Service of the United Kingdom, and the Centre Evelyne et Jean Kestemberg in the 13th *arrondissement* of Paris – promoted by such distinguished analysts as Liliane Abensour and Alain Gibeault, whose journal *Psychanalyse et Psychose* contributes significantly to the debate about psychoanalysis and psychosis. In Scandinavia there is considerable interest in a treatment of psychosis based on a psychoanalytic orientation – thanks, particularly, to the driving force of enterprises like the Turku Schizophrenia Project in Finland and of such people as Yrjö Alanen, one of its founders. The late Murray Jackson did supervision in Scandinavia for many years, and published a collection of an interesting series of clinical cases treated with an average of two sessions weekly for five years, which was deemed sufficient for the positive evolution of very dramatic cases of psychosis. His experience is recorded in the still topical and instructive volume *Weathering the Storms: Psychotherapy for Psychosis* (Jackson, 2001).

An important international association that organically and systematically considers the psychoanalytic treatment of psychoses is the International Society for the Psychological Treatment of Schizophrenia and Other Psychoses – now called International Society for Psychological and Social Approaches to Psychosis – of which our colleague Ira Steinman of San Francisco is a member. Steinman's contribution to our collection is an interesting essay that demonstrates how an analyst can effectually manage a psychotic situation both analytically and pharmacologically, thus countering the widespread tendency to offer a psychotic patient an analyst working in tandem with a pharmacologist and if possible integrated by a third figure who works as a consultant for the family. San Francisco is also the location of the Center for the Advanced Study of the Psychoses, co-founded and for years directed by the late L. Bryce Boyer and Thomas Ogden, who have both written numerous distinguished articles and books, many of which have been translated into a variety of languages.

The question of how to structure the psychoanalytic and pharmacological setting(s) essential to the treatment of psychoses is only one of the controversial features of this kind of treatment. And the existence of various controversial points is a sign of the complexity of the field with which we are concerned. Among the elements about which there is general agreement we would list: the importance of a stable work environment; keeping the work anchored to the here and now as much as possible; a greater active presence of the analyst, so as to increase the possibility of managing the hostile communications that endanger both the treatment and the patient's implied safety in perilous situations in the course of treatment. Among the contended points we note a different way of conceiving the support setting, the corrective emotional experience and the role and manner of offering interpretation (Waldinger and Gunderson, 1987). These differences will also be manifest to the reader in the following essays, which have been chosen with a belief in the advantages of a perspective that fosters the greatest possible conceptual openness as regards differences of approach in psychoanalytic intervention in psychoses.

It is also part of our orientation here to understand the term *psychosis* in an inclusive way that – starting with the Freudian concept that posits a primary conflict with reality in psychosis (Freud, 1924a, 1924b) – comprises the more severe forms, such as schizophrenia and schizophreniform disorders, but also acute psychoses, including those that are limited in duration, as well as those in which the psychotic part of the personality (Bion, 1957) clearly takes the upper hand, as is the case of personality disorders. Paul Williams, in his detailed essay, offers us an important example of the difficulty involved in treating these psychotic forms.

In analytic work we must take account of the complexity of the psychotic patient, who cannot be fitted into well-defined explanatory models. There co-exist in him, together with the straightforwardly psychotic parts (characterized by extremely primitive defenses, first of all ego-fragmentation), experiential areas that are distinctly regressive or involve the negation of wishes (with a tendency to have an anorexic orientation towards life) and relatively healthy parts. The analyst must then collaborate with the healthy parts in order to foster a psychic rearrangement that will permit the two of them to continue with their work and allow the patient to have some stability in her affective attachments. The risk one runs is that one may erroneously take for a healthy part of the personality what is in fact the result of a purely cognitive adaptation to reality.

It should be noted that, in psychoanalytic theory, there is a general tendency – whatever the idiosyncratic formulations of individual authors – towards considering psychosis a "black hole" in the affective and mental representation of one's body and of one's relationship with reality (Freud, Winnicott, Bion, Lacan, Aulagnier, Tustin, Grotstein, Ferrari). Empowering the patient to expand his subjective experience, which had been distorted by his incapacity to give personal sense to his own life, is the main aim of therapy.

The thinking defect that is characteristic of psychosis so extensively damages the barrier between the unconscious and the conscious that this barrier does not manage to function appropriately, with the consequent risk of hallucinations, delirium and confusion. The aim of analysis is a form of learning from experience (Bion, 1962) that can make it possible to restore a functional separation/communication between the unconscious and the conscious. This cannot be realized "directly" through a classic interpretation of unconscious fantasies. The psychotic patient's use of language is very fragile and can at times result in neologisms. This does not impede the possibility of helping the patient spontaneously give shape to thoughts and emotions that were previously inaccessible, encouraging the analysand to let his subjective reality progress towards more organized and shared forms of thinking. Thus the analyst can support the psychotic analysand's tendency to conceive reality as an "oneiric" protofunction (Bion, 1992) that tends to organize experience, by creating a membrane or barrier of communication and differentiation between the conscious and the unconscious.

Psychotic patients pose awkward problems for all schematizations of analytic work that are based on the commonplaces of orthodoxy. For

example, the indiscriminate and often arbitrary use of transference interpretation, improperly employed as a litmus test of the analytic authen-
ticity of interpretation, is not advisable in the therapy of psychosis, as is
clearly pointed out here in the pieces by De Masi and Lombardi. And by
the way, it should be borne in mind that the prestige accorded to transference interpretations in official psychoanalytic circles has never been
backed up by empirical research, and that the few empirical studies that
do exist on the subject show an inverse relationship between frequency
of transference interpretations and therapeutic results (Crits-Christoph
and Connolly Gibbons, 2002; Høglend, 2004). Among the various kinds
of psychotherapeutic approach dedicated to the needs of borderline
patients, i.e., Mentalization-Based Treatment (MBT), advanced by Peter
Fonagy, Dialectical Behavior Therapy (DBT), promoted by Marsha Line-
ham, and Transference-Focused Psychotherapy (TFP), based on the ideas
of Otto Kernberg, only the last-named approach envisages an unequivo-
cal concentration on the transference, since it is intentionally addressed
to the less serious cases on the borderline spectrum, whereas the afore-
mentioned other two kinds of therapeutic intervention are aimed primarily at improving emotional control and the capacity for introspection
(Munich, 2011).

We refer here to these approaches because, for all the significant differences between them, each of them has to do with an attempt to reorient the psychoanalytic process in the light of the pressing needs that the
so-called difficult patient presents. We do in fact believe that it is possible
to construct an analytic approach that includes some judicious modifications to classic treatment so as to be appropriate to the levels of functioning on which these analysands are accessible. This would include a change
in the traditional technical parameters that, far from being an obstacle to
analysis, conceived in the strict sense, should instead lead to an enrichment of it, and to rendering it more responsive to the clinical needs of the
present, by distinguishing the particularity that the working through of
the most archaic levels implies as compared to the working through of
the more evolved relational levels. Given that "a flexible approach on the
supportive-expressive continuum is used today by a majority of dynamically oriented therapists" (Munich, 2011), we find it impossible to conceive of an evolution of psychoanalysis – one that is realistically oriented
towards including most patients, not excepting severe cases, who today
undertake analytic treatment – without the use of intelligent and justifi-
able flexibility built on the foundations of clinical observation.

There are, however, those who maintain that there has never actually
been an orthodox model of classical psychoanalysis, or at least that such
a thing was never used clinically to the extent that is generally believed.
But despite the real possibility that the "classic model" is not much more
than a fantasy, such a model continues to dominate official psychoanalytic

discourse and to pervade training programs, thereby impeding the development of new techniques and new therapeutic interventions of a psychoanalytic nature (Fonagy, 2010; Luyten, Blatt, and Mayes, 2012). Since those who have not received orthodox training are more at ease with new techniques, one wonders whether there isn't in fact the risk, of which Renik (2012) warns us, that the future of psychoanalysis will have to be ensured by analysts with no connection whatsoever to official channels of training, or even by professionals who use psychoanalytic tools without recognizing any connection to psychoanalysis.

Kernberg (1975, 1992) valorizes the psychoanalytic interest in difficult cases with considerable psychotic processes and in psychosis in general. He observes that the theory that pharmacological treatment supersedes the need for a psychotherapeutic approach based on psychoanalytic knowledge is altogether false. Not only does he find the role of psychoanalysis decisive for the understanding and treatment of psychosis, but, he also stresses, the psychoanalytic exploration of psychosis is essential because it can brilliantly illuminate the psychodynamics of less severe cases.

The need to reorient our discipline towards exploratory work that is open to innovation, and to a sense of play (Winnicott, 1971), as well as being firmly attached to an empirical base, has recently been confirmed by Luyten (2015), who underscores the need for psychoanalysts to re-examine – unashamedly – the cornerstones that support psychoanalysis, which they have always tended to take for granted; otherwise orthodoxy and rigidity, which still dominate some parts of it, could lead to an irreparable decline of the clinical and intellectual activity of our branch of science. Luyten also notes that the therapeutic results that can be achieved in analysis arise not so much from particular changes induced by interpretational interventions, as instead from the extent to which the analysis can activate a new epistemological capacity in the patient, together with social awareness. All of this seems to correspond with what we find in practicing the psychoanalysis of psychosis, as well as with the spirit with which we have chosen the essays that make up this book. The psychoanalysis of psychosis is decisively fostered by the mental openness of the analyst, by the ability to learn from the patient and by an orientation that can encourage in the analysand a burgeoning receptivity towards new experiences, supported by their working through in the session.

A brief mention is reserved for the problems related to pharmacological treatment of psychotic disturbances and its integration in the analytical process. This issue can be considered a part of that discipline known as *psychodynamic psychopharmacology*, which is characterized by its particular attention to factors such as transference and countertransference dynamics, treatment adherence, placebo and nocebo responses, and conscious and unconscious factors related to ambivalence.

Such factors have a special importance in the field of psychoses where pharmacological treatment is more urgent, the decision between a split or unified treatment is more problematic and the transferral dynamics are more violent because they are conditioned by omnipotence, a sense of emptiness and anger. The drug could in fact be viewed as a fantasmatic object endowed with omnipotence, even though it remains a concrete object.

The problem can perhaps be summarized in the following question: can the drug contribute to reducing the fragmentation of the self, to strengthening insight and oneiric capacities, favoring the participation in the analysis without activating a dangerous analytic disinvestment and undesirable shifts of transference outside of the analysis? We believe that these are open questions that need to be addressed in every single treatment utilizing the collaboration between the psychoanalyst and the psychiatric consultant as effectively as possible.

A note on the historical development of the psychoanalysis of psychoses

At this point we would like to present a brief overview of some of the protagonists in the clinical research of the psychoanalysis of psychoses over the course of a century of psychoanalysis. This review does not have any pretense of completeness since an exhaustive coverage would require at least a volume in itself. We would just like to give an idea here of the varied research that has characterized the psychoanalysis of psychoses over time and the diverse psychoanalytic traditions with some examples of powerful intuitions that are often still valid today.

At the beginning of the 20th century Eugen Bleuler from the psychiatric school of Zurich had already introduced an initial optimistic perspective stating that schizophrenia could be arrested or made to regress, independently from its state of evolution. The Swiss school at the time of Carl Gustav Jung was an important reference point in stimulating a psychoanalytic interest in psychosis. Freud in his letter of 13 August 1908 to Jung writes that his intention was to nominate Jung as his successor as long as he applied his discoveries on neurosis to psychoses. Jung, however, was always clear in his skepticism about directly transferring Freud's theory of the libido to psychoses because he believed that their manifestations were too complex to be explained simply by a loss of erotic interest (see Conci, 2000, p. 275).

Among Freud's students interested in psychosis Victor Tausk must be mentioned: a "rarely-gifted man", as defined by the father of psychoanalysis in his obituary (Freud, 1919), who tragically took his own life in 1919 at the age of 42. He is renowned chiefly for his brilliant essay "On the Origin of the 'Influencing Machine' in Schizophrenia" (1933), in which he described several cases of 'somatic paranoia', where a machine or an external box acted as a "suggestion-apparatus", creating somatic sensations and visual hallucinations, and conditioning the body of the person. In the delusional state the body loses its substantial physiological statute and its normal manifestations, such as peristaltic movements, become the expression of external demonic forces. The crisis of normal reference to the real body in schizophrenia has proved today to be a powerful intuition that leads to certain aspects of current research on the relationship between body and psychosis.

Among the pioneers of the treatment of psychosis in Freud's first Viennese circle, Karl Abraham (1916) noted the possibility of establishing a therapeutic relationship with patients suffering from manic-depressive psychosis, despite their evident difficulty in manifesting a transference. These experiences did not align with Freud's own orientation, who considered psychotic patients incapable of establishing a transference relationship. Later Paul Federn (1952) confirmed that the retreat of the psychotic from reality is never complete, giving rise to the possibility of activating a positive transference towards the analyst. Conversely the eventual emergence of a negative transference made the interruption of the treatment advisable. Federn can be credited for emphasizing the role of boundaries, stressing that the damage that characterizes the psychosis is concerned principally with the loss of the boundaries of the self, which must therefore be constructed in the course of the psychotherapy. The possibility of further exploring the negative aspects of transference was instead a specific feature of the Kleinian school.

Beginning with the analysis of infants during the 1920s in German countries, Melanie Klein emigrated to Great Britain, where she applied her theories to the psychoanalytic treatment of psychosis. She studied the mechanisms of paranoia at the root of depressive psychosis (Klein, 1935, 1940), advancing her knowledge of primitive mechanisms above all with the study of the *projective identification* (Klein, 1946). This is a complex clinical concept that attempts to describe the destructive dynamics characteristic of the psychosis, emphasizing the role of the annihilation of parts of the self, together with the splitting and projection of the good and bad parts into external objects, as occurs – according to Klein – in the earliest phases of the mother-infant relationship. The unconscious fantasies on the sadistic-oral level are constantly in the foreground of Kleinian attentions: they are directly elaborated in the transference with the analyst and woven together with the reparative orientations of the subject.

The school of Melanie Klein has made a particularly rich and varied contribution to the exploration of the psychoses thanks to influential analysts including Hanna Segal, Wilfred Bion, Donald Meltzer, Herbert Rosenfeld, Edna O'Shaunessy and Salomon Resnik. The theories of these authors are widely known, and to conserve space on this occasion, we will limit our discussion to some aspects of Herbert Rosenfeld's contribution, since he demonstrated a particularly systematic dedication to the exploration of the psychoses. It must be remembered that the Kleinian approach to psychosis has had an original development in South America, both in the Argentinian school of psychoanalysis thanks to the pioneering role of Enrique Pichon Rivière – continued further with the work of David Rosenfeld, Salomon Resnik and Horatio Etchegoyen (Etchegoyen and Zysman, 2005) – and in Brazil through the influence of Frank Philips and Virginia Bicudo (1964).

Herbert Rosenfeld's most significant contributions (1965, 1987) concern the confusional states, destructive narcissism and the difficulty of projective identification management during analytic therapy. While Freud considered that the central conflict of psychosis played out between the Ego and reality, Rosenfeld emphasized the role of conflict between the destructive and constructive aspects. He stresses that in the passage from the schizo-paranoid position to the depressive state a confusion may arise and the distinction between good and bad becomes difficult to discern, activating confusion between fantasy and reality, and patient and analyst. In the most serious confusional states schizoid mechanisms may be activated that can cause fragmentation of the Ego. Splitting and fragmentation lead to an excess of projective identification and states of depersonalization. Rehabilitation occurs through a reconnection of the fragments favored by the growth of libidinal impulses.

According to Rosenfeld, psychoanalytic therapy passes through a narcissistic object relationship, that is, the connection with the object characterized by indifferentiation and confusion, invested in an omnipotent manner. If the analyst wants access to the psychic world of the patient, the analytic relationship must deal with this state dominated by projective identification – which is mainly understood as a defense against an extreme anxiety of separation. The analytic task is hindered by the fact that the destructive narcissistic aspects are perceived as more attractive than libidinal ones because they strengthen the sense of omnipotence. The idealization of the 'bad' parts of the self entails an organized attack against the constructive aspects of the personality. This psychopathological organization denies feelings of dependence in relation to the separated object, primarily the analyst, and leads to significant emotional impoverishment. Rosenfeld's interpretation of projective identification places the accent on primitive states of symbiosis with the mother where communication occurs through an osmotic modality, such that the patient's anxiety states can transform themselves into bodily states of the analyst. The patient's suffering can manifest itself also in the body of the analyst through sleepiness or somatic malaise, inhibiting the latter's capacity for concentration and thought.

Influenced by Melanie Klein's object relationships theory, but characterized by a distinctly personal approach, Ronald Fairbairn (1952) emphasized the insufficiency of an interpretative approach that is not supported by specific attention to the totality of the relationship between analyst and analysand. For Fairbairn psychoanalysis is difficult to reconcile with a psychology conceived predominantly in terms of 'impulse', as it happens with Freud's libido theory, since the analyst's personality contributes to the therapeutic process in a determinate way. Fairbairn's position in relation to the treatment of psychoses has such significance and relevance today that it warrants a citation: "any tendency to adhere with pronounced rigidity to the details of the classic psycho-analytical technique, as standardized by Freud more than half a century ago, is liable to defensive exploitation, however unconscious this may be, in the interests of the analyst and at the expense of the patient; and certainly any tendency to treat the classic technique as sacrosanct raises the suspicion that an element of such a defensive exploitation is at work. Further, it seems to me that a complete stultification of the therapeutic aim is involved in any demand, whether explicit or implicit, that the patient must conform to the nature of the therapeutic method rather than that the method must conform to the requirements of the patient" (Fairbairn, 1958, pp. 378–379). His approach was developed chiefly by Harry Guntrip (1962), who, among other things, posed the problem of whether the psychotherapeutic technique was able to provoke emotional experiences sufficiently intense as to produce personality alterations, since the emotional experiences produced by pathological models had been extremely intense.

The psychoanalysis of psychoses in North America was represented primarily by Abraham Arden Brill, who worked in the Burghölzli psychiatric clinic in Zurich as a young man, going on to play a central role in importing psychoanalysis to the United States. He influenced the ideas of Harry Stack Sullivan (1940, see Conci, 2000), who offered a powerful contribution to the clinic of psychosis by considering psychosis a disorder in which the total experience of the individual is reorganized. He acknowledged the patient and analyst's distinctive personal uniqueness, stressing the need to intervene with psychotherapy before contact with reality is completely compromised by the illness. According to Sullivan, the doctor's preconceived ideas may constitute a serious obstacle in establishing communication with the psychotic patient. Hence it is necessary to avoid premature interpretations that are not supported by attentive observation of the patient. The respect for the psychotic patient's subjectivity and his or her acute sensitivity guides the *interpersonal interaction* as a determining factor in the psychotherapy of the psychosis. Sullivan's work has been enormously influential on various generations of American analysts.

Active in the William Alanson White Institute of New York, Silvano Arieti (1955, 1974) was one of the leading promoters of psychotherapy of schizophrenia in the years between 1950 and 1970. Born in Pisa in 1904, he emigrated to the USA to escape from the Fascist movement after having attained his medical degree. He considered psychosis an important human experience that is able to benefit from an interpretative approach stimulating the patient's *basic trust*, which is crucial in not interrupting his or her relationship with reality. According to Arieti the biological and psychodynamic approaches are not opposing paradigms but rather complementary orientations. Only psychotherapy is able to remove the conflicts at the root of schizophrenic disorder, correct the psychopathological patterns and initiate the stimulation of the organism's regenerative psychological powers to regain lost ground. Arieti had a particular interest in the schizophrenic patient's thought disorders: these patients utilize archaic thought processes connoted by the 'primary process' (Freud, 1900), in which condensation and displacement are dominant, allowing an escape from the patient's own anxieties. Inspired by von Domarus (1944), Arieti calls this archaic form of thinking 'Paleological Thought', stressing its unrelatedness to the normal logic based on Aristotelian non-contradiction principles.

Another author who made a key contribution to the role of logic in schizophrenia is Ignatio Matte Blanco (1975, 1988). He was trained in the 1930s in London, then became professor of Psychiatry at the University in Santiago del Chile and finally immigrated to Italy in the 1960s. Matte Blanco proposed an original interpretation of the Unconscious described by Freud (1900, 1915) making use of logical and mathematical concepts. He reformulated the unconscious functioning in terms of infinite sets and 'bi-logic', differentiating two contrasting types of logic: the bivalent logic, which strictly follows Aristotelian logical order, and symmetrical logic, which operates 'like an acid' that annihilates all logical differentiations. The dominance of symmetry is particularly relevant in children's intense emotions, but it is also a characteristic of the psychotic patient's mental functioning. These patients are continuously at risk of falling into a 'formless infinity' in which the normal categories of space and time disappear (Lombardi, 2015).

The American analyst Harold Searles treated eighteen chronic schizophrenics with intensive therapies that were undertaken over various durations, from a minimum of a few months to more than ten years. Half of these people were treated in the analyst's consulting room and the other half in their hospital rooms. The foundation of Searles' therapeutic work was based on a radical honesty with respect to himself and to the mindfulness of his own feelings, impulses and fantasies. The therapeutic symbiosis – that is, the reciprocal incorporation between the analyst and the patient in which the personality of one devours the personality of the other – is, from Searles' point of view (1965), a condition that is constantly present in the treatment of the psychosis, and the therapist should take into account his or her tendency to incorporate the personality of the patient. Psychotic patients are characterized by an intense dependence need that they tend to distance from their conscience, not daring to reveal it to anyone. The needs centered at the oral level include the desire to be nursed and caressed, together with the desire to be constantly loved, protected and guided. The therapist can be negatively influenced by anxiety and guilt, discouraging the patient's dependence needs when instead the acceptance of these needs may be instrumental in helping the analysand to abandon infantile omnipotence.

According to Searles the unconscious effort to drive the other person crazy occupies a central place in schizophrenia. If in a certain sense the desire to drive the other person crazy is a universal phenomenon that involves all human beings, in the psychotherapy of psychosis this attempt is particularly active. Another aspect of Searles' most original contributions (1960) concerns the role of the non-human environment. At the beginning of the development of the Ego, the infant is undifferentiated not only towards the human components of its environment but also towards the non-human components: the infant is in a symbiotic relation with both and attributes a profound meaning to them. The investment of non-human objects allows the person to shift upon them a part of the feelings directed towards the mother, which would otherwise risk being excessive. In turn, the emotional reaction of the mother allows the infant to differentiate between the animate and the inanimate, and that which is human and that which is not. In the psychotic patient the effort required to reach this result may prove to be an impossible task. The ability of the analyst to tolerate the role of the non-human object in countertransference provides the patient with the emotional mediation necessary in humanizing and differentiating it from the inanimate, and this is decisive for a positive result in analytical treatment.

The clinical research of the psychoanalysis of psychosis in France reveals an original development. Evelyne Kestemberg, together with Lebovici and Diatkine, elaborated the analytical psychodrama, deriving it from the original by Moreno (1947). This technique was utilized as the chosen therapy both for adolescents who often rely on acting and for psychotic patients. The analytical psychodrama allows work on a concrete level that adheres to reality, creating through its mechanisms those traces of existence that the psychotic anxieties had blocked from registering in the psyche. The representation of the external space facilitates in this way the acquisition of an internal space. The psychodrama allows the analytical treatment of the deficiencies of symbolization or of verbalization, distributing on the group of co-therapists a type of transference that would be intolerable in a traditional analytic relationship (Kestemberg and Jammet, 1987).

Kestemberg (2001) distinguishes two fundamental forms of psychosis: delusional psychosis and "cold" psychosis. The former includes paranoia, schizophrenia and delusional psychoses, while the latter includes mental anorexia and certain forms of mania and melancholia. The clinic of anorexia displays a fetishistic cult of the skinny body ideal that often entirely eliminates the world of object relations. Autism, auto-eroticism, exclusion of libidinal exchange and denial of alterity characterize cold psychosis. The narcissistic hardening of these patients is intent on avoiding loss, which is perceived as intolerable and impossible to symbolize. This constant quest for dissatisfaction is sustained by a control of the death instinct. Evelyne Kestemberg's work was followed in the Center Evelyne et Jean Kestemberg by the work of well-known analysts, including Liliane Abensour (2008) and Alain Gibeaut (Aisenstein and Gibeault, 1991).

Piera Aulagnier, née Spairani, was an Italian by birth and medical training. Having moved to France, she was analyzed by Lacan, and later was to detach herself from him to found the so-called Quatrième Group within the French psychoanalytic movement. Her contribution is based on an original understanding of psychosis, together with a general theory of becoming a subject. According to Aulagnier (1975) parents, in the moment when they interpret a newborn's needs, give meaning to a biological reaction that would otherwise be senseless. If instead the meaning is imposed externally, the so-called "violence of interpretation" inhibits the subjective development of the infant's psyche, becoming a source of "psychotic potentiality".

Aulagnier's work considers the Freudian metapsychology insufficient in psychosis, placing particular value on the relationship with language, with reality and with representation, where the pictogram is considered the most archaic form of psychic metabolization. The psychotic condition should be the result of three conditions: (1) the original and its pictograms meet an external reality that does not lend itself to reflect a state of total union, thereby resulting in rejection and a desire of self-annihilation; the situation deteriorates if successive meetings with the external reality are not able to cure this initial wound; (2) "In its turn, the primary has sought in vain in the outside-self for signs that might allow it to find in the locus of the Other the cause of a state of pleasure that one may link to one's desire and, what is more, signs that would deny one's phantasies of rejection, which would help one to recognise that the world and the other's body are also loci in which pleasure is possible, in which desire may be fulfilled"; and finally (3) "the I encounters in the space in which it must come about, in the statements that must establish it and which will constitute it, *the order of having to be*, whereas *whenever it becomes*, in each image of itself that it tends to cathect, it comes up against the prohibition of being that form, that image, that moment, as soon as they are presented as *its* choice" (Aulagnier, 1975, p. 226).

Active in France and Germany during the years 1960 to 1980, Gisela Pankow concentrated on the psychotherapy of psychoses and schizophrenia, employing a perspective that places the relationship of the subject with her own body at the center of the analyst's attention. Pankow (1969) reformulated the concept of *Spaltung*, or psychotic disassociation, placing a focus on the destruction of the tie with the body, rather than on the loss of a sense of reality. The patients, who are not able to establish a relationship of traditional transference centered on the recognition of the external relationship, organize a relationship of corporal exchanges that Pankow calls *Mitleiblichkeit*. The dissociation of the being-in-the-body entails a destruction of every spatial and temporal dialectic in the patient, as well as a paralysis in the world of desire: the relationship with one's own body thus becomes the center of the psychoanalytical elaboration. The space-time structure connected to the anatomical-physiological functioning of the body is a reference parameter for the mind that allows the growth of a realistic space-time organization, which is able to contrast with the disorganized pressure of the psychosis.

A brief outline of the book

The articles that follow attempt to explain the reasons for active exploration of the psychoanalysis of psychosis in a variety of cultural and methodological contexts. We made a point of asking for contributions from Italian, other European and American authors from different psychoanalytic backgrounds, but with a shared commitment to a pragmatic engagement with the psychoanalytic psychotherapy of psychosis. Even with their diverse perspectives, and their differences of style and language, they still have in common – as the reader will note – an empirical and experiential grounding that is reflected in each and every chapter.

Didier Houzel, in the first chapter, introduces the notion of psychosis and autism in the child, and invites us to distrust etiological simplifications, or simplistic explanations that can easily unleash intolerance on the part of the parents of these children, in part because, in the past, they were irrationally accused of "lack of affect", which was to be seen as the origin of the child's disorder. Psychosis in children is instead to be considered in relation to a representational deficit. As far as the approach to treatment goes, it is essential to bear in mind the actual context if one is to set off on the individual psychoanalysis of a child, and hence it should be conceived as an intervention "with the greatest possible frequency and the longest possible duration", whatever the rigidly pre-established rules may be. Inspired by the example of Frances Tustin, Houzel highlights the value of an intervention that works on the level of the container-contained relationship (Bion, 1970), and hence on the so-called transference onto the container (Houzel), as a more primitive level than what Melanie Klein identified as infantile transference based on projective identification.

John Kafka, the eminent Washington, D.C., psychiatrist and psychoanalyst, bases his contribution about psychosis on a reexamination of his experience with Chestnut Lodge – a distinguished psychiatric institution in Rockville, Maryland, about an hour's distance from Baltimore – which for many years offered residential treatment, based on psychoanalytic principles, of seriously disturbed patients. Kafka – author of the informative book *Multiple Realities in Clinical Practice* (1989) – considers the importance, for the seriously disturbed patient, of a "sense of agency", i.e., a sense of identity based not only on his/her capacity to interact constructively with external reality, but also on his/her ability to organize important aspects of internal functioning, such as the one that deals with temporality. He underscores the role of the various ways of considering psychosis, such as, for instance, the expression of a deficiency or of a conflict: a difference of perspective that permeates the contributions of historic theorists like Ping-Nie Pao and Harold Searles. A decisive factor in the Chestnut Lodge experience was the role of Frieda Fromm-Reichmann, who brought into play her unique capacity for entering into communication with seriously disturbed patients, by responding with flexibility and empathy to both the psychotic and the non-psychotic levels of communication.

Franco De Masi has offered an essay that recapitulates his own experience of the psychoanalysis of psychosis, starting from a reconsideration of the cases of Alvise and Ada (treated by Paola Capozzi). Alvise presented psychotic ideation, which receded with analysis, but re-emerged during his struggle with his degree thesis, when he reacted with the delusion that the CIA wanted to kidnap him and take him to the United States: an explosion that would seem to have the characteristics of a catastrophic change (Bion, 1970), in which the change represented by the bachelor's degree and the new world opening before him is experienced as alien to his very personality. De Masi attributes this re-emergence of the psychosis to insufficient analysis of the unconscious motivations underpinning the first psychotic episode, and backs up his hypothesis with statements by Arieti and Searles. De Masi's study of the material from the analysis of Ada allows him to hypothesize that dreams can function as predictors of a new psychotic explosion. He then goes on to consider the importance of states of infantile withdrawal – characterized by dissociation from reality – in the genesis of subsequent delusional states in the adult patient; the role of pathological organization, in which the patient is in thrall to a sensory fixation with pleasure; and the distinctive characteristics of the psychotic transference.

Riccardo Lombardi begins his essay by reappraising the significance of the psychoanalytic treatment of psychosis, which should be divested of its 'omnipotent' sense of bringing recovery from an illness: a dynamic equilibrium between the psychotic and non-psychotic parts of the personality is of concern to everyone, however healthy or ill he or she may appear from an external phenomenological viewpoint. Schizophrenia and severe psychoses show the use of a characteristic way of thinking that reveals the logical functioning of the unconscious at its deepest levels. The working through should proceed towards reinforcing the reality principle. Together with a series of orientative psychoanalytic hypotheses that are basic for the understanding of psychosis, Lombardi underlines the importance of the role played by phenomena of body-mind dissociation in fostering the onset of an evident psychotic disorder. A briefly recounted analytic treatment of a clinical case illustrates his position. If the most urgent task of a psychoanalytic intervention in psychosis is to encourage the growth of mental phenomena, then the mind needs to base itself on a body/affect/thought continuum: there can be no evolution towards the mental level that does not start with the recognition of one's own body and the respect for the sensory matrices of thought. The working through with a psychotic patient must be focused on the primary needs this sort of patient has, i.e., to establish communication with his- or herself, and to activate phenomena of perception and self-awareness.

Mark J. Blechner, on the basis, first of all, of his rich and, in human terms, intense experience, as a young therapist, of the treatment of psychotic patients, stresses the importance of working in the open air and in natural surroundings. To make the most of this approach, one must devise a particular therapy for each patient, seeking to understand whatever might involve the analysand in meaningful communication and emotional connection. In keeping with this profoundly interpersonal perspective, the listener chooses her answers to her interlocutor, bearing in mind not only the semantic contents but also the other dimensions of the communication, such as its tone, its implicit emotion and the accompanying bodily attitude. The therapist's contribution to the dialogue is shaped, to a great extent, by the other's response. Blechner's therapeutic strategy, as he outlines it here, involves the analyst's reaching an agreement with the sane part of the patient's communications, which requires considerable sensibility, as well as a capacity for attentive listening, on the part of the analyst. If the therapist focuses on the other's madness, the dialogue seems crazier and there is an increase in the anxiety of both participants. If instead the therapist responds only to what is rational and meaningful in the patient's communication, the dialogue makes the patient seem saner and can actually make him saner.

Michael Robbins presents a clinical report about the evolution of Sara, a 28-year-old paranoid schizophrenic, who was in analysis for eleven years. After a very brief account of some of the ups and downs of Sara's life, he concentrates on her first few years of analysis, in which the main goal was to create an atmosphere in which Sara's compulsion to act out disruptively might be contained. The psychoanalytic focus was particularly to promote thinking and communication, and it benefited from the protective effect of her hospitalization at the time. Robbins emphasizes the importance, in terms of the patient's positive development, of the analyst's decision not to urge her to free associate: thus he points out the danger that can arise from an analyst's idealistic attachment to a traditional technique, which, however, in serious cases, can expose the analysand to the risk of disorganized thinking. The active support of mentalization and attempting to establish constructive visual contact with the patient were, on the other hand, an important driving force in the analytic relationship in this case.

For Stefano Calamandrei, the main cause of psychotic disorders is the absence of an auto-erotic filter for emotional intrusions on the part of the object. In place of the missing filter, psychotic patients, to keep at bay these strong emotional stimuli, make use of denial, externalization of the self and narcissistic investment in the environment. Reality experienced as an extension of the self leads to a narcissistic investment that is not defensive, but is instead the consequence of the diffusion of the subject in the human and non-human environment. Nondifferentiation between me and not-me creates, in the transference, an obstacle to mutual holding and evenly poised attention. The analyst who is perceived as part of the patient's internal world is the object of a despotic relationship that is subject to abrupt changes. Every supposed shortcoming of the analyst gives rise to profound disappointment quite unlike resentment towards an external object. The real object of the patient's anger is her own helplessness, and this results in intense self-denigration. In Calamandrei's view, the psychotic patient's transference develops on two different but coexistent planes. The first is manifest: autistic withdrawal, which creates an insurmountable barrier between patient and analyst. The second, which is hard to detect, is a disguised symbiotic dimension: the patient's narcissistic world is projected and deposited within the analyst and in the setting.

For Sarantis Thanopulos, psychosis arises from the breakdown of an important area of subjective experience in the primary relationship with the mother. The breakdown takes place just when the experience is about to take shape: in favorable conditions it remains engraved on the psyche as a potentiality. The tendency of a compressed and deformed subjectivity to start growing again meets, however, with strong opposition because it exposes the subject to the risk of undergoing a repetition of the breakdown. A part of the patient is still alive enough to be able to dream, so that the analyst can still analyze fantasies and interpret dreams. This gratifies the analyst and supports the relatively sane part of the patient. The tension between interpretative truth and the truth of delusion, with which the patient tries to fill the yawning gap, helps the patient's subjective truth to find a way of approaching reality and of taking shape. The first, if indirect, expression of this truth is found in the destabilization of the mental and emotional order of the analyst.

The "reverse side of thinking" is the concise expression Giuseppe Civitarese uses to indicate the great contribution Bion made to the understanding of typical psychotic thinking, which is characterized by attacks on linking, dream-thoughts in the process of dreaming and thinking, and hence an attack on the very process of attributing meaning to experience.

The "reverse side of thinking" is the result of introjection, on the part of the newborn or baby, of the mother's incapacity to contain his emotional state, and is based on the delicate mechanism of the so-called transformations in hallucinosis, which, for Bion, are a feature, albeit varying in gravity, not only of seriously disturbed patients, but also of the psychotic part of the mind of each of us. A clinical illustration shows how the analyst's *reverie* puts into effect his willingness to dream the dream the patient hasn't dreamt and thus to "allow the O of the session to evolve: to go beyond conscious identification, comprehension and the mere analysis of phenomena". According to the author's own reinterpretation of Bion, "the understanding of psychosis, of the reverse side of thinking, is based on a radically social theory of the subject", and hence the analyst must work more on mental containers, and especially on the development of thinking and of containing emotions, than on thoughts and emotions as contents in themselves.

An analysand's dreams when periods of analytic holidays impend present Luigi Rinaldi with the opportunity to reflect on the relation between dreaming and psychosis, and in particular on the knotty problem of the presence, quality and function of dreams in psychotic states. What emerges from his clinical experience and his analysis of the literature is that, when the psychotic process is not in an acute phase and has not invaded the entire mental structure, it is possible to dream. In these cases, however, the partial or total failure of the dream-work, which can be traced back to deficient symbol formation and to concrete thinking, does not lead to sufficient metabolization of the day's residues, and thus does not result in the fulfillment of repressed desires or in protecting sleep from the assaults of instincts or external reality. What is preserved, however, is the dream's function of representing the self and its attempts to integrate current and past emotional experiences, including those that are stored in the non-verbal memory. Thus dream regression can even manage to illustrate a deficiency in the integration of body and mind, and the vicissitudes of the transference can be represented in sensory and physical terms. It's a matter, in these cases, of representations that derive from the re-proposal, performed by the psychosis, of the pictographic register (Aulagnier, 1975), which reflects, mirror-like, the earliest experiences having to do with the primary relation, and describes how this "primitive process" can be a sort of pre-form of subsequent fantasies of fragmentation, annihilation and loss of Ego boundaries.

According to Paul Williams, pathological organization of a psychotic nature works in parallel with the non-psychotic part of the personality, which keeps track of and opposes it. When the pathological organization gains the upper hand, any opposing sentiments or doubts – a prerogative of the non-psychotic part of the personality – are not tolerated. Only the certainties welling up from sexual and aggressive fantasies that have not been worked through are deemed acceptable. The analyst's principal task is to make communication intelligible by distinguishing, in both the transference and the countertransference, between the patient's non-psychotic needs and his or her systematic psychotic distortions. By paying attention to both of the patient's modes of communicating and thinking, the analyst can introduce into the discourse what he or she has understood – stimulated by a spirit of curiosity and interest – about the non-psychotic part of the patient's mind. The analyst essentially navigates between the sane part of the patient's mind, the patient's anger and the impact of these fluctuating positions on the relationship with him or her, thus making room for mutual exploration of the patient's polarized experiences that may result in an authentic expression of feelings. With time this may even lead to the painful process of disentanglement from the pseudo-protection offered by the pathological organization of the patient's mind.

The fourth part of the book examines the problem of the interaction between psychoanalysis and psychopharmacology in the treatment of psychoses.

Ira Steinman presents an approach in which the psychoanalyst (who is a psychiatrist as well) also manages, where required, the psychopharmacological aspect of the treatment, with a moderate use of drugs during acute phases – whenever anxiety is rampant and blocks all forms of psychotherapeutic activity – then gradually reducing the doses of the drug(s) as the patient learns to control those psychological processes that seemed at first to be incomprehensible and terrifying. With illustrations from two clinical cases, he shows us how the treatment proceeds, with the customary psychodynamic analysis of past events, of phenomena of the transference and the countertransference, and of affective states during the period in which the symptoms appeared. In this way he helps the patients to understand the symbolic meaning they assigned to hallucinations and delusions, and to identify the traumatic events that led to Ego-fragmentation and psychosis. To that end, it is essential, in his opinion, that the therapist reach what Harry Guntrip calls the "inner core of the self", and that he or she be quite sure that it is possible to "peel the onion" and get to the source of the most bizarre and extreme psychotic phenomena.

With his well-composed contribution on the relation between pharmacological and psychoanalytic treatment for psychotic disorders, Giuseppe Martini aims to fill a void caused by the fact that this subject, although of enormous importance, is not to be found with any frequency in psychoanalytic journals. In his consideration of the literature he inclines towards the contributions of those authors who call for a new discipline – psychodynamic psychopharmacology – that recognizes the central role that meaning and interpersonal factors play in psychopharmacological treatment. If one accepts this premise, it would seem to follow that patients who are in analysis and who take psychiatric medication, instead of being prey to a flattening of emotions and "dehumanizing *experiences*", as was thought in the 1980s, can get from it a potentiation of their insight and of the ability to remember their dreams, and be helped to recompact their fragmented Egos, and, in general, to participate more fully in the analytic experience, which, in the absence of psychoactive drugs, would be impossible for them. Martini then dwells on theoretical and methodological questions so as to refute the presumed contradictory practice among psychoanalytic therapy and psychopharmacology. He then discusses the emotional, relational and transferential transformations arising from the use of these drugs. He finishes by illustrating, with lively clinical examples, the indications and contraindications of a unified setting (in which the psychoanalyst also prescribes medicines) and of a separate setting (in which the psychopharmacologist works as a backup to the analyst) in acute psychosis, schizophrenia and bipolar disorders.

References

Abensour, L. (2008). *Psychotic Temptation*. Trans by D. Alcorn. London: Routledge.

Abraham, K. (1916). The first pregenital stage of the libido. In *Selected Papers*. London: Institute of psychoanalysis and Hogarth Press, 1927, pp. 248–279.

Aisenstein, M., and Gibeault, A. (1991). The work of hypochondria – A contribution to the study of the specificity of hypochondria, in particular in relation to hysterical conversion and organic disease. *International Journal of Psychoanalysis* 72: 669–680.

Arieti, S. (1955). *American Handbook of Psychiatry*. New York: Basic Books.

Arieti, S. (1974). *Interpretation of Schizophrenia*. New York: Basic Books.

Aulagnier, P. (1975). *The Violence of Interpretation. From Pictogram to Statement*. Trans by A. Sheridan. Hove and East Sussex: Brunner-Routledge, 2001.

Bicudo, V.L. (1964). Persecutory guilt and ego restrictions – Characterization of a pre-depressive position. *International Journal of Psychoanalysis* 45: 358–363.

Bion, W.R. (1957). Differentiation of psychotic from non-psychotic personalities. In *Second Thoughts*. London: Karnac Books, 1967, pp. 43–64.

Bion, W.R. (1962). *Learning from Experience*. London: Karnac Books, 1984.

Bion, W.R. (1970). *Attention and Interpretation*. London: Karnac Books.

Bion, W.R. (1992). *Cogitations*. London: Karnac Books.

Conci, M. (2000). *Sullivan Rivisitato*. English Ed. *Sullivan Revisited*. Trento: Tangram, 2010.

Crits-Christoph, P., and Connolly Gibbons, M.B. (2002). Relational interpretations. In Norcross, J.C. (Editor), *Psychotherapy Relationships That Work*. Oxford: Oxford University Press, pp. 285–300.

Etchegoyen, H.R., and Zysman, S. (2005). Melanie Klein in Buenos Aires. *International Journal of Psychoanalysis* 86 (3): 869–894.

Fairbairn, W.D. (1952). *Psychoanalytic Studies of the Personality*. London: Tavistock.

Fairbairn, W.D. (1958). On the nature and aims of psycho-analytical treatment. *International Journal of Psychoanalysis* 39: 374–385.

Federn, P. (1952). *Ego Psychology and the Psychoses*. New York: Basic Books.

Fonagy, P. (2010). The changing shape of clinical practice: Driven by science or by pragmatics? *Psychoanalytic Psychotherapy* 24 (1): 22–43.

Freud, S. (1900). The interpretation of dreams. *Standard Edition*.

Freud, S. (1915). The unconscious. *Standard Edition*.

Freud, S. (1919). Victor tausk. *Standard Edition*, 17.

Freud, S. (1924a). Neurosis and psychosis. *Standard Edition*, 19.

Freud, S. (1924b). The loss of reality in neurosis and nella psychosis. *Standard Edition*, 19.

Gabbard, G.O., and Westen, D. (2003). Rethinking therapeutic action. *International Journal of Psychoanalysis* 84: 823–841.

Guntrip, H. (1962). *Personality Structure and Human Interaction. The Developing Synthesis of Psychodinamic Theory*. London: The Hogarth Press.

Hoglend, P. (2004). Analysis of transference in psychodynamic psychotherapy. *Canadian Journal of Psychoanalysis* 12: 279–300.

Jackson, M. (2001). *Weathering the Storm: Psychotherapy for Psychosis*. London: Karnac Books.

Kafka, J.S. (1989). *Multiple Realities in Clinical Practice*. New Haven, CT: Yale University Press.

Kestemberg, E. (2001). *La Psychose Froide*. Paris: PUF.

Kestemberg, E., and Jammet, P. (1987). *Le psychodrame psychoanalytique*. Paris: PUF.

Kernberg, O. (1975). *Borderline Conditions and Pathological Narcissism*. New York: Aronson.

Kernberg, O. (1992). Psychopathic, paranoid and depressive transferences. *International Journal of Psychoanalysis* 73: 13–28.

Klein, M. (1935). A contribution to the psychogenesis of manic-depressive states. *International Journal of Psychoanalysis* 16: 145–174.

Klein, M. (1940). Mourning and its relation to manic-depressive states. *International Journal of Psychoanalysis* 21: 125–153.

Klein, M. (1946). Notes on some schizoid mechanisms. In *Envy and Gratitude and Other Works*. London: The Hogarth Press, 1975.

Luyten, P. (2015). Unholy questions about five central tenets of psychoanalysis that need to be empirically verified. *Psychoanalytic Inquiry* 35: 5–23.

Luyten, P., Blatt, S.J., and Mayes, L.C. (2012). Process and outcome in psychoanalytic psychotherapy research: The need for a (relatively) new paradigm. In Levy, R.A., Ablon, J.S., and Kaechele, H. (Editors), *Handbook of Evidence-Based Psychodynamic Psychotherapy. Bridging the Gap Between Science and Practice* (2nd ed.). New York: Humana Press/Springer, pp. 345–359.

Lombardi, R. (2015). *Formless Infinity. Clinical Explorations of Matte Blanco and Bion*. London: Routledge.

Matte Blanco, I. (1975). *Unconscious as Infinite Sets*. London: Karnac Books.

Matte Blanco, I. (1988). *Thinking, Feeling, and Being*. London and New York: Routledge.

Moreno, J.L. (1947). *The Theatre of Spontaneity*. New York: Beacon House.

Munich, R.L. (2011). The psychoanalytic approach to psychosis: Commentary on Kafka. *Journal of the American Psychoanalytic Association* 59: 49–57.

Pankow, G. (1969). *L'Homme et sa Psychose (Man and his Psychosis)*. Paris: Flammarion.

Renik, O. (2006a). An analyst questions the self-perpetuating side of therapy. Interview by Benedict Carey to Owen Renik. *New York Times*, 10th October.

Renik, O. (2006b). *Pratical Psychoanalysis for Therapists and Patients*. New York: Other Press.

Renik, O. (2012). *Sydney Pulver Lecture.* Unpublished paper. Philadelphia.

Rosenfeld, H. (1965). *Psychotic States. A Psychoanalytic Approach.* London: The Hogarth Press.

Rosenfeld, H. (1987). *Impasse and Interpretation.* London: Tavistock.

Saks, E.R. (2007). *The Center Cannot Hold. My Journey through Madness.* New York: Hyperion.

Saks, E.R., and Evans, O.B. (2011). Psychoanalysis and the psychoses: Commentary on Kafka. *Journal of the American Psychoanalytic Association* 59: 59–70.

Searles, H.F. (1960). *The Non Human Environment in Normal Development and in Schizophrenia.* New York: International University Press.

Searles, H.F. (1965). *Collected Papers on Schizophrenia and Related Subjects.* London: The Hogarth Press.

Sullivan, H.S. (1940). *Conceptions of Modern Psychiatry.* New York: Norton.

Tausk, V. (1933). On the origin of the "influencing machine" in schizophrenia. *Psychoanalytic Quarterly* 2: 519–556.

Von Domarus, E. (1944). The specific laws of logic in schizophrenia. In Kasanin, J.S. (Editor), *Language and Thought in Schizophrenia: Collected Papers.* Oakland CA, University of California Press, 1944.

Waldinger, R., and Gunderson, J. (1987). *Effective Psychotherapy with Borderline Patients: Case Studies.* New York: Macmillan.

Winnicott, D.W. (1971). *Playing and Reality.* London: Tavistock.

Part I

General perspectives on the psychoanalytic experience with psychosis

Chapter 1

Child psychosis

An impairment in the work of representation

Didier Houzel[1]

The origin of the concept of child psychosis

The word "psychosis" appeared in the context of Germanic romantic psychiatry (Karl Friedrich Canstatt, 1841; Ernst Baron Von Feuchtersleben, 1845). At the time, the issue was not the child, but rather one of describing "mental diseases", to be distinguished from "neuroses", nervous diseases. During the whole of the nineteenth century, mental diseases in children were ignored, with the exception of the treatise by Paul Moreau de Tours (1888), who simply recognised the possible presence, before puberty, of psychic symptoms described in the adult. When Kraepelin (1899) described "early dementia", he scarcely envisaged a pre-pubertal outbreak of the disease, since he attributed it to a sort of brain intoxication resulting from the genital pressure of puberty, even if he accepted that 5% of future schizophrenics had already presented symptoms in childhood. It is striking to note that, for more than a century, while adult psychiatry was increasingly isolating different syndromes better, child psychopathology was limited to mental retardation and character disorders. The developing mind of the child was therefore considered as a consciousness of the present instant, dominated by uncontrolled or poorly controlled instinctual tendencies, thus incapable of developing a pathological form of functioning due quite simply to a lack of overall organisation.

The first to isolate a form of infantile psychosis was the Italian psychiatrist Sancte de Sanctis (1906) when he described "very early dementia", which he distinguished clearly from mental retardation and regarded as a specific form of child psychosis. Eugen Bleuler (1911) acknowledged that a small proportion of schizophrenias occurred in childhood, and it was after Bleuler that the notion of "infantile psychosis" developed. H. W. Potter (1933) was the first to use the expression "child schizophrenia", an expression that gradually gave way to that of "infantile psychosis" as a refinement of child psychiatric clinical material made it possible to isolate different forms of psychoses: autistic psychoses (Kanner, 1943; Asperger, 1944), symbiotic psychoses (Mahler, 1952), deficit-based psychoses (Misès, 1968), psychotic dysharmonies (Misès and Barande, 1963).

This spadework in the field of child psychopathology during the twentieth century was considerable. It should be noted that it was largely based on psychoanalysis which had highlighted the dynamics of psychic development; while this is admittedly dependent on the innate equipment of the child, it is necessarily deployed within relationships with the key figures around him/her in a subjective and intersubjective history. Psychic development could no longer be conceived merely in terms of maturation, but as a dynamic complex including organic factors, as well as subjective and intersubjective factors, and even social and cultural factors.

As a result of a seesaw movement, the likes of which psychiatry has been familiar with since its foundation, all this painstaking clinical and nosographical work had to yield in the 1980s to a vast nosographical catchall, mixing once again what had been patiently distinguished – autism, retardation, dementia – in an uncertain continuum baptised sometimes as "pervasive developmental disorders" and sometimes as "autistic spectrum disorders". There were many reasons for this return to non-differentiation. I will insist on one of them that seems to me to be crucial. I will call it the *aetiological a priori*.

The question of aetiology

In the same year, 1979, two events combined to give an exclusive place to the organic aetiology of infantile psychoses. The first was the publication in the *Journal of Autism and Developmental Disorders* of an editorial written by Eric Schopler, Michael Rutter, and Stella Chess (1979) which rejected the dynamic psychopathological approach that had prevailed hitherto in the study of infantile autism in favour of an exclusively organic aetiology impeding the development of the brain (embryological, perinatal or genetic). The second event was the publication by L. Wing and J. Gould (1979) of their research based on a hereditary aetiology of infantile autism which had led them to extend their investigations to the collaterals of the child affected. This led them to define a *triad of social impairments*: communication disorders, socialisation disorders, and restricted and repetitive interests, a triad that has become the basis of modern classifications (DSM, International Classification of Mental Diseases).

The problem is not the hypothesis, which is entirely legitimate, of an organic, genetic or other origin of the autistic syndromes, but the hypostasis of this hypothesis as a certitude excluding any other hypothesis, giving rise to endless debates between the upholders of organogenesis and those of psychogenesis.

The *aetiological a priori*, which I am denouncing here, seems to me to be at the heart of the sterile debates agitating professional and associative circles. In this respect, I equally denounce the *aetiological a priori* of certain psychoanalysts, an *a priori* that has its source, moreover, in the key article

by L. Kanner (1943) in which he described autistic parents as lacking emotional warmth. We know that he subsequently deeply regretted having
adopted this position, one that was no doubt dictated by the fashion of
that era known as "relational psychopathology" which flourished in the
United States of America with the dominant figures of Frieda Fromm-
Reichmann (1950) and Harry Stack Sullivan (1953).

We know the use that B. Bettelheim (1967) made of this *aetiological a
priori*, and how he was bitterly and legitimately reproached for doing so.
Other currents of psychoanalysis have brought their influence to bear in
the same direction, in particular that arising from the teaching of Jacques
Lacan, of which one of the chief representatives was Maud Mannoni
(1964).

These *a prioris* must be denounced, whatever their origin. It should be
added that psychoanalysis does not have a role to play in this aetiological debate. It is not concerned with "aetiologies", but with "meaning".
Another form of causality is involved, it is true, but a form that is quite
distinct from what the philosopher Aristotle (2005) called "efficient causality", describing it rather as "final causality", a form that modern epis-
temologists call "intentionality" or alternatively "reason". This underlies
what the philosopher W. Dilthey (1883) called "comprehensive psychology", to be distinguished from "explanatory psychology", a distinction
that K. Jaspers (1913) took up by distinguishing between a "comprehensive psychopathology" and an "explanatory psychopathology".

Psychoanalysis is concerned with meaning and not with aetiology, as
S. Freud had asserted in 1897 in his famous letter to Fliess (the so-called
"letter of the equinox", dated 21 September 1897): "I no longer believe
in my neurotica. . . . I was so far influenced (by this) that I was ready to
give up two things: the complete resolution of a neurosis and the certain
knowledge of its *etiology* in childhood" (see Masson, 1985, pp. 264–265)
(my emphasis).

Psychoanalysis: an inescapable
therapeutic reference

I think that the first thing to do with an autistic or psychotic child corresponds to what the American philosopher W. V. O. Quine (1960) called,
following N. L. Wilson (1959) the "principle of charity", which consists in
crediting one's interlocutor with a maximum of rationality in what he/she
expresses, on the condition that we extend this requirement of rationality to the unconscious mind. In other words: the expressions of the child,
whatever they may be, must be considered as carriers of meaning, most
often unconscious.

An error that is often made is to treat the communication of these children in a neurotic or characteropathic way. If an autistic child creates a

mess in the room, the therapist is tempted to say to him/her: "You're doing that to make me angry", as if a conscious intention had dictated the child's act. In fact, it is not a matter of a conscious intention, but rather of what I propose to call an unconscious intention or alternatively a *mise en scène*. This links up with the notion, which I find very fruitful, of Francisco Varela, Thompson, and Rosch (1993) of *énaction*, derived from the English *enactment*, which means *mise en scène* in the theatrical sense of the term. The central idea defended by Varela is that the brain and the mind are not apparatuses for recording passively what the subject perceives in the external world, but dynamic systems in interaction with this external world, including the human environment, which are capable of creating and enacting new forms arising from this interaction. In the classical language of philosophy and of psychoanalysis, we speak of representation (*Vorstellung*), which should be understood in the sense, not of a true copy, but of a creation of the mind. The hypothesis that I want to examine is that autism spectrum disorders, irrespective of their aetiology(ies), result from a failure of this work of representation.

In the notions of *enaction* and *representation*, there is a reference to intentionality: the psychic apparatus, to use the expression that Freud borrowed from Fechner, cathects the world, not passively but actively, obeying innate requirements that govern the equilibrium and stability of the body just as much as those of the mind. The reference to intentionality is essential in psychology, psychopathology and psychoanalysis. The philosopher Franz Brentano (1874), who was Freud's mentor, had defined psychic phenomena in terms of their intentionality: "consciousness is consciousness of something", he said, reaccrediting thereby the thought of Aristotle and the scholastics. But for him it was obvious that all intentionality was conscious: if I perform an act, if I say something, it is because I want to obtain such and such a result or transmit such and such a message. I think that one of Freud's fundamental discoveries was what may be called "unconscious intentionality": I do something, I say something, I think something, I am well aware of it, but I do not know what meaning it has. Freud (1901) showed that a slip of the tongue, a bungled action, a dream or neurotic symptom had a meaning, but a meaning of which the subject himself is unaware. Each of the phenomena cited is conscious, but its aim is unconscious. It is in this sense that I speak of unconscious intentionality.

It is this kind of unconscious intentionality that we come across in autistic behaviours. It is as if the child were showing through his (or her) behaviour his inner state which, moreover, he does not clearly perceive himself. Saying to the child I mentioned earlier, "Perhaps you are showing me how much disorder you feel in your head" is much more adequate than attributing him with conscious intentionality. It is, in fact, as if he were enacting his own psychic state which he cannot think about himself or communicate. We must then be very attentive to the circumstances surrounding this enactment, circumstances that must be described in detail in order to give full meaning to what the child is showing: "You feel totally overwhelmed in your head because this or that person is not there, or because we did not do the same things as usual". A commentary of this kind has a chance of calming the child down, at least temporarily, thanks to the meaning that it offers.

This does not mean, however, that one should let the child do anything he wants, without setting limits. Too often the error has been to think that unlimited tolerance was possible and that it would one day lead the child to reconciliation with his human environment. Experience shows that there is always a limit to an adult's tolerance, however gifted and patient he or she may be. It also shows that leaving the child without limits helps preserve his sense of omnipotence, which is particularly frightening for him, and feeds the vicious circle in which he is caught: for him, if there is no limit, it is because any limit would be unbearable, so he has to struggle in an omnipotent way against every external constraint instead of reconciling himself gradually with the world by accepting its rules.

The containing function

One of the major difficulties in working with children belonging to the autism spectrum is to combine, in the right proportions, the indispensable psychic availability and receptivity he/she needs with the necessary limits to his/her destructiveness. This balance allows for what Wilfred Bion (1962) called a *containing function*, which is the psychic task that the mother must fulfil for the infant and the therapist for his/her patient. The model he proposes is based on the mother/baby relationship within the dyad: the baby has intense somato-psychic experiences but cannot deal with them psychically, that is to say, give them meaning; he can only evacuate them outside of himself through his crying, gestures, mimic expressions, muscular tensions, etc. The mother must be receptive to all these messages, which make her experience similar states to those the baby is experiencing, albeit less intensely. Above all, she has the possibility of giving them meaning and, of course, of responding to the child by giving him/her the appropriate care as she sees fit. But what is important to understand is that, in her ministrations, the mother does not content herself with satisfying the corporal needs of her baby; nor does she content herself with providing him with the psychic relaxation and bonus of pleasure associated with this satisfaction. She also provides meaning for what he was experiencing, and so gradually the child, on the basis of his past experiences, will be able to attribute meaning himself to what he is experiencing.

The studies of two experimental psychologists have recently lent remarkable support to the hypothesis of the mother's containing function and elucidated the notion of unconscious intentionality that I am putting forward. The studies in question are those of Gergely and Watson (Gergely, 2004) on what they call *social bio-feedback*. These two authors were interested in studying the imitation of the infant by his mother. They have shown that mothers imitated the mimic expressions of their baby, but in a slightly exaggerated way and with a note of irony. They make the assumption that babies are not aware at the beginning of their own emotional states and that they become conscious of them only by seeing these excessive and somewhat mocking imitations of their mothers. They refer to the technique of *feedback*, by means of which it is possible to become aware of the variations of a physiological state of one's own body, for example, blood pressure, by associating these variations that are normally not perceived with an external stimulus, for example, a sound which, for its part, is perceived. The subject, then, gradually perceives his blood pressure variations even in the absence of an external stimulus. Some gifted subjects are even able to control more or less the variations of the physiological state in question. This is what fakirs do. In *social biofeedback* it is not a matter of becoming aware of a physiological state, but rather of an emotional state that is initially unconscious. To achieve this the mother's imitation must be congruent; that is to say, it must correspond closely to the emotional state expressed by the infant, and further it must be marked in such a way that the infant can understand that the mother is not expressing her own emotional states but rather is reflecting his own emotional states. An incongruent or unmarked imitation merely confuses the issue and impedes the infant from identifying with his own internal states.

Psychic bisexuality of the containing function

Bion described the containing function as a purely maternal function. My experience of treating autistic children has led me to make the hypothesis that this containing function is in fact bisexual. It must combine, in the right proportions that evolve over the course of time, aspects of maternal availability and receptivity and aspects of paternal consistency and limitation. This bisexuality of the containing function needs to be rediscovered when one is caring for a child belonging to the autism spectrum, and it is essential that it is the same person who provides the complementary aspects of the maternal and paternal poles. I would like to point out on this subject that although the mother draws on her maternal identifications to become a mother in her turn, she also has paternal identifications that help her not to let herself be invaded by the demands of the child, which by nature are unlimited. The autistic child is no more capable than the infant of entering into a truly triangular relationship and of sharing a relationship with several partners. It is only subsequently that he or she will become capable of doing so if things go as well as possible. The therapist's recourse is thus not to call on a third party to establish with the child what he or she believes to be a triangulation, but to obtain help in discovering or rediscovering in him or herself the right maternal/paternal equilibrium that I have referred to in the relationship with the child.

The orientation of an autistic child towards this or that form of care depends primarily on the necessities of this containing function. If the child is oriented towards a specialised institution, it is because he or she needs an adapted concrete setting that allows the carers to provide this containing function, that is to say, being both receptive and consistent with regard to the child's behaviours and modes of relating. As soon as the child is able to tolerate the frustration imposed by a group situation, it is better to let him or her benefit from a period of more or less adapted schooling.

It hardly needs stressing that multiple measures are necessary when taking care of these children. We are no longer in the era when there was a clear opposition between psychotherapeutic treatment and educative and pedagogical care. The child needs both. He or she needs educative care for the purposes of socialisation and pedagogy to help him/her discover without fear the surrounding world and to understand it; great progress has been made since the 1980s in this pedagogical approach, which must be very progressive and structured. But the child also needs therapeutic care in order to get out of the vicious circles in which he/she is trapped by the autistic or psychotic processes, which in turn helps him/her to benefit as much as possible from the educative, pedagogical and leisure experiences that are on offer. I will focus here on individual psychotherapeutic forms of care.

I am going to look in detail at this last aspect of the measures that can be proposed to an autistic or psychotic child: an individual psychotherapy on as frequent a basis as possible and for as long as possible. I want to stress that by insisting on this aspect of the treatment, I am not overlooking either the work that needs to be done with the parents or all the work of elaboration that takes place within institutions.

The principle of the treatment

The general principle of any analytic treatment is to help the patient give (or give again) psychic form to what he/she is experiencing inwardly. Freud borrowed the term of German philosophical vocabulary to denote these psychic forms that it is a matter of creating or rediscovering: namely, the term "representation" (*Vorstellung*). We speak, then, of a *work of representation*. The experience, now secular, of psychoanalysts and of their patients has amply showed that what has not been experienced in the psychic world and which, for one reason or another, could not be represented is inevitably a source of mental disturbance and suffering. Freud accounted for this

phenomenon using the scientific models available in his time, those in particular of thermodynamics. Thus he put forward the hypothesis of a psychic
energy, the *libido*, which sometimes cathects representations, guaranteeing
it a peaceful outcome and favouring harmonious psychic development and
functioning, and sometimes, for lack of finding an outcome in representations, manifesting itself in the form of anxiety; finally, it is also sometimes
expressed through psychopathological symptoms which are a result of
mechanisms aimed at fighting against anxiety, but at the price of certain
limitations in development or in mental functioning.

Nowadays, other models are available and, I think, more adequate to
account for certain aspects of the process of analysis. We can understand
now, which was not the case in Freud's time, that, under certain conditions, processes of self-organisation can take place within a dynamic system which lead to the creation and stabilisation of forms, here psychic
forms that can be grouped together under the generic term "representation". The whole art of the psychoanalyst is thus to create the conditions
permitting such self-organisation.

Melanie Klein (1930) spoke of *symbol formation* to denote this same process. She drew on the theory of object-relations in which the object, that
is to say, the person cathected, does not only have the role of permitting
instinctual drive discharge, but also of receiving and transforming the
primitive communications of the child. In this context, she made the fundamental discovery in 1946 of "projective identification", a mechanism
with which the subject unconsciously splits his mind and projects a split-
off part of himself into another mind, either to get rid of it or to protect it
from his destructive tendencies. She called the transference based on this
projective identification the "infantile transference". Equipped with this
new concept, many Kleinian analysts became passionately interested in
the psychoanalytic treatment of the most severe forms of psychopathology in both the adult and the child.

Among these Kleinian authors, I would like to stress the contributions
of Frances Tustin (1972, 1986, 1990, 1992), who discovered in autistic children a still more archaic level than those described by Melanie Klein, who
herself had identified more archaic levels than those described by Freud.
The level explored by Tustin in particular corresponds to what Bion (1962),
who was her analyst for fourteen years, called the *container/contained relationship*. This will lead me to describe a more archaic transference than the
infantile transference explored by Melanie Klein, itself more archaic than the
transference neurosis as described by Freud. But before doing so I would
like to say a few more words about the analytic process in general, as it can
be envisaged nowadays in my view.

In total, I think that the best way of characterising the analytic process
is to acknowledge that, throughout the treatment, there is both a bringing to light of pre-existing representations but which are repressed in the

Unconscious, and a creation of new representations within the dynamic system of the transference/countertransference relationship between the analysand and the analyst. For this to occur, processes of stabilisation must be set up at the heart of this dynamic system so that the instinctual and emotional turbulence is not suppressed or left to its own devices, but channelled into stable forms that are the support of our representations, thoughts and symbols. The psychoanalytic exploration of autistic children leads me to think that these processes of stabilisation unfold in several phases, each corresponding to a prevailing mode of transference. The transference modes that I have identified are the following: the *transference on to the container*, the *infantile transference*, the *transference neurosis* and the *end of the treatment*.

Each of these stages of the elaboration of the transference corresponds to an ever higher level of stabilisation: the elaboration of the transference on to the container leads to delimiting in a stable way the frontiers of the self; the elaboration of the infantile transference leads to the stabilisation of the internal world; the elaboration of the transference neurosis leads to the stabilisation of sexual identity.

The transference on to the container

It is very common at the beginning of the treatment. In fact, it is as if the child were pouring into the therapeutic situation his/her own psychic states and had to discover the possibility of reuniting, conserving and rediscovering them. All these functions correspond to the *containing function*. The psychotherapist offers him-/herself as a containing object by showing the child how, from one session to another, he/she has kept all the messages that the child has communicated to him/her and how he/she is trying to link them up with each other. It is of course somewhat artificial to identify a period that is more specifically devoted to this containing function of the transference. In fact, the analyst plays this role of container for the projections of the child throughout the entire treatment. It is nonetheless useful to accord a prominent place to this function of receptivity and of gathering together at the beginning of the treatment, and in particular to accept the need to wait as long as is necessary before offering the child interpretations on the content, because if they were made prematurely, they would be felt to be persecuting. F. Tustin (1972) showed that the autistic child experienced in a traumatic way what he/she had felt to be a premature psychic birth; that is to say, he/she became aware too early that his/her libidinal object is separable from his/her own body. It is important to avoid reproducing this trauma in the treatment. Initial work needs to be done in connection with this transference on to the container with the aim of integrating or reintegrating the psychic bisexuality in the child's constitution.

In the psychoanalytic exploration of the autistic child, we are dealing with a pathology of alterity. Being able to distinguish oneself from others, to establish a frontier between Self and the Object, to tolerate being separate from others and everything that that supposes in terms of a gap, limits, differences and frustrations is what is at stake in the relationship with *a container* (or *envelope*) endowed with bisexual qualities combined in the right proportions. I think that without a bisexual container, there can be neither Self nor Other; there is either a spreading out on the surface of juxtaposed sensory experiences as in autism (Meltzer et al., 1975) or forceful penetration of the object and entanglement in which any differentiation of the Self and of the Object is impossible, as in psychoses.

Frances Tustin (1992) drew attention to the deep splits that operate in autistic children between these qualities of the psychic envelope which are expressed through oppositions between contrasting sensory qualities: dry and humid, rough and smooth, hard and soft, hot and cold, etc. She linked these split sensory qualities to a splitting of the *psychic bisexuality* of the first container. It is as if, she says, for the psychotic child, the rapprochement between paternal/male qualities and maternal/female qualities was felt to be destructive and catastrophic:

> Gradually, "soft" sensations become associated with "taking in", with receptivity. "Hard" sensations become associated with "entering" and "thrusting". At some point, these become associated with the infant's bisexuality. "Hard" thrusting become "male", and "soft" receptivity become "female". When, on the basis of a co-operative suckling experience, the "hard" entering nipple and tongue are experienced as working together with the "soft" receptive mouth and breast, then a "marriage" between "male" and "female" elements takes place.
>
> (Tustin, 1992, pp. 100–101)

In this citation, Tustin suggests that the male elements are penetrating, while the female elements are receptive. In fact, I am assuming that bisexuality is situated at a more archaic level, in which male elements *do not penetrate* female elements: they serve, it could be said, as reinforcement for the maternal container, just as certain buildings need buttresses to ensure their stability. I think, therefore, that it is very important to acknowledge that it is the same containing object that must possess in the right proportions female/maternal and male/paternal qualities. Any paternal element dissociated from the container is likely to be felt to be threatening, persecuting and destructive. This is probably what happens in autistic children, who split psychic bisexuality at a very early stage.

In analytic treatments, it is above all by elaborating the countertransference that the psychoanalyst can help the child reintegrate the split psychic bisexuality of his/her containing object. Tustin insisted a great deal on the necessity of demonstrating both great availability and great receptivity, but also a certain firmness in conducting the treatment. This involves a combination of the maternal/female and paternal/male aspects of the containing function.

The infantile transference

Analysis of the *infantile transference* is the second stage. We use the term "infantile transference" as a way of representing relations with others characterised by trust in the containing capacity of the other, but also by a massive fear of rivals who could expel the subject from his/her place, occupy it entirely and threaten violent retaliation if he/she tries to get it back. This corresponds to what one feels with a very young child who is very eager to have the attention he/she is receiving but very mistrustful towards any other child, and equally towards an adult who might take attention away from him/her. This is a phase during which fantasies are particularly violent, like those, moreover, that can be found in the fairy tales or comic strips that children love or that they sometimes enact in their nightmares: a world of monsters, witches, ghosts, etc. Melanie Klein's work was focussed on this analysis of the infantile transference. It has two essential characteristics: the first is that it corresponds to a part-object relationship, that is to say, a relationship with an object endowed with physical and psychic qualities, but devoid of its own desire and will, of personal history; the second is that it is essentially based on projective identification (Klein, 1946).

The transference neurosis

This corresponds to the oedipal period described by Freud. It is during this period that the child organises his/her sexual identity and the ideas he/she has of the attributes and roles of each of the sexes. But this does not occur without conflict or anxiety. The fabric of this transference neurosis consists in rivalry with the parent of the same sex and a particular form of anxiety linked to this rivalry, which concerns the representation of the subject's own sexual capacities. Freud called this type of anxiety *castration anxiety*. When the autistic child reaches this level of organisation, it can be said that he/she has already travelled a considerable distance and is beginning to resemble psychically all the other children in the world. In the best of cases, he/she may reach this phase of development. Unfortunately, the majority of autistic children do not reach this phase or only in a fragile way. Indeed, one of the characteristics of the process of treating autistic children is the instability of the most elaborate phases of development. They have been reached, but it takes nothing at all to plunge the child again into his/her previous modes of functioning. The psychoanalyst and the parents therefore need much patience to help the child consolidate as best as possible the phases of his/her development.

The process of termination

This is particularly difficult to describe. Can a psychoanalytic treatment ever be said to be finished? The best criterion for terminating a psychoanalysis is the observation that not only is the child managing to adapt him-/herself to new environments, but that he/she is continuing between the sessions, and particularly during the holidays, to make significant progress by him-/herself. Once again, it is to a criterion of stability, associated with criteria of evolution and creativity, that I am referring.

Clinical illustration

I will conclude by illustrating with clinical material a few stages in the treatment of a child whom I followed for a long time for a severe autistic syndrome, on a basis of three sessions per week.

The parents had manifested their concern about the delay of the boy's psychomotor development and particularly about the fact that he had not begun to speak. Furthermore, they had noticed behaviours that they described as "strange": he would bang his head on the ground or against walls, and make rocking movements back and forth. Towards the age of twenty months he gave his parents the impression that he was withdrawing from the world, that he was "in his own bubble"; he manifested restricted interests like opening and closing doors, and listening to music; he did not develop any symbolic play; finally, he would take hold of an adult's hand to obtain what he wanted and did not point his finger.

Extracts from the material of the analytic treatment

After playing games in the first few sessions that involved dispersing everything that could be found in the room such as coloured pencils, papers, toys and so on, he wanted to gather up the objects and to control the containers. In particular, he was very interested in the boxes of modelling clay that were in his material and in the lids for closing them. He soon uttered the word "lid", which was the first word I heard from his mouth.

After two months, he began to show interest in water. He mainly played with hot water and said "hot", then "it's hot" while touching the water with his hand. I said to him that it was hot whenever we saw each other again. During the following sessions he played at spraying the room with water; he tried to suck the tap, which he could not reach with his mouth, but he said "Mummy" several times as he was playing with the water or while looking at it. One day, after playing with water by trying to get hold of the stream of water, he came and put his head right against my belly, which I interpreted to him as a wish to get into my belly and to be like a baby in his mother's womb. After this interpretation, he leaned backwards, and I had to hold him to stop him from falling (this evoked a fantasy of birth in me). Then he turned round and placed his back against me as if to have some support. After that, he emptied the boxes of modelling clay of their contents and wanted to leave. I interpreted that he may have had the impression he had made me completely empty by taking everything that I had inside me (from my notes I realised that this could correspond to a postnatal maternal depression, as if his birth had emptied his mother) and that he then wanted to leave because he felt I was dangerous.

In these first sessions, we can see him constituting a transferential containing object for himself. It is the attention, regularity and availability of the therapist that characterise this container. But the child needs to represent this for him-/herself very concretely in a close physical relationship that is evocative of a fantasy of returning to the womb. This containing object has, of course, maternal qualities, but it must at the same time, as I have said, have paternal qualities closely interwoven with its maternal qualities. A purely maternal container would be attractive and seductive, but also engulfing and annihilating.

Gradually, trust in the containing object and in its qualities increases. The child can project into it his/her libidinal and aggressive contents without fearing a threatening backlash. But then a new problem emerges: the child feels he/she must defend this very precious container against all possible rivals and derive the maximum of benefit from it. Frances Tustin described what she called the fantasy of the "nest of babies":

> In this phase, when the child is beginning to be able to bear the awareness of a clear distinction between himself and other people, there invariably develops a fantasy which I have come to call the "nest of babies" fantasy. This is associated with the notion that there are "special babies" who are given "special food". (John called it "egg-da".) My "brain children", the children in my mind whom I am felt to feed when I am preoccupied and averted from them, are sometimes felt to be the recipients of this special food. There is the fantasy that he (the patient/the child who is receiving my therapeutic milk) is in competition with predatory rivals on the other side of the "breast" who want to snatch the nipple away from him – to take away his chance of life and sustenance.

> (Tustin, 1972, pp. 177–178)

I have put forward the hypothesis (Houzel, 2000) that at the moment when the child gains access to alterity and begins to become aware of his/her inner psychic life, it is as if every content of the treatment room could be experienced as representing rival babies who remain permanently present in the therapeutic setting and who, in this respect, are supposed to profit, in the child's absence of this special food of which Frances Tustin speaks and of which the child feels deprived between the sessions.

Later, I saw the beginnings of a transference neurosis emerge in this child in which unconscious fantasies were becoming organised in relation to the primal scene and the theme of castration: one day he arrived a bit ahead of time and saw me in the company of a female psychologist. Once we were in the treatment room, he asked me, "Why was there a lady?" and then, "Where did the lady go?" I told him that I didn't know. He concluded that she had gone home. He then started saying to me: "If you want, I can break your feet, legs, knees, etc.", including my head and hair. Then he started banging a metal cupboard which resounded, and he counted the blows that he dealt. Suddenly he asked me if he could go to the toilet. When he returned I asked him what had made him think of doing a pooh. I got no response, but he started banging on the metal cupboard again while counting and making me count the blows, which I accepted to do once or twice, but then I stopped. He told me to touch my feet, my legs, etc. I did this once, but then refused to continue while pointing out to him that he seemed to want to prevent me from thinking by making me do what he wanted, perhaps because he had seen me arrive with the lady and he was afraid that I was thinking about her rather than him.

For the first time, he sat down and drew some scribbles with each coloured pencil in turn. He covered the paper with his scribbles in all colours. Then, he drew with three coloured pencils together and made less compact forms that resembled clouds.

His language is now well developed, and he is learning things at school. He still presents some bizarre forms of behaviour, but is quite well socialised. The most interesting thing recently has been the development of a game of make-believe: before, whenever he emerged from his autistic isolation, marked by repeated water games, he would rush towards me in an attempt to bite me, which, of course, I did not allow him to do. He does not do that anymore now. He plays dînette with me; we pretend to eat delicious dishes together which seem to me to reflect the quality of the fantasised and emotional exchanges that have developed between us. From now on, he can manage these encounters with the help of representations and no longer needs to act out. Could it be that treating an autistic child consists first and foremost in helping him/her to think?

Note

1 Translated by Andrew Weller.

References

Aristotle. (2005). *Physics, or, Natural Healing*. Trans by G. Coughlin. South Bend: S. Augustine's Press.

Asperger, H. (1944). Die autistischen psychopathenin kindesalter. *Archiv für Psychiatrie und Nervenkrankeiten* 117: 76–136.

Bettelheim, B. (1967). *The Empty Fortress*. New York: Free Press.

Bion, W.R. (1962). *Learning from Experience*. New York: Basis Books.

Bleuler, E. (1911). *Dementia Praecox or the Group of Schizophrenias*. Trans by J. Zinkin. New York: International Universities Press, 1950.

Brentano, F. (1874). *Psychology from an Empirical Standpoint*. London: Routledge, 1995.

Canstatt, K.F. (1841). *Handburch der Medicinischen Klinik*. Stuttgart, Germany: Enke.

Dilthey, W. (1883). *Introduction to the Human Sciences*. Princeton: Princeton University Press, 1995.

Feuchtersleben, E. Baron von. (1845). *Lerbuch des Ärztlichen Seelenkinde*. Vienna: Gerold.

Freud, S. (1901). *The Psychopathology of Everyday Life*. S.E. 6. London: The Hogarth Press.

Fromm-Reichmann, F. (1950). *Principles of Intensive Psychotherapy*. Chicago: University of Chicago Press.

Gergely, G. (2004). The social biofeedback theory of affect-mirroring: The development of emotional self-awareness and self-control in infancy. In Fonagy, P., Gergely, G., Jurist, E.L., and Target, M. (Editors), *Affect Regulation, Mentalization, and the Development of the Self*. London and New York: Karnac Books, pp. 145–202.

Houzel, D. (2000). Le fantasme du nid aux bébés. *Journal de la psychanalyse de l'enfant* 27: 83–106.

Jaspers, K. (1913). *General Psychopathology*. Trans by J. Hoenig and M. Hamilton. Baltimore: The John Hopkins University Press, 1957.

Kanner, L. (1943). Autistic disturbances of affective contact. *The Nervous Child* II: 3217–3250.

Klein, M. (1930). The importance of symbol formation in the development of the ego. *International Journal of Psychoanalysis* 11: 24–39.

Klein, M. (1946). Notes on some schizoid mechanisms. *International Journal of Psychoanalysis* 27: 99–110.

Kraepelin, E. (1899). *Lerburch der Psychiatrie* (6ème édition). Leipzig: Barth.

Mahler, M. (1952). On child psychosis and schizophrenia – Autistic and symbiotic infantile psychosis. *Psychoanal St Child* 7: 266–305.

Mannoni, M. (1964). *The Retarded Child and the Mother*. London: Tavistock, 1973.

Masson, J.M. (1985) (Editor). *The Complete Letters of Sigmund Freud to Wilhelm Fliess, 1887–1904*. Cambridge, MA: Belknap.

Meltzer, D., Bremner, J., Hoxter, S., Weddell, D., and Wittenberg, I. (1975). *Explorations in Autism: A Psychoanalytic Study*. London: Karnac Books, 2008.

Misès, R. (1968). Problèmes nosologiques posés par les psychoses de l'enfant. *La psychiatrie de l'enfant* 11 (2): 492–512.

Misès, R., and Barande, I. (1963). Les états déficitaires dysharmoniques grave. Ètude clinique de formes précoces intriquant relation psychotique et symptomatologie de type déficitaire. *La psychiatrie de l'enfant* VI: 1–78.

Moreau de Tours, P. (1888). *La folie chez les enfants*. Paris: Baillière.

Potter, H.W. (1933). Schizophrenia in children. *American Journal of Psychoanalysis* 6: 1257–1270.

Quine, W.V.O. (1960). *Word and Object*. Cambridge, MA: MIT Press.

Sanctis, S. de. (1906). Sopra alcune varietà delle demenza precoce. *Rivista sper di Frenatria* XXII: fasc. 1 and 2.

Schopler, E., Rutter, M., and Chess, S. (1979). Change of the journal scope and title. *Journal of Autism and Developmental Disorders* 9 (1): 1–10.

Sullivan, H.S. (1953). *The Interpersonal Theory of Psychiatry*. New York: Norton.

Tustin, F. (1972). *Autism and Childhood Psychosis*. London: The Hogarth Press.

Tustin, F. (1986). *Autistic Barriers in Neurotic Patients*. London: Karnac Books.

Tustin, F. (1992). (Revised Edition). *Autistic States in Children*. London and New York: Tavistock/Routledge.

Tustin, F. (1990). *The Protective Shell in Children and Adults*. London: Karnac Books.

Varela, F., Thompson, E., and Rosch, E. (1993). *L'inscription corporelle de l'esprit*. Paris: Seuil.

Wilson, N.L. (1959). Substances without substrata. *The Review of Metaphysic* 12 (4): 521–539.

Wing, L., and Gould, J. (1979). Severe impairments of social interactions and associated abnormalities in children: Epidemiology and classification. *Journal of Autism and Developmental Disorders* 9: 11–29.

Chapter 2

Chestnut Lodge and the psychoanalytic approach to psychosis

John Kafka

The 100th anniversary of the American Psychoanalytic Association was celebrated in the February 2011, volume 59 issue of the *Journal of the American Psychoanalytic Association*, for which I was asked to write a relevant article about the treatment of psychosis. Comments on my paper by three colleagues and my response to these comments are also in this issue. Because I had been asked to write broadly about the development of the psychoanalytic treatment of psychosis in America, my own theories and clinical material are presented in a very condensed form. They are much more fully developed in my book *Multiple Realities in Clinical Practice*. By the way, I did not choose the title of the Italian translation of my book, *Le Nuove Realtà, Percezione e psycoanalisi*.

Psychoanalysis and the treatment of psychosis

The study of psychosis has a long history in psychoanalysis and so does the debate about the suitability of psychoanalysis for treatment of schizophrenia. Nathaniel London (1973), in his "An essay on psychoanalytic theory: two theories of schizophrenia," gave an overview of the contrasting psychoanalytic views that psychosis is on a continuum with neurotic disorders, i.e. a conflict theory of schizophrenia versus a view that specific ego defects characterize psychosis. Freud thought that the schizophrenic cannot be treated psychoanalytically because his/her narcissistic libidinal withdrawal prevented the development of transference. That seemed to have remained Freud's basic position, but Ping-Nie Pao (1973) has called attention to some of Freud's other ideas about schizophrenia that are dispersed in various papers. Here is an example: "Freud did not seem to have dealt with thought disorder adequately. This deficit, however, was supplemented in two later papers (1915a), (1915b), in which he distinguished thing-presentation and word-presentation of an object and suggested that, in schizophrenia, *words* and not things are subjected to the primary psychic process" (p. 470). While he remained interested in the theory of schizophrenia, Freud's belief in the un-analyzability of schizophrenic patients also led to his lack of interest in the first psychoanalytic hospital organized by István Hollós, an analysand of Paul Federn.

In contrast to Freud's theory that the schizophrenic's basic pathology consists in the withdrawal of libido from external objects, Federn (1952) theorized that the ego *boundary* (my italics) was not sufficiently cathected. If there are not enough border guards, the ego cannot differentiate which stimuli come from the outside or which originate inside, whether they are perceptions or hallucinations. Federn was one of the early analysts who was interested in working with psychotic patients. His clinical approach was based on this theory. It is not surprising that one of his analysands, István Hollós, made the first attempt to operate a psychoanalytically informed hospital for psychotic patients. István Hollós, co-founder with Ferenczi of the Hungarian Psychoanalytic Association, directed such a hospital before World War I. "Already in the 1910's he was convinced that the 'liberation' of the mentally ill from the chains of their stigmatization will only become possible if society arrives at a psychoanalytic under-standing of its own madness, if nurses are taught that there is meaning in psychotic talk, and if caregivers analyze *their* Unconscious . . . and inte-grate the 'mad' parts of themselves." (Pestalozzi, Frisch, Hinshelwood, and Houzel, 1998). Federn's approach to the treatment of psychotics that influenced Hollós also implied that psychotics had *sane* parts that could be used therapeutically. Nevertheless, Federn thought that the therapist who had treated the patient during the psychotic episode might be con-taminated by psychosis for the patient and that treatment by a new, not contaminated, analyst of the same patient was preferable. At Chestnut Lodge, we found it preferable *not* to change therapists.[1]

The vision of those who started treating schizophrenic patients at Chest-nut Lodge resonated with the philosophy of the first psychoanalytic hos-pital. At Chestnut Lodge, from the very beginning, there was also a belief that there were sane parts to the psychotics that could be used in the thera-peutic work with these patients.

The early history of Chestnut Lodge and its move toward psychoanalytically informed treatment of psychosis

How did Chestnut Lodge evolve? A few words about its history and how it became a center for psychoanalytically informed treatment of severe pathology, eventually a unique institution.

Dr. Ernest Bullard, father of Dexter, had been a superintendent of a state hospital for the insane in Wisconsin. He wanted a hospital of his own and bought the Woodlawn Hotel in 1908, and Chestnut Lodge was born in 1910. Ernest Bullard was the only physician until 1925, when Dexter arrived. From then on, Dexter was in charge. His formal psychiatric training had consisted of two months at the Boston Psychopathic Hospital. Frieda Fromm-Reichmann was hired in 1935. Julia Waddell (1964), who became the Chief Nurse, writes that, when she arrived on May 12, 1935, the nursing staff consisted of a superintendent of nurses, two RNs, and five aides. She writes, "Orientation was unknown. . . . I was expected to go on night duty that evening. . . . Some medical students had been hired to 'cover' night duty in exchange for room and board and they would call for me at 4 o'clock to . . . meet the patients. A week or so later, about two o'clock in the morning I heard someone come onto the porch. . . . 'I'm Dr. Dexter Bullard. You must be Miss Blankenhorn (Mrs. Waddell's maiden name) . . . glad to have you here'. . . . The admission of patients was handled quite differently (at that time). We got no preview of what was coming . . . one night I was told a patient was to be admitted . . . the doorbell rang. The medical student and I went to the door and a mother and her 21-year-old son were standing on the porch arguing . . . the son said 'Mother, I can't leave you here.' The mother said, 'I certainly can't leave you in a place like this.' Which was the patient? I could not decide. So I kept them both all night. Dr. Bullard could settle this in the morning. The next night, when I came on, neither was there" (p. 123).

Dr. Douglas Noble (1963), describing a somewhat later phase in the early development of Chestnut Lodge, writes,

> Underlying the therapeutic program was the theory that the schizophrenic patient because of early hurts to his ego required a long period of affectionate care in which his trust in another person would be restored and intensive psychotherapeutic work would then become possible. In accordance with this concept, patients were encouraged to self-realization and exposed to very little frustration in the hospital. The patient was always right. This led to much frustration of the nursing personnel and staff, especially since the method was obviously susceptible of exploitation. Patient's privileges were reviewed frequently, sometimes by different doctors with not a little crossing of wires. Frieda Fromm-Reichmann and Dexter Bullard were remarkably faithful to their therapeutic concepts, often at the cost of great discomfort to themselves. In an early paper, Dexter Bullard describes a session with a patient who hurled an ash tray at him; there was another occasion on which he sat at the door of a room of a patient in a panic because the patient had a sheet of glass which he broke into pieces and threw at the therapist. Dr. Frieda Fromm-Reichmann tells of sitting on a bench beside a patient for an hour daily for several weeks while the patient remained silent. Then one day, he placed a newspaper in her accustomed seat saying that he did not wish her to dirty her dress. Most of the work, however, was less dramatic than these episodes would indicate. Dr. Bullard was at work every

morning at eight o'clock for his first hour and saw several patients daily in analysis. I recall Freida Fromm-Reichmann's trudging up the stairs to the fourth floor every night for weeks to see a schizophrenic patient who would not talk with her at any other time. There was, in other words, great interest but much drudgery. Some of the things that were done were later discarded but they were learned the hard way.[2]

(pp. 93–103)

From such beginnings, Chestnut Lodge developed into a unique institution – a place with about 100 patients and about 20 psychiatrists who had four to five sessions a week with each of their individual patients, and these psychiatrists met at least once a week in a small group with their colleagues; a place where senior staff members supervised junior members; where the psychiatrists, most of whom were psychoanalysts or were in psychoanalytic training, met at least once a week in staff conferences with members of the nursing and psychiatric aides staff, the social workers, one or two psychologists, the recreational staff, occupational, art and dance therapists; and one weekly all hospital meeting for patients and staff together! Add to this that there was quite an active social life among staff members, making Chestnut Lodge a hotbed of interpersonal activity. Work with psychotic and other severely disturbed individuals stirred up existential and deep intra-personal issues and contributed to an intellectually and emotionally charged atmosphere experienced by staff members.

I was a staff member from 1957 to 1967, although I continued to work with a few of my patients for several additional decades. In retrospect, I think that those of us who were interested in being therapists of psychotics in some way resembled a group of anthropologists who wanted to understand and to find a way of communicating with the inhabitants of psychosis-land. Perhaps, we also shared with anthropologists the temptations and the dangers of going native. I believe the unique culture of Chestnut Lodge, with its structure of supervision and small and large group discussions, offered an emotional and intellectual supportive framework – an arena to work through, or at least on, the profound counter-transference feelings associated with intense involvement with psychotic and other very disturbed individuals.

I have already referred to Dr. Noble's comment that some of the lessons learned in the early phases of his work at Chestnut Lodge were learned the hard way. These hard lessons consisted precisely in the findings of what does not work in the long run, even if it seemed successful for the moment. Both negative and positive findings from very extended longitudinal studies may be very different from the findings from quite time limited ones. Staff members who published what they learned are those who are known to the wider psychoanalytic community, but there were others who learned much and taught much to the rest of us and who never published anything. Dr. Milton Hendlich, for instance, remarkably successful in treating extremely traumatized patients, conveyed to us his therapeutic strategy of spending much time with his patients exploring every detail of their positive, not traumatic, memories.

The freedom to experiment with group and individual therapeutic approaches eventually led to a menu of theories and practices of Chestnut Lodge that included just about all the diverse approaches to treatment of severely disturbed patients that are described in a monograph entitled "Psychoanalytic psychotherapy in institutional settings" (Pestalozzi et al., 1998, p. xvii), for instance, the psycho-social nursing emphasis in the Cassel hospital. Chestnut Lodge also worked with a halfway house. Work was expanded by including families who lived at a great distance from the Lodge. Together with the social work staff, I was allowed to start a program in which visiting families could stay for several days in the Frieda Fromm-Reichmann cottage. I mention these developments now because they resonate with the radical shift in the asylum system that was created in Italy. Some of its architects were acquainted with the work done at Chestnut Lodge. In the Italian system, the program for each patient was supposed to be "tailor made." This was true to an even greater extent at the Lodge. Here is a brief description of the Italian system: "New patients are treated with different sorts of 'tailor-made' provision on a home and community basis, according to four different models as previously defined by Janssen: the *bifocal* model, with emphasis on a dual therapeutic relationship, *the small integrated-group model*, based on individual intervention involving the interaction of several professional figures and models, including, for instance, psychotherapeutic, pharmacological, and rehabilitative; the *community model*, based on the tradition of the 'therapeutic community'" (Pestalozzi et al., 1998, p. xvii).

At Chestnut Lodge, all these models were applied with "tailor-made" variations in emphasis and timing to all patients. Individual therapists at the Lodge experimented with many approaches that are now often parceled out as "educational," "rehabilitative," etc. modalities. The mainstay of treatment, however, was always a minimum of four or five times per week psychoanalytic individual therapy.

The development of therapeutic approaches to psychosis

Despite the intense interaction of the Chestnut Lodge staff members with each other, the large body of their publications cannot be called the work of a Chestnut Lodge *school*. The books and papers are very much of individuals with different theoretical and technical ideas and styles. There are, however, some common elements: all Chestnut Lodge authors recognized, on the one hand, the importance of using the healthy part of the individual patient and, on the other hand, the importance of following the patient into his/her psychotic world. The latter was seen as a prerequisite for establishing contact with such patients. Readers of the literature by Chestnut Lodge authors may note, however, that they differed in their focus on one or the other of the polarities of the "healthy" or the psychotic parts. References to classical ego-psychology, for instance, are especially elaborated in Ping-Nie Pao's papers (1973, 1983), and immersion in the world of psychosis is prominent in the writings of Harold Searles (1963). These differences in emphasis not only reflect differences in personal style but may also be an echo of the dual psychoanalytic theories of psychosis as *defect* or *conflict* (London, 1973; Kafka, 1997).

A theoretical discussion of these two views was never a central concern of Frieda Fromm-Reichmann, whose name is most closely associated with Chestnut Lodge. A refugee from Nazi Germany, she came to Chestnut Lodge in 1935. She had a broad background in psychiatry, neurology, and psychoanalysis, and had already published neurological and psychoanalytic papers. Jarl E. Dyrud (1989) has shown how these earlier experiences influenced her later work. After coming to Chestnut Lodge, she published and lectured widely. Her patients, students, supervisees, and colleagues contributed to a volume published on the occasion of the 50th anniversary of Frieda's coming to Chestnut Lodge (Silver, 1989). This volume, which also includes verbatim transcripts of some of her remarks in staff conferences, gives a vivid picture of her personality, her style, and her work. Frieda is described as forceful, intensively engaged, and direct especially as explicitly addressing the "healthy" and the psychotic parts of the patient at the same time. Jacob Arlow (1989) writes, "Hers was a special ability to understand a patient's metaphoric language but, more than that, she had the ability to communicate the understanding in a way that helped to create for her patients a bridge that led from metaphor to simile to objective communication. It was her special gift not only to understand the nature of the unconscious conflicts hidden behind the patient's delusion and metaphors, but also to use language that indicated to the patient that he was being understood. This perhaps was the first step on the road to recovery" (pp. 181–182).

Interviewed by Laurice McAfee (Silver, 1989), Joanne Greenberg, the author of *I Never Promised You a Rose Garden* and perhaps Frieda's best known patient, indicates that from her perspective, "the personalities have to fit in therapy and if the symptoms are metaphors, the therapist has to be someone who understands those metaphors or at least is amenable to learning them so that when they appear in the therapeutic dialogue, the right amount of weight is given to them" (p. 523). Concerning the polarity of the sane and psychotic parts, Joanne Greenberg's comments are particularly informative. Frieda told her that "you must take me with you," that she, Frieda, knows nothing about mental illness and that Joanne has to be her teacher (pp. 515–516). On the other hand, Greenberg speaks about the danger of being understood on the psychotic level. "People would tell you what perceptive things a patient had said. The thing is I want to choose my perceptions. I don't want them to come out of some kind of unconscious soup. I want it to be something I choose to say, not something that says me." Joanne added that being understood in that state felt horrifically dangerous: "I don't know how Frieda got around that. I remember the danger. . . . It's bigger than you are. It's more powerful. It can kill" (p. 528). "Maybe the strongest thing I'd like to say ever to anybody is that creativity and mental illness are *opposites*, not complements. It's a confusion of mental illness with creativity. Imagination is, includes, goes *out*, opens out, learns from experience. Craziness is the opposite: it is a fort that's a prison" (p. 527).

We have to note that this is Greenberg's retrospective view. There is no reason to believe that Fromm-Reichmann could have made any contact with a patient without acknowledging and following her into her psychotic world. What is striking is that, from the very beginning, Fromm-Reichmann functioned in both the non-psychotic and psychotic worlds. This is a useful approach that I also discovered and elaborated by noting that the schizophrenic patient may move in and out of psychotic mental organization very rapidly from second to second and that the therapist who speaks on the psychotic and non-psychotic level is more likely to be on target at some point. I also believe that the patient may be reluctant to let the therapist know, at least early in the therapeutic work, when he is more or less psychotic. This is one area where the patient, aware of his inadequate functioning generally, may feel that he can be "one up" on the therapist.

The great part of the literature emanating from Chestnut Lodge describes the efforts of the therapists to comprehend psychotic functioning and the counter-transference developments while working with such disturbed patients. This is a dominant feature in Harold Searles' work. In his paper (1963) "Transference psychosis in the psychotherapy of chronic schizophrenia," he describes his "realization that even the most deep and chronic symptoms of schizophrenia . . . emerge . . . (as) the manifestations of . . . (an) unconscious effort . . . of the patient . . . to maintain, and to become free from, modes of relatedness which held sway between himself and other persons in his childhood and which he is now fostering unconsciously . . . in . . . his relationship with his therapist" (p. 249). In Searles' view, the utter helplessness that the therapist feels may reflect the patient's helplessness in dealing with a disturbed parent. "Even the most . . . 'crazy', manifestations of schizophrenia come to reveal meaningfulness and reality-relatedness not only as transference reactions to the therapist, but, even beyond this, as delusional identifications with real aspects of the therapist's own personality" (p. 280). My personal reaction to Searles' moving descriptions of counter-transference developments is influenced by my experience of having been supervised by Searles for many years. At times, he spoke of the importance for a therapist of psychotic patients to ensure one's own emotional survival. One function of the kind of counter-transference examination that Searles described made prolonged work with psychotic patients tolerable. The scope and depth of Searles' counter-transference explorations did permit him to have contact with some almost inaccessible patients. His encouragement for me to have a "no-holds barred" search for my own raw emotional reactions proved valuable also in my work with both non-psychotic and psychotic patients. Searles' writings on counter-transference found a profound echo in many psychoanalysts including many who were not working with severely disturbed patients. Counter-transference reactions may be related to the patient's experiences in childhood, but Searles' implied view that these childhood experiences are a major etiological factor for schizophrenia is not now widely accepted. Willick (2001), for instance, points out that a psychoanalytic theory of the etiology of schizophrenia has "very serious inadequacies in the care taking person" and has not stood the test of time (p. 27). It should also be noted that Searles referred to schizophrenic patient efforts "to become free from, modes of relatedness which held sway between himself and other persons in his *childhood*" (my italics) (p. 249). Here Searles does speak essentially of a schizophreniogenic parent and does not dissociate himself from a view of an etiological factor in schizophrenia.

Other Chestnut Lodge authors do not propose a primary etiological theory of schizophrenia. Donald Burnham (1969), for instance, wrote that the schizophrenic's personal need for contact and his/her fear of contact are a central dynamic that the therapist also experiences in his/her counter-transference reactions. In his foreword to a book by Burnham, Gladstone, and Gibson (1969), *Schizophrenia: The Need-Fear Dilemma*, Robert Cohen wrote,

> the authors are not proposing a primary etiological theory of schizophrenia. We . . . do not know . . . how the ego defect develops. It may be inherited, constitutional, experiential, or the result of some biological imbalance. What the authors attempt to explain is the nature of the human experience of the schizophrenic individual, and they offer a structural psychological theory to account for his observed behavior and reported feelings, relating these to vicissitudes in the course of personality development. Any theory of schizophrenia which purports to be complete must include a consideration of these issues, and must take into account the schizophrenic's adapted as well as his maladapted behavior.
>
> (p. xv)

Joanne Greenberg's comments about the danger of being responded to on the psychotic level and the need to be contacted at that level are also an expression of a "need-fear dilemma," the need, and the fear, of contact with psychosis. Joanne Greenberg said, "I feared that when I would not be sick, that if I gave that up, since madness and creativity were equated in my mind at the time, I would have to give the latter away and then not have anything" (McAfee, 1989, pp. 517–518). As already mentioned, Paul Federn thought that the therapist who worked with the patient when he/she was in his/her most psychotic regressed phase had become contaminated with psychosis and that it would be best if another therapist worked with the patient after he/she was no longer in such a deeply regressed phase. This definitely was not the experience at Chestnut Lodge. The patient who was not abandoned during descent into, and escape from, a deep psychotic state may feel that he/she can convey or teach something about that experience to his/her therapist or "train," as one of my patients told me.

In some psychoanalytic presentations and panels on psychosis, no clear distinction is made between patients in deep psychotic states and those patients who are relatively well-functioning with "psychotic aspects of the personality." This lack of distinction contributes to confusion and seemingly contradictory views of a connection between psychosis and creativity.

Joanne Greenberg insisted that there is nothing creative about psychosis. When Donald Burnham studied the psychotic episodes of Strindberg in great detail and made a connection between psychosis and creativity, he did so by emphasizing the creativity it takes to *transform* (my italics) the psychotic experience into a new and broader vision (Burnham, 1973; Kafka, 2009). Ping-Nie Pao (1983) is particularly clear in differentiating three levels of psychosis and gives an example of his interview with a patient on each of these levels. In a sense, he counts on the patient's creativity and metaphoric understanding in a case of "apparent contact with reality but severe thought disorder" (pp. 147–154) and in a case of "intermittent loss of reality contact and visible panic" (pp. 154–161). In a consultation with a patient who shows "lack of reality orientation and [is] almost mute" (pp. 161–167), Ping-Nie Pao's concern is primarily with understanding the patient's panic and helping her to become less frightened.

So far, I have specifically referred to the writings of Fromm-Richmann, Searles, Donald Burnham, and Ping-Nie Pao. I cannot do justice here to the wealth of books and papers that originated at Chestnut Lodge. An annual symposium was held at Chestnut Lodge. The papers presented at these symposia were collected in private booklets and were not published more widely.[3]

Among the papers written by Chestnut Lodge staff members are the studies of McGlashan (1984, 1986) that are widely cited to discredit the value of psychotherapy in the treatment of psychosis. These studies were a major and ambitious project. Many more papers and spin-offs followed the three main papers that described the methodology and results of the follow-up and long-term outcomes of schizophrenia, the affective disorders, and borderline personalities. The papers are complex. McGlashan is far from condemning all interpersonal, dynamic, or psychoanalytic therapies, but his conclusion, that intensive psychotherapeutic work with chronic schizophrenic patients was not effective, had considerable impact. McGlashan (1984) wrote,

> The most striking findings relate to our schizophrenic population. These findings are clear: two of every three schizophrenic patients treated at Chestnut Lode were chronically ill or marginally functional at follow-up. The result is distressingly familiar; schizophrenia in its chronic form tends not to respond to treatments of known effectiveness with other difficulties. This outcome certainly did not derive from inadequate effort, at least in the psycho-social sphere where treatment was an active, intense, and prolonged endeavor. The psychopharmacologic aspects of treatment, on the other hand, were undoubtedly inadequate by today's standards since psychoactive drugs were not used systematically until well into the 1960s. Nevertheless, the results are clear; by and large the treatment as it was constituted failed to alter the momentum of this disease toward lifelong disability.
>
> The findings are not unequivocally negative. Recoveries and functionally adequate outcomes occur in one of every three of the schizophrenic patients studied. Furthermore, this has been observed among some of the most chronic and 'hopeless' cases in the hospital. These developments, of course, are of particular interest, including the degree to which they can be predicted and/or related to particular therapeutic interventions. These developments may also justify trials of intensive residential treatment in schizophrenic patients who have run the gamut of therapeutic interventions to no avail.
>
> (p. 600)

I find McGlashan's phrase "not unequivocally negative" somewhat misleading. If one considers that we are dealing with a population of deeply psychotic individuals who had not improved with any other treatment and for whom hospitalization at Chestnut Lodge was the "last resort," having relatively positive outcomes in one-third of this population is remarkable!

Brigitte Bechgaard (2003), chief psychologist at the Copenhagen University Hospital, has criticized McGlashan's work. She published an article with the aggressive title, "Lessons in how to ruin a study in psychotherapy effectiveness: a critical review of the Follow-up study from

Chestnut Lodge" (pp. 119–139). While she mentions various Chestnut Lodge research publications on psychotherapy that McGlashan co-authored with Dingman, Gedo, Goodrich, Fritsch, Keats, Miller, and Nayfack, she directs sharp and detailed criticism at McGlashan's second paper: "Long term outcome of schizophrenia and the affective disorders." She writes, "Originally, the follow-up study was intended as a study of the psychotherapeutic process and its outcome. While widely referred to as a follow-up study, it is not possible to make conclusions about psychotherapy from the study. Data about the psychodynamic aspects of therapy have been collected but never analyzed. Additionally, the study does not fulfill the requirements of a psychotherapeutic outcome study. The conclusion of the current review is that as the study turned out, it only allows one to draw conclusions about different kinds of illness courses and predictor factors" (abstract, p. 119).

Without discussing the merits and limitations of McGlashan's study nor the merits and limitations of Bechgaard's critique, we cannot claim that, looking at results statistically using Kraeplinian criteria, the work at Chestnut Lodge led to the *cure* of a *majority* of chronic schizophrenics by psychotherapy alone. It is the *individual case* that yielded Chestnut Lodge's richest fruit. We can speak of personal and conceptual yields. What all of us who worked at Chestnut Lodge learned are the personally transforming self-searching effects of profound contact with raw psychosis and the consequent opening, deepening, and widening of therapeutic range with all of our patients. We could communicate some of these attitudes and skills to students and colleagues. Depending on our individual interests, we also had the opportunity to harvest the more conceptual fruits of unusually intensive, detailed, and prolonged single case studies, and clusters of such studies. As already mentioned, McGlashan (1984) recognized that "adequate outcomes . . . among some of the most chronic and hopeless cases . . . are of particular interest" (p. 600). This brings to mind Heinrich Klüever's influential lectures I attended at the University of Chicago in which he stressed that most major advances in *all* fields resulted from the study of *exceptions*. These lectures were particularly influential because they were addressed to an audience of mainly statistically oriented psychologists. Chestnut Lodge also provided us with the exceptional opportunity to study the unique characteristics of each patient.

It was clear to us just how different from each other were patients with the same formal diagnosis. Ian Hacking (2009), in an article entitled "Humans, aliens and autism," writes about the many forms of autism being studied today and says, "If you know about one autistic person, you know about *one* autistic person" (p. 46). We could say, "If you know about one schizophrenic person, you know about *one* schizophrenic person." Saying this, of course, does not diminish the importance of studying any features that may characterize most or all schizophrenics.[4]

Chestnut Lodge provided an unique opportunity to observe, in great detail, patients during the periods of *transition* – in and out of the most severe psychotic states. Wherever short hospitalization periods and early discharge are practiced, these particularly interesting moments of transition are missed. Furthermore, we could continue to treat our patients when they were functioning on a good level. Elsewhere, that treatment would have been stopped, curtailed, or reduced to "medication management." At the Lodge, we could explore what kind of treatment was desirable and possible during periods when the patients functioned on a non-psychotic, frequently high and highly creative, level. Sometimes, during such periods, psychoanalysis without unusual "parameters" was the treatment of choice, although the *overall* course of treatment did not fit with a description of "classical" psychoanalysis because of the modifications at times of psychotic crisis.

Moments of transition – in and out of the most severe psychotic states – are of such particular interest because at least some patients, especially those who function on a very high level during some periods, are interested in teaching us something about *their* experiences and about *their* world. When one such patient, after many years of treatment, was discharged and moved to another city, I referred her to a colleague in that city. She would not accept this referral and insisted on coming to see me, although it had to be at a reduced frequency. She told me, with the apparent lack of humor of some schizophrenic patients, "It took me so long to train you."

A theory rooted in the Chestnut Lodge experience

Here is a condensed formulation of one theory, based on what Chestnut Lodge patients have taught me. This theory and related theories are in my book *Multiple Realities in Clinical Practice* (Kafka, 1989) and my paper "The romantic and classic visions in the therapy of psychosis: a personal perspective and an evolving theory of schizophrenia" (Kafka, 1997). The central theory deals with the schizophrenic's object world.

The schizophrenic's objects

I have already made a brief reference to Nathaniel London's review (1973) of the history of psychoanalytic efforts to understand schizophrenia. One can distinguish a unitary from a specific theory. London (1973) writes, "The Unitary Theory asserts an essential continuity between schizophrenic and neurotic behaviors . . . and considers intra-psychic conflict and defense as primary determiners." "Such an assertion . . . strains our available knowledge of these mental states so disparate in phenomenology and likely aetiologies. . . . The Specific Theory is focused on a deficiency in mental representation" (p. 190).

My work with schizophrenic patients also led me to focus on mental representations, the schizophrenic *objects*. My observations at the Lodge led me to disagree with Arieti's (1963) influential theory of a specific different schizophrenic *logic* (p. 59), and this, in turn, led to my hypothesis that schizophrenics apply our *common* logic to specific schizophrenic objects. Schizophrenic patients have taught me that *combinations of characteristics* can be more *constant* than any "person," self or other, and any "object" in the usual psychoanalytic sense. They have taught me that, in order to comprehend them, it is useful to decipher these combinations of characteristics as their own, their idiosyncratic, relatively more constant objects, their "atmospheric objects," as I call them. An example is a patient who, during an acute psychotic episode, had called a particular nurse "Heidi." After emerging from this acute episode, she explained to me that she never thought the nurse was "Heidi" but that the combination of being blonde and having a foreign accent had evoked in her an atmosphere she could hold on to, the atmosphere of the book *Heidi* that she had loved since her childhood. She could not hold on to the identities of actual people, not mine nor her own. In our language, the "object constancy" of common or common-sense objects was missing or, at least, less stable. It can be objected that, after all, there must have been such constancy since she always called the same nurse "Heidi" (Kafka, 1989, pp. 28–29). But, if we keep in mind the rapid fluctuations of levels of psychic organization and disorganization that we observed in our Lodge patients, the relatively greater stability of "atmospheric objects" becomes comprehensible. All object formation, all "object permanence," involves the acceptance as "identical" of patterns of stimuli that are not exactly the same. Patterns of stimuli that differ in some respects from each other are accepted as subjectively equivalent, and thus all psychological "objects" are based on subjective equivalences. Even the psychological existence of "a table" requires the subjective equivalence of the different visual patterns that result when the table is seen from different angles. This is usually called "object permanence." Psychoanalytically understandable defenses play a role in more complex emotionally charged object constancy, such as a constant mother image that includes the *bad* withholding mother and the *good* giving mother. We know that affect influences our experience of time, that objectively identical intervals can be subjectively different and that objectively different intervals can be subjectively equivalent. Our psychological object world, therefore, is an ever-changing web of spatial and temporal subjective equivalences, a model that has a good fit with current neuroscientific ones.

Still pertinent to the topic of the schizophrenic's object formation is a hypothesis that perceptual acts recapitulate the ontogeny of perception, the development of perception. Studies of perceptgenesis support the idea that developmentally early perceptions are more synesthetic and less sensory specific than later perceptions. Adult perception – as shown in the micro-temporal dissection of the process in tachistoscopic experiments – recapitulates autogenetic developments. Ordinary object formation involves more or less complete recapitulative cycles that lead to subjective equivalences – objects – that are our "common-sense" objects. I hypothesize that schizophrenic objects represent subjective equivalences resulting from a mixture of completed and aborted recapitulative perceptual cycles involving rhythmic distortions. It is possible to think of a conflictual basis for aborted perceptions, but it is at this juncture that disturbances in biological rhythms – perhaps genetically based – play a role in the etiology of schizophrenia. Effects of psychopharmacological agents may be due to changes they induce in biological rhythms. I believe that many schizophrenic patients shift rapidly between different levels of psychic organization, for instance, between an atmospheric object organization as exemplified by the Heidiness example and a level of a more specific *personal* world. A therapist, however, who assumes that the patient experiences these extremely rapid changes in levels of functioning and who therefore approaches the patient on multiple levels (of functioning) at the same time is more likely to be "on target."[5] At Chestnut Lodge, our therapeutic approach was informed by the recognition not only that some schizophrenic patients had these micro-temporal fluctuations in levels of functioning, but that some were able to comprehend and feel at ease in highly complex and abstract domains while at the same time they may have been severely deficient in problem-solving abilities needed for daily functioning. This has specific implications for therapeutic technique. I would work with a patient, as already mentioned, on cognitive problems such as are involved in ordering in a restaurant or using a telephone while, at the same time, dynamically exploring, as a specific example, the connection of the emotional history of a patient's close ties and identification with her father and with the patient's peculiar body sensations when she informs me that she "has her father's legs and therefore could not shave them."

As already mentioned, my theoretical ideas are more fully developed in *Multiple Realities*, and so are some ideas that are generally applicable for the treatment of psychotic persons. They include the therapist's readiness to communicate practically simultaneously on psychotic and narrowly "realistic" levels because it is assumed that patients fluctuate rapidly in and out of psychotic modes, fluctuations that are not detected by the therapist. The notion of the atmospheric object is, I believe, of central importance in our understanding of schizophrenic thought disorder.

The theoretical background of this notion is more fully developed in *Multiple Realities*, but my realization of its implications keep expanding.

An atmospheric object, for instance, and an atmospheric self-object, a *not* narrow "I," have no sense of agency.

The recovering schizophrenic patient insists on her need of a sense of agency. Joanne Greenberg, for instance (p. 33 of JAPA article, February 2011), states, "I want it to be something I choose to say, not something that says me." In the psychotic state, there is no "I" at the center. Elyn Saks' story of her recovery in her book *The Center Cannot Hold* (2007) is the story of a passage from a center that cannot hold to an "I" at the center.

Besides ideas that are generally applicable to the treatment of persons with psychosis, case material illustrates how the therapist tailors his/her approach to the individual situation. An example is a case in which a specific trauma played a prominent role in the etiology of a psychosis. While dream analysis frequently does not play a prominent role in the therapy of psychotic persons, work with dreams in this case had a specific function.

> Eleanor M, who had her first acute episode after she had acquiesced to her mother's request that she be present in the operating room during the mother's exploratory surgery; when the mother was opened up, she was found to have a widespread malignancy. Eleanor was also the main caretaker of her dying mother, and the notion that a sedative she gave her mother killed her was at times an important element in her delusions.
>
> Eleanor was diagnosed as schizophrenic on the basis of all the usual criteria by the staffs of several hospitals. She showed particularly flamboyant pathology: hallucinating and wildly agitated, she was denudative, smeared herself and the walls of seclusion rooms with menstrual blood, and was destructive of property and sometimes assaultive. During more than fifteen years of psychotherapeutic work with her, I found the role of dreams in her treatment an important one, as I shall describe below.
>
> Eleanor was eventually able to leave the hospital, the frequency and severity of acute episodes diminished radically, and during the last eight years only one brief hospitalization was necessary. (Medication, on the whole, did not play a significant role in her management or treatment.) When she did not need to be hospitalized, Eleanor functioned quite well as a wife, mother, and participating member in community affairs. Her preoccupation with violence in her waking life was limited to a fascination with crime and criminals, wars, and catastrophes. Her selection of movies, television shows, and newspaper and magazine articles was almost exclusively based on such interests. Her dream life was characterized by prolonged periods during which she reported hundreds of rather repetitive dreams dealing with amputations, mutilations, and bloody scenes.

Thus, Eleanor presented contrasting pictures: she was prim and proper when not psychotic, but her dream life and psychotic periods were full of gore. Over the years of working with her, I developed a technique of using gory language in talking about her dreams and impulses ("You wanted to smash her skull and smear her brains all over the wall"). But again and again I told her my reasons for doing so, spelling out the idea that her attempts to compartmentalize such material might contribute to the psychotic episodes. [Note: This is an example of my multiple levels of communication. To avoid "intellec-tualization," psychoanalysts sometimes mistakenly refrain from mak-ing "intellectual" comments when they are appropriate.] In Eleanor's treatment there were long periods when the therapy resembled some of the therapeutic work done with cases of battle fatigue during and after World War II. (For example, war movies were shown to soldiers who had experienced major dissociative episodes in battle. Showings of these movies were interrupted from time to time, and when the lights were on, Red Cross girls offered the soldiers tea.)

Despite the use of such techniques, recognition of transference ele-ments and the genetics of the conflict had their place in Eleanor's ther-apeutic. The emphasis was, however, as Andre Green put it, "not [on] the dream's latent content but the dreamer's experience."

(Kafka, 1989, pp. 121–123)

Another tailor-made individual therapeutic maneuver resulted from my accidental discovery that a patient had psychosis-free periods after awakening. I developed this unusual therapeutic maneuver with an often assaultive paranoid schizophrenic patient. Some psychotic features had probably been present prior to his military service, but his overt severe psychosis became manifest some time after he served in a combat zone and sustained a head wound. Neurological consultants thought that the head wound did not explain the psychosis on anatomical grounds, namely that others with anatomically similar neurologic damage did not have psychotic features. The patient's uncontrolled violence was such that he spent much time and all his nights in an isolation room. After he attacked me several times in my office, we had our sessions in the isola-tion room. A psychiatric aide sat just outside the room during my session with this patient. One morning, the patient was asleep when I arrived for our session. I woke him up and discovered to my surprise that I hardly recognized him. He greeted me, was free of delusions, showed no signs of hallucinations. All this changed rather quickly after seven minutes. He became his old psychotic self. From then on, I timed my sessions such that I would almost always find him asleep. The seven-minute psychosis-free pattern continued for more than a year, but during this time his overall condition did not improve. This was the case despite the fact that during

the seven-minute periods, the patient frequently spoke about family conflicts and his anger toward his father. He seemed to remember our con-
versations about these matters from one to the next psychosis-free period,
but, as mentioned, his condition did not improve, and his family moved
the patient to another institution.

The seven-minute pattern was discussed with neurologists and other
colleagues and examined in the context of ideas about sleep, awakening,
and dreams in schizophrenics. A general discussion of dreams in psychosis can be found in *Multiple Realities*.

With or without the use of medication, we have to confront the fact that
there are states in which some schizophrenic patients are unreachable.
These are the times when we can only wait. But the therapist's presence –
again and again – at those moments of entry and exit from the psychotic
episodes form a kind of bond that may permit the patient to communicate
to the therapist in a subtle manner the need for hospitalization. A patient
who had been discharged telephoned me to say that she wanted to visit
the Lodge and complain to Dr. Bullard about her previous hospitalization,
which had been against her will. Her violence had previously forced her
family to admit her to the hospital with the help of several attendants.
Her phone call essentially informed me that now she sought voluntary
hospitalization.

Psychotic processes and contemporary psychoanalysis

Most analysts would agree that the question if there is a continuum
between neurosis and psychosis has essentially been answered, at least in
the sense that conflict theory alone does not *explain* schizophrenia. Psychoanalytic therapy based only on conflict theory is not an effective approach
to treating psychotics.

I have already commented on the clinical use of the "atmospheric object"
in work with schizophrenic patients. Once alerted to the "atmospheric
objects" notion in psychotic patients, an awareness enhanced by the work
at Chestnut Lodge, we discovered transference and counter-transference
to the "atmospheric object" elements in all our patients. For example,
I offered an early Monday morning session to a patient with marked
obsessive-compulsive features whose passive-aggressive characteristics
played havoc with his professional career. He said, "Monday morning is
my father – get to work – you never finish anything and you never finish
anything right." I had become the atmospheric Monday morning demand.
Perceptual recapitulation is always at work. We are both atmospheric *and*
more personally defined objects to many of our patients, and they are both
to us. As the range of pathology of our psychoanalytically treated patient
population expands, we find that some of their functioning is primarily in

the atmospheric transference realm and that for some we are so personally *real* that we never assume a more atmospheric resonance that would be useful in their lives. This widening and deepening of our comprehension of deeply disturbed patients at Chestnut Lodge refined our approach to patients with lesser degrees of similar "ego defects."

The atmospheric object, as observed in the schizophrenic patient, gives us a conceptual bridge to the understanding of features of some non-psychotic patients. Much of contemporary psychoanalytic literature[6] deals with such patients, for whom interpretation is insufficient but for whom hard to specify moments of intense interpersonal affective resonance are crucial.

Let us return to the connections between the atmospheric object, the atmospheric self-object, and the self that experiences a sense of agency. The focus is often on the analysand's sense of self, its vicissitudes, and the sense of reality. An object – in the usual psychoanalytic meaning – is *personified* and so is a "self-object." A *person* experiences him-/herself as having the power of agency. An atmospheric object does not have a sense that it can make decisions and influence "reality." The existence of the link between "personified" objects – including self-objects – and reality is best illustrated by observing the effects of a lack of a personified self-object.[7] A patient told me, "There are thoughts and feelings around but I don't know whose they are." Descartes' "cogito, ergo sum" (I think; therefore, I am) does not hold. The same patient told me that he had to close the door on his finger to make sure that the car and his finger did exist. He also told me that he wanted to travel to California to make sure that California existed and was not only on a map. Working with patients whose sense of self and common-sense reality is so deeply disturbed but who maintain a sense of atmospheric reality through which we can make contact with them can help us in our treatment of patients who have less severe, less persistent, but qualitatively similar "ego deficits."

Conclusion

Work with the psychotic patient as a unique individual confronted the therapists with the deepest questions about our emotional and intellectual lives. Chestnut Lodge provided the opportunity to deal with these questions in depth because it recognized and fostered the importance of the single case, the single individual.[8] The Chestnut Lodge legacy of the importance of the single case is in sharp contrast to the regressive tendency in much of current psychiatry to focus on the single *symptom*. In a *Schizophrenia Bulletin* article on Freud's Schreber case, McGlashan (2009) wrote, "A case like Schreber's is sufficiently removed from our contemporary clinical scene to be useful in germinating questions that would otherwise never ever occur to us as we run from one modern patient to another" (p. 480). The psychoanalytic therapist at Chestnut Lodge did see cases like the Schreber case. That is why some questions occurred to the therapists: questions that they could pass on to a wider psychoanalytic and psychiatric community. Pursuing these questions in conditions quite different from Chestnut Lodge need not deprive any "modern psychiatric patient" of access to basic humanistic psychiatry. Some understanding of severe pathology gained at Chestnut Lodge and related therapeutic strategies are also valuable in the treatment of non-psychotic patients in a psychoanalytic patient population with an ever-widening range of pathology.

Notes

1 A brief digression here about Hollós' personal fate. During World War II, he and his family were rounded up in Hungary and taken to the shores of the Danube in Budapest, where they were forced to stand naked. People were being shot and thrown into the river when, for some unknown reason, the shooting stopped. In a letter to his former analyst, Paul Federn, Hollós described his feelings during this episode. In this letter, Hollós spoke of a melting away of ego boundaries in this moment of expectation of death. This comment is of special interest in light of Federn's (1952) theory about ego boundary cathexis. To return to Hollós' personal fate, he was saved by the Swedish diplomat, Wallenberg, who went house to house to give Swedish passports to Jews who were to be deported.

2 Other histories of Chestnut Lodge cover developments after the wider use of medication. These include the forward written by Dr. Dexter Bullard, Jr. (pp. xix–xxi) and the introduction written by Ann-Louise Silver (1989, pp. 1–12) in the book she edited, *Psychoanalysis and Psychosis.*

3 *Chestnut Lodge Symposium: Papers Presented on the Fiftieth Anniversary 1910–1961. Contents: Whitehorn, John C. "Alienation and Leadership." Rioch, David McK. "The Sense and the Noise." Stanton, Alfred H. "Milieu Therapy and the Development of Insight." Jackson, Don D. and Weakland, John H. "Conjoint Family Therapy: Some Considerations on Theory, Technique, and Results." Cohen, Robert A. and Cohen, Mabel Blake "Research in Psychotherapy: A Preliminary Report." Schulz, Clarence G. "Case Report of an Obsessional Patient." Will, Otto Allen, Jr. "Paranoid Development and the Concept of Self: Psychotherapeutic Intervention." Searles, Harold F. "Sexual Processes in Schizophrenia." Burnham, Donald L. "Identity Definition and Role Demand in the Hospital Careers of Schizophrenic Patients." William Alanson White Psychiatric Foundation, Inc., 1961. Printer: Port City Press, Inc.* This book first appeared in *Psychiatry* as a supplement to Volume 24 #2, May 1961: the Chestnut Lodge Symposium issue.

4 One brief comment about autism: childhood schizophrenia and autism were once considered the same or closely connected condition. Since then, studies of the two have mostly gone in different directions. In retrospect, I recall that some Chestnut Lodge patients, diagnosed as schizophrenic, had marked autistic spectrum features. I believe the relationship between these conditions deserves renewed study, and a re-examination of some of Chestnut Lodge case studies may be of interest.

5 Joanne Greenberg described how Frieda Fromm-Reichmann, in a sense, treated the patient's delusional gods as "real," substantial, by herself being angry at them and at the same time telling the patient that, if she wants to, she can keep these crazy delusions (McAfee, p. 518).

6 For instance, Fonagy and Target (2007) wrote, "Only slowly does the uniqueness of his own perspective differentiate so that a sense of mental self can develop" (p. 917). Stern et al. (1998) wrote, "A 'moment of meeting' can create a new intersubjective environment and an altered domain of 'implicit relational knowing'" (p. 909). These words describe experiences reported by some patients, and with particular clarity by Joanne Greenberg, at Chestnut Lodge. One of my patients attributed a marked improvement in his condition to the simple words of a psychiatric aide, "You have a choice." The choice was between going, or not going, on an excursion with some other patients. I want to emphasize, however, that I do not believe in the transformational magic of these words. The patient may have been given many choices previously. Also unknown are the multiple factors that may have made it possible for this patient to hear and respond to these words at that particular time. The history of a relationship between this patient and the aide also must have played a role. I do want to emphasize that the sense of agency is well illustrated by Joanne Greenberg's description of her treatment by Frieda Fromm-Reichmann.

7 A *sense* of agency should not be confused with agency proper. Many neuroscientific findings, using neuro-imaging, show that actual *agency* – decisions and initiations of action – precedes a conscious *sense* of agency (Stoerig, 2006; Libet, 2004; Wegner, 2002). To bridge this confusing gap, I have explored elsewhere the connection between consciousness and time sense, the link between the experience of *now* and the sense of agency (Kafka, 1987, 1992).

8 This is in line with medical progress, the trend and anticipation that individual constellations of DNA and social and environmental factors rather than disease entities will determine individual treatment strategies.

References

Arieti, S. (1963). Studies of thought processes in contemporary psychiatry. *American Journal of Psychiatry* 120: 58–64.

Arlow, J.A. (1989). Delusion and metaphor. In Silver, A.S. (Editor), *Psychoanalysis and Psychosis*. Madison, CT: International Universities Press, pp. 173–182.

Bechgaard, B. (2003). Lessons in how to ruin a study in psychotherapy effectiveness: A critical review of the follow-up study from Chestnut Lodge. *Journal of the American Academy of Psychoanalysis and Dynamic Psychiatry* 31: 119–139.

Burnham, D.L. (1973). Restitutional functions of symbol and myth in Strindberg's *Inferno*. The sixteenth annual frieda fromm-reichmann memorial lecture. *Psychiatry* 36: 229–243.

Burnham, D.L., Gladstone, A.I., and Gibson, R.W. (1969). *Schizophrenia and the Need-Fear Dilemma*. New York: International Universities Press.

Dyrud, J.E. (1989). The early Frieda, and traces of her in her later writings. In Silver A.S. (Editor), *Psychoanalysis and Psychosis*. Madison, CT: International Universities Press, pp. 483–494.

Federn, P. (1952). *Ego Psychology and the Psychoses*. New York: Basic Books.

Fonagy, P., and Target, M. (2007). Playing with reality: IV. A theory of external reality rooted in intersubjectivity. *International Journal of Psychoanalysis* 88: 917–937.

Freud, S. (1915 a). Papers on metapsychology. *Standard Edition* 14: 201.

Freud, S. (1915 b). A metapsychological supplement to the theory of dreams. *Standart Edition* 14: 217–235.

Hacking, I. (2009). Humans, aliens and autism. *Daedalus, Journal of the American Academy of Arts and Sciences* 138 (Summer 2009): 44–59, 46.

Kafka, J.S. (1987). On the question of insight in psychoanalysis. Presentation: Symposium of psychoanalysis and psychosis. *American Academy of Psychoanalysis* 1987: 18–28.

Kafka, J.S. (1989). *Multiple Realities in Clinical Practice*. New Haven and London: Yale University Press.

Kafka, J.S. (1992). Consciousness and the shadow of time. In Leuzinger-Bohleber, M., Schneider, H., and Pfeiffer, R. (Editors), *Two Butterflies on My Head. Psychoanalysis in the Interdisciplinary Scientific Dialogue*. Verlag and Berlin: Springer, 1992, pp. 87–95; and IPSO Newsletter Anniversary Edition, Summer 1991.

Kafka, J.S. (1997). The romantic and classic visions in the therapy of psychosis: A personal perspective and an evolving theory of schizophrenia. *Psychiatry* 60: 209–221, Fall 1997.

Kafka, J.S. (2009). Commentary on 'restitutional' functions of symbol and myth in Strindberg's *Inferno*. On schizophreniform crisis and on schizophrenia. *Psychiatry* 72 (2): 139–142.

Libet, B. (2004). *Mind Time: The Temporal Factor in Consciousness*. Cambridge, MA: Harvard University Press.

London, N. (1973). An essay on psychoanalytic theory: Two theories of schizophrenia. Part I: Review and critical assessment of the development of the two theories. Part II: Discussion and restatement of the specific theory of schizophrenia. *International Journal of Psychoanalysis* 54 (2): 169–193.

McAfee, L.I. (1989). Interview with Joanne Greenberg. In Silver, A.S. (Editor), *Psychoanalysis and Psychosis*. Madison, CT: International Universities Press, pp. 513–533.

McGlashan, T. (1984). The Chestnut Lodge follow-up study. I: Follow-up methodology and study sample. II: Long-term outcome of schizophrenia and the affective disorders. *Archives of General Psychiatry* 41 (1984a): 573–601.

McGlashan, T. (1986). The Chestnut Lodge follow-up study. III: Long-term outcome of borderline personalities. *Archives of General Psychiatry* 43 (1986): 20–30.

McGlashan, T. (2009). Psychosis as a disorder of reduced cathectic capacity: Freud's analysis of the Schreber case revisited. *Schizophrenia Bulletin* 35 (#3): 480.

Noble, Douglas. (1963). Early days at the 'The Lodge'. *The Ninth Annual Chestnut Lodge Symposium*, Friday, October 25, 1963, Rockville, MD: Privately published, pp. 93–103.

Pao, Ping-Nie. (1973). Notes on Freud's theory of schizophrenia. *The International Journal of Psychoanalysis* 54: 469–476.

Pao, Ping-Nie. (1983). Therapeutic empathy and the treatment of schizophrenia. *Psychoanalytic Inquiry* 3: 145–167.

Pestalozzi, J., Frisch, S., Hinshelwood, R.D., and Houzel, D. (1998) (Editors). *Psychoanalytic Psychotherapy in Institutional Settings. The EFPP Clinical Monograph Series*. London: Karnac Books for the European Federation for Psychoanalytic Psychotherapy in the Public Health Services.

Saks, E.R. (2007). *The Center Cannot Hold: My Journey Through Madness*. New York: Hyperion.

Searles, H.F. (1963). Transference psychosis in the psychotherapy of chronic schizophrenia. *The International Journal of Psychoanalysis* 44: 249–281.

Silver, Ann-Louise. (1989) (Editor). *Psychoanalysis and Psychosis*. Madison, CT: International Universities Press.

Stern, D.N., Sander, L.W., Nahum, J.P., Harrison, A.M., Lyons-Ruth, Morgan, A.C., Brushweilerstern, N., and Tronick, E.Z. (1998). Non-interpretive mechanisms in psychoanalytic therapy: The 'something more' than interpretation. *International Journal of Psychoanalysis* 79: 903–921.

Stoerig, P. (2006). The impact of invisible stimuli. *Science* 314: 1694–1695.

Waddell, J. (1964). The evolution of nursing at Chestnut Lodge. *The Tenth Annual Chestnut Lodge Symposium*, Friday, November 6, 1964, Rockville, MD: Privately published, p. 123.

Wegner, D.M. (2002). *The Illusion of Conscious Will*. Cambridge, MA: MIT Press.

Willick, M.S. (2001). Psychoanalysis and schizophrenia: A cautionary tale. *Journal of the American Psychoanalytic Association* 49: 27–56.

Chapter 3

A personal path to analytic therapy for psychosis

Franco De Masi

How can we work analytically with a patient who seems to have no apti-tude for thought and is engrossed in a hallucinatory sensorial world, as occurs when treating a psychotic patient?

Generally speaking, discussions on issues concerning this kind of patient and his/her respective therapy are not so common among analysts. Train-ing does not always provide seminars on the subject, and should a pupil wish to talk over a psychotic patient's case, finding an expert's listening ear among the older colleagues might not prove so easy.

The book's promoters therefore deserve thanks for this renewed effort to cast light on a difficult and complex area of our discipline. From vari-ous viewpoints, psychoanalysis does, in fact, seem to have had its woes when it comes to examining the psychotic state in depth and discussing constructively complexities surrounding therapy for this kind of patient. Psychosis in a certain sense still seems like a besieged citadel whose walls have been but merely scratched by those in the past endeavouring to make their way in and conquer it.

When examining analytic literature in this field (from Freud, to Bion, to Rosenfeld, and to Lacan or Piera Aulagnier), what we can see is a set of important contributions that did not, however, come to produce one single theoretical and clinical fabric capable of enlightening us on psycho-sis and the peculiarity of its therapy. And if we are to consider things as they stand today, it must be said that one complete and shared psychoana-lytic theory of psychosis still does not exist. I feel I have acquired much clinical knowledge of the psychotic process and the way in which we can intervene to favour the illness being overcome, but a theory I likewise do not have.

So here I would like to set out my path to understanding the nature of the psychotic process, and describe how I devised an analytic approach for these patients. Initially, my path saw several temporary successes that were then marked by unforeseeable lapses back into illness. The lapses were what kept pushing me towards trying to understand what it was in my analytic approach that was not working, and from there a better understanding of the psychotic process and its apparent unpredictability followed.

Failures

Until the age of forty, I worked in a psychiatric hospital, where I treated many psychotic patients and also witnessed their distressing and irremediable regressions. In a like manner, I observed partial remissions, too, but could not understand the reasons behind improvement. These experiences have remained etched in my mind, and often I have thought about the destiny of many individuals who, once having entered psychosis, never managed to come out of it again. After leaving the hospital, for a long time I was very careful not to undertake analysis with psychotic patients; analytic work and psychosis in my mind seemed an impossible fit.

In spite of the care I took, I was unable not to accept Alvise, then twenty-five years old, as my patient.[1]

He came from a city a long way away from Milan, and even though it was July, with the summer holidays in sight, he wanted to begin analysis immediately. His determination struck me, and perhaps this was what made me decide to see him. His analysis began in September at four sessions per week in an analytic setting. Alvise had spent some time in a psychiatric hospital in his hometown and had had psychotherapy for several months with a psychotherapist who then sent him to me. His stay in hospital had lasted two months, during which time he was treated with psychotropic drugs because of a severe psychotic breakdown.

His breakdown had culminated in attempted suicide: while on holiday, he hurled himself off a flyover, under the delusional conviction that he harboured a diabolical power that made him totally destructive. Other diabolical presences were at work, too, often in the shape of animals, such as black dogs, while, to the toll of bells or bursts of gunfire, the world proclaimed mass suicides. Alvise had felt that he could telepathically enter others' minds, bring about their suicide, and, thinking he was in touch with God (divine and terrifying voices declared catastrophic truths), he was convinced that his condemnation was final.

After eight years of analysis, the patient's conditions had improved so much that his parents persuaded him to complete his university studies, which he had suspended quite some time before that (he needed only to pass one exam and do his thesis).

Despite displaying discomfort for and intolerance to intellectual work, the patient accepted his parents' suggestion. In order to work on his thesis, Alvise needed to cut his weekly sessions from four to two. (During the second part of his analysis, he had rented a studio flat so that he could continue to do four sessions per week, given the distance between his hometown and Milan.) His analysis halved and the tension of preparing his thesis difficult to bear, Alvise had a new psychotic breakdown during the summer holidays while separated from his therapy. This time the auditory hallucinations were not experienced as perturbing (which they had been in the first breakdown), but as a special quality that made him unique, to the extent that he believed the CIA was searching for him in order to abduct him, take him to the United States and make him work for the American government.

Due to the new psychotic breakdown and a series of adverse circumstances, it was not possible to analyse his idealisation of his madness. Alvise and myself both ended up feeling discouraged, and he did not come to his sessions anymore. After his analysis ended, I received news from his father that he had gone back home, was living a narrow life and regularly took antipsychotic medication.

Ten years on, I received a telephone call from Alvise asking to see me again. He warmly greeting me when we met, and I learned he had in the meanwhile graduated and was making work plans. Despite this, I got the impression that he still considered acoustic hallucinations, this time centred on neighbours, as real facts.

When this analysis was over, I reflected a great deal on the case, and asked myself what had been lacking in my therapeutic approach. I realised I had focussed much of my analytic work on analysing the psychotic Super-ego that underpinned the hallucinatory state. Alvise had in actual fact improved and could tolerate awareness of his ongoing psychotic catastrophe. It is likely that the urge for 'recovery', which was overly premature and mainly sustained by his parents, had favoured a return to psychosis.

The main question that came up in my reflections was whether I had really understood the origin and dynamics of the delusion. I asked myself if I had actually managed to get to the bottom of the original psychotic episode, that is, whether I had understood how the patient had entered psychosis. In retrospect, it seemed that I had not, because each time I had tried to share and relive the sequences of the psychotic episode with the patient, I found he put up very strong resistance: either it was difficult for him to remember, or he tried to trivialise what had happened. In actual fact, I had to acknowledge that I had given up on doing a systematic analysis of the first psychotic episode because of the patient's resistance, and focussed instead on his need to repair the psychic damage so that his mental functioning could be recovered. I came to understand only once the analysis had ended that the original psychotic episode had been there between us like an uncomfortable third.

I would like to recall two important thoughts that, after the case of Alvise, have always stayed in my mind.

The first is by Arieti, who stated in his book *Interpretation of Schizophrenia* (1955):

> An important point to be considered is the relevance of the original episode. It is not just a precipitating event; it is a very important dynamic factor, without which the patient would have been able to check, or even compensate, his psychotic propensity.
>
> (p. 909)

The second is by Searles (1979):

> Schizophrenia cannot be understood simply in terms of traumata and deprivation, no matter how grievous, inflicted by the outer world upon the helpless child. The patient himself, no matter how unwittingly, has an active part in the development and tenacious maintenance of the illness and only by making contact with this essentially assertive energy in him can one help him to become well.
>
> (p. 22)

After the unfortunate ending of the therapy with Alvise, I would like to underline how important I feel it is to work constantly on reconstructing the original psychotic episode, from which the patient's subsequent readiness to be delusional derives. Within all possible limits, the analyst must return to the past and reconstruct how the patient entered the delusion construction that very first time. I cannot underline enough that always to be borne in mind is that the first psychotic breakdown leaves an indelible mark in the mind: subsequent delusional experiences, which may be considered as different versions of the first, are built onto this matrix.

Dreams in the psychotic state

When working with a psychotic patient, a real difficulty is not being aware of the pathogenic nature of psychotic functioning. Held by the fascination of the psychotic part's flattery, the patient will more often than not conceal the existence of his/her psychotic part from the analyst, who, at times, is taken by surprise at the sudden appearance of a breakdown.

One path allowing me access to this problem was understanding the meaning of dreams in the psychotic state, as, at times, they describe in detail what the psychotic patient does not communicate verbally.

Approximately fifteen years ago, I formed a study group of colleagues who had psychotic patients in analysis. Paola Capozzi was in the group, a patient of hers having had a psychotic episode. When the group examined the material on Ada, the patient, we felt that she did not present psychotic symptoms. The material was on anxieties linked to a depressive state subsequent to the psychotic episode, and these were connected to a collapse of identity. Interpretations on the transference, especially those concerning fear that the analyst would be unable to understand and support the patient, managed to enable Ada to overcome moments of anxiousness and distressing feelings of emptiness.

The first part of this analysis was unexpectedly shaken by a new psychotic episode. The patient had agreed to her father's request to go on a cruise with him, and, while on the cruise and having foregone two weeks of sessions, Ada began to feel delusional about being sexually aroused by her father, who was perceived as the devil.

To better understand what had stood in the way of foreseeing the new psychotic episode, and what we had possibly not understood, together with Paola Capozzi I looked again at all the material preceding the psychotic episode. Our attention focussed on a series of dreams in which the patient seemed to have anticipated and virtually foreseen the new episode. These dreams had not been analysed because, on the one hand, they were so terrifying that the patient had brought no associations whatsoever, and on the other, they seemed truly bizarre and 'alien'. Rereading them in retrospect facilitated considering them as 'signs' of a new psychotic episode that, unfortunately, both patient and analyst had not opened their eyes to. The analytic work henceforth carried out consistently on the 'psychotic' dreams was extremely important to the positive outcome of this analysis. It enabled the patient to gradually become more aware of the danger exercised by the psychotic part's allure, and her own progressive submission to its power. This approach also brought an understanding of the origin and development of the patient's two previous psychotic episodes.

From the very first consultations with these patients, it is clear that they are unable to use thought to understand their own mental state. Their bizarre dreams, apparently without meaning, reflect this. A more careful assessment, however, reveals that such dreams are so bizarre because they are the product of the psychotic part of the personality.

This makes the dreams useful, though, as they fulfil an important communicative function: they often anticipate the development of a psychotic episode and warn of the danger the patient is facing. In order to distinguish this type of dream from others that we are more used to understanding and interpreting, I have proposed to distinguish between *thought-dreams* and *delusion-dreams*. The latter are not suited to symbolic interpretations because they do not imply a hidden meaning, nor do they represent a veiled transference communication.

Infantile psychotic withdrawal

A further knowledge source of mine for the psychotic process is as supervisor of analytic therapies with severely ill children, my involvement on an individual and group basis stretching over fifteen years. This constant contact with cases of severely ill children has further opened my mind with regard to adult psychotic patient treatment, given that the child analyst must always stay in touch with archaic and primitive functions of the mind; moreover, the psychopathological constructions leading to breakdowns, at times irreversible in adulthood, are already present in severely ill children. Our mind lives and develops if it draws food from human relationships, if it grows amid affects and emotions, and if it is nourished by values and ideals. Environmental circumstances or early emotional communication distortions within the family create a backward motion in the psychotic patient. Whereas the normal child progressively widens her horizons and knowledge, the child who is destined to become psychotic takes the reverse path: she closes herself off in a *psychic withdrawal*, in a world made up of gratifying sensory fantasies that detach her from real life. She uses the mind not so much to understand herself and her surrounding reality, but to produce pleasant perceptions and stimulations. Dissociation from psychic reality, or, in other words, the foundation for future delusion development, takes shape in the psychic withdrawal, which gets its start in childhood. Some children clearly manifest this, accurately describing their state of withdrawal into fantasy during their sessions.

Melanie Klein's enlightening words on this subject are as follows:

> Then there is the child who lives in phantasy, and we can see how in their play such children must shut out reality completely and can only maintain their phantasies by excluding it altogether. These children find any frustration very intolerable because it reminds them of reality; and they are quite unable to concentrate on any occupation connected with reality.
>
> (Klein, 1930, p. 253)

Winnicott echoed this when he described a patient who, from the age of two, had drawn a clear line of separation between fantasies and relations with real objects. Winnicott portrayed her as a girl who, while playing other people's games, was constantly engaged in fantasying. Her attraction to the world of fantasy had prevented her from becoming a whole person and drained her life of meaning: 'Gradually she became one of the many who do not feel that they exist in their own right as whole human beings. [. . .] while she was at school and later at work, there was another life going on in terms of the part that was dissociated. [The main part of her] was living in what became an organized sequence of fantasying' (Winnicott, 1971, p. 29).

Children who are predisposed to developing psychosis are often ignored by parents who do not distinguish between a normal attraction towards the world of games, and the construction of a fantasy world that is dissociated from reality. This mental state is often taken for their child's calm, serene attitude. Profound distortion of psychic reality that takes shape in infantile withdrawal favours distance being created between these children and their peers (they often do not know how to play sharing games); it stops them learning from experience and from their relations with adults, and generates dependence on an omnipotent system made up of false constructions.

During the analysis of adult psychotic patients, we can reconstruct the childhood withdrawal condition and understand how the child's dissociation from reality was ignored or even involuntarily encouraged by the parents. Once the withdrawal forms, the illusory, omnipotent grandiosity the child gains from it keeps him there. He becomes unable to integrate into his school and peer community, and has trouble learning, because he now lives mostly in a world of dissociated fantasies.

Psychotic transformation

The role of withdrawal in the construction of the psychotic state, a pathological organisation studied for the first time by Steiner (1993), cannot be underestimated. It operates along self-produced sensory lines, forming a reality dissociated from the rest of the personality, 'another reality' constantly provided for by the patient's imagination. It is the seat from which the psychotic part of the personality then proliferates.

Bion (1957) hypothesised that the patient tends to destroy thought because of pain intolerance. It is conceivable that this destruction follows a long path since childhood via the patient's withdrawal into a sensory reality of fantasy that replaces the ability to think. Destroying thought function is not a direct process, operating the mind recurrently undergoing transformations for the sake of pleasure. The mind is employed as a sensory organ that produces grandiose, eroticised or ecstatic mental states that, once they peter out, leave behind intolerable holes and voids. Indeed, it is my belief that the delusion constructions do not develop in order to fill unbearable holes or relieve anxiety, but they also produces holes and anxiety that are laid bare as the delusion dies away.

Psychosis develops via progressive regression in which the individual disinvests in psychic reality (relational) and withdraws into her own bodily and sensory personal space. To carry this operation out, the patient must disconnect herself from cognitive brain functions that keep her in contact with psychic reality, in particular with the function that discriminates between what is internally and sensorially produced and what exists outside and is independent of her.

Over a long period, the psychotic part, that which sensorially creates a new reality, coexists alongside the healthy part, but in the end, the former tends to dominate the latter until it completely colonises it. When the healthy part has been totally taken over by the ill part, a psychotic breakdown occurs, which often requires hospitalisation. Anxiety is unleashed when the conquering process by the ill part over the healthy part is at its peak. Here, the patient feels lost but can no longer turn back. At this point the perception of irreversible psychic catastrophe comes through, that is, *Wahnstimmung*, which for psychiatry of the last century corresponds to the dramatic beginning of the psychotic process. This is the exact moment the process of hallucination is at its highest.

Bion wrote the following on the matter:

> The patient feels imprisoned in the state of mind he has achieved, and unable to escape from it because he feels he lacks the apparatus of awareness of reality which is both the key to escape and the freedom itself to which he would escape.
>
> (Bion, 1967, p. 39)

In other words, a psychotic patient becomes a prisoner of false identities he has constructed because he no longer possesses the apparatus of awareness of reality, this being the only thing that could help him construct a real identity. During therapy, it is important to spend time working with the patient to make him aware of the risk his mind runs should he allow himself to be seduced by the psychotic part. This is easier said than done, as the psychotic part presents itself to the patient as a pleasant condition, the analyst therefore often being kept in the dark about this propensity towards delusion. As previously mentioned, insidious conquering by the psychotic part is frequently well represented in some apparently bizarre dreams that can, however, openly describe the process.

Following are the main points my work with psychotic patients is based on, my analytic technique permeated by them still.

1 psychosis originates in infantile withdrawal during childhood;
2 delusion develops out of this withdrawal; it encysts in the mind, and tends to reproduce; and
3 a sign of progress is when the patient shares his delusion with the analyst and can recognise its pathogenic nature. Analysing dreams that describe the dynamics of the psychotic state is useful in order to reach this point.

When a psychotic patient is taken into one's care, it is important not to underestimate the progressive nature of the psychotic process, and to sense immediately the dangerous direction the patient may take. Differently put, we need to know how the psychotic mind works and what the risks during the course of treatment are.

Unlike before, today with drug therapies we can reduce the extent of psychotic symptomatology and intervene positively even during an episode. Usually, when psychotic patients go to an analyst, they are already on psychotropic medication prescribed during their hospitalisation; if this is not the case, an agreement needs to be come to with the patient so that, before beginning the analysis, he can consult a psychiatrist who will see him regularly during the treatment. I prefer this practice, as it is extremely difficult to send a patient to a colleague that he does not know when a psychotic episode occurs. Naturally, it is important to choose a psychiatrist who looks upon analytic therapy empathically and takes great care not to interfere with it.

Beyond the dynamic unconscious

Psychoanalytic technique, the basis of clinical work, consists in understanding the patient's mental state and then describing her experiences in order to activate her understanding of her own mental processes. Freud's goal was this, but the theoretical base he worked on was the *dynamic unconscious*, and he operated to weaken the defences, censorship and repression, in particular, in order that the patient be made aware of the nucleus of hidden truths underlying her suffering. When we process emotions, most of our perceptions are made unconscious. Once processed unconsciously, emotional facts acquire meaning and are integrated into the complex of personal emotional experience. Dreams provide evidence of this constant binding and lending emotional meaning to what we have experienced. Repressed content in the dream gets resolved, and we can thus trace back through association the experienced emotional reality.

The complex problem about analytic technique when treating psychosis derives from the fact that the disorder does not concern the dynamic unconscious, but a more basic mental malfunction that, *outside awareness*, makes the patient distort the function of thought.

Whereas the neurotic patient uses repression to bind anew the conflictual experience in her unconscious, the psychotic patient destroys the tools that would enable the unconscious to understand mental experiences. This latter kind of patient is unable to repress and unconsciously process emotional experience (she is unable to 'dream'), and, consequently, cannot benefit from work carried out by the dynamic unconscious. In other words, psychotic patients do not possess symbolic thought, and, in particular, they are unable to use emotions, conscious or unconscious, to understand psychic reality.

The analyst cannot therefore use with the psychotic patient the mental tool kit that can help the neurotic patient, but must leave aside what she has learnt from her personal analysis, from clinical practice with other patients and from discussions with her colleagues.

The psychotic patient is unable to think, because his mind is saturated with sensory elements that will then form the foundations of his delusions and hallucinations. These concrete sensory elements cancel out the inner world, pervade and dominate mental processes and obstruct the ability to dream because they 'imbue' the mind sensorially. Dreams do not therefore correspond to symbolic processing, but portray concrete facts given that they lack 'dream work'.

Yet another aspect of psychosis is that, once pathological change has occurred, it is stubbornly persistent, like a mutation, a lava flow that does away with the pre-existing structure and the healthy part of the personality. The analyst's countertransference bewilderment lies here, as she witnesses the disappearance of the collaborating part of the patient, with whom she had hitherto been able to converse.

Together with other authors (Federn, 1952; Bion, 1957, 1967; Little, 1958), I believe that the patient in a psychotic state cannot, as previously stated, use repression and symbolic functions. All of this prevents the establishment of the transference, as would occur with neurotic patients. It is particularly difficult when a psychotic transference develops in its place, as this risks leading the analytic process towards a dangerous impasse. The psychotic transference does not express the re-emergence of the patient's childhood past, but represents contamination of the analytic relationship by his delusion. This is why, unlike transference neurosis, it is not a useful tool with which to bring about change, but the opposite, it essentially being an obstacle to analytic progress.

In order to understand the difference between the neurotic and the psychotic transference, it is useful and sustainable to draw an analogy in structural terms between the transference construction and dream work: in the therapy of neurotic patients, unconscious emotional activity that invests another subject, the analyst, must occur in order that a transference be established. Like the dream, the transference is open to numerous meanings that the analyst can interpret to take the patient to a past or present emotional experience, or to the perception of a split-off and projected part of the self. In the neurotic transference, the repressed and the conscious reality are both present and projected into the analyst, who, as a transferential object, maintains an *as if* position halfway between fantasy and reality. This analogy between the structure of the dream and that of the transference also explains why the neurotic patient stays in an open and doubting position and accepts the transference interpretation as he does the analysis of a dream. This being the case supports the neurotic patient's ability to 'dream' the transference, and hence to create it, whereas the psychotic patient is unable to do so because of his inability to 'dream'. When a psychotic transference is produced, patients concretely project their delusional belief into the analyst, who becomes its captive.

Propaganda in the analytic relationship

A principal problem with psychotic patients is that they live amid confusion, between the psychotic and the healthy part. They do not recognise the psychotic part as an ill part, but consider it as an alive, intelligent part, which ultimately gives pleasure (as in erotic or grandeur delusions, for example).

For the psychotic patient, what gives pleasure equals what is good, as is the case with perverse patients. This is a key point when treating psychotic patients; the first therapeutic goal is to help the patient distinguish between the psychotic part and the healthy part. The delusion nucleus and its pathogenic power must be examined session after session to help the patient develop awareness and thinking ability that will limit her delusion production.

The psychotic construction of virtual and parallel worlds is so seductive that it prevents the patient from recognising its pathogenic nature. When these worlds appear in clinical material and dreams, it is important to describe them in detail to the patient, otherwise she will allow herself to be conquered by the pathological structure.

The analyst's intervention needs to focus on analysing confusion between what is pleasant for the functioning of the mind, which is erroneously matched to what is good for it, and what instead is dangerous. Demolishing the psychotic propaganda helps the patient free herself from the appeal of the psychopathological construction. Consequently, the healthy part can then be helped to develop.

It is this world of delusion, dissociated from reality, that the patient needs to be helped out of, and she needs to be taken back to a way of functioning where the rules of psychic reality and emotional ties are accepted and considered indispensable to mental survival.

A clinical example that clearly illustrates the patient's confusion between the healthy part and the ill part, and how the patient, deceived by the psychotic part, tries in turn to deceive the analyst, is this clinical sequence from the therapy of Agnese, whom I followed in supervision.

Some months before the start of analysis, Agnese had been admitted to the psychiatric department of the hospital in her town for an acute psychotic episode. The apparent symptoms were characterised by auditory and visual hallucinations and by an ideational disorder of a delusional nature that inclined strongly to interpretation and magic thoughts. The medical history gleaned from her relatives when she was admitted was not very extensive. She remained only a short time in the ward and when she was discharged she seemed to have recovered a sufficient hold on reality, although she still appeared very evanescent.

The psychotic episode had manifested itself suddenly and Agnese rapidly demonstrated an apparent recovery. She was entrusted as an outpatient to a psychiatrist who prescribed psychotropic drugs and sent her to a female analyst some months later for therapy. After about two months of face-to-face consultations, Agnese accepted the proposal to start analysis at four sessions a week lying on a couch. The analyst believed it was also useful to talk to the patient's parents to inform them of the difficulties inherent to the therapy and to sound out their willingness to support their daughter. The mother, in particular, appeared very anxious and during therapy it became clear that she tended to blame Agnese for her admission to hospital as well as for her illness.

At the beginning, Agnese never missed a session. In the first months she was accompanied by her mother, then, gradually, she managed to come alone. Initially she seemed inexpressive and fearful, perhaps still immersed in a delusional atmosphere that she tended to conceal. She was sad and lifeless as though, on coming out of the psychotic crisis, she had become depressed, empty, and without her bearings. In some sessions she let a few memories of the difficult relationship with her parents emerge. She said that when she was fourteen she had been slapped by her mother and forcefully taken back home because she had been caught holding hands with and kissing a boy from her school that she had fallen for. Agnese said that since then she had always refrained from going out with boys because she was frightened of her parents' possible reaction.

In fact, during adolescence she never tried to have an autonomous life away from her parents. She had never been on holiday alone or with a group of friends. Moreover, she rarely went out with her girlfriends, and this made her feel even more isolated from the world.

We can suppose that it was then that Agnese began to construct her psychic withdrawal, which took on the semblance of a love nest in which to take shelter, a fantastic world in which symbols and signs reinforced what she herself was creating. The delusion that led to her admission to hospital was, in fact, of an erotic nature. The protagonist was an old school friend who had fallen in love with her, followed her, spoke to her, was present everywhere, but who was never visible because, in her words, he always hid himself from her eyes. Agnese's mental state was characterised by frenzy stimulated by visual and auditory hallucinations that referred to the presence and to the signs left by her loved one.

Marco, the protagonist of the delusion, had indeed been one of her schoolmates. But he had disappeared from her life, and Agnese had neither kept company with him nor set eyes upon him since. Striking was that Agnese remembered he had been the leader of an aggressive gang that constantly made fun of her and played a part in isolating her even more in class. Agnese's delusional withdrawal had also served to completely overturn the frustrating reality she had experienced: Marco now loved her and could not live without her.

Following is material from a session in the fourth month of analysis.

> *The patient enters smiling and rather evanescent: 'I will describe my dream: I was living inside a videogame; the walls opened and closed at my command depending on whether I said "open file, close file". But when I opened it some people approached wanting to come in; they were dangerous. It was a constant opening and closing. I wanted to open so that I could get out but I was obliged to close to protect myself. I am always afraid. Even yesterday when I went to Milan with my mother I was afraid, and when I got home I breathed a sigh of relief.'*

It would seem that in this dream Agnese is describing her psychotic functioning: she can create a videogame that replaces psychic reality, opening it and closing it at will. But then the psychotic system becomes threatening: Agnese can no longer master it and risks being held prisoner with no way out.

In a subsequent session, about a month before the summer holidays:

> *'I'm happy today because I had a nice dream, not an anxious one. I was with my friends from high school, but only those I got on well with, including Franca and Emilia. We were at a school near the coast. I had to do a computer test, and my friends had a maths test. At a certain point I confided in them about what had happened in September* (when she was admitted to hospital). *Then I asked them to get the medicine that I have to take. They were very caring and understood me, but the absurd thing about the dream is that Marco arrived too* (the character from the delusion), *and he didn't make fun of me or treat me badly; in fact, he told me that he would like to go out with me as long as I stop being stand-offish. Then I woke up calm and peaceful.'*

The dream is apparently calm and positive. In the first part Agnese manages to talk to her friends about her psychotic breakdown and even remembers the antipsychotic medication she has to take. But at this point, Marco, the protagonist of her love delusion, unexpectedly appears. It really does seem to be a peaceful dream, but a closer look shows that it is highly ambiguous.

Why does Marco appear suddenly in the dream? Why is the school at the seaside?

With this material in hand, her analyst might wonder whether this is not a case of the patient trying to convince her in the transference that everything is fine (as she does with her two friends in the dream), that she has recovered her mental health, while in actual fact she is secretly preparing another delusional meeting with Marco on the brink of the summer holidays (the school is on the coast).

In the next session, Agnese still seems apparently quite calm:

> *'It's a time in which I'm thinking about the future; even simple things make me euphoric. I'll give you an example: I bought a cream for cellulite to use in the summer, it's a nagging thought, I do nothing but think about the holidays. I bought a new swimsuit. I spend hours in front of the mirror. It's such an exhilarating thought that it makes me feel hyperactive. Then I started chatting to Daniele, and we spoke about everything, films, theatre, sport. Every time I go to the coast I dream of meeting someone who will turn my life around, and perhaps I'll run away with him.'*

The conclusion we can draw from this sequence of sessions is that the patient is preparing another psychotic episode, since the summer break is approaching and her analyst will not be there. The cellulite cream might allude to the beginning of a new euphoric sexual phase.

In fact, within a short space of time the same delusional atmosphere of the original psychotic episode is recreated. Agnese begins to miss sessions and, while she tells her parents she is going to the analyst, she prefers to wander about town in a paradelusional manner. Only a prompt and attentive psychiatric intervention and the resumption of regular sessions, after just a short holiday break, were to prevent re-admission to hospital.

This brief clinical example serves to demonstrate how the delusion, once established, tends to re-present itself, and also how it seduces the patient, who, confused about its pathological nature, in turn tends to do the same with the analyst in the transference.

In this case the lure of the aroused and ecstatic state was strongly enticing, and the approaching summer break from analysis reinforced the psychotic part. Agnese, having always lived a spent and isolated life, seemed to perceive the delusional part as an intoxicating experience of freedom.

The moment the patient produced the dream of the school at the seaside she was at risk, the delusional part already having created collusive complicity with the healthy part. Despite the patient's reticence, which is not a good sign, as it is often the determining factor in new relapses, the dream in this case shows the psychotic part's manoeuvrings and its bid to seduce the analyst.

It is therefore absolutely crucial that the analyst can capture traces of the psychotic part in the dream.

This clinical material on Agnese exemplifies how the dreams of some patients can acquire the predictive value of an impending psychotic crisis. Examining the delusion and working through how it came to form must be key focus points in an analysis like this one, requiring long, constant work.

The explosion of a psychotic episode leaves indelible traces and requires laborious reconstruction. Always to be borne in mind is that once an episode comes to an end, even though not manifest, a psychotic nucleus remains active, like a plant that has been cut but whose roots are still alive below the surface of the soil. For this reason, it is desirable to intervene before the psychosis presents its dramatic clinical manifestation, and likewise to have in therapy those children with clear but probably unrecognised symptoms that will lead to the psychosis developing in adulthood.

Conclusion

As analysts we are in a privileged position when we work with psychotic patients. We can listen, session after session, to a patient who continues to confide in us and in our method. No other clinician has the same opportunity as we do to learn from one single patient in a psychotic state from which he is trying to free himself. Therefore, it would be preferable if analysts could unite their forces to study this mental state in order to better understand the extent to which a reparative process of this complex illness can be promoted.

In my view (De Masi, 2000), damage done by psychosis has its origins in basic functions of the mind, those that underlie emotion perception and thought construction, which are needed to maintain our mental life but do not belong to the repressed unconscious. These functions take shape in the original mother-child relation, and towards adulthood become structures on which dynamic unconscious functioning (repressed) is based.

Among the numerous contributions of the contemporary landscape that have cast light on the importance of these primitive functions outside awareness, I shall cite the work of Beebe, Lachmann, and Jaffe (1997) only.

These authors seek to shed light on early interactive structures that originate in the way mother and child communicate emotionally during the first year of the child's life, before the use of verbal language. Their reciprocal interrelations organise experience and create patterns that the infant learns to recognise, remember and expect. These dyadic experiences later constitute the unconscious organisational structures that underlie personality. The authors speak of a 'prereflective' unconscious as opposed to a dynamic unconscious; they claim, moreover, that the newborn's representations will be symbolised above all in the nonverbal representation system. This is why, as stated earlier, I believe the psychotic disorder is on a different level from that which interests the repressed unconscious, whose exploration has permitted the origins of neurosis to be widely clarified. Psychotic functioning prevents the symbolisation of experience because the patient lives predominantly in a dissociated sensory withdrawal, an alternative to the construction of psychic reality, where mechanisms are created that alter psychic reality and personal identity through a pathological identification with grandiose and omnipotent figures created in fantasy. Such characters, made concrete and real, become mixed up with residual fragments of the patient's *real identity*, producing depersonalisation or confused states.

Each psychotic patient carries her specific psychotic islands that are subject to reactivation for internal or external reasons. Consequently, in analysis the course of these patients is unpredictable, it often being the case that precisely when vitality returns and an attempt at recovery seems possible, sudden relapses are triggered. Overly rapid improvements turn out to be false, as well-being unexpectedly turns into a condition of excitement.

It is difficult to decide when the therapy of a psychotic patient can be considered as carried forward sufficiently so that stability over time is achieved. Improvement should consist not only of an end to clinically psychotic functioning (that is, coming out of the delusion and hallucinations), but, more importantly, of acquiring stable emotional competence that will help the patient understand psychic reality and tolerate frustrations inherent to relating with the human world.

Before the clinical manifestations of their illness, these patients had been unable to establish a true personal identity. When their episode occurred, their precarious identity collapsed. The trigger is often connected to a break with an idealised bond that served as adhesive for their personality.

Not by chance psychotic breaks appear as if from nowhere during periods of transformation, from adolescence to adulthood, for instance, a transition that requires a firm base of emotional stability. During therapy, these patients try to find their previous equilibrium and seek to reconstruct the same adhesive pseudo-identity of the past. And it is these pseudo-recoveries that more often than not give false hope to family members, and the therapist.

Progress in therapy needs to be assessed in terms of new emotional experiences that structure a true personal identity, and in real terms this means a long and difficult path that goes beyond the disappearance of clinical symptoms.

I have sought here to set out the main and inevitable difficulties that emerge in therapeutic work with psychotic patients. These are facts I have gathered in my work as a therapist and supervisor. Only by taking such difficulties into account can we perfect a *specific* technique for these patients, who are apparently distant from us, but once understood in their lived experience and in their particular world, give unexpectedly positive therapeutic responses.

I must specify that patients I have had in my care are those in which the illness did not act chronically, leading to deterioration. They are individuals either at risk or who, despite struggling against one or more psychotic episodes, have maintained part of their personality apparently alive.

Note

1 An account of this patient may be found in my book *Vulnerability to Psychosis* (De Masi, 2009).

References

Arieti, S. (1955). *Interpretation of Schizophrenia* (2nd ed.). London: Crosby Lockwood Staples, 1974.

Beebe, B., Lachmann, F., and Jaffe, J. (1997). Mother-infant structures and presymbolic self and object representation. *Psychoanalytic Dialogues* 7: 133–182.

Bion, W. (1957). Differentiation of the psychotic from non-psychotic personalities. *International Journal of Psychoanalysis* 38: 266–275.

Bion, W. (1967). *Second Thoughts. Selected Papers on Psycho-Analysis*. London: William Heinemann Medical Books.

De Masi, F. (2000). The unconscious and psychosis. Some considerations on the psychoanalytic theory of psychosis. *International Journal of Psychoanalysis* 81: 1–20.

De Masi, F. (2009). *Vulnerability to Psychosis*. London: Karnac Books.

Federn, P. (1952). *Ego Psychology and the Psychoses*. London: Routledge.

Klein, M. (1930). The psychotherapy of psychoses. In *Contributions to Psychoanalysis 1921–1945*. London: The Hogarth Press, 1965, pp. 251–253.

Little, M. (1958). On delusional transference (transference psychosis). *International Journal of Psychoanalysis* 39: 134–138.

Searles, H. (1979). The schizophrenic individual experience of his world. In *Countertransference and Related Subjects: Selected Papers*. New York: International Universities Press.

Steiner, J. (1993). *Psychic Retreats*. London: Routledge.

Winnicott, D. (1971). Dreaming, fantasying and living: A case history describing a primary dissociation. In *Playing and Reality*. London: Tavistock.

Chapter 4

Psychosis and body-mind dissociation

A personal perspective on the psychoanalysis of acute crises and of schizophrenia[1]

Riccardo Lombardi

Those who think of psychotics as the degenerated and vacant patients of the old-style insane asylums, or else are reminded of Jack Torrance's uncontainable homicidal rage in the final scene of the film *The Shining* (Kubrick, 1980), may attribute a romantic notion of omnipotence to people who engage in psychoanalytic work with psychosis. And it *is* true that when psychosis has been present for decades, degenerative biological processes, together with the shutting out of reality, take over, so that the patients in question cannot be helped by psychoanalysis.

But all forms of psychosis must not be lumped together indiscriminately: every case should be evaluated separately to determine the actual possibility of analytic treatment's being beneficial. Thus we can attempt to guard against backsliding into the doubts that made Freud, first of all, opine that psychotics do not respond to analysis. These doubts seem occasionally to crop up again amongst analysts, at times in the guise of a fascinated deference to psychopharmacology, despite the revolutionary contributions of Klein, Fromm-Reichmann, Arieti, Bion, Sullivan, Searles and the multitude of other analysts who have dared to approach the most severely disturbed patients through analysis. It's hard to avoid wondering whether the gap between psychoanalysis and psychosis has not been widening in recent years.

"Curing" psychosis

On more than one occasion patients of mine have ridiculed me for my inability to cure their psychoses. And from a certain point of view how can one say they were entirely wrong? Is psychosis really "curable" by means of psychoanalysis?

The notion of simply "curing" psychosis seems to stem directly from a schizoparanoid assumption that the so-called "sick" part of the mind is to be neutralized and eliminated, instead of being integrated within one's internal dialogue and the general context of the personality. If the concept of a cure is absolutized according to this way of thinking, then it is certainly true that psychosis cannot be cured by psychoanalysis.

But if instead we consider the intervention of psychoanalysis in the context of the interaction between what Bion called the psychotic and the non-psychotic areas of the personality (Bion, 1957), then the whole situation is different. The psychoanalysis of psychosis would then address the growth of the non-psychotic part of the personality and work towards a progressive reduction of the psychotic area, through developing the perception of and familiarity with the patient's own psychotic activity.

If the presence of a genetic and constitutional component in psychosis is a matter for neurochemists of the brain, the analyst's attention is directed towards the mental perspective, which is used as a driving force that can, in some cases, bring about change on the physical level as well.

It is best, however, to proceed with care, since psychosis covers an endless territory, specifically because of the fragmentation of space-time parameters that it involves, to the point that exhaustive answers to the questions it poses would not even seem to exist. In approaching psychosis we are confronting mystery, the unknown or indeed the unfathomable – given that its concrete manifestations evoke the "noumenal" dimension of reality (Kant, 1781) and the most profound levels of the mind.

Given the questionable nature of any absolute pronouncement about psychosis, only the personal experience of treating patients with this problem can give empirical coherence to our knowledge of the field, so that I find that I prefer clinical accounts to general propositions. It is hardly by accident that any psychoanalytic session with a psychotic patient demonstrates that every one of our hypotheses is destined to be superseded or replaced by fresh data from the next session. And this brief work as well is not intended as an exception to the necessarily partial and provisional nature of any assertion on the subject.

Bion delivered a *coup de grâce* to the etiological approach to psychoanalysis, so I shall limit myself to an essentially pragmatic mode, focusing on the strategic possibilities of intervention in psychosis.

The discussion that follows is based on a few hypotheses – which I have verified in clinical practice – such as the conflict between the ego and external reality (Freud, 1923, 1924), the destructive and fragmentating attacks of projective identification directed against the personality (Klein, 1935, 1946) and the conflictual relationship between the psychotic and non-psychotic areas (Katan, 1954; Bion, 1957). In a more contemporary perspective I find that these assumptions can be significantly enriched by taking account of a structural discord between the body and the mind (Ferrari, 2004; Ferrari and Lombardi, 1998; Lombardi, 2002): when the conflict between the internal urgings of body and mind becomes unbearable it ends up in a body-mind dissociation, which becomes a basic obstacle to the activation of mental functioning in a psychotic. The body-mind dissociation that we encounter in psychosis can be correlated to the problem of saturation (Bion, 1967), together with other polarities in psychosis, such as that between order and disorder (Prigogyne, 1988) and finite and infinite (Bion, 1970; Matte Blanco, 1975, 1988; Bria and Lombardi, 2008; Lombardi, 2009b).

The body is understood as the point of origin of symbol formation, so the bodily instinct (Freud, 1915) must find correspondence and containment in an abstract formulation that can represent it (Bion, 1963). Everyone's body has unique characteristics, which are biological before they become psychological, and hence any sensory datum, as it begins to develop towards emotion and thought, already has personal characteristics (Ferrari, 2004). Psychosis, in relation to this trajectory, acts as an interference on the axis of body-affect-thought development (Lombardi, 2009d).

The analyst's *reverie* (Bion, 1962) and the analytic working through can help to facilitate the patient's mental growth. At the same time, we must bear in mind that the mental operations of notation and containment (Freud, 1911) take place within the analysand and are therefore conditioned by his/her responsibility and intentions.

All of this means that a psychoanalytic approach to psychosis should be based on the internal structure and inclination of the analysand's mental functioning rather than on a historic or reconstructive perspective. In other words, the disorder is not in the past, but in the criteria that are active in the present and that unfold, in most cases, before the eyes of the analyst.

Intervene as soon as possible

When dealing clinically with psychosis, it seems advantageous to intervene at once – if possible, in the very context of the first psychotic episode. This is particularly the case for psychoses in adolescence and for incipient schizophrenia (Lombardi and Pola, 2010). Such an episode has an enormous traumatic impact that can be attenuated by making use of the analytic instruments of containment. Receiving a psychotic patient in a psychoanalytic session during an acute phase can make it possible to foster the analysand's mental presence in the midst of a condition of chaos, which would otherwise tend to annihilate every form of rational thought.

For the analyst, receiving a patient in an acute condition is correlated to the recognition of the structural role played by catastrophic phenomena in mental functioning (Bion, 1970; Matte Blanco, 1975), so that no thought exists that does not, at its most profound levels, include the oscillations between fragmentation and integration (Lombardi, 2009b).

Analytic interaction during an acute psychotic episode has the merit of rendering containable and – for the purposes of experience and perception – utilizable those phenomena that, if left to themselves, would vanish into chaos. The analytic working through encourages an integration of intense emotions, awareness and thought, and it fosters belief in the resources of the mind and the value of the analytic relationship. Moreover, the analyst who chooses to wait out the acute episode misses a valuable chance to work on the disorganized levels of the mind where psychosis originates, without even having any guarantee that the psychotic disintegration will not unexpectedly well up again, since explosive moments can reappear in subsequent years. If episodes recur in the course of the analysis, the analyst should carefully explore the regressive meaning or, on the contrary, the developmental value of the episode itself, and avoid regarding it as a crisis and a pathology.

Going about it

It seems unlikely to be able to intervene beneficially in psychosis in the traditional way employed for patients who are relatively well adapted to reality. Given the multifactorial matrix – biological, environmental and psychological – of this condition (Grotstein, 2001), work with a psychotic is perforce teamwork: the analyst is joined by a pharmacological psychiatrist and by a consulting analyst for the family. The trespassing of psychotic disorder into external reality requires constant monitoring, particularly in certain critical moments, so that analytic work seems a realistic option only when reliable professional support is available for the people most affected by this spilling over of the patient's malaise. Some colleagues prefer to manage the pharmacological treatment themselves, in part so as to foster a complete emancipation from psychoactive drugs (*v.*, *e.g.*, Steinman, 2009, with its exceptionally rich back-up of case studies). I have, however, always benefited from teamwork, not least because it can ensure continuity of support for a severely disturbed patient during unavoidable interruptions of analysis and hence the absence of the analyst.

Pharmacological treatment is based on accepting the undeniable presence of biological components that accompany psychotic manifestations, and indeed it would now be thought criminal to treat a psychotic patient without considering the neurochemical factors at play. Medication makes it possible to reduce the disengagement from reality and lower the level of psychotic anxiety, thus fostering the analytic relationship and the analytic dialogue. Only the psychoanalytic working through, however, is capable of showing the importance of psychotic symptoms, giving them dynamic meaning; of encouraging the growth of the entire personality; and, with time, of creating the conditions of internal containment that make it possible to suspend the medication.

The analytic dialogue

The first goal to aim for in the psychoanalysis of psychosis is the continuity of the analytic dialogue, which should follow the criteria of simplicity and evidence. Some theoreticians place interpretation in the foreground

(Rosenfeld, 1965, 1987); others emphasize the role of deficit and empathy (Fromm-Reichmann, 1959; Killingmo, 1989), or instead the importance of integrating a supportive orientation and interpretative elements (Blechner, 1995; Williams, 2010). I feel, however, that it is essential to have a dialogic and interactive approach that can provide a constant support for the very weak resources of the psychotic analysand's ego, thus encouraging a tendency to correlate different mental elements and nourishing the patient's faith in his own communicational and perceptual resources.

This means that an analytic attitude of listening and affective acceptance of the patient seems in general to be contraindicated in the psychoanalysis of psychosis. Such an attitude, while it may be useful with mentally well-integrated patients, is, instead, not helpful in terms of the primary need to actively encourage a sense of reality in the psychotic patient, confronting him with the importance of self-observation and a continuous dialectic, which has been attacked by the thought defect that characterizes his internal organization. The analysand's traditional position – stretched out on the analytic couch – can also be contraindicated in many cases, and the patient should be free to place himself where he feels most at ease in the analytic office: activating eye contact within the analytic relationship can in fact help the patient to maintain attention and vigilance, which are useful for a certain functional articulation of thought, when this is at risk of crumbling before the very eyes of the analyst.

Internal world and external world

The analyst, with *binocular vision*, considers the patient's internal organization and external reality, emphasizing the most urgent implications.

The modes and forms of mental functioning on which the analyst tends first of all to dwell are not less *real* than other aspects of the patient's life; in fact they deserve careful consideration because they lay the foundations of the patient's links with reality.

A patient who had been suffering from explosive manifestations was having recurrent dreams of a clogged toilet, and finally she dreamed that she was on the toilet seat, repeatedly trying to flush away the feces that were filling the bowl, and, in the dream itself, she raised her eyes for the first time to look around her and discovered that the WC was in a state of serious neglect: many tiles had even come away from the walls. From that moment forth, looking after her own external reality became a primary aim of hers. This also implied an analytic adjustment befitting the analysand's newly acquired orientation towards reality.

A part of the external world is the family environment of the psychotic patient. Generally, families that are strongly motivated to back up the patient's development and his entry into real life turn out to be able to support his analysis, even during the dramatic periods of destabilization and

regression that can easily crop up in this sort of treatment. This destabilization can also be useful in offering a crucial form of personal experience, in
that the patient can learn in a transformative way from his errors. It should
be mentioned, however, that there are no treatments guaranteed to be free
of risks, including even the most extreme risk – death – when one is dealing with psychosis, since an integral part of the disorder is challenging the
limits imposed by reality. A patient of mine, for example, when faced with a
very painful bereavement, had reacted with a delusional denial of her loss,
involving, among other things, a continual defiance of death, so that when
the traffic light at an intersection was red she drove full speed ahead. Obviously the survival of a patient in cases of this sort cannot be guaranteed by
any form of psychoanalysis, although such situations of danger can be used
by the analyst for a working through of the analysand's challenge to death
and the real danger of dying brought on by this behavior.

To return to the family environment, I should mention that the evolution brought about by psychoanalysis can provoke a crisis in a family
arrangement based on atemporality and relational equilibria that are basically fictitious and unstable. Consequently one may encounter dangerous
obstructionism on the part of the family, leading even to the interruption of
the analysis. The role of the consulting analyst who has been looking after
the family can be crucial in seeking to sort out the conflicts that may even
affect the functioning of the family members. Some families may be hostile to
change in the patient, and may disguise their hostility, expressing skepticism
about the possibility of evolution in their psychotic relative. In these cases
they may use the transitory destabilization as a justification for interrupting
the analysis, thus precluding the analysand's achieving any independence.

Fundamental intersubjectivity and working through focused on the patient

The intersubjective level is the starting point as well as the arrival platform
in the psychoanalysis of psychosis: in building an experience of exchange,
understanding and trust become an essential springboard for creating a
relational connection with the patient. Given the weak reality sense of the
seriously disordered analysand and the danger of a delusional takeover,
the analytic relationship should be treated first of all in terms of its implications about reality, and the limitations of the setting should be employed
to reinforce an awareness of this intersubjective reality.

The psychotic patient suffers from a condition of saturation – a being
too full, which the patient sometimes perceives as being too empty – that
urgently requires bringing into play an internal metabolism. Saturation
causes an inability in the analysand to accept the interpretations of the
transference, as well as – because of concrete thinking – symbolic and
reconstructive interpretations.

The transference is nonetheless "total", as Melanie Klein understood. I tend to welcome this transference, and I leave relational phenomena in the background, in order to help the analysand move towards himself. In this way the analysand can activate a first capacity for self-observation and give a wide berth to internal sensory pressure. And saturation can gradually make way for the construction of a mental space. With the progressive expansion of the mental space, there come to be the conditions for the working through of the relational "other", whereas a premature emphasis on otherness risks creating internal disengagement and imitation.

As Ferrari explains it (2004), the transference consists of contemporaneous horizontal (relational) and vertical (intrasubjective) relationships. The initial working through particularly favors the development of a "vertical relationship" in the analysand, so that he can discover himself and the potential offered by an internal body-mind dialogue. This process should not be confused with a "one-person psychology", since it contains very powerful relational implications, such that the analyst must make use of a special capacity for involvement and *attunement* so as to foster the patient's access to insight of his own internal condition.

The profound levels

The patient, in his communications with the analyst, displays the modes and forms that are characteristic of him: the analyst can recognize them as such, and they can become an element of the analytic relationship. Freud (1899) discovered in dreams a totally ego-driven dimension that could be translated into the multi-dimensionality of the mind. Bion (1962) observed how a dream infiltrates the entire analytic session, so that every communication becomes a potential entry way to the patient's most profound levels. The formal arrangement of the thinking apparatus, the patient facing himself, the mind facing the body, and also the body facing the mind, the craving for and the terror of the infinite, and the transference onto space-time all take shape and are represented in the analytic relationship. The analyst "becomes" (Bion, 1970) that part of herself that corresponds to the analysand so as to understand and communicate on the same wavelength as the patient's intrasubjective levels, thus responding to the urgent need to define parameters of subjectivity and differentiation, as well as to create the conditions for the activation of the mind.

Schizophrenic logic and the "unfolding" of symmetry

The logic of the psychotic patient has different characteristics from the normal Aristotelian logic to which we are accustomed. It is a logic that has been infiltrated by the primary process (Freud, 1899), in which condensation and displacement play a significant role. This is what has been called *paleological thinking* (von Domarus, 1944; Arieti, 1955), in which an object is considered identical to the logical class to which it belongs, and hence the asymmetrical distinction between objects, people, situations, etc. is thrown out of kilter. The paleolithic aspects of thought act like "an acid" that slackens and then destroys logical distinctions, to the point where every kind of recognition and thought becomes impossible. The devastating effects that the so-called principle of symmetry (Matte Blanco, 1975) has on the psychotic patient mean that the analyst must devote his attention to the *unfolding* of all the symmetrical forms that crop up in the session, in order to foster plausibly realistic communication, the development of affects and the recognition of reality (Lombardi, 2006, 2010a; Niemi and Lombardi, 2008).

Helping the patient's use of language to evolve

The seriously disordered patient is likely to lack distinct elements of subjectivization, i.e., of that precise identifactory core that some English-speaking theorists call the patient's "agency". From this point of view it seems out of place to stress the narcissism or the relational perversion of these patients, since their problem is essentially the result of insufficient narcissism.

The psychotic doesn't clearly grasp his own reasoning, and is certainly not up to defending it, but this does not imply that he doesn't have reasons, perceptions or positions of his own. Even his use of language may be compromised or reduced to extremely condensed forms, having been infiltrated by the primary process, so that the analyst is addressed by the patient in oracular mode, which "neither reveals nor conceals, but gives a sign" (Heraclitus).

The analyst is then called upon to work on the precursors of organized language, or "language registers" (Ferrari, 2004; Lombardi, 2004), so that they can evolve towards more realistic and comprehensible modes. In this perspective, delusions and hallucinations can be taken not as the pathological symptoms they unquestionably are, but as potential forms of valid communication.

The development of these modes is greatly influenced by the relational dynamics: it is up to the analyst to find a way of reaching the analysand and establishing a transitional language with symbolic potential (Ekstein and Caruth, 1969; Winnicott, 1971) that can release the analysand from solipsistic imprisonment.

Analysis of models and mental theories

Analytic theories, because they are notoriously so abstract, are far removed from the pressing need to organize the material one encounters during an analytic session (Bion, 1962). In general, resorting to analytic theories at such a time is indicative of the analyst's anxiety when faced with the unknown in the form of the enigmatic communications of the analysand. Thus one should never allow the presence of Psychoanalysis with a capital P – a corpus of pre-established knowledge – in an analytic session. The analyst can, instead, consider psychoanalytic theory outside of the sessions, so as to compare her experience with the current state of received knowledge.

Instead of emphasizing symbolic contents or historic reconstruction, analytic work with psychotics should concentrate on observing the modes and forms of mental functioning. Mental models (Bion, 1962; Lombardi, 2003a, 2004) can help to introduce progressive levels of abstraction in the analysand's communications, which are overburdened with concreteness. Abstraction makes the set-up of internal functioning definable and communicable.

Working through on these levels makes it possible to foster the patient's awareness of his recurrent attitudes and to have him assume responsibility for his own mental functioning, which can thus become internally manageable. Observing the patient's internal functioning is a function of the analyst's *reverie* (Bion, 1962), i.e., of the analyst's capacity for feeling the patient's primary needs, amongst which are included the needs to generate and deal with abstractions and to develop perceptions and self-knowledge.

Hate, destructiveness and negative transference

Activating the mental metabolism of hate in a psychotic patient is essential to forestalling situations of acting out that could be dangerous for the analyst or lead to the interruption of treatment. It is important for the analyst to maintain a relational distance – i.e., not force the development of a positive transference, nor, certainly, a condition of dependence – so as to allow the patient to bring his hate directly into the transference when necessary. The experience of negative transference facilitates the elaboration of hate, reinforces the patient's faith in himself and readjusts the analytic relationship, fostering intersubjective differentiation. Given the patient's thinking defect, negative transference can, in certain circumstances, take on dramatic proportions, so that it is not surprising that theorists like Federn (1943) have advised the interruption of treatment in such an eventuality. Negative transference can also become homicidal transference. This can be due to a situation of particularly violent splitting, such that the patient, when she succeeds in gaining access to her hate, finds it in its concrete and infinite form. In a patient with suicidal tendencies, homicidal transference can also be a sign of a development that becomes the antechamber to a representation of the most stealthy and unconscious destructive components of the personality. Analyzing homicidal levels is also important in that the seriously disordered patient can have a homicidal relationship with his own mind, so that this working through can make it possible to emerge from a condition of mental death. The analyst's capacity to contain direct attacks and keep her own internal love and hate integrated is essential to readjusting the most extreme phenomena that may appear in a session, bearing in mind that a certain quota of affectionate feelings and of hate-love ambivalence is always present, even in the most aggressive patients. Nevertheless, there are real risks for the analyst, so it hardly needs saying that this kind of analysis contains a variable that is strongly tied to personal motivation. But in this situation too, it seems valid to say, "Nothing ventured, nothing gained".

Transference onto the body and the body-mind dialogue

Amongst the most telling theories about psychotic patients and the so-called borderline cases are those that consider thought as independent of sensations, and the mind as separate from the body (Laing, 1955; Lombardi, 2000, 2004, 2007b). In the most discordant cases, body and mind are like incompatible, indeed opposed, entities – as is particularly evident, for instance, in psychoses associated with eating disorders. "I'd like to be a baby balloon", an analysand told me, reducing to one sentence her anorexic and incorporeal ideal. "For me everything becomes absolute", another patient commented, expressing her bulimic oscillation between being "all body" – and eating limitless amounts – and being "bodiless" – devoid of sexuality and prey to a relentlessly ascetic ideal.

The passage from body to mind in psychosis can reach the limits of what is possible, like – to use a gospel phrase dear to Freud – a camel trying to pass through the eye of a needle (see Lombardi, 2009a). But analysis can catalyze a transference onto the body and help set in motion a body-mind dialogue in the analysand (Lombardi, 1992, 2003b, 2005a, 2006). At the same time the body – together with the spatio-temporal organization that belongs to it – can come to be the pivot for constructing a sense of personal identity as opposed to the paralyzing maelstrom of annihilation anxiety (Lombardi, 2008, 2010b, 2011a).

Time and psychosis

Time for a psychotic is like teatime for the Mad Hatter: his watch is stopped and always shows that it's time for tea. But the psychotic hates time, as an element outside his control that brings him face to face with limitations (Bion, 1967; Kernberg, 2008), with the result that life and death may even seem altogether indistinguishable (Lombardi, 2007a). Confronting the discovery of linear and irreversible time can unleash extreme acting out, even homicide and suicide (Lombardi, 1985, 2011b). Time can be the object of an actual "theft of time" – as in Michael Ende's novel *Momo*, which Alberto Schon (1985), with dazzling insight, recognized as a prototype of the primary levels in mourning (for the clinical implications, *v*. Lombardi, 2009c). But before hating it, the psychotic may entirely ignore time – as a category inherent in mental functioning (Kant, 1781) – and hence may respond in a very intolerant way to a working through that places the relationship to time in the foreground (Bonaparte, 1940; Lombardi, 2003b, 2005b).

Psychosis and regression

Analytic work with psychosis should *contain* regressive urges and foster a progressive orientation. Attending the patient's progression can be an arduous challenge to the analyst's own resources. Discerning in my face the distress brought about by a dramatic session consisting of a patient's screams, tears, insults and desperation, the said patient suddenly stopped dead in her tracks and asked me, "Do I cause you so much trouble? Do I? But what's all this trouble for? Why are we born? Who is it that makes us be born?"

The psychotic's ambition would seem in some way to *not have been born*, in keeping with the fantasy of not being exposed to the dangers, instability and precariousness of life. In *The Birth of Tragedy* (1862), Nietzsche recounts the legend of King Midas, who hunted out the sage Silenus to ask him about the best and most desirable thing for man, and received the following reply, "Not to have been born, not to be, to be nothing. But the best thing for *you* is to die soon" (Italian translation 1972, pp. 31–32), which could serve as a model of concision in describing the component of aggravated inertia in the psychotic conception of the world. Developing, with great originality, Bion's ideas about catastrophic change, Tustin (1972, p. 111) describes negativism and non-communication as ingredients that are essential to autistic barriers that protect the autistic child from contact with pre-verbal ontological anguish and with the need for the working through of hate connected to psychological birth.

The psychotic shows a particular sensibility about ontological problems – as I learned, during the years of my specialization in psychiatry, from Salomon Resnik (2001), with his unique ability to articulate clearly about both psychoanalysis and phenomenology. Often it is precisely the experience of an acute phase – in which hate takes on explosive volcanic characteristics – that catalyzes the breaking down of autistic barriers and of counterfeit forms of adaptation to reality, thus fostering the patient's access to actual space-time and the world of genuine relations.

Compared to conditions of "non-existence", with their bi-dimensional and imitative shams, a psychotic crisis can often be an opening up – an attempt to approach a vital dimension composed of meaning and awareness – and an analytic intervention can be the decisive element in promoting the propulsive force implicit in the crisis, and differentiating it from the formless mass of expulsive and destructive detritus.

"Psychosis: it's something else" (*La psychose: c'est autre chose*), Liliane Abensour liked to remind me, so as to underscore the difference between the psychoanalytic conception of psychosis and the medico-psychiatric one that simply regards it as a pathology. Her book, which has been catching on, although, unfortunately, only after her death, makes it clear that she had in mind a close connection between psychosis and the "subliminal ego" of André Breton and the Surrealists: "Distinct from the unconscious, this area, situated beneath the threshold of consciousness, unorganized and sometimes fruitful, is this not precisely what inhabits psychotic patients? A place of non-contradiction, of non-differentiation of the real from the imaginary, of life from death, of the past from the future" (Abensour, 2008, p. 166).

Pulled into this subliminal area by the relationship with the psychotic, the analyst is faced by "an avalanche of sensations that reject any form" ("une avalanche de sensations qui repoussent toute forme", Cioran, 1971, p. 24).

Counter-transference, bodily counter-transference and the analyst's working through

Constant working through of the so-called counter-transference is essential to attending the psychotic analysand's evolution. The term "counter-transference" seems, regrettably, reductive, in that the experiences that are integral to analysis of this kind can have a profound transformational effect on the analyst and involve her capacity to "evolve" – as Bion put it – towards an unknown self, as they draw her nearer to areas that are generally repressed. Thus the patient becomes, for the analyst, like Dante's Virgil, and can lead her to the circle of profound experiences (Lombardi, 1987). Hence it can be helpful to experience treating psychosis while undergoing one's own analysis, since this kind of experience introduces a further dimension of depth to that analysis. The area in question involves, first of all, the somatic origins of distinctly concrete thinking – as in Freud's "Dingvorstellung" (1915) and Ferrari's concept of the "Concrete Original Object" (1992). The analyst faces notably complex experiences, which are difficult to translate or transmit, an inevitable concomitant of attempting to approach asymbolic and pre-verbal areas; she takes in the somatic precursors of emotions and thoughts that are in the course of being defined in the analytic process, and tolerates within herself the development of new and unknown sensations, or actual transitory somatic phenomena, both during the session and outside of it. This "somatic counter-transference", as we may call it, requires a great commitment and the investment of energy, as well as caution in managing one's own life. The body's emergence in the foreground in these cases must not be confused with reactions due to unanalyzed culs-de-sac, resistance or containment deficits: what it does first of all is indicate a presence. The body "is there", because the analyst "is there", in fact – before being there as a thinking subject – she is there as an actual and bodily person relating to an analysand who is, in the bud, just as real and bodily. Thus the analyst accompanies the analysand's transference on to the body, his taking bodily shape and becoming real. So the analyst must undergo not only the problem of containing her hate in the counter-transference (Winnicott, 1947), but also a sort of "primary maternal preoccupation" – i.e., that emergence of the "psyche-soma", with considerable involvement of the unconscious, that Winnicott (1956) attributed to pregnant women. This experience can be even more complex for the analyst, to the extent that "difficult" patients in treatment are more than one person. In addition, the analyst's mind can be called on – in situations of great pressure in the analytic relationship – to dream along with the patient, or even "in place of" the patient, paving the way to primary forms of representation and organization of his internal world.

It should, however, be borne in mind that if one is to endure this type of experience it is extremely important, as Fromm-Reichmann (1959) points out, for the analyst to have a personal life, separate from her professional endeavors, from which to draw independent satisfaction.

The limits of the counter-transference

The involvement of asymbolic and pre-verbal areas implies a non-direct link between sensation and thought, a condition that is only increased by the serious discord in the body-mind relationship of these patients. Hence the analyst must be able to accompany body and mind experiences separately, as an expression of the functional dualism (Damasio, 1999) that characterizes the human animal. Accordingly, the analyst must cultivate an "objective approach" (Tustin, 1981) that makes good use of the analyst's observant mode, with its roots in the specialized sense organs directed towards external reality (Freud, 1911; Bion, 1962). Accepting the patient in his entirety composed of sensations, emotions, bodily language and verbal symbolization is thus essential. Verbal communications must be understood in their multiplicity of communicative levels – from the concrete to the symbolic, from the intrasubjective to the external relational – selecting as necessary the level that is most urgent and likely to further the analytic process. This all implies not allowing oneself to be guided only by one's own internal sensations – which may well be deceived and thrown off track by the condition of internal saturation the patient is experiencing – but instead being careful to take in the analysand's objective communications, and to compare the characteristics of this level with one's own counter-transferential response.

A clinical experience

Having on various occasions engaged in psychoanalytic treatment in the course of a patient's acute psychotic episode, I shall now pause to consider some passages from a psychoanalytic intervention in a case of schizophrenia. There are serious limitations to this kind of intervention due to the incrustation of inevitable degeneration, particularly when, as here, the patient's psychosis has for years been unchallenged as it acted on his personality. I've already alluded to the fact that, in psychosis, the annihilation of the idea of time and the dissociation from the body are central. These characteristics are connected to the unstable spatio-temporal organization caused by a thinking defect, to which significant attacks on linking contribute (Bion, 1959).

So we'll have a look at a few moments from the analysis of Gennaro, a 50-year-old schizophrenic with a long history of hospitalization for acute episodes that included delusions and manic agitation. Despite considerable pharmacological treatment, the patient's persecutory symptoms had worsened, to the point where he feared his family might be poisoning him, and he presented agoraphobic anxiety and a stubborn refusal to practice any form of bodily hygiene, so that, in the sessions, he emanated an almost unbearable stench. He had already undergone a long psychotherapy in the past, which had been complicated by certain concrete benefits that the therapist had sought to obtain from the patient. I saw the patient four times a week for about six months; shortly before the summer vacation he interrupted the treatment in an aggressive climate of manic excitation. Indeed, although at the beginning of our relationship Gennaro had idealized me to excess, with the passage of time he developed an intense negative transference and even made open threats of physical aggression. This setting in motion of hate in the transference was accompanied by a clear improvement of his symptoms, so that the interruption was backed up by the resolution of the urgent problems that had motivated his request for analysis in the first place.

My psychoanalytic work with Gennaro had at once seemed very nearly impossible, because his problem challenged the most elementary condition of the analytic setting, i.e., the physical presence during sessions of the analysand, without which it was impossible to start on any form of working through. He, instead, would frequently arrive for his session at the time when it should have been concluding or almost concluding, putting me in the paradoxical position of having to choose between my connection to him and my respect for the temporal parameters of the setting, which are representatives of the existence of an external reality with its concomitant limits. This problem was a clear expression of Gennaro's psy-chotic conflict with reality, so that his own self and reality excluded each other by turns. The situation seemed also to establish a dramatic body-mind dissociation, condemning him never to be present in the physical space of his sessions, just as he kept his mind outside of the actual space of the body that belonged to him. Extreme conflictual situations of this sort can jeopardize any real possibility of psychoanalytic intervention: they require some form of pragmatic adaptation of the normal parameters of the setting, and so I allowed myself – flexibly and in keeping with keen observation of the process moment by moment – to introduce a temporal violation of the setting, at least to the extent that might make it possible to effect some form of working through, while being equally careful not to lose my sense of analytic space-time, and of space-time altogether. Thus, according to how things were going, I might lengthen his sessions by 5, 10 or 20 minutes – whatever gave me the impression that something had been noted by him in terms of his experience. In his most compromised moments I decided to offer him the chance to make up on the same day for the session he had missed through lateness or absence, without asking for an additional fee.

The subject of time appeared even in our first encounters, and then constantly returned in Gennaro's sessions. "I got up late. I didn't realize what time it was" became a frequent refrain. And time indeed seemed completely extraneous to the horizon of his mental notation. To this was added the chronic cancelation of time with his uncontrollable obsessive-compulsive symptoms, which led him to repeat the same behavior dozens of times: "I always repeat the same things, I'm outside of life". His grave symptoms created a violent hate and rejection of himself, thus forming a vicious and deadly circle, according to which he could not accept himself because he was "physically damaged" – as he was wont to say – and this "dogma" of non-acceptance stood in the way of any real possibility of experience and evolution within his actual condition. So now we can have a look at some aspects of the analytic work with this patient in the midst of a session. He starts out by saying that he generally doesn't manage to arrive on time because he doesn't notice that time is passing while he's getting ready, and then he adds:

G: *It's as if time didn't ever pass.*
RL: *Time that passes implies mourning.*
G: *Do you mean death?*
RL: *What meaning are you thinking of?*
G: *That if time is passing we're moving towards death.*
RL: *So we may conclude that you blot out the perception of time,
            in the belief that this way you can do away with death. Despite
            your delusion, the risk of death continues to exist, and all you*

	succeed in doing away with is your own *time, the time that could allow you to live.*
G [*reflectively*]:	*This could be what happens.* [after a pause] *I was thinking about how my repetitions work. For instance: when I looked at the empty envelope, and then I looked away, and I just couldn't remember what I had seen. So then I have to look again, and so on, ad infinitum.*
RL:	*How would you explain it?*
G:	*I'd say it goes back to the prohibition about looking at the female genitals, to the prohibition in the sixth commandment: Thou shalt not commit adultery!*
RL:	[I ascribe his reply to the intellectualization and psycho-analytic indoctrination he received in his previous psychotherapy.] *You're looking for excitation rather than seeing reality for what it is, instead of looking in order to see. For example, when there's an empty envelope, you may see empti-ness, but then you cancel it because you feel it's threatening, as if it were death. And so you seek to do away with death.*
G:	*There must be something like that involved. But according to you, do I believe that I'm immortal?*
RL:	*What would you say?*
G:	*After death life goes on, that's what I believe.*
RL:	[I have the impression that his psychotic functioning is surfacing, i.e., his psychotic denial of death.]
G:	[after a pause, he seems more uncertain; his tone of voice changes as he adds]: *Even though the body certainly putrefies.*
RL:	[I'm surprised by his change of course and consider it very positive that he keeps his non-psychotic resources working during our dialogue, as evinced by his recogni-tion of a realistic component of death, the putrefaction of the body. I attempt to take advantage of this percep-tion of his to bring up his dissociation from his body, so I show my surprise, seeking to make use of his percep-tion to link it to his denial of his body and his lack of per-sonal hygiene] *Aha! So this is why you don't want to have anything to do with your body!? And why you let it putrefy with filth!?*
G:	[very disoriented, and it seems to me that he has been struck by my intervention, which has got to the heart of his dissociation; he reacts slowly, drawing out his words] *Ah, yes, yes . . . that must be it . . . But what I fear most is the death of my soul. According to the way I was brought up, you have to be wary of life's temptations so as not to consign your soul to perdition.*

RL: So, to avoid the death of your soul you just renounce living:
            you're barricaded at home, as if you were already buried.
G: I behave like certain monks who shut themselves up, far from
            the outside world, to avoid temptations.
RL: Like hermits?
G: Exactly!

Here I pointed out that by behaving this way one provokes a chronic frustration that one then avenges by having only sexual thoughts, as was the case with him, shut up at home. This was a rather imprecise description, given that at this point it had become clear that his compulsive eroticization was essentially a response to the condition of internal death that Gennaro forced on himself in his would-be omnipotent attempt to control death.

We had meanwhile reached the end of the session, and I stood up, as I usually do to signal that a session is finished. The analysand's reaction was somewhere between astonished and desperate – almost at the point of tearing his hair. I was struck by the vividness of his emotional reaction, which was much more like that of a normal person than his usual impassible, frigid and intellectual manner. And indeed he exclaimed, "Good God! Are three quarters of an hour over already?!" In response I pointed out that at least this time we had been able to have a session, unlike the lateness-ordained nothing – or almost nothing – he had in general grudgingly allowed himself. And this lateness now seemed connected to a desire not to grant himself anything, just so as to avoid the distress of facing an end, a void.

The session we've been considering brings out various elements, including the correlation between the denial of time and the terror of death – which has been underlined by various other authors such as Bonaparte (1940), Arlow (1984), Hartocollis (1972) – as well as the connection between these anxieties, dissociation from the body and agoraphobia. His amazement and pain when faced with the end of the session became a decisive opportunity for Gennaro to *experience limitation* as part of a link to a reality that could not dispense with his actual existence. The working through created the conditions for catalyzing the beginning of tolerance for limitations, which would allow him to approach both reality in general and a self that was still radically rejected because of being "too disordered and damaged" or, in other words, "too" limited.

I find this material particularly striking as a demonstration of how the dissociation or denial of the body could lead Gennaro, in his everyday life, to let his body become and remain putrid, which served to confuse life with death, since both were characterized by a "putrefied" body – what I, following Matte Blanco, have characterized as a symmetrization of the life-death dualism (Lombardi, 2007a). Working through this area makes it possible to reduce the psychotic colonization of the body and the body-mind dissociation, allowing the analysand to re-appropriate a realistic anxiety about death. In the case at hand, amongst the results of this phase of analytic working through, there was, most significantly, Gennaro's collaboration in arranging to have a pair of shoes made to order, which allowed him to leave home and walk, whereas previously the deterioration of his condition had been reinforced by the impossibility of going out because he had no shoes to put on, since some foot deformities kept him from wearing any shoes one can usually find ready-made.

About six years after this first phase of analytic work, Gennaro returned for a second but brief period of analysis. He seemed in much better shape: his personal hygiene was distinctly improved, he trimmed his beard, he went out and had more contact with life. He appeared to be more mentally present and his delusional symptoms were more constantly challenged by his now lucid consciousness. He said that he had come back mostly to thank me for the work we had done together, which he believed he had digested little by little during the six-year interim, and he felt that this had made possible the improvement from which he was benefiting. His recognition of the importance of a connection with time returned in this second analytic period in the form of a significant dream in which his discovery of time was represented in a very original way, with evident connections to his personal history and his family relationships.

Conclusion

Before finishing, I'd like to express my hope that familiarity with the primitive levels of the border between body and mind – where life itself, experience and thought are organized out of a formless mass – might help us to respond to the challenges that clinical psychoanalysis faces in an ever more complex and constantly evolving world. From this perspective, it does not seem absurd to me to believe that the exploration of psychosis could be – now more than ever before – a decisive opportunity for psychoanalysis to expand its horizons.

Note

1 This chapter has been translated into English by Karen Christenfeld.

References

Abensour, L. (2008). *La tentation psychotique*. Paris: Presse Universitaire de France.
Arieti, S. (1955). *Interpretation of Schizophrenia*. New York: Brunner.
Arlow, J. (1984). Disturbances of the sense of time – With special reference to the experience of timelessness. *Psychoanalytic Quarterly* 53: 13–37.

Bion, W.R. (1957). Differentiation of psychotic from non-psychotic personalities. In *Second Thoughts*. London: Karnac Books, 1967.

Bion, W.R. (1959). Attacks on linkings. In *Second Thoughts*. London: Karnac Books, 1967.

Bion, W.R. (1962). *Learning from Experience*. London: Karnac Books.

Bion, W.R. (1963). *Elements of Psychoanalysis*. London: Karnac Books.

Bion, W.R. (1967). *Second Thoughts*. London: Karnac Books.

Bion, W.R. (1970). *Attention and Interpretation*. London: Karnac Books.

Blechner, M. (1995). Schizophrenia. In Lionells, M., Fiscalini, J., Mann, C., and Stern, D. (Editors), *Handbook of Interpersonal Psychoanalysis*. Hillsdale, NJ: Analytic Press, pp. 375–396.

Bonaparte, M. (1940). Time and the unconscious. *International Journal of Psychoanalysis* 21: 427–468.

Bria, P., and Lombardi, R. (2008). The logic of turmoil: Some epistemological and clinical considerations on emotional experience and the infinite. *International Journal of Psychoanalysis* 89: 709–726.

Cioran. (1971). *Le crépuscule des pensées*. Paris: L'Herne.

Damasio, A. (1999). *The Feeling of What Happens. Body and Emotion in the Making of Consciousness*. New York: Hartbace & Co.

Ekstein, R., and Caruth, E. (1969). Levels of verbal communication in the schizophrenic child's struggle against, for and with the world of object. *Psychoanal Study Child* 24: 115–137.

Federn, P. (1943). *L'analisi della psicosi*. Torino: Boringhieri, 1953.

Ferrari, A.B. (2004). *From the Eclipse of the Body to the Dawn of Thought*. London: Free Association Books.

Ferrari, A.B., and Lombardi, R. (1998). Il corpo dell'Inconscio. *MicroMega* 3: 197–208.

Freud, S. (1899). The interpretation of dreams. *Standard Edition* 5.

Freud, S. (1911). Formulation on the two principles of mental functioning. *Standard Edition* 12.

Freud, S. (1915). The unconscious. *Standard Edition* 14.

Freud, S. (1923). Neurosis and psychosis. *Standard Edition* 19.

Freud, S. (1924). The loss of reality in neurosis and psychosis. *Standard Edition* 19.

Fromm Reichmann, F. (1959). Psychoanalysis and psychotherapy. In Bullard, D. (Editor), *Selected Papers of Frieda Fromm Reichmann*. Chicago: University of Chicago Press.

Grotstein, J. (2001). A rationale for the psychoanalytically informed psychotherapy of schizophrenia and other psychoses: Towards the concepts of 'rehabilitative psychoanalysis'. In Williams, P. (Editor), *A Language for Psychosis*. London and Philadelphia: Whurr Publishers.

Hartocollis, P. (1972). Time as a dimension of affects. *Journal of the American Psychoanalytical Association* 20: 92–108.

Kant, E. (1781). *Critique of Pure Reason*. Houndmills, England: Palgrave Macmillan.

Katan, M. (1954). The importance of the non-psychotic part of the personality in schizophrenia. *International Journal of Psychoanalysis* 35: 119–128.

Kubrick, S. (1980). The Shining.

Kernberg, O. (2008). The destruction of time in pathological narcissism. *International Journal of Psychoanalysis* 89: 299–312.

Killingmo, B. (1989). Conflict and deficit: Implications for technique. *International Journal of Psychoanalysis* 70: 65–79.

Klein, M. (1935). A contribution to the psychogenesis of manic-depressive States. In *Love, Guilt and Reparation & Other Works 1921–1945*. New York: Delta.

Klein, M. (1946). Notes on some schizoid mechanisms. In *Envy and Gratitude and Other Works*. London: The Hogarth Press, 1975.

Laing, R.D. (1955). *The Divided Self*. London: Penguin.

Lombardi, R. (1985). Lutto e psicosi. In De Risio, S., Ferro, F.M., and Orlandelli, H. (Editors), *La psicosi e la maschera*. Roma: IES Mercuri.

Lombardi, R. (1987). Funzione di guida dell'analizzando nel trattamento psicoanalitico delle psicosi. *Neurologia Psichiatria Scienze umane* VII (1): 1–14.

Lombardi, R. (1992). Corpo e Psicosi. In *Ferrari A L'eclissi del corpo*. Roma: Borla.

Lombardi, R. (2000). Il sogno e la rete di contatto corpo-mente. In Bolognini, S. (a cura di), *Il sogno cent'anni dopo*. Torino: Boringhieri.

Lombardi, R. (2002). Primitive mental states and the body. A personal view of A. B. Ferrari's concrete original object. *International Journal of Psychoanalysis* 83: 363–382.

Lombardi, R. (2003a). Mental models and language registers in the psychoanalysis of psychosis. An overview of a thirteen-year analysis. *International Journal of Psychoanalysis* 84: 843–863.

Lombardi, R. (2003b). Knowledge and experience of time in primitive mental states. *International Journal of Psychoanalysis* 84: 1531–1549.

Lombardi, R. (2004). Three psychoanalytic sessions. *Psychoanalytic Quarterly* 73: 773–814.

Lombardi, R. (2005a). On the psychoanalytic treatment of a psychotic breakdown. *Psychoanalytic Quarterly* 74: 1069–1099.

Lombardi, R. (2005b). Setting e Temporalità. In Giuseppe Berti Ceroni (a cura di), *Come cura la psicoanalisi?* Milano: Franco Angeli.

Lombardi, R. (2006). Catalizzando il dialogo tra il corpo e la mente in un analizzando psicotico. [Una prospettiva bi-logica] *Rivista Psicoanal* 52: 743–765.

Lombardi, R. (2007a). Sull'essere: dispiegamento della simmetrizzazione vita-morte. In Ginzburg, A., and Lombardi, R. (Editors), *L'emozione come esperienza infinita*. Milano: Franco Angeli.

Lombardi, R. (2007b). Shame in relation to the body, sex and death: A clinical exploration of the psychotic levels of shame. *Psychoanalytic Dialogues* 17 (3): 1–15.

Lombardi, R. (2008). The body in the analytic session: Focusing on the body-mind link. *International Journal of Psychoanalysis* 89: 89–110.

Lombardi, R. (2009a). Through the eye of the needle: The unfolding of the unconscious body. *Journal of the American Psychoanalytical Association* 57: 61–94.

Lombardi, R. (2009b). Symmetric frenzy and catastrophic change: A consideration of primitive mental states in the wake of Bion and Matte Blanco. *International Journal of Psychoanalysis* 90: 529–549.

Lombardi, R. (2009c). On the psychoanalytic working-through with a psychotic patient at the crossroad of death, time and life. Letto a IPA Conference, Panel 'Psychosis and regression', Chair L. Abensour, Discussioni di D. Rosenfeld e A. Silver, Chicago, 30 luglio.

Lombardi, R. (2009d). Body, affects, thoughts. *Psychoanalytic Quarterly* 78: 126–160.

Lombardi, R. (2010a). Flexibility of the psychoanalytic approach in the treatment of a suicidal patient: Stubborn silences as "playing dead". *Psychoanalytic Dialogues* 20: 269–284.

Lombardi, R. (2010b). The body emerging from the "neverland" of nothingness. *Psychoanalytic Quarterly* 79: 879–909.

Lombardi, R. (2011a). Body, feelings and the unheard music of the senses. *Contemporary Psychoanalysis* 47: 3–24.

Lombardi, R. (2011b). Identité et mise à mort dans la psychose. *Psychanalyse et Psychose* 11.

Lombardi, R., and Pola, M. (2010). Body, adolescence and psychosis. *International Journal of Psychoanalysis* 91: 1419–1444.

Matte Blanco, I. (1975). *Unconscious as Infinite Sets*. London: Karnac Books, 1978.

Matte Blanco, I. (1988). *Thinking, Feeling and Being*. London and New York: Routledge.

Niemi, T., and Lombardi, R. (2008). Run or die: Bi-logical phenomena at the body-mind border. *Scandinavian Psychoanalytic Review* 31: 95–104.

Nietzsche, F. (1862). *The Birth of Tragedy*. New York: Oxford University Press, 2000.

Prigogyne, I. (1988). *Entre le temps et l'éternité*. Paris: Fayard.

Resnik, S. (2001). *The Delusional Person: Bodily Feeling in Psychosis*. London: Karnac Books.

Rosenfeld, H. (1965). *Psychotic States*. London: The Hogarth Press.

Rosenfeld, H. (1987). *Impasse and Interpretation*. London: Tavistock.

Schon, A. (1985). 'Momo' di Michael Ende o la leggenda del tempo rubato. *Rivista Psicoanal* 31: 405–406.

Steinman, I. (2009). *Treating the 'Untreatable'*. London: Karnac Books.

Tustin, F. (1972). *Autism and Childhood Psychosis*. London: Karnac Books.

Tustin, F. (1981). *Autistic States in Children*. London: Routledge.

Von Domarus, E. (1944). The specific laws of logic in schizophrenia. In Kasanin, J.S. (Editor), *Language and Thought in Schizophrenia: Collected Papers*. Oakland, CA: University of California Press, 1944.

Williams, P. (2010). *Invasive Objects. Minds Under Siege*. New York and London: Routledge.

Winnicott, D.W. (1947). Hate in the countertransference. In *Collected Papers: Through Paediatrics to Psycho-Analysis*. London: Tavistock, 1958.

Winnicott, D.W. (1956). Primary maternal preoccupation. In *Collected Papers: Through Paediatrics to Psycho-Analysis*. London: Tavistock, 1958.

Winnicott, D.W. (1971). *Playing and Reality*. London: Tavistock.

Part II

Communication and empathy with the psychotic analysand

Chapter 5

Aspects of clinical work with psychotic patients

Mark J. Blechner

I have been working in psychotherapy with psychotic patients for 43 years. Rather than give an extensive theoretical discussion of psychosis, of which there are already many in our literature, I would like to describe some of the peak formative experiences in my career, some of the essential principles of my own clinical work, and my observation of other people's work with psychotic patients. I will consider especially the importance of affective and nonverbal communication, the role of stigma in exacerbating psychopathology, the importance of the psychic concerns just before the first psychotic break, and the interrelationship of hallucinations, delusions, and dreams.

Communication: emotional, musical, and verbal

The first extended clinical experience in my life was with Larry, a severely autistic 10-year-old boy. Larry's mother hired me, a 19-year-old college student, to spend a few afternoons a week with him. She probably wanted to get him out of the house for a while, but also hoped that I could achieve something therapeutic. At the time, I had just a few psychology courses under my belt. I had read *The Empty Fortress* (Bettelheim, 1967), but that hardly prepared me for Larry. He was echolalic, hardly speaking at all except to repeat the last three or four syllables of whatever he heard. He also had annoying habits, like saying, "PSoff!" (a neologistic condensation of "Pants off") and then actually pulling his pants off, with no concern about where he was. He liked to eat large amounts of plain mustard. He also liked to climb up on banisters, crouch down, and defecate. I had all the therapeutic enthusiasm of a young psychology major, and I would take Larry on outings to museums, to the beach (this was in Chicago, where the beach was just down the block), to parks, and to other places. Being out in the natural world helped open new experiences for him. It brought him into contact with many helpful people, and it allowed him to be in situations where we really enjoyed one another. I would engage my friends in the role of co-therapists, and we all did everything possible to bring Larry into communicative contact with other human beings.

We even invented a kind of music therapy for him. We taught him a song of nonsense syllables, which took the word "Piccolomini," and rearranged the syllables and accents over and over (see Figure 5.1). It was the perfect thing for an echolalic boy, because we could stop singing at any point, and he would fill in the next two or three missing syllables. For example, if we stopped with "Picco," he would say "lomini." This song-game got him into a kind of wordless verbal communication that felt, nevertheless, very connected emotionally. After two years of such work with Larry, he started speaking, which was as surprising to his mother as it was to me. It taught me the value of working with a patient in a natural way and in a natural setting. It also began my realization that with psychotic patients, you must invent a new therapy for each patient, learning about whatever can engage the patient in meaningful communication and affective engagement.[1]

I once supervised a male graduate student in psychology, who was hired by a family to spend several afternoons a week with their adult schizophrenic son. That work was also conducted out in the world and was very helpful to the patient. They would go on what I thought of as therapeutic adventures together, and formed a kind of preadolescent bond that the patient had never had and, as we know from Sullivan, is essential in development. This bond included some shared grandiosity, which was something the patient and my student had in common, but the student could be aware of it and regulate it in himself and in the patient.

As we become older and more established, we may be less likely to work with patients in such innovative ways. This is unfortunate. In our education we may learn sophisticated techniques and theories. These

Piccolomini

Figure 5.1 Piccolomini

are useful, but we should keep ourselves open to experimentation and fresh approaches. We should avoid what Berlioz said of Saint-Saens: "He knows everything but he lacks inexperience. (Il sait tout, mais il manque d'inexpérience.)" While we learn of the importance of the psychoanalytic frame, we must not forget that it is in shared activities that an affective connection can be forged, which with psychotic patients may form the groundwork for therapeutic advances.

Ann-Louise Silver, one of the leading psychoanalysts at the residential treatment center for psychotics Chestnut Lodge, was once invited by a German hospital to read a paper about her work with psychotic patients, but her invitation was suddenly canceled. An official of the hospital wrote to her, "You may not read your paper at my hospital. It shows too the deterioration of Chestnut Lodge, where you take the patient to restaurants. This is the work we expect from our specially trained nurses, escorting them to the rehabilitation programs. . . . Here at our hospital we follow the principles of Fromm-Reichmann (Silver, 1997, p. 245)." Yet Fromm-Reichmann did go on outings with psychotic patients, as have many other leading therapists.

The issues of both status and gender are captured by the admonition of the German hospital that such work belongs to the nurses. The implication is that women with lesser degrees can do this; men and doctors should not.

The relationship between human communication and schizophrenic pathology has been fundamental to interpersonal psychoanalytic thinking since Harry Stack Sullivan's time. It was said that when Sullivan talked to a schizophrenic patient, the patient did not sound schizophrenic. My best friend in college, Daniel Kozloff, had the same ability, and he was my first great teacher about working with schizophrenics. Daniel had no psychiatric training, although he did have a schizophrenic older brother.

Many years ago, I visited Daniel in California, where he lives, and while we were walking down the streets of San Francisco (which has many homeless schizophrenics), I observed his skill once again. We were standing in front of a movie theater, looking at what they were showing, and a blatantly psychotic man walked by and started to talk about the movies that were there in a very crazy way. In a couple of minutes, Daniel had him engaged in a quite serious, interesting conversation. What did he do? He focused on what there was in the man's speech that made sense and addressed mainly that. He amplified what was serious in what the man said, and developed an interesting idea from it, which he restated. The man agreed with Daniel, and developed it further. In this mini-conversation, there were great lessons in working with schizophrenia, and probably, too, in working with any psychopathology.

Daniel had never read Sullivan, but he had discovered on his own what Sullivan had discovered. Sullivan (1956) divided a schizophrenic patient's communications into three categories: (1) those that are understandable; (2) those that are of questionable meaning; and (3) those that are thoroughly not understandable. The therapist, Sullivan thought, should attend primarily to communications in the first category, and occasionally to those in the second category. Regression can often be limited by the therapist actively making contact with meaningful elements in the patient's speech. Frequently, in the midst of irrational statements, a psychotic patient will become briefly clear, perhaps in relating an anecdote of which he is proud and which is a repository of what little self-esteem he has left. Those moments are precious, Sullivan taught, and require an inquisitive response from the therapist. If you focus on those communications, you will go a long way toward making contact with a psychotic patient.

There is a basic lesson in this about human communication, which extends beyond our work with schizophrenics. In any dialogue, the listener always picks and chooses what she will respond to in the other person's statements. This has to do with semantic content and with other dimensions of the communication, including tone, implicit emotion, and attitudes. This is a profoundly interpersonal view – that one person's contribution to a dialogue is seriously shaped by the response of the other person. If A says something with crazy elements, and B focuses on the craziness (a common mistake of beginning clinicians), the dialogue will sound crazier and everyone's anxiety will escalate. If B responds only to what is rational and meaningful in A's statement, the dialogue will make A sound saner, and may actually make A *be* saner. Who we are is very strongly shaped by whom we interact with.

My first dramatic experience of this principle came when I worked at the Illinois State Psychiatric Institute. I spent much time working in the locked back ward with patients who were thought to be hopeless and had been hospitalized for decades. There, in 1972, you could still see syndromes like "word salad," where patients utter mixed-up jumbles of words that seem to have no meaning. I learned something very important from those visits: No matter how seemingly degenerated the thinking of a longtime, hospitalized schizophrenic, there were glimmers of rational thought if you were willing to hear them. Some patients who seemed mostly involved in their own fantasy worlds occasionally showed remarkable concern for me and my interest in what they were saying.

For example, one elderly man told me he was a member of a delegation from outer space. I found his story to be fascinating and asked him many detailed questions about his mission. He answered my questions, more or less, sounding crazier and crazier, but in the midst of his stream of words I heard the phrase "Don't believe a thing I tell you" uttered without pause or demarcation, just part of the string of what he was saying. Then he resumed the crazy talk and went on to tell me that he was a Moslem specializing in circumcision, but I had heard his message.

The ability to communicate with anyone, especially with psychotics, is a skill that I think is gradually being lost today in mainstream psychiatry. When I was doing my internship at the New York State Psychiatric Institute at Columbia-Presbyterian, a very manic woman was admitted to the inpatient unit where I worked. She was not assigned to me, but her presence was an issue for everyone on the unit because she talked constantly, with pressured and very abusive speech. This was in 1977, just at the time that the Psychiatric Institute was being completely reorganized, with many of the psychoanalysts being fired and psychopharmacologists taking over. In line with the "new" psychiatry, the daily unit conferences were obsessed with fine-tuning the patient's medication. The woman's medication was adjusted over and over, but still she caused a ruckus and did not seem improved.

At that time, Alberta Szalita was teaching a case seminar to the interns and residents. In this seminar, one of us would interview one of our own inpatients in front of the entire staff. After about 10 or 20 minutes of this, Dr. Szalita would step in and continue the interview in her own fashion. The resident responsible for the troublesome manic patient started the interview, hardly getting a word in edgewise, while the patient blabbered on and on, her speech pressured and abusive. Then, Dr. Szalita stepped in and asked the patient about something she had said. The patient said something, and Dr. Szalita tried to clarify it, but the patient jumped in with her pressured speech. Dr. Szalita said, with great vehemence, "Why are you interrupting me?" All of a sudden – really for the first time in two weeks – the patient stopped talking. They then continued the interview for some 20 minutes, in a relatively normal fashion, with some real clarification of the issues in the patient's life. I knew then the power of a firm, sincere, interpersonal intervention.

Schizophrenia, paranoia, and stigma

Schizophrenics often feel isolated from humanity, and the first task of treatment is to meet them as a fellow human being who accepts them, respects them, and shares their humanity. The beginning of any therapeutic work with a schizophrenic patient is to establish contact. This often requires considerable patience and ingenuity, for the psychotic patient may be extremely frightened or hostile (Benedetti, 1987). Fromm-Reichmann (1939) sat every day for a month with a mute patient whose only responsiveness was to say "Don't leave" on two occasions. It is often left to the creativity of the therapist, what Hill (1955) called the artistic functions of the analyst, to find a way to make contact with the patient, to be admitted to the patient's emotions and inner world.

There can be many sources of the schizophrenic's terror. Extreme fear and shame are some of the central affects before the first schizophrenic break. Sullivan (1956, p. 184) wrote: "The things that become terrifying and generalized in these primitive processes are the cultural mandates – the prohibitions and proscriptions – that I have not been able to live up to, or to live with."

The way the patient feels that he or she has failed to live up to standards of humanity can vary, and the psychoanalyst must keep an open mind. In much of the twentieth century, psychiatry was influenced by Freud's idea that paranoia and paranoid schizophrenia were caused by unacceptable homosexual impulses (Freud, 1911). The idea was that a person defensively transformed his love for another man. "I love him" became "I hate him," which then became "he hates me." Since then, decades of psychiatrists assumed that there was an intrinsic link between homosexuality and paranoia. But in 1962, Edwin Weinstein, an Interpersonal psychoanalyst and neurologist, went to the Caribbean, and found that homosexuality was not the main source of stigma there; instead, infertility was the most shameful thing. Weinstein (1962) found that paranoid schizophrenics in the Caribbean had more frequent delusions about infertility than about homosexuality.[2] This suggests that paranoia may be essentially linked not to homosexuality, but to social stigma. Paranoid schizophrenics often feel accused of whatever trait is most stigmatized by the culture they live in. Sullivan (1972) saw that homosexual pre-occupations among paranoid schizophrenics were not necessarily indicative of the source of the psychosis (as Freud thought), but could instead provide an explanation for plummets in self-esteem and feeling scorned and hated.

Although we should not presume that homosexuality causes paranoid schizophrenia, there are patients who are both schizophrenic and homosexual. For them, would isolation from the pressure of anti-homosexual hatred and prejudice have therapeutic value? Sullivan tested this very hypothesis in the late 1920s, when he established his ward for young schizophrenics at the Sheppard and Enoch Pratt Hospital near Baltimore. The ward had an astonishing 86% cure rate for schizophrenics, and this was before the advent of neuroleptic medication (Perry, 1982). Sullivan was famously skillful at making a connection with very cut-off patients. Sullivan also developed milieu therapy; every aspect of living in the ward was carefully thought out to lessen the patients' anxiety and help them find new pathways to secure living.

This is well-known. But what seems to be less well-known is that Sullivan's ward was a gay male ward. In the 1970s, a psychologist named Kenneth Chatelaine interviewed the last surviving people who had worked on Sullivan's ward, and published their revelations in his book *Harry Stack Sullivan: The Formative Years* (Chatelaine, 1981). The description of the ward and of Sullivan is noteworthy for its frankness. The staff, hand-picked by

Sullivan, were either openly homosexual or extremely easy-going about it. The staff and the patients were all male. No female nurses were allowed even to come into the ward. The staff members were encouraged to talk casually to each other about homosexual experiences, to let the patients feel that it was not something to be ashamed of or afraid of.

It would be extraordinary today if someone established a gay psychiatric ward in a major hospital. It is even more extraordinary that Sullivan did it back in 1930. That took courage. It also represented a brilliant insight into the factors that can lead to serious mental illness and the best approach to helping such patients. Even today, when attitudes towards homosexuality are better than they were in the past, every gay and lesbian person knows how difficult it is to cope with anti-gay hostility. Prejudice against gays and lesbians is still considered acceptable in much of society.

What effect does this have on the mental health of young gays and lesbians? As we know, the effect is highly detrimental. The rate of teenage suicide has been estimated to be three times higher for gay youth than for straight (Archuleta, 1998; Paul et al., 2002). And in people disposed to mental illness, either because of a genetic predisposition, a traumatic history, or other factors, the added stress of anti-homosexual hatred can push them over the edge into psychosis. Sullivan showed, with his ward, that when you remove such a person, even temporarily, from exposure to such hatred, the potential for therapeutic gain can be enormous.

I have myself not set up a ward for gay and lesbian psychotics. But interestingly, just by being an openly gay psychoanalyst, I have had quite a number of patients come to me who might have been accepted into Sullivan's ward. These patients had been burned in various ways by anti-homosexual prejudice in the mental health system.

I cannot relate to you all of these experiences, but I will give you one example that captures the problem. In the early 1990s, I was consulted by a 33-year-old man for treatment. His presenting complaint was that he felt lost, professionally and personally. He impressed me as very private and cautious. When he called for an initial appointment, he got my answering machine. He told me the name of the doctor who referred him, but didn't tell me his own name and telephone number, so I had to telephone the referring physician to get that information. In our first session, when I asked the patient where he worked, he hesitated for a long time and did not want to tell me.

You may feel that this man was paranoid. But as his story unfolded, I learned that there was good reason for his caution. When he was eighteen, he went away to college, and found that he was sexually attracted only to men, a fact that he had suspected but tried to ignore during high school. He knew that his religious family would disapprove of his homosexuality, and so he became extremely anxious about it. On a vacation, he returned home. His father noticed his agitation, and asked him what was bothering him. He blurted out to his father that he was gay. The family sent him to a psychoanalyst immediately. When the patient tried to bring up his homosexuality, the analyst said, "Well, of course, doing things with girls is fun." As you can imagine, the patient was not encouraged to tell this man more. Instead, he retreated more and more into himself. He then was hospitalized for two weeks with electro-shock treatments every other day. This had no effect on his sexual orientation, but it certainly taught him to beware of the homophobia in his parents, in psychiatry, and in society in general. He waited a dozen years to seek psychotherapy, and did so only when he could be sure to find a therapist who was openly gay himself.

We obtained his hospital records, and they were fascinating. They showed a diagnosis of paranoid schizophrenia, based on the fact that: "The patient claims people are saying he is a homosexual." Well, he *was* claiming that people were saying he was a homosexual, because they were, and he was. The use of ECT was unconscionable. And remember, this was not in a rural hospital. It was in a major New York area hospital in the late 1970s.

Sullivan found that removing a gay man temporarily into a hospital environment that was accepting of his sexuality could facilitate remarkable clinical improvement (Blechner, 2009; Wake, 2011). The ramifications of this finding have never been fully appreciated, nor have they been adequately tested in other groups that suffer discrimination. For example, we know that Black Americans are diagnosed with schizophrenia three times more frequently than White Americans (Bresnahan et al., 2007). In the United Kingdom, the racial disparity for schizophrenia diagnosis is much higher (Morgan, McKenzie, and Fearon, 2008; Morgan et al., 2010). But what we do not know is: Would it help Black people diagnosed with schizophrenia to be in a ward where racial prejudice is eliminated as much as possible, and would this lead to better recovery rates? As far as I know, this experiment has not been conducted. There have been all-Black hospitals, but these were set up by Whites to give substandard care (Randall, 2004). There have not, to my knowledge, been all-Black hospitals set up by Black medical professionals with the explicit intention of giving excellent care, free of prejudice, analogous to Sullivan's ward for gay men.

The first psychotic break

All people have certain areas of experience that they completely dissociate, what Sullivan called the "not-me." In most of us, the "not-me" makes an appearance mostly in dreams, but in the schizophrenic, the "not-me" breaks the psychic barrier into consciousness, where it wreaks havoc with reality testing and can appear in hallucinations and delusions. While some psychoanalysts have traditionally focused in therapy on the earliest periods of life, Sullivan's theory suggests, instead, an intense examination of the period immediately preceding the first psychotic break (Blechner,

1995). That era will contain within it some of the focal anxieties, the essential "not-me" experiences (accompanied by uncanny emotions like dread and horror), and the core areas of vulnerability that led to panic and the subsequent psychotic solution. One must seek the essentials of the disaster to self-esteem that are the fundament of the schizophrenic reaction. Success and accuracy lie in detail and consistency. If the delusions of a paranoid patient are directly and vigorously challenged, they may yield, and the earlier schizophrenic panic will re-emerge. Although terrifying, this regression to the primal psychotic panic may be a promising development in therapy, since the patient, with the help of the analyst, can confront the primal anxiety with other means than psychotic solutions, so that a different integration may be achieved (Sullivan, 1956).

Often, the delusions and hallucinations experienced before and during the first psychotic break will be most amenable to understanding, but you must pay attention to the specifics of the person's life, just as you need to do with the interpretation of dreams (Blechner, 2002, 2002a, 2002b). Consider a patient who felt that his brain was receiving broadcasts from a distant planet with a Spanish name. If you knew that he lived in New York City but was raised in East Los Angeles (a Hispanic neighborhood), and that he had a strong ambivalence toward his economically poor but culture-rich background, you would have a much better idea of the affective experience and ambivalent loyalties portrayed in the delusion. Knowing that, the clinician can choose not to confront the delusional system, per se, but merely to work with the patient's inferiority feelings with respect to the far-away world, and his dissociated affection and yearning for it, expressed in the delusional broadcasts from that world.

Hallucinations and delusions become dreams

In some patients who improve, the content of the hallucinations and delusions may, later in treatment, start to appear in dreams as the waking psychotic experiences diminish or disappear (Blechner, 1983). Ms. T, a young psychotic woman, was the youngest child in a large family. Her father abandoned the family when she was 6 months old, and thereafter visited the children rarely. When he did, the visit often ended with his beating up his wife. He once threw Ms. T at the wall. Ms. T never saw him after she was 5, because he moved to a distant city. She was raped by one of her brothers when she was 9. She developed a mutually symbiotic tie with her mother, which she tried to break several times during her adolescence. She returned to live with her mother at age 19, and was still there when she began psychoanalytic treatment with me at the age of 26. She could not hold a job for more than a few months and had many paranoid fantasies. She had been in several therapies; she counted eight therapists whom she had seen before me, all women, with whom she had worked for relatively brief periods, never more than a year. A dominant issue at the start of her treatment was her fear of men, and she was immediately fearful and distrusting of me. She came to her first session carrying a tree branch, which she waved at me menacingly.

The first dream that she reported to me occurred during the first week of treatment: "I dreamt last night that I was a man."

Ms. T's first dream is a simple statement, and it contained a direct message to the analyst that could easily have been missed in the deluge of paranoid statements that flooded her waking communications. It was as if the patient were saying, "I felt relatively safe with you in our first session, and I had always thought that only if I were a man would I be able not to fear you as a man. To feel safe with you meant to me that I must be a man. You would then not rape me as my brother did, nor would you beat me up as my father did."

Four years later, after major therapeutic gains in reality testing, affective stability, and her ability to trust, she reported the following dream:

> I was supposed to take a horse from here to Melrose, near Bryn Mawr. Since I didn't have one of those horse trucks to deliver it, I'd have to take a risk. I didn't know if I could ride it on the highway. I called Sally, in Villa Nova. I couldn't ride because it was dark. I parked the horse in the Bronx.

The dream illustrated her capacity for verbal symbolization, which had developed dramatically during the analysis. In the dream, Villa Nova, i.e., New City, stood for the major career change she was about to embark on and also for the new home in which she was about to start living. By this time in the analysis, Ms. T had made many constructive changes in her life, of which she prized most highly an extended romantic relationship with a man. Moreover, her psychic approach to the world had changed considerably. Many of her paranoid fears had been analyzed, and she was able to think symbolically and humorously. She even made jokes about her former nonverbal symbols. Thus, a few months after this dream, she came cheerfully to her session waving two wooden dowels. I immediately thought of our first session, when she came in with the branch. She pointed out their double meaning to her. While reminiscent of her extreme defensiveness in our early sessions (the branch that she had waved at me in the first session), the dowels, which she was using to build a rather impressive piece of furniture (a fulfillment of one of her longtime ambitions), were a sign of her increased self-sufficiency and competence.

Arieti (1963) reported a similar incorporation of psychotic material into dreams after effective treatment. He worked with a patient who had delusions that the Russians were invading the city and had interpreted the red sunset over the Hudson as a divine warning that the whole world would become red. Arieti traces this to a letter from her parents announcing that

they would come for a visit to New York. The patient had left her conserva-
tive family for New York's Greenwich Village, to live in a wild way that
her parents, and she (to some degree), would disapprove of. As the patient
improved, she dreamt that she was being chased by her parents all over
New York City. She saw in this dream scenes similar to those she saw in
her acute delusional state, including the scene around the Hudson River.
She was afraid and kept hiding. Finally, however, she felt she did not care
whether the parents caught her or not. They would not hurt her. She decided
she had nothing to hide and went toward the parents to meet them.

Similarly, Marcus (1992, p. 189) describes a delusional patient who believes
that a crown is waiting for him in the White House and tries, in fact, to get
into the White House to retrieve it. He is treated with medication and psychotherapy, and the delusion abates. At first the patient gains insight that his
delusion is actually a wish. Eventually, the patient is freed of the preoccupy-
ing fantasy, and the delusion then appears periodically as a dream.

Jung (1907) has drawn our attention to the relationship between mental
processes in dreams and in waking psychotic experiences with his famous
statement: "Let the dreamer walk about and act like a person awake, and
we have the clinical picture of dementia praecox." In good psychoanalytic
treatment, as the psychotic patient's waking emotional life becomes richer,
as conscious thinking becomes more lucid and uncontaminated, and as
the capacity for interpersonal relatedness improves, the patient's dream
life becomes more "psychotic" in structure, what I call the "reallocation of
madness" (Blechner, 2001). The dreams become more complex, with more
bizarreness and sudden shifts. Psychotic thinking is shifted to where it
belongs, in the unconscious and in dream-life.

In summary, psychoanalytic work with psychotic patients requires the
analyst to be creative in how he or she makes emotional contact with the
patient, creates a safe environment, counters the effects of stigma, and
works through primal anxieties. It is common for contemporary psychiatrists to assume wrongly that the diagnosis of schizophrenia means that
a blunted life is inevitable (Saks, 2007). A good psychoanalytic treatment,
while difficult, can make the difference between a life of aimless despair
and a life of emotional connection, productivity, and satisfaction.

Notes

1 Silver (1997) also describes engaging a schizophrenic patient musically by singing together. Lombardi (2008) describes the resonance of musical associations
and powerful affects in psychoanalytic sessions.
2 Macalpine and Hunter (1953) argued that Schreber was childless and that his
fantasies were not essentially homosexual, but cross-gendered; we are more
familiar today with the differentiation of sexual orientation and gender identity
(Blechner, 2015). Schreber fantasized himself as a woman being impregnated,
which would allow him not to be childless.

References

Archuleta, M. (1998). *Suicide statistics for lesbian and gay youth: A bibliography.* http://isd.usc.edu/~retter/suicstats.html.

Arieti, S. (1963) The psychotherapy of schizophrenia in research and practice. Psychiatric Research Report No. 17, American Psychiatric Association.

Benedetti, G. (1987). *Psychotherapy of Schizophrenia.* New York: New York University Press.

Bettelheim, B. (1967). *The Empty Fortress.* New York: Free Press.

Blechner, M. (1983). Changes in the dreams of borderline patients. *Contemporary Psychoanalysis* 19: 485–498.

Blechner, M. (1995). Schizophrenia. In Lionells, M., Fiscalini, J., Mann, C., and Stern, D. (Editors), *Handbook of Interpersonal Psychoanalysis.* Hillsdale, NJ: Analytic Press, pp. 375–396.

Blechner, M. (2001). *The Dream Frontier.* New York: Routledge.

Blechner, M. (2002a). Hallucinations. In Erwin, E. (Editor), *The Freud Encyclopedia.* New York: Routledge, 2002, pp. 251–252.

Blechner, M. (2002b). Delusions. In Erwin, E. (Editor), *The Freud Encyclopedia.* New York: Routledge, 2002, pp. 141–142.

Blechner, M. (2009). *Sex Changes: Transformations in Society and Psychoanalysis.* New York: Routledge.

Blechner, M. (2015). Bigenderism and bisexuality. *Contemporary Psychoanalysis,* 51(3): 503–522.

Bresnahan, M., Begg, M., Brown, A., Schaefer, C., Sohler, N., Insel, B., Vella, L. & Susser, E. (2007). Race and risk of schizophrenia in a US birth cohort: Another example of health disparity? *International Journal of Epidemiology* 36: 751–758.

Chatelaine, K. (1981). *Harry Stack Sullivan: The Formative Years.* Washington, DC: University Press of America.

Freud, S. (1911). Psycho-analytic notes on an autobiographical account of a case of paranoia. *Standard Edition* 2: 1–82.

Fromm-Reichmann, F. (1939). Transference problems in schizophrenics. *Psychoanalytic Quarterly* 8: 412–426.

Hill, L. (1955). *Psychotherapeutic Intervention in Schizophrenia.* Chicago: University of Chicago Press.

Jung, C.G. (1907). The psychology of dementia praecox. Trans by R.F.C. Hull. In Jung, C.G. (Editor), *Collected Works,* Vol. 3. New York: Pantheon Books, 1960.

Lombardi, R. (2008). Time, music, and reverie. *Journal of the American Psychoanalytic Association* 56: 1191–1211.

Macalpine, I., and Hunter, R. (1953). The schreber case – A contribution to schizophrenia, hypochondria, and psychosomatic symptom-formation. *Psychoanalytic Quarterly* 22: 328–371.

Marcus, E. (1992). *Psychosis and Near Psychosis.* New York: Springer Verlag.

Morgan, D., Charalambides, M., Hutchinson, G., and Murray, R. (2010). Migration, ethnicity, and psychosis: Toward a sociodevelopmental model. *Schizophrenia Bulletin* 36: 655–664.

Morgan, C., McKenzie, K., and Fearon, P. (2008) (Editors). *Society and Psychosis.* New York: Cambridge University Press.

Paul, J., Catania, J., Pollack, L., Moskowitz, J., Cachola, J., and Mills, T. (2002). Suicide attempts among gay and bisexual men: Lifetime prevalence and antecedence. *American Journal of Public Health* 92: 1338–1345.

Perry, H. (1982). *Psychiatrist of America. The Life of Harry Stack Sullivan*. Cambridge, MA: Harvard University Press.

Randall, V. (2004). An early history: African American mental health. Retrieved January 24, 2013, from http://academic.udayton.edu/health/01status/mental01.htm.

Saks, E. (2007). *The Center Cannot Hold: My Journey through Madness*. New York: Hyperion.

Silver, A.-L. (1997). Chestnut Lodge, then and now. *Contemporary Psychoanalysis*, 33: 227–249.

Sullivan, H.S. (1956). *Clinical Studies in Psychiatry*. New York: Norton.

Sullivan, H.S. (1972). *Personal Psychopathology*. New York: Norton.

Wake, N. (2011). *Private Practices: Harry Stack Sullivan, the Science of Homosexuality, and American Liberalism*. Rutgers, NJ: Rutgers University Press.

Weinstein, E. (1962). *Cultural Aspects of Delusion*. New York: Free Press.

Chapter 6

Psychoanalytic therapy of a chronic paranoid schizophrenic woman[1]

Michael Robbins

A few years ago I was unexpectedly contacted by Sara, a former patient whose treatment had concluded more than two decades previously. She was passing through the community where I practice, and she wanted to say hello and tell me about her subsequent life. Her 11 year therapy had included several hospitalizations as well as intermittent and prolonged periods of time on phenothiazine medications.

Sara was 28 when she consulted me because a condition of discharge from a hospital where she was then a patient was that she first find a therapist. She was drab, overweight, and conveyed an impression of indeterminate gender. Her gaze was vacant, she had a flat whispery voice, she made no eye contact, and her discourse was vague. As we talked she reported a sensation that the top of her head was lifting off, and she said she was hearing voices that were harassing and frightening her. She said it was difficult to think clearly since thoughts would "short-circuit" and make strange connections so that she could not understand what others were saying or express herself sequentially.

Space does not permit inclusion of Sara's history, but as time passed I learned such things as that her psychotic hallucinations and delusions had commenced 19 years previous, when Sara was 9. At that time her nuclear family, including an unstable, hostile, rejecting mother, a distant, critical father who was preoccupied with his career, two older brothers, and a younger sister, was permanently disrupted when her mother was hospitalized for two years for a mental illness, and her father obtained a divorce and remarried. At this time Sara developed magical ritualistic behavior, for example around the number 8, which she eventually told me represented breasts, and she began to hallucinate. As she became adolescent Sara regularly ran away from home to skid row areas of cities where she would involve herself with men who abused her sexually in exchange for food and a place to sleep. At age 15 she was arrested and admitted to a public mental hospital where she received phenothiazine medication and therapy. After six months she was expelled for abusing drugs. Despite this chaos Sara managed to complete high school with high grades, and over the course of subsequent years punctuated by hospitalizations, to graduate from a good college.

During our appointments Sara would sit near the door with her head averted, her coat on and purse clutched to her lap; and she often bolted out the door a few minutes early. Her posture was rigid, and her gestures and facial expressions were contorted and contextually inappropriate. She was detached, her voice was flat, whispery, and without affect, and she did not make eye contact. There were long silences sometimes punctuated with *sotto voce* mocking laughter or muttered curses and gibberish about shapes and patterns. She had auditory and visual hallucinations. She believed bombs were planted in the walls and planes and missiles were about to attack and kill her. Our sessions consisted of a curious triadic relationship among Sara, myself, and a kind of Greek chorus of female voices that terrorized her as they instructed her how to cope with the dangerous world she was in and the horrible consequences that would ensue if she disobeyed them. "They" would require that she deprive herself of food and sleep and undergo various punishments in order to avoid being killed. "They" developed an immediate mistrust and dislike for me and told her they would punish her if she got involved with me because I wanted to kill her. My subjective sense was one of helplessness and defeat, because "they" seemed to control "her" behavior, and I was unable to talk to "them" directly. Nonetheless, occasional astute observations she made and her large vocabulary led me to believe she was unusually intelligent.

Sara was a nocturnal creature. Her voices would not let her sleep. In the middle of the night she often drove her car long distances following big trucks. She frequented bars, pool halls, and gambling casinos and involved herself in the culture of darkness, warmth, drinking, drugs, loud noise, pimps, prostitution, and abuse, sexual and otherwise. Her goal was to prove that no matter what was done to her it did not upset her emotionally; in that way she could believe she was in control and superior to those around her. Her self-destructiveness included depriving herself of sleep and food, smoking heavily, inducing accidents and injuries, and then ignoring the pain and damage. Not only were such attitudes and behaviors of no concern to her, but she was thoroughly convinced that she was taking care of herself better than anyone else could.

In her previous extensive contacts with psychiatrists she believed she had acted crazy because that was what was expected of her, and she was contemptuous because she believed she was successful in fooling them. She soon became frustrated because she felt that unlike others, I gave her little clue about what I wanted from her. However, most of her attention seemed directed toward what "they," her voices, were telling her, and what she was "seeing" about the dangerous world she was in and how to deal with it, in the case of therapy "telling" her not to relate to me at all.

After a time there appeared transient indications of a wish to relate to me including brief eye contact and flashes of feeling, consisting of deep sadness and incipient tears, and a rage including wishes to "scream bloody murder" and kill everyone.

In our 14th hour she recounted her first dream: There was a cylindrical eight story building open inside and resembling a great family dining room, with tables and chairs floating around. One false move and one could take a dangerous fall. Her sister was dying. A clown began to entertain everyone and pushed her sister over the edge. Subsequently I learned that "8" represented breasts.

She missed an appointment, and I learned that she had gone to Las Vegas and put herself in dangerous situations. She admitted being angry and wanting to kill me because I had gotten her to like me despite the warning from her voices that I would kill her. Her test for whether she liked someone was whether she thought she could kill them with a gun; she acknowledged she would have trouble shooting me. When she violated the commands of her voices that she was not to sleep more than 4 hours at night, "they" terrified her the following night with the belief that she had jumped from an airplane and her parachute would not open, and "they" regularly arranged punishments for her after any occasion in which she might have been more open and communicative with me.

During the 28th hour I prescribed trifluoperazine. However, it seemed to have no discernable effect. After five months we had our first substantial separation when I took a summer vacation, and despite the fact I gave her a number where she could reach me she decided I was not coming back, hence she stopped the medication.

There ensued the first of numerous interchanges that challenged my sanity. One day she informed me that she had never really hallucinated and the stories she had been telling me were manifestations of her ability to fool and manipulate people, including "shrinks" for whom she had great contempt. She described how in the past she had played the roles of a heroin addict in withdrawal, a tough street person, a good girl, and a scholar. She seemed sincere and acted more mature and integrated. After a few sessions in which she was able to talk more directly about her struggle against feelings and dependency and there was no sign that she was hallucinating, I felt both pleased and deeply unsettled. How could I have been so gullible? I consulted informally with two colleagues in an effort to make some sense of what was happening, but it did not allay my sense of helplessness and confusion.

Around eight months after commencing therapy Sara reported a visit to her mother, who had casually inquired whether Sara had stopped therapy yet, expressing her assumption that, as in the past, Sara would find it valueless. Soon after eight months of therapy Sara became acutely paranoid. She wondered if the wiring was connected to explosives, if I had a gun in my drawer, and if I was about to strangle her. Between therapy hours she went to a bar, got drunk, and invited attack. When she became so agitated that she paced my office and said she was going to escape to a distant city I arranged for her admission to the hospital in which I worked, where she remained on a locked ward for the next one and a half years.

Sara immediately barricaded herself in her hospital room. In terror that staff were trying to kill her she assaulted them, and in order to contain her they had to put her in seclusion and sometimes restraints. In the seclusion room she would huddle in corners, grimace and make strange body movements, bang her head against the wall, twist and smash her hands violently, glance around the room apprehensively, and pick at her face. She experienced visual projections of disembodied fragmented floating parts, and hallucinated voices either threatening her with terrifying scenarios or "protecting" her by commanding that she act in ways that were self-destructive in order to prevent terrible things from happening to her. When released from seclusion she managed to escape from the hospital several times and place herself in dangerous situations.

Shortly after her admission I increased the frequency of our sessions from three to four per week, a frequency we maintained until near the conclusion of our work together. Sara remembered feigning sleep as a child, so her father would carry her to bed, as she knew he would not do so if she asked. She told me how she often drove off in her car in the middle of the night and followed big trucks for hundreds of miles, so as not to feel lonely. Despite her paranoid terror of me and the admonitions of her voices she admitted that she was "getting a few crumbs." Between meetings she wrote me a remarkable letter. "I really think I am alive, and if I think about it I get so sad and I get really angry. When I sit in the room with you and I let myself believe you are there I feel so safe I just want to sit there forever. But I can't seem to be able to believe it for very long afterwards. I had no idea what I was getting into by entering therapy and I'm scared and I do hate you, but I also wish I could be with you every minute." Over the ensuing weekend Sara briefly escaped from the hospital in near zero temperature without a coat.

As Sara began to show more neediness and emotion on the ward some of the staff began to believe that her therapy was making her sicker. After one of her brothers raised questions about her need for hospitalization Sara wrote to her family:

> I am not dependent on the hospital, in fact I have trouble even asking staff for a towel or for change. I have been operating under the delusion that I am very confident in taking care of myself and trying to persuade everyone as well as me that this is the case, but it is not. Hanging out on skid row, getting beaten up, putting myself in very dangerous situations wandering around the streets of the big city in the middle of

the night totally paranoid, in my apartment all day in what my therapist calls psychotic terror, alone and pretty nuts. My ability to come off as rational, functioning, jobs, school, talk to people etc. is an integral part of the craziness. When I sit with another person I focus on them entirely, try to figure them out and organize my own self around information I can pick up. It could be described as human saran wrap, week ego boundaries. The day I arrived in the hospital I thought the staff was going to kill me. I ended up in four-point restraints flat on the mattress with my arms and legs strapped down. I am struggling for my life here because I have gotten crazier as the years go by. I am fighting myself, the part that hates the whole god damn world and doesn't want anything to do with anyone, that part is supported by my saying shit to me like 'I hate Dr. Robbins,' and I tell myself to get the hell out of the hospital. Part of the treatment is forming a real human relationship with him, telling him I hate him for exposing me to all the rage, sadness, feelings, and that I like him. I have to practice asking for things and saying no to people. I need a safe place to take risks.

This lucid, insightful letter about her capacity to be fraudulent turned out to be yet another example of the very fraudulence, as subsequent events showed how little of what she wrote she really meant.

Year two

Preceding a short separation Sara became more detached, and I commented that she was trying to leave before I did. That night she escaped from the hospital into a cold, rainy night. She returned for our final meeting before my absence, and I pointed out that she was creating a world of rejection, misery, and abuse and trying to believe that she could control it by not acknowledging how much it disturbed her. She remarked to me sheepishly, "I'm addicted to you; a Robbins addict." It was a cold, wintry day, and shortly after telling me of her wish that I would surround her, she said she had an urge to go out into the woods and lie in the snow were she was convinced it would feel warm and secure. I wondered if she was trying to make me feel responsible for the distress she felt when I was gone, and her laughter confirmed the accuracy of my speculation. She told me how as a child she spent much time in the basement of her house, hiding from her mother, and how she taught herself to use dangerous power tools without any sense of fear, even though on more than one occasion she had come close to electrocuting herself. Then she remarked that she had been using power tools in the hospital shop and had told the supervisor that she was frightened. She was stunned when he responded that he was glad to hear it, and if she were not afraid he would no longer allow her to use the tools.

She became almost catatonic. I talked with her about how her delusions and hallucinations were reflections of the fear and rage she was unable to bear, but this confused her and made her hate and fear me and wonder if I was driving her crazy. She gave me a self-portrait. In addition to revealing her considerable artistic ability what was striking was that it looked like an aerial view of a landscape consisting of geometric plots, each filled with busy designs and a large empty space in the middle. She was aware of urges to do violence to me, and her paranoid-determined violent behavior on the ward led to her spending much time in restraints and seclusion. Her trifluoperazine dosage was gradually increased, and when there was no discernible improvement chlorpromazine was added. Because she was convinced that the staff had gone crazy and attacked her I asked a staff nurse to join a session. Sara was confused when told that her assaultive, destructive behavior could evoke powerful responses from others. For the first time she felt rage at her family for their failure to appreciate her needs, and she began to raise objections when her mother and brother ridiculed psychiatrists and mental hospitals and said she had no need to be in a mental hospital, but she also expressed rage at me for making her know this.

Remarkably, considering her out of control states, Sara's capacity to seem rational and logical proved very effective in convincing hospital staff that she was normal and simply feigning illness. Over the course of the second year on several occasions the ward psychiatrist and staff raised serious questions about whether therapy was harming her and whether I should stop seeing her. The staff acted out their belief in various ways including waiting for two days after Sara escaped from the hospital before notifying me.

Sara was beginning to note the passage of time in relation to the rhythm of our appointments. She worried about my forthcoming summer vacation. She admitted having feelings of caring about me, and when I asked her what they were she pointed mutely to her heart. She was able to acknowledge that the hospital was her home for now and decided to keep a diary when I was away.

When I left she escaped and bought a plane ticket to France, where her father had sent her to live with a friend after her mother's hospitalization, but she changed her mind and returned to the hospital, where she involved herself with a male patient who was known for his violent behavior.

When I returned from my summer vacation Sara said that she was enraged that I had left her but that it had not been safe for her to leave me until I returned. She gave me a diary entry she had written: "I am really lost; I am 1,000,000 miles away and I don't know where that is. I have all these fantasies about taking off with him, staying stoned, drunk, getting pimped out, beaten up. I want to cry and scream and hit people and I am so angry. You know I am really smart. I am creative and imaginative

I could've done a hell of a lot with myself, and here I am coming up on 30 and I am sitting in a nut house kissing a fucking psychopath. I am so angry at you. I want to scream, tear the room apart." She then lost control, and when restrained and placed in the quiet room she giggled, hallucinated, and banged her head against the wall. Yet again I experienced a sense of helplessness and hopelessness similar to what she seemed to feel about relating to another person.

The administrative psychiatrist increased her dose of chlorpromazine again. Sara learned that the staff had serious doubts about her therapy and that our relationship might be in jeopardy. She was very distressed and correctly surmised that she was setting others up to enact her hatred and her confusion of sanity and craziness, the part of herself she now associated with the attitudes of her parents. Sara tried to talk to her mother about her feelings of having been neglected, and she told me that in response her mother became enraged, called Sara a bitch, threw an ashtray against the wall, and resisted efforts of staff to calm her. Our responses to her story were curiously congruent; I wondered if Sara had imagined all this, and Sara herself did not find anything remarkable about her description of her mother's behavior. Interestingly, her mother's crazy behavior was subsequently confirmed in its particulars by a staff member who had been present. This led to Sara's recollection of an incident from early childhood when her mother, in a rage, had literally thrown Sara and her siblings around the room. After telling me this Sara experienced herself fragmented in pieces sitting in several different areas of the room, one part running away from me, and another feeling attached to me and sitting near me as protection against her mother.

We had another review conference in which the nursing staff voiced their near unanimous belief that therapy was not working and that my treatment was making Sara regress. When Sara escaped from the hospital I was not notified by the staff although it was customary hospital procedure, and first learned about it more than a day later when I found a message from her on my answering machine telling me she had "split" and assuring me she was safe and would return. Sara had gone to Las Vegas but resisted the prompting of her hallucinations to walk the streets late at night. She had also resisted calling me for fear it would make her have feelings and hence "fall apart." On return she talked of her urge to "split" again, and we realized that splitting really meant cutting herself off from her feelings. Sara was genuinely confused about whether medication was making her better or as she put it, "driving her crazy," and she was aware of a belief that her food was being poisoned. I regularly questioned my own sanity, and often I did not know what to believe.

Sadness, anger, and related childhood memories began to surface more regularly, and Sara looked forward to her hours with me and reported a feeling of security she claimed was entirely novel in her life. Yet she told me she was much more comfortable relating to an assaultive patient on the ward. I responded that while she longed for caring, the only treatment she seemed able to tolerate was a reflection of her own hateful, uncaring attitudes.

Her condition improved, and she was allowed to leave the hospital and come to my private office for therapy appointments. She adopted a motherly role toward an adolescent female patient who repeatedly ran away and got herself into destructive predicaments. It was around this time that her mature sense of identity began to emerge. But yet again she became paranoid and assaultive, and fought off all efforts to help her. Her privileges to leave the hospital were curtailed, and she required restraint and seclusion in the quiet room. Then she was able to talk about her rage-filled fantasies of ripping herself apart and blowing up the hospital and me. She felt her head swelling and occupying all corners of the room.

I had the impression that she did not seem to be attending to anything I said, but she laughed and tried to convince me that my perceptions were not accurate. I suggested she might tape-record her sessions to help her determine the truth (Robbins, 1988), and she agreed to do so. Sara was responsible for the taping, and the tapes were in her possession to use as she chose. Once again I had to deal with my helplessness and uncertainty about what use she might make of the recordings. However, she soon informed me that she was learning how little she actually listened to me. She told me this was the first experience in her life of a caring relationship with another person in which her needs were satisfied, and the realization made her depressed and enraged. Caring was a chink in her armor and a threat to her "independence." She remembered an incident in which her mother had taken her and her siblings sailing and threw them in the ocean in order to teach them not to be frightened and prove to herself that she could rescue them if need be. Soon afterward Sara again escaped from the hospital, went to a bar, got drunk, and had casual sex. When she literally tried to tear her face off she was put back in restraints. There she told me, "you can only destroy what you have."

Year three

Sara was again confined to the seclusion room because she had begun to tear at the skin on her face in an admitted effort to tear her face off. I shared with her my feelings of helplessness and distress, and we both marveled at the power of her hatred. She regained some self-control and became very sad as she realized her drive to destroy what was important to her. She realized that she was trying to drive me crazy. Sara gradually regained more consistent self-control, and discharge planning began. She began to drive to her therapy appointments at my office, which was now in my home some distance from the hospital grounds. When her car would not start after an appointment she frantically pushed it away from my house and down a nearby hill and almost into a main street full of rush-hour traffic, so terrified was she that I might notice her predicament and she might have to ask for help.

After 26 months and 355 hours of therapy, and one and a half years of hospitalization, Sara moved to a halfway house. She anticipated my summer vacation with terror and articulated her fear that I was abandoning her to the clutches of a crazy woman. We agreed that the woman was no longer her mother but part of herself. She realized how unaware she tended to be of injury, illness, fatigue, hunger, and sexual feelings and for the first time was frighteningly aware that her self-protective instincts were deficient and that the things that upset most people did not bother her. I added that the things that signified home to most people such as intimacy terrified her. Finally Sara concluded that she might need to return to the hospital while I was gone, and immediately she felt better. She said she loved me, and she gave me a gift of a lovely ceramic car she had made, which she called her "get away" car.

But caring and insight became more infrequent, and I found myself responding to lengthy silences and paranoid detachment with sleepiness and boredom. When she noticed this Sara articulated wishes to tease and torture me and put me in a dark place so that I would feel trapped and alone, give up hope as she had done, detach myself from my body and feelings, and go crazy. She was relieved next hour to find I was still intact. These ideas alternated with memories of having such things done to her, first by her mother, then her brother, and ultimately some of the sadistic men she had apprenticed herself to.

When we separated for my month-long vacation Sara went to London, where in fact she knew no one, but she called to reassure me that she was well and taking care of herself, and she sent me a card from Freud's house.

She was pleased to see me on my return and seemed positive about our relationship and aware of her problems with self-care, but her characteristic paranoid withdrawal and muteness followed, with discussions of my drowsiness and detachment as responses to her wish to drive me crazy as had been done to her. It seemed that we were immobilized in the throes of a mutual struggle for sanity in the face of hopelessness and resignation to losing our minds. I told her I was thinking about recommending re-hospitalization, and to my surprise she cried, felt closer to me. She construed my setting limits on her as the actions of a good parent. She felt pleasure when a policeman stopped her for speeding. She dreamed chickens had escaped the coop and a raccoon was about to kill them. She told me that her mother never made enough food for her and forced her to eat things she did not want, and associated to how she performed fellatio on abusive men in the belief she was controlling them.

In the fall Sara began constructive planning and returned to graduate school. But once again she pulled the rug of sanity and reality out from under me. She said, very convincingly, that she was upset because she had been untruthful with me and that she really did not hallucinate, and the stories of abuse and skid row were fabrications. She said when she was in London and had wanted attention and sympathy she went to a restaurant and convinced the waiter that she was a bereaved widow revisiting the scene of her marriage. I felt shocked and a bit sick to my stomach, and I wondered aloud whether I could trust my senses about what was real. Sara tried to convince me that she was telling me these "truths" because our relationship was deepening and she cared, but I felt suspicious, a bit para-noid as I struggled with what was real. Fortunately I observed and pointed out that she was sitting in the farthest corner of the room and showing no emotion. In response she reported that the room was becoming animated in sinister and threatening ways and she feared that I was going crazy.

She told me life was becoming meaningful to her, that she was taking better care of herself, and she expressed gratitude. For the first time in her life she took a stuffed animal to bed with her. She asked her mother for permission to see her mother's hospital records so she might find out what had really happened to her as a child. To her surprise her mother agreed. But her mother did not follow through. After dreaming she was in a world of seductive vampires and had to decide whether to swallow a concoction and become like them Sara again asked her mother. This time her mother got angry and accused Sara of trying to persecute her. Sara began to express rage at her mother and a wish to kill or drive her crazy, but her talk was punctuated by disruptions, self-derision, and the sen-sation of choking and suffocating. She wrote me a letter that included: "I hate the whole fucking world. Not only does my head get splintered up but the room goes to pieces and words get blasted into meaningless let-ters. So the four walls of the room no longer join and I don't feel safe here. Everything gets unglued. I get so angry I just want to blow up the world. Where the hell are you?" She seemed more aware of how identical her own attitudes and behaviors were to those of her mother and how unreli-able and inconsistent both of them were.

Sara then revealed that she did not believe her mother had been in a mental hospital or had been mentally ill, and she subscribed to the family belief that her mother had been hospitalized for a physical problem. None-theless I received detailed records of her mother's hospitalization along with her permission to share what I thought appropriate. Sara wondered whether they contained information about whether her mother cared about her. After reading the notes I responded that there was little con-cern about her marriage or her children. Sara told me she was chopping up her thoughts and physically choking back massive rage and that she might kill me. When Sara reported delusions of a terrifying woman in the doorway of her room at night I read her a nursing report that mentioned her mother's abusiveness, threats of violence and suicide, running away, periods of disorientation and immobility lasting for hours, and her mother's terrifying hallucinations of a persecutory old woman. We realized how similar she and her mother were and how much she had been invested in her efforts to control her mother's behavior by invisibility and compliance.

Year four

Sara shared fantasies of having a home and her husband of her own, but then she withdrew and told me that she was crazy and that there was a bomb bursting in her head. Around the time of her birthday she struggled with feelings of homelessness and wishes to be my little child on the one hand, and terror of me because I looked crazy, associated with the urge to speed, get picked up by the police, attack them, and get killed. Eventually she sought help from the staff at the halfway house and was briefly and constructively re-hospitalized. She said, "if I'm going to feel all this stuff then I want to have people around all the time to share it with."

She went to a family gathering at her mother's house and told one of her brothers how important he was to her and how angry she was at some of the ways he treated her. He became angry, withdrew, and uttered a mocking laugh she was very familiar with. To Sara's surprise her mother empathized with her and attempted to stop the quarrel. Sara moved out of the halfway house and into a house she rented jointly with several women. At night when she began to be terrified and paranoid she hugged her stuffed animal. My summer vacation approached. After another episode of rage and fantasies of bombing and destroying the entire east coast Sara laughed and told me that she had fooled me yet again, this time into believing that we were getting closer. When she observed my drowsiness in response to her detached silence she vehemently asserted that it was because she didn't want me near her. She wished to go to a foreign country where she did not speak the language so there could be no communication. I commented that that country was called the land of backward schizophrenia.

Nonetheless she managed our separation well, obtained a job as a pre-school teacher's aide, and undertook more course work. Her teaching experience exposed her to scenarios of infants crying for their mothers and mothers claiming them. She felt overwhelming sadness and rage, associated her feelings to my vacation, and voiced confusion about whether she was a small child and I had in fact abandoned her. She reported that at the end of the previous hour she had stood outside the office door wanting to knock and tell me she needed a hug for security. Instead she went to a bar and got drunk. The theme was that an abandoned child feels so overwhelmed with pain that eventually she no longer wants anyone to come back and make her aware of it.

After another period of paranoid detachment she remarked that going crazy was a terrible price to pay for not being able to say no to her mother, and the nature of the current conflict emerged. Her mother had recently had surgery, and Sara had been driving her mother to the hospital for her treatments. She recalled a childhood incident where she had hidden from her mother but her mother had found her, hit her, and told her that if she saw her again she would cook her in the oven and eat her for dinner. She began to keep a diary between sessions in the form of letters to me. She wrote, "I would like to kill a lot of people and they don't know it but really I don't want to kill you. I wish I could give you a big hug and tell you how I feel, that I am so lonely and so tired and so scared and I can't sleep. I know it won't be you that kills me, it is my feelings that I think will kill me; feeling good, safe, loving you, wanting to hug you and never leave. I think of you sitting in your chair and I feel warm inside and safe and so sad I can hardly bear it, like I could cry forever."

She told me about the summer that she was sent abroad when her father was dying, and she remembered visiting an old baker to whom she became very attached. He had an endearing pet name for her, and she recalled wishing that he would adopt her. I had a familiar sense of surprise and disorientation learning of this hitherto unmentioned oasis of caring in her life. But the very next hour Sara informed me that she had listened to her tape-recording and realized that what she told me was what she had wanted to believe, whereas in fact she had only run errands for the baker. She described her terrifying mother, tall and wiry, "wired up" all the time. I recalled some of her delusional preoccupations with electricity and some of the near serious mishaps she had made when she did electrical wiring; she laughed and related this to her wish and fear to hold on, adding: "if the voltage is high and you hold on with both hands the current will go through your heart and kill you."

Sara decided she needed to talk with me about sex since she wanted to have children of her own, and she was beginning to show some interest in men. She remembered the experiences she had when she performed fellatio, and how she transformed her feelings of helplessness and the wish to vomit, to hit, and to bite off the penis into a sense of mastery and control in which she felt superior, in control, and belittling of the man for being so insanely excited. I suggested that real control was based on consistency, knowledge of her emotions, and selective action based on that knowledge. She responded that for the first time in her life she felt listened to and attended to, and she realized that the more she accepted her upset feelings the less she hallucinated, and she was sleeping better at night.

Year five

Another birthday approached. Sara imagined that I came over to her and removed a tiny baby from within her and nurtured it. She recalled that her mother was unable to remember any of the children's birthdays. I gave her a birthday card and wrote, "we all deserve the opportunity to be special to someone. I hope you won't let the misfortunes of your past imprison you so that you won't have yours." Her response was a fragmented combination of tense laughter, sadness, anger, and flat words of thanks. I had upset her expectation that I would not remember.

She began to envision a future and for the first time felt hopeful. She was doing very well at school and would become a full-fledged teacher the following year. But she fought with me over everything, remained withdrawn, and would allow a bit of contact only just before the end of an hour. We began to wonder whether the best she could do was to be like a squirrel that gets its nut and then runs. She reported a nightmare in which she was with a former patient who was wheelchair-bound, her hands and feet amputated, and Sara was hugging her and trying to estimate just how much she was capable of learning to do. We talked about her chronically hunched over posture in the office, which was an effort to deny the existence of her body and sexuality. She was literally unable to sit back. When she tried she felt dizzy and nauseated with powerful sensations of terror that she would be attacked, ripped apart, and annihilated. She told me this was why she had never felt safe enough to wear a skirt.

She received her Master's degree, and at graduation fellow students and teachers expressed caring for her and described her as gifted and creative. She told me that for the first time in her life she felt optimistic and excited and had even purchased a dress to wear to a job interview. She was certain she now had enough control that she would not become psychotic during our upcoming summer separation. When we resumed she had begun a full-time teaching position.

She dreamed she was observing a person of indeterminate gender who was wearing a plastic raincoat and who set her or himself on fire. No one paid attention. The victim was amazed to find out that he or she had not died but the coat had melted into the person's body. After this she recalled a childhood incident when her mother's sailboat tipped over, throwing her into the water with the sail on top of her. Because she had followed her mother's instructions and had worn a life preserver she was trapped beneath the sail and could not get out. Sara was less rigid physically and emotionally, and more spontaneous. She was more sensitive to temperature and pain. She sat a bit closer to me in the room, spontaneously clapped her hands when she said something, and wanted to examine an object of interest in my office. At times she sat back and relaxed, and once yelled in an angry voice, "fuck you." These gestures and expressions of emotion terrified her. She feared she would be attacked, but she realized it was her who had been attacking everything both of us did or said.

For the first time she began to worry about real problems of her life like finding a caring husband rather than about her hallucinations and delusions. She realized that she wanted to have children and that there were now men she liked, and she would be forced to talk to me about sex if she wanted a man in her life. We concluded that this idea was a concrete reflection of her belief that in order to get any semblance of attention or affection she was forced to perform oral sex. She perceived me as a crazy man, out of control of my sexuality and sadism, and she concluded I had been trying to disrupt our relationship by prematurely forcing the subject of sex on her. Nonetheless she took the unprecedented step of telling her oldest and perhaps only male friend that she cared about him. He responded that he did not reciprocate her feelings. She fled to a pool hall, where she proceeded to take out her pool stick and defeat every man who would play with her.

Despite her concern that I would not want her to do it, Sara planned a holiday trip abroad with a friend. She gave me a small gift before leaving and shook my hand, demonstrating a violent physical oscillation I now associated with alternating holding on and breaking off. At the beginning of our separation Sara had the first dream that she could recall in which I figured, which she told me on her return. She was in my office, and there was a big window against which lay a monstrous dead whale. It seemed normal to her that it was there, until my teenage daughter came along and Sara asked her what the whale looked like from the outside. Sara saw me approach from another building and feared I would get angry at my daughter for talking to her. She related the dream to her deadness identity and to a childhood memory of seeing people pick apart a dead whale that washed up on the beach. "Dead whale" became an important therapy metaphor for the state of being she continued to strive to achieve.

Year six

Sara uncharacteristically showed emotional upset at a family dinner, and when she tried to leave, one of her brothers followed her. She burst into tears as they shared their mutual mistrust of others and the belief that the ability to be detached and unfeeling represented control, and her brother hugged her. Sara angrily blamed me for this. Soon thereafter she reported a nightmare in which she had entrusted the care of her students to someone else and went off and forgot their existence. When she remembered and returned it was evident that something terrible had happened to one of the students. I told Sara that I knew what had happened, that it had been unbearable for the student to be left alone so she had gotten herself beaten into unconsciousness.

When her first teaching year ended students, their parents, and faculty expressed praise and gratitude to her. But once again our relationship seemed stalemated, and when our summer vacation separation approached she wrote me a letter: "you shouldn't bother with me and should take a painkiller and sleep. You know I do hear you and I feel I am being attacked because it is not too pleasant what you're saying. I just want to tell you to go to hell and take your damn caring with you because I want to blast everyone to hell especially someone who cares. It is becoming clear what I want and what I don't want and I didn't get and that clarity makes me so angry it scares the hell out of me." She then dreamed that someone killed her brother, cooked his appendix, and gave it to her to eat as though this were normal. In the dream she was terribly upset, screamed, and then awoke. It turned out that the brother image represented things she liked and valued in her life, whereas her cannibalism represented the killing of caring. As my summer vacation approached Sara reproached me for leaving, saying, "look who you're leaving me with!"

When we met in the fall Sara told me how constructive her month had been. She had purchased a house of her own in a safe neighborhood, was being assertive and creative at work, and had maintained a sense of me within her that helped her make good decisions. As usual there was another side. She began to miss appointments and then reported a dream in which she had spilled coffee on the lovely dining table she had purchased for her home, and in order to avoid awareness of the contrast between the marred area and the rest of the tabletop she hacked it to pieces.

Sara told me she was afraid she might wear two mismatched shoes to a forthcoming parents' meeting, and she realized this represented how little dialogue there was between the caring and hating parts of herself. I suggested that she try to find names for each one and that she sit in different chairs in the office when talking from each position. She called the two parts "black" and "red," and over the next five weeks we elaborated the characteristics of each. Ms. Black turned away from me and muttered curses. When expressing Ms. Red she told me that Ms. Black was thoughtless, ignorant, rigid, hateful, and destructive, and possessed a vocabulary limited to name-calling. She began to panic and said that I did not understand that she would punish herself for this conversation once she got herself alone. She dreamed her house was burning down, she walked down a dark, empty street with burns on her feet, but she did not seem to care. She told me how she had burned some food and burned her hands removing it from the oven, and she twisted her fingers violently. At the same time she began to express horror at the Ms. Black part of herself, calling it mean and "Neanderthal." But she felt frightened and told me that her mind was exploding and her thoughts were flying apart, and she was barely able to speak.

When Sara told me how she had cared for two children at school who had been injured I contrasted her capacity to care with her refusal to take care of herself. She responded by telling me how she was walking around with a hole in her shoe, that she habitually drove without a seatbelt, that she allowed her house to remain a mess, that she did not allow herself sleep, and that she physically tortured her hands so badly when expressing her caring for me that she worried that she might break her fingers. After sharing her impulse to travel to a nearby city where the news media reported a mass murderer had been killing women Sara reported a nightmare. She had cancer and was being her own doctor. She took slices of herself and put them in the oven to incubate, and they grew to be monstrous, black, gross, and disgusting. She said, "if I lock up this Neanderthal part then I will have lost the only part that has ever taken care of me and I will feel intolerably alone."

In our last hour prior to a separation she admonished me to take care of myself so that nothing would happen to me and she would not be heartbroken. I responded that she needed to take care of herself, which meant bearing her feelings. She struggled against the urge to cry. She imagined having me sit next to her and put my arm around her so that she would feel secure and be able to fall sleep. But she panicked until she realized that it was because her image of me had changed into that of her mother, with long fingernails, ready to strangle her.

Year seven

After reiterating her belief that she had to perform oral sex in order to have a relationship Sara realized that it was after her mother's hospitalization that she began to run away and get men to abuse her and force her to do that even though it made her choke and want to vomit. She began to cry. She knew she had been breast fed and began to wonder what it had been like. On Sara's birthday, our 998th hour, I gave her another card, on which I wrote: "I am sorry I can't be the loving mother you never had. And I can't take away your memories and feelings about never having had one. But I would like to help you put these things where they belong so that you can get some love in the future." Sara clutched it for the entire hour, interrupted at times by the feeling that her mother was about to take it from her, and at other times by her own wish to get away. She told me that she had kept on her person for half a year the other card I had given her. At the conclusion of this hour she said, quite unaware, "I'm going to take care of myself even if it kills me!"

After another deadening stalemate I remarked somewhat facetiously that I needed a consultation from her. Little did I know I was mobilizing her ability to write, think, reflect, and be artistically creative, presaging some of her later accomplishments. In response she began to bring me a series of documents, beautifully illustrated as though they were children's stories, with the theme that holding onto her mother was a barrier between us and that she needed to face her rage and tears over having had no mother. She wrote about how she had been destroying her life and our relationship, adding: "I don't want to spend my life doing a Woody Allen impersonation. The pendulum has been swinging for 35 years, without any joy, love, sadness, company. I want more with you and I want the rest of my life also. I want lots of things but the minute you show up I don't want anything but to drive you nuts and run." There followed a section written in red ink to indicate the thoughts of Ms. Red, which concluded with "so I waste my time getting revenge on you who has never hurt me in any way and in reality getting revenge on myself, carrying out my mother's misdirected revenge on me." After a sentence in black starting with "this is a bunch of bullshit" she concluded in red that she was taking courses with me, "feelings 101" and "elementary language."

Year eight

Preceding my summer vacation the stalemate between the two sides of Sara intensified along with her anger at me no matter what I did, and I struggled during her hours with the urge to lose consciousness and fall asleep. During our separation she enrolled in an educational program abroad, and when we resumed in the fall she was tanned, well dressed, and had lost weight. She talked enthusiastically about her adventures, new relationships, and the future.

She was distressed that she had a dream in which I appeared because it indicated my importance. We were sleeping in separate sleeping bags, entirely zipped up, on a beach on the northern coast. We had been there a long time, there was water and a line of seaweed over much of us, and she was half awake. This clear illustration of our relationship was most troubling to Sara – our disengagement, the deadness, and endlessness. She admitted that she missed me and had pretended the teddy bear she now used for comfort represented me, but then she called herself a "stupid jerk."

She said with regret that despite her love of children she would probably never be able to have any of her own because she was now in her mid-30s. I likened the way she led her life to how she customarily waited until the end of therapy hours to get anything from our relationship and wondered if she might be inventing a new form of self-punishment by making herself wait until it was too late in life to get what she wanted. As she struggled over her heartbroken, childlike longing to cry, be comforted, and fall asleep, she tried to cover herself with the blanket on my couch, but her striking motor inability to hold it enacted her difficulty holding onto caring feelings. Sara told me she had gotten drunk and had slept with a "loser" who lived in her neighborhood for some time. She began to hallucinate cursing commentary on her relationship with me; she told me that over the holiday she had felt rejected and excluded from my family. I suggested and she agreed that she resume trifluoperazine.

For perhaps the first time she allowed medication to help her, and she allowed herself to think and talk about what was happening. Almost immediately her hallucinations diminished, and she became calmer and better able to sleep, to focus attention and concentrate and organize her life. She recalled her struggles in the hospital to fight off the effects of medication and felt terrified that she was allowing someone to get into her mouth and influence her. She tried to sit closer to me and had a fantasy of being dragged back into the corner by her hair. I encouraged her to identify the parts of herself by moving from one chair to another again. In the "black" chair she talked about her contempt for human beings, relationships, and her own well-being. In the "red" chair she told me she had made a new female friend, had joined a health club, and was expressing anger more appropriately when people mistreated her. At the end of this hour she reported "a splitting headache."

Disturbing memories of performing fellatio made her consider whether this had been a repetition of her breast-feeding experiences. She talked about being force fed and having to pretend that she enjoyed it while experiencing sensations of suffocation, gagging, and wishes to bite. She remembered it was after her mother was hospitalized that she began to run away and engage in the enslavement relationships that involved sucking the penis to ejaculation. She had a sudden urge to suck her thumb. She dreamed she and her brother were attempting to escape from her home of origin through an underground garage but her mother came along in the car and flattened them. She dreamed of travelling down a jungle river with a guide. On the last part of the journey they went over rapids and she fell overboard, swallowed water, and drowned. She felt certain that the dream and memory of almost drowning under the sail when her mother's boat capsized related to her breast-feeding experience. She recalled her mother in the kitchen, cursing, threatening, throwing things, baking a cake, and making the children sit in a circle on the floor and one by one lick the remains of the batter from her finger.

She recalled her terror watching her mother shaving her legs, and watching her newborn sister lose a piece of umbilical cord. Perhaps her mother had done something to her. She had the urge to sleep with a man, and I wondered if this was her way of assuaging doubts about her gender. To my surprise Sara agreed and began to talk about the feeling that she had been "ripped off" and forced to be a girl in a world where boys got everything. She recalled childhood activities using a blowtorch in her basement, which she now believed were efforts to construct a penis. She was apprehensive that I might want "a blow job" from her.

She wrote me a letter in which she described a dream: "I was searching for something but there was this demon following me around in the shadows killing people. It was like some robot that ripped the tops of people's heads off and ate their brains and hands. It killed everyone that I saw or talked to. What a vivid picture of what I am doing! The monster is obviously me and I can't kill it and you can't kill it because all it does is constantly tried to kill you. I don't think you really understand what a monster I am. I get you where it hurts. I get you to care about me and try to help and then kick you in the head over and over."

We returned to the subject of castration and discovered that she believed all children are initially male. Males have power and control, but they are "pricks, have brains in their crotch." Some children get "ripped off" and become eunuchs. In my notes subsequent to this session I subsequently realized I had written, "it is like pulling teeth to get her to continue to think about this." She realized that getting beaten up and "ripped off" and trying to control the penis and get it inside her was re-enacting her struggle to get a penis as well as the feeding struggle with her mother. She realized that she tried to control me by withholding her thoughts and feelings, withdrawing, and "ripping me off."

Year nine

She reported a "splitting headache" as she contemplated the part of her that wanted to be close to people and the part that was enraged at human beings. She missed hours and made the tape recorder malfunction. She picked fights with me over everything and wanted to "kick my balls." She resumed sleeping with an old boy-friend and hallucinating. She insisted on stopping the trifluoperazine because it made her feel drunk. I suggested it was helping her wake up, but she was adamant, and I decided she needed to bear the consequences of her decisions. The thoughtful work that had characterized recent sessions stopped as well. She walked in front of her car after parking it on a hill without setting the break and nearly succeeded in running herself over. When she said that I looked like I felt helpless I readily assented. She felt as though we were saying good-bye and she were attending her own funeral. After a long silence she said that it was pointless, that she was not going to change, and that although she would miss me, tomorrow would be our last hour. Perhaps she was right, I thought, and in any case I felt I needed to accept her right to control her life, so I shared my concern for her and my sadness.

Sara called me soon thereafter to say she had reconsidered, and she told me her fantasy had been to quit therapy, stop caring, quit her job, and drive off. We agreed that she wanted to take a trip from the city of caring and loving to one of hatred, insanity, and perhaps suicide. She talked about how little it would disturb her family if this were to happen, and I responded that I cared and it would distress me deeply. She was touched and cried. When she left the session she discovered that she had locked herself out of her car and had to return to the office for help. The next hour, after preliminary curses, she said she had been relieved to find herself locked out of her car because she was certain that had been her unconscious effort to keep herself from driving off and quitting, and this was the first instance she could recall in which her unconscious motivation had been constructive!

Unlike other positive moments in our work this incident heralded a permanent change. Sara no longer seemed psychotic. She told me that to her surprise she had never been this depressed before without having delusions and hallucinations. She decided to cut back to once weekly therapy. We met at this diminished frequency for another year and a half prior to terminating, and although our relationship remained stalemated there was no recurrence of hallucinations or delusions. Sara reported progressive expansion in the areas of close friendships and work. She began to develop an identity as an educational crusader as evidenced by meteoric career advancement and the high esteem in which she was held by other educators, parents, and most of all the children she taught. It became clear that the extent of her professional ambition and effort would be the only limiting factor in the success of her career.

About seven months after we decreased the frequency of her appointments Sara gave me another one of her illustrated letters as a kind of Christmas gift. After summarizing her accomplishments she concluded: "from the quiet room to this. That is saying a lot. For a huge chunk of each day I am happy, enjoying myself, challenged. You stuck by me. Thank you for your amazing patience and caring. I did everything I could to drive you away, and I continue to keep you at a distance with all the ways I have worked out over the years. But at the same time I take little pieces of our friendship and use them to patch my broken heart. You have given me a good life with friends and a satisfying job. You have also, like you said a long time ago, given me choices. My happiness with what I have now fuels my rage and urge to destroy you and my feelings, destroy myself. But much of me wants more and thinks that I can go further."

Although she realized it was unlikely that she could attain her goal of intimacy with a man without further intensive work with me, each gesture in that direction was regularly followed by some form of destructiveness. She seemed to be saying "I won't" to the prospect of more intensive emotional involvement with me. Finally I suggested that she was saying by her angry negative behavior what she was unable to say in words, namely that she did not wish to go further in therapy. Then it turned out that Sara did not want to experience the intense sadness of termination, either. She seemed to want to continue our cyclically ambivalent contact endlessly. She seemed no more capable of saying goodbye than she was of continuing our work. We agreed to her wish to visit and report to me every half year or so, in the hope that eventually she might be able to reach a more definitive decision of one kind or another. During one such interval she wrote me:

> There are nights when I get so depressed and feel helpless and angry and want to die, but I can survive them, I have control and know more clearly that the feelings will not kill me. I do not take drastic action anymore. Often I don't pay attention to my feelings and it is only when I get very close to being psychotic that I force myself to

figure out what is going on. You helped me to do this many, many times. I can do it myself now. Thank you for your patience and caring. Thank you for giving me choices. You sat there for years waiting for me to show up. You ran the risk of holding out your caring and being rejected over and over and over. I know that I didn't entirely arrive, but I am happy. I know that it is not ideal that I carry you around in my head as a watchdog. Ideally it should be me that does this but the part of me that wants to destroy all caring and all life is very powerful and I need you there in my mind as a third-party.

After another hiatus in our sessions Sara returned and informed me that she had made a very satisfying relationship with a man she described as kind and intelligent. She shared the surprising news that they had a good sexual relationship because she realized that in order to retain her sanity during sex she had to reserve the right to ask him to stop lovemaking at any time, a condition he was willing to honor. He lived in a distant city, and they had concluded that in order to decide whether they wanted to make a commitment to one another they would first need to live together. This awareness coincided fortuitously with Sara's conclusion that in order to advance her career she needed to change jobs and get a Ph.D. and this might just as well be done in the city where he lived. She knew I would be pleased, and she had come to say goodbye. She expressed moving tears of farewell and gratitude.

Epilogue

More than 20 years elapsed before Sara unexpectedly contacted me and came to visit. I felt I was in the presence of an impressively mature woman with a solid sense of self who made direct eye and emotional contact with me, had a sense of values and purpose, and was highly intelligent and articulate. She described a very satisfying marriage to the man she had told me about in that final session. She and her husband had adopted a very disturbed adolescent boy and raised him to a constructive and mature manhood. In her career as teacher and educational innovator she was greatly valued by colleagues and by the community. She had resigned her position some years previously after a dispute with authorities in which she had the backing of her colleagues and the community, and obtained a Master's degree in creative writing. She had written and illustrated a coming of age novel for 9–12 year olds that had been published and very favorably reviewed and was at work on a second one. She had never required further therapy or medication. Remarkably what she recalled most about our work was not things I had said to her, but my unwavering patience and caring during her long periods of silence and disengagement.

Discussion and conclusion

Space considerations preclude more than a superficial reference to my theoretical orientation, which is spelled out in detail elsewhere (1993, 2002, 2011, and under review). It has roots in Freud's seminal work on the primary process (1900, 1911). In fact most serious efforts to comprehend psychotic mental processes can be traced back to Freud's model, though each subsequent theorist has obscured this fact by employing idiosyncratic conceptual terminology and failing to acknowledge theoretical indebtedness to Freud. These include Klein's theory of splitting and the concrete body-mind she called phantasy; Bion's theory of failure of alpha functioning and dreaming that ordinarily creates a gradient between conscious thought and unconscious process, with resultant evacuation of raw beta elements in the form of delusion and hallucination; and Matte-Blanco's (1988) model of symmetric and asymmetric logic.

Freud believed that the primary process is the underpinning not only of dreaming but of the severe psychoses. Nonetheless his writings are confused and vacillate with regard to whether it is the structure of the unconscious mind that is by definition invisible to direct observation and can only be inferred from perturbations of normal thought, or whether it is nothing more than an arcane variation of symbolic thought. He was also confused about whether it is a normal, mature way that the mind works or whether it is immature and pathological. As a result he failed to appreciate its major conscious role in mental life. The theories of those who followed him reflect similar confusion. I have proposed a model of primordial consciousness and elaborated how it is of importance equivalent to that of reflective symbolic thought and is responsible for many aspects of life, including, in addition to psychosis, dogmatic belief systems, aspects of creativity, parent-infant bonding, spirituality, and much more.

Primordial consciousness is syncretic or holistic. Sensations and perceptions are neither differentiated in terms of inner self and external world nor integrated into a cohesive self, hence it supports contradiction and what from a thoughtful perspective is unreality as well as mental disintegration. Its imagery is concrete and pictorial rather than symbolic, as evinced by Sara's oral confusions about breasts, penises, medications, and words. It is a language of the body and of undifferentiated affect, psychosomatic-motoric, and these elements rather than the logic of thought drive its narrative. It does not differentiate ideation or image from actuality and action. In dreams when motor discharge is paralyzed it is reflected in non-symbolic imagery. It is a system of belief rather than reflection. Sara's mental activity, though qualitatively different from reflective, logical, realistic symbolic thought, was quite conscious, in contrast to Freud's belief that the primary process is unconscious. What is true, however, is that she could not thoughtfully reflect on it.

Sara's therapy consisted of enactment of a struggle for sanity, and probably for life itself. Which of us would succeed in "treating" or changing the other? Without thoughtful awareness Sara set out to sadistically persecute me in such a way as to undermine my trust in caring and in other people, and in my own sense of reality and sanity, to make me experience rage, despair, and hopelessness, and force me into a thought-numbing state of despair and paranoid psychosis such as she must have experienced at the hands of her mother as a child. It was my task to maintain my belief in my sense of reality and caring and demonstrate to her that one could not only survive such assaults, but bear the unbearable feelings and metabolize them into thoughtful, differentiated, and controlled emotions.

Particularly in the early years the work required creation of a holding environment capable of containing her urge to act destructively and to flee, an environment that promoted thought and communication instead. The availability of a supportive long-term hospital environment was essential in this regard, and it was sorely tested by Sara's destructiveness not only to herself, but toward both myself and ward staff by undermining our sense of reality and pressuring us to enact toward one another the unintegrated rage and suspiciousness that she was unable to represent, bear, and think about.

Sara was not encouraged to free associate, insofar as this would have promoted disintegration and undermined her reflective and integrative capabilities. Instead, I tried to establish eye contact as an essential element of our relationship, and meaning was uncovered by dialectic interchanges in which I tried to hold in mind what I thought she was communicating to me by her behavior, gestures and facial expressions, speech peculiarities, and prosody, as well as her actual words; to mirror my impressions back to her as thoughtful speculations; and to encourage her to confirm or deny their accuracy.

Note

1 Reprinted in a shortened and modified version from Robbins, M. (2012). The successful psychoanalytic therapy of a schizophrenic woman. *Psychodynamic Psychiatry* 40: 575–608, with permission of Guilford Publications, Inc. This version of the chapter first appeared in Robbins, M. (2019). *Psychoanalysis Meets Psychosis: Attachment, Separation, and the Undifferentiated Unintegrated Mind.* Abingdon and New York: Routledge.

References

Freud, S. (1900). The interpretation of dreams. *Standard Edition* 4–5.

Freud, S. (1911). Formulations on the two principles of mental functioning. *Standard Edition* 12.

Matte-Blanco, I. (1988). *Thinking, Feeling, and Being: Clinical Reflections on the Fundamental Antinomy of Human Beings and World.* London: Routledge.

Robbins, M. (1988). Use of audiotape recording in impasses with severely disturbed personalities. *Journal of the American Psychoanalytic Association* 36: 61–75.

Robbins, M. (1993). *Experiences of Schizophrenia*. New York: Guilford.

Robbins, M. (2002). The language of schizophrenia and the world of delusion. *International Journal of Psycho-Analysis* 83: 383–405.

Robbins, M. (2011). *The Primordial Mind in Health and Illness: A Cross-Cultural Perspective*. London and New York: Routledge.

Robbins, M. (under review). Revisiting the nature and relationship of conscious and unconscious mind.

Chapter 7

The psychoanalyst and psychosis

The bull in a China shop

Stefano Calamandrei

The psychoanalysis and psychotherapy of a patient affected by a serious psychopathology must be undertaken in full awareness of what is distinctive about psychotic mental functioning. The daily observation of psychosis which has been carried out in recent years, both in individual and in group sessions, and especially in rehabilitative psychiatric facilities, has enabled us to understand the defensive mechanisms which are behind this kind of disturbance. This relatively new knowledge shows that one of the most significant points for the effectiveness of psychoanalytic therapy consists in the quality of the therapist's mental disposition. In fact, the inner psychological disposition of the therapist should be framed according to a mode of listening which identifies psychosis as principally a relational disturbance, and hence we must be aware that one of the vertices of the problem is located in the mind of the therapist who is confronted with the difficulties of comprehending the psychotic world. If the psychoanalyst starts to understand, to intuit something, of how the other feels, she will be able to erect an empathic bridge so that the psychosis will no longer be, or remain, alien; thus a possible, even if very complicated, therapy will begin.

Psychotic mental functioning

Sassolas (2011) summarises the distinctive psychology of the psychotic mind, identifying how the massive intervention of the main defence mechanisms, setting aside individual differences, tend to flatten out the mental world, making everyone who is blocked by these defences seem alike and impoverished. The psychological characteristics, the defence mechanisms of this mind which appears "alien" to us, are characterised above all by an intense "denial" of the existence of their own internal world. These patients wish to wipe out all their mental contents, anything that is happening inside them, whether it is the event which has just occurred or, most often, its emotional and mental repercussions. The patients tend to defend themselves by not acknowledging the elements of their own feelings, and they are not aware that they deceive others and themselves. This does not mean they are telling a lie, simply that they are committed to denying that they have had any sensation. We can consider this mechanism as a form of control which has the purpose of avoiding any possible emotional perturbation, since this would not be bearable. Another intensely used mechanism is "projection" of their own psychological contents outside themselves, resulting in a more or less complete externalisation of their own feelings, a thorough expulsion of their mental life. This mechanism is not exactly a true projection of a certain emotional content nor a projective identification, but a substantial outward projection of their internal world: rather than try to acknowledge their own feelings, assuming they have been obliged to perceive them, they are compelled to attribute them to the external world. However, I do not believe we should think of this as a structured move by an Ego using such a mechanism in a capable and organised manner, but should rather bear in mind that it is the action of a mind not yet well integrated – in Winnicott's sense, still dispersed into the environment – which is making use of this primitive mode to an extreme extent. As a consequence, the stimuli which may arouse emotions are rationalised and personified, as in paranoia, systematically organised so as to be controlled: but when this happens, another mode is also used at the same time, one which tries by means of a metaphor to give meaning, to comprehend what is happening.

Another very important defensive mode is that of resorting to "acting out", using actions by which an emotional perturbation can be avoided: in other words, instead of feeling a sensation, a psychotic performs an action, an act, a personified projection with which he tries to get rid of that "something" which might be experienced. When we are relating to such patients, it may happen that, stimulated by our presence, they behave in a way that has the sole purpose of regaining their distance from us, such as a fugue or a bizarre action. Sassolas maintains that the incomprehensibility of such behaviours or such thinking – that is to say, psychotic bizarreness – arises when the act of expulsion is added to denial. In this way, the conditions are created which cause the therapist to run into great difficulties of comprehension. It must be considered that, in relational situations, which are often of high emotional intensity for those who, like psychotics, are psychologically fragile, it is a common characteristic of these patients to be frightened by what is happening to them since they realise that they are not in control of such powerful defence mechanisms. Indeed, when these defensive modes are put into action, they function intensely and automatically, and create more emotional difficulties than they solve. The patient has the wholly reasonable sensation that she is not the protagonist of her own psychic life. When we are faced with such people, in our empathic listening and our transference rather than in our countertransference, they seem to be empty, impoverished, with no past, no history or identity, seeming instead to be much like one another. It would be easy to fall into the error of thinking that they really are empty, a sensation which causes us suffering. This particular "feeling" which arises in the therapeutic encounter with a psychotic person is essentially due to the fact that another intense mechanism is being set in motion: the "avoidance" of any relationship. In the psychoanalytic session this difficulty acquires a determining significance, since such a lack of relationality is perceived by the therapist as the setting up of a particular distance by the patient. This does not allow that "mutual holding" which, in my opinion, is necessary so that the analyst can develop his ability to listen with a freely floating attention. It can seem difficult to maintain the relationship when there appears to be a void in front of us, one that we perceive in a very different manner from the way we perceive our own feeling of solitude, which can paradoxically seem more "rich" to us, and less solitary. However, we must be aware that there is not a void but emptied people who have been forced to get rid of their own mental life and to scatter it into the environment and into other significant figures around them. In this projection of their own internal world as well as their emotions, patients also get rid of their abilities, their qualities: and so they disenfranchise themselves and are left impoverished. We can consider this dispersal as a distinctive consequence of the failure to integrate the narcissistic aspects of the transference, with the result that the patient is no longer present in her own life, and can no longer take responsibility for herself since she has not internalised the parental functions, the so-called good object. This necessary form of withdrawal from others depends on the fact of having to reduce and avoid everything that stimulates her psychic life since the emotions it evokes reveal its existence, and the suffering becomes unbearable. Every time there is an encounter with another person, there is the possibility of being struck by an intense emotional stimulation on both narcissistic and libidinal levels, and of undergoing an excessive release of mental sensations. The only defence that ensures self-preservation is the avoidance of the stimulating relationship. I think that the fundamental deficiency in psychotic disturbance consists in the absence of an established apparatus for autoeroticism or para-excitation which would make it possible to bear the emotions evoked by the other's presence and to set up an adequate filter against the object's emotional intrusions. This is why, instead of the autoerotic filter, psychotic patients are compelled to use symptoms as defences, so as to keep every relationship and its connected emotions at a distance. If we can consider psychosis from this point of view, I think we will be able to understand that its symptoms, perhaps its entire psychopathology, are only a highly individual way of restoring the right relational distance, because these are people who are not equipped with an internal filter which might defend them against such intrusions and the emotional stimulations coming from the environment and from emotionally important people.

Searles (1979) had earlier identified how, rather than experiencing sadness and other feelings, even simple ones, the patient preferred a state of delusion since he regarded his own psychic life, his own emotional experience, as a danger. Hence, the change that is necessary for addressing psychosis with the psychoanalytic instrument consists in trying to adapt our therapy to the particular quality of the pathology with a modification which consists essentially in changing the therapist's psychological disposition and way of entering into a relationship, rather than in modifying the setting or the other parameters of classical psychoanalysis. This is so that we can come face to face with a psychic functioning which appears to be different from our own (and which, in some cases, we need the serenity to admit into our transference), rather than in the various degrees through which the pleasure principle is expressed. In other words, we are compelled to match ourselves to a mind which uses its defence mechanisms not to manage an internal conflict which might be developing within their own psychological structures, but to protect themselves from psychic life and from the intensity of the internal world and, at the same time, from the relationship with us. As a result of the expulsion of their own mental life, and the dispersal of the self into the environment, caused by the lack of integration of the narcissistic transference, there is a strong "narcissistic investment in external reality". Reality, indeed, is experienced as an extension of themselves; however, this narcissistic investment is not exactly a defence mechanism but an inevitable consequence of the diffusion of the self into the environment, both human and non-human, caused by the more or less serious persistence of the undifferentiation between me and not-me which is left waiting for a process of integration. During therapy we can understand that, given that the external world is part of themselves, there is a different concept of setting, and this makes the relationship very taxing. This characteristic of the setting is made clear to us by a particular quality of the transference which stops us using free-floating attention, and I would call it the absence of a minimum level of mutual holding, precisely because we, the carers, are included in the external world. As we are part of this world, an extension of their inner world, the relationship with us is a tyrannical one subject to abrupt variations since we are not experienced as separate and independent objects. As a result, there is great sensitivity to any deficiency in us, and indeed we often cause a profound and particular disappointment which I would sum up as narcissistic rage. However, this narcissistic rage has a distinctive character in that, instead of being directed at the object, it is turned against themselves and their own powerlessness, with an intense self-devaluation. This is because the patient has not been able to put things in reality or in the other into a relationship: he considers them a part of himself, like, for example, a limb or a function, and so the disappointment which results has a different quality from resentment towards an object, from being disappointed by a person outside. This rage is coloured by a feeling of giving up, a feeling of failure, the habit of a chronically frustrated omnipotent act. As a result of denial, the externalisation of the self, and narcissistic investment in the environment, the patient appears to the therapist to be defending himself with another mechanism, that of "autistic withdrawal and isolation". But Bleger (1967), having earlier identified these problems, said that this is the presenting characteristic of symbiotic transference. This particular type of transference actually develops on two co-existent levels: the more manifest one, more visible to us, is the autistic aspect of withdrawal which sets up an insurmountable barrier between us and the patient; the other, which becomes apparent only with difficulty even to the therapist, is the symbiotic aspect, less obvious and more concealed. On this second level, the patient's narcissistic world is projected and deposited inside the therapist and into the setting.

Psychosis is therefore an illness of the Self, a disintegration or, rather, a permanent and protracted non-integration which obviously goes against attempts to make a precarious reorganisation of the fragments, so that such attempts end up creating incongruous aggregations. For example, some primitive states of mind, like normal infantile omnipotence or normal self-confidence, can achieve great intensity, bizarrely and in a state of isolation, leading to detached psychotic grandiosity. In the same way, primitive experiences of fusion can, instead of being felt as agreeably empathic, be reconstrued psychologically as influencing forces coming from other people, usually with hostile intent. This does not mean there cannot be spaces for the possibility of an object-relation, but the therapeutic process should be capable of going beyond the most external and defensive aspects of the personality. The good session of psychotherapy should permit a new and extended experiencing of the oscillations between pre-psychological chaos and the certainly provided by primitive fusion with the therapist, so as to enable the gradual structuring of the personality's narcissistic bases. For the therapist, psychotic and borderline personalities entail having to confront chaotic states of mind (Rinaldi, 2003), which the observer's empathic instrument is almost incapable of comprehending. When we are introduced to a patient, the best differential diagnosis we can make to identify these disturbances is one which identifies psychosis as that degree of psychological fragmentation and disturbance in thought and affectivity where we are no longer able to help with our empathy. In my opinion, it is in these situations that the most difficult work begins for the psychoanalyst, who is the only professional who can have the strength of spirit to consider these difficulties as referring also to herself: that is, as a disturbance of the relationship, one which involves her own ability to understand the other, an ability to understand which can also be strongly conditioned by a too strict adherence to one's own theories. Indeed, we should be able to accept that our difficulty in responding with enough coherence to the patient's communications (in the broad sense) may be due to our finding it impossible to use our most precious clinical tool for these levels, which is empathy. So we must be able to make our patients understand that we know they are vulnerable and wounded, that we understand when they show us that things are going to pieces, that we must above all try to integrate, to give a psychological meaning when they present us with disjointed constructions. In this context, we can say that not only is psychoanalysis the most appropriate tool for treating psychosis, but it is precisely the figure of the psychoanalyst as therapist who, thanks to his sensitivity and empathy, is the only one who can be capable of moving productively within the patient's inner world. In fact, being included in the externalised inner world, he must know how to use all his sensitivity in moving like a careful bull in a China shop, in order to restore those conditions, both of holding and of object-relation, which enable the gradual structuring of the narcissistic transference and hence a greater integration of the patient's personality.

Maria (aged twenty-one) is in analysis three times a week, face to face, after an initial phase on the couch (in fact, being in a delusional state, she was not only unable to associate, but thought I was telepathic and so she attempted a magical fusion, remaining silent for long periods). She finds her convictions confirmed above all when I try to interpret her states of mind, when I am able to intuit them, so as to create an empathic bridge. One of the last sessions begins with her telling me that during the night she had had an anxiety attack which has left her shaken, during which she saw her room fill with tangible, concrete demonic presences. The first part of the session is devoted to the detailed description of how the devils came to visit her: she is genuinely distressed and completely believes what she is saying. The whole session unfolds in a climate of great excitation, with the sensation on my part of being in the presence of a state of psychotic collapse. My countertransference is one of dismay and a break in empathic communication and understanding: the certainty with which I speak, its detachment from any emotion and inner content, detaches me from Maria and her "comprehensibility"; I am observing an "alien" phenomenon. With resignation, I feel the urge to act, to depart from my listening stance, and think I should act as a psychiatrist. Reflecting on this, almost seeking an individuality of my own in order to react to the great emotional pressure she is putting me under (because at the same time she wants to convince me about the existence of evil and the devil, the real concreteness of her visions), without too much conviction, but as if to assert that there is nevertheless a psychological level related to this massive, concrete externalisation, I ask the patient if perhaps she hadn't first of all had a dream.

Maria: Yes, it all started with that, I dreamed that the devil (*This surprises me*) came into my room, took me sexually, wanted to change me, wanted me for himself. (*She carries on talking about the reality of the images in which the sexual act continues, even once she was awake, describing the physical sensation of feeling the weight of the devil's body on top of her.*)

Analyst: (*With the impression of building something in the void, a typical countertransferential sensation when faced with patients who "empty" themselves, but wishing to bring her malaise into the session and into the transference, I reflect on the fact that in her description we have passed from dispersal among many figures to a single figure.*) Maybe you dreamed the fear you have of me, the fear that I might possess you and want to change you. You see me as a dangerous and very powerful figure, too close to you.

Maria: (*She seems to calm down, does not object to my interpretation of her delusion, accepts it, and seems more at ease.*) A syringe came into my mind, an overdose of Milkshake, and superpowers.

Analyst: (*Interpreting the visions, to give them a communicative sense.*) You seem afraid of me as if I were the devil, but you envy my superpowers, and you'd like to be soothed and strengthened.

Maria: Don't say that, did you say it or not? Now, here from the left, there was a voice. It was saying, "You must protest," I'm suffering. I have to explain a problem to you, a secret, from this point on, I start being afraid of the end of the session. Because I don't know how to behave, in every way I have to make it end in a precise way. I don't know if I should tell you this because if I do it might get worse. If we do the same thing at the end of the session it's a drama, it's a "mirror", I leave and I feel empty. But instead, if we make a "cross" at the end of the session (*She makes the sign of the cross*), I mean something different, that's all right. It's always been like this, with my other psychotherapies too, the last thing you do is important and there's always this problem. With my last therapist we always mirrored each other and it was a disaster. That's why, when I leave, I can't cope with it, and I spit, I need a smoke, and I suddenly go backwards and forwards, I do absurd things. When there's a mirror I'm not in control any more, I can't bear submission, I wouldn't be me any more.

Analyst: (*I am making an effort to adapt to this explanation of the relationship because it subverts the concept of attunement, which I considered positive, and her desire for silent magical, telepathic communication, but I intuit that the problem is feeling alone: separateness.*) Help me understand: when we make the cross it's as if we were making an exchange, a meeting of mind or body or memory, an enrichment. So, you take something away and don't feel alone any more. But if there's a mirror instead, a harmony, you feel rejected and then you feel alone. I think it may really be the problem of separation, how to separate in such a way that you can take something away, be enriched, but still be yourself.

Maria: You knew it already, you're telepathic, I told you before but you go on denying it. I hate myself because you are a genius with superpowers. I feel I'm in debt, I've got so much guilt.

The session has got too long and tiring, she can't cope with being in my presence any longer, the words do not fill the tension that's developed: we finish with the ritual of the cross, but this time I understand it. If she says "Good evening", I'll have to say something different, not the same, like "Goodbye".

Narcissistic features in the session

When we are faced with a patient who has externalised her inner world, the therapeutic mental stance we must adopt, besides being very alert to the relational distance, is an awareness that we must construct a holding which may be able to permit the integration of the patient's personality. One of the fundamental deficits in psychosis is the failure to form regulatory narcissistic structures which constitute the founding nucleus of the personality, operating silently and, in adult life, without our being aware of them. These structures are formed thanks to the optimal experience of the object's capacity for response when it is still experienced predominantly as environment, and is not perceived as separate or distinct from the infant. During the early phases in which the Self is being constituted – that is, before the mother becomes an object subjectively perceived by the infant in the non-me space and ambivalence develops – "It is helpful to postulate the existence for the immature child of two mothers" (Winnicott, 1965). These are "the object-mother and the environment-mother", and they

> describe the vast difference that there is for the infant between two aspects of infant-care, the mother as object, or owner of the part-object that may satisfy the infant's urgent needs, and the mother as the person who wards off the unpredictable and who actively provides care in handling and in general management. What the infant does at the height of id-tension and the use thus made of the object seems to me very different from the use the infant makes of the mother as part of the total environment. . . . It is the environment-mother who receives all that can be called affection and sensuous co-existence; it is the object-mother who becomes the target for excited experience backed by crude instinct-tension.
>
> (pp. 75–76)

The main deficiency during the development of the future psychotic patient seems to be not having been able to make use of a tranquil relationship with the environment-mother. The very lack of development of "ego-relatedness", as Winnicott calls it, contrasting it with "id-relationship" (ibid., 30), has contributed to the fragility of the structures that are the narcissistic bases of the personality, which promote subjectivation, autonomy, and being "able to enjoy solitude" or "buoyancy". This concept, being "able to enjoy one's own solitude", has been elaborated by J. M. Quinodoz (1991), who sums up in Kleinian theoretical language how internal security is structured thanks to the introjection of the good object. Psychosis comes about when the structures of the personality have not been sufficiently internalised during the process of development through identification and the elaboration of the narcissistic transference directed to the environment-mother. In fact, if the new-born infant can discover that the object-mother survives the episodes dominated by the drives, the oral-sadistic fantasies, he must also be able to count on a continuous and stable relationship with the environment-mother, who "has a special function, which is to continue to be herself, to be empathic towards her infant, to be there to receive the spontaneous gesture, and to be pleased" (Winnicott, 1965, p. 76). In the conditions of immaturity which apply to the period prior to the possibility of introjecting the good object, the infant must start becoming able "to be alone" in the presence of another person who is sustaining him, by the gradual introjection of aspects of the relationship with the environment-mother. Optimal frustration and the tolerant parental stance enable the permanent incorporation into the psychic organisation of positive mnesic traces of the satisfaction of partial drives, what Freud called "organ pleasure" (Freud, 1915a), which then, through introjection and identification, go to constitute the majority of the mind, that part which is silent and not repressed. The result of these acquisitions will lead the infant, and the patient, to master the mechanism which will enable her to address the instinctual demands which arise in her and neutralise them. In the treatment of psychotic patients we must be aware that the setting brings about an ideal situation for working on the psychological structures which regulate the narcissistic equilibrium and constitute the narcissistic bases of the individual. Indeed, analytic sessions are organised to promote an ideal frustration, directing the patient towards a displacement of instinctual gratification or reassurance towards a neutral space for play, towards the spontaneity and introspection of free association, towards a tranquil relationship similar to the one with the environment-mother. Recognising the value of these features, we could define the session as a new experience in which one learns to be alone in the presence of another person, and as the creation of a space in which we can be sanely non-integrated. Thus, stimulating the verbalisation of every associative thought is like inviting a new "spontaneous gesture": that is, reconstituting the optimal situation for the development of healthy narcissism and the integrative structuring of the Self. Clinical practice shows us that without the constitution of a stable narcissistic base it is not even possible to experience, in a "real and lively" way, the impulse coming from the world of the instincts because the relationship with the other would remain too emotionally excitatory and destabilising, and so the Self would be forced to set itself up along the lines of compliance and falsity.

Dependency as the search for the environment-mother and autoeroticism

Deficiencies in narcissistic structuring usually emerge at the end of childhood, when adolescence begins, revealing that the autoerotic function has not been able to develop normally. For this para-excitatory capacity to be fully established it needs to evolve from a correct hallucinatory satisfaction of desire which we can identify as one of the constituent elements of a good object's internal permanence. In fact, sensoriality, when it is not protected by the filter of autoeroticism, has to direct and intensify a contact in the relationship with the object. Autoeroticism is formed thanks to the intermittent reinvestment of the mnesic traces of hallucinatory satisfaction, a reinvestment which gradually becomes more independent of the expression of the initial need. In the sphere of primary identification, the hallucinatory satisfaction of pleasure is the first way of performing alone the maternal function of a protective screen against excitations. The shadow of the object endures in the quality of the autoerotic function, but, once it has been acquired as such, this develops autonomously as "functional" identification, creating an internal space of "intrapsychic play" which allows representational data to be dealt with through subsequent displacements. The possibility of displacement will allow the introduction of the "small differences" which are essential for psychic functioning because of how they enable the work of transformation which avoids direct discharge down hallucinatory or motor-perceptual routes, and the stimulus-response short circuit.

In order to be able to move out of the state of dependency, it must be possible to separate oneself from the object through a process of internal displacement which may lead to the utilisation of an internal representation of the object: that is, to the processes of symbolisation in place of the real presence. We know that temporality begins in the passage from separateness to separation: that is, when we can conceive the other's existence and bear its loss. Until that moment – that is, until the capacity for separation is acquired – there remains only the mechanism of spatial, phobic concreteness: in other words, the search for an impossible relational distance. This leads to a stalemate which can last throughout life and is, for me, perhaps the best definition of psychosis: on the one hand the impossibility of being autonomous because of the narcissistic structures' excessive fragility, and on the other hand the necessary search for a holding, a dependency that is not too "objectual". Indeed, the very desire felt for the object can be perceived as a narcissistic threat because it puts subjectivity and identity in danger. A subject with a fragile narcissistic base is forced to clutch on to perceptual data, to overinvest the external objects he depends on. For this reason, he becomes hypersensitive to variations in relational distance since it is his only possible defence: the object acquires great power through the desire it provokes. In this case, the only possible survival strategy is not to have desires, as is perceptible in psychotic patients, who manifest a profound and unconscious inability to know what they desire. Action becomes the means for overthrowing what they fear they will undergo and for recovering control over the external world, since they are not capable of representing it to themselves, the Ego being frozen by the massive weight of the affects and constrained into a flattened psychic space. The subtle play of displacing representations is replaced by more archaic mechanisms such as projection, reversal into the opposite, and turning back on oneself. The solidity of the narcissistic base is therefore the filtering factor (of para-excitation or autoeroticism) in relation to the attraction of the object, and we begin to perceive the defect when the relationship with the parents changes quality in adolescence, when autonomy should emerge and residual dependency is coloured by incest. Then dependency is displaced towards the psychosocial environment, which becomes used above all as a counterinvestment to internal reality, functioning as a holding environment, and will be all the greater when there has been no internal working through of the narcissistic transference in relation to the so-called environment-mother (Jeammet, 2005).

Structural identifications arise from the work of mourning

The mode in which identifications are structured as the result of a separation is addressed by Freud in *Mourning and Melancholia* (1915b), when he describes the withdrawal of libido from the invested object and the consequent passage from fusion to the development of a function. His description derives from an analysis of the effects on the Ego of the loss of the object and the forces that are mobilised until the Ego "is persuaded by the sum of the narcissistic satisfactions it derives from being alive to sever its attachment to the object that has been abolished" (p. 255). This is achieved by the narcissistic identification which the Ego sets up to try and compensate itself for loss. With the patients I am describing, structuring the narcissistic base means having to address the dual work indicated by Freud since, besides abandoning the love-object (that is, effecting and bearing separation), they must also learn to give up the satisfaction of an unmodified infantile desire which has been maintained as such through the traumatic absence of the object. In other words, we are in the phase of separateness where there is still a marked degree of indistinctness between environment and Self. Hence, before being able to work through mourning, we have to address the work which Freud called melancholy: that is, the constitution of a narcissistic base which enables the displacement of the object-investments. In normal mourning, when we are in the presence of a sufficiently healthy Ego which has learned to be separate, to remain alone, the process can take place thanks to the displacement of investment towards new objects, so that the Ego can convince itself that it can survive by the sum total of narcissistic gratifications. Instead, in melancholy this is not possible since the Ego cannot detach itself from the environment-mother because it is still not differentiated from her. Freud attributed this impossibility to the Narcissistic Choice of Object whereby the Ego is in a fusional relationship with its sustaining environment, and so experiences detachment as an intolerable loss of part of the Self.

In the moment of separation, according to Freud, love for the object, the need we have of it, is transformed into an introjection within the Ego, an identification with the absent other. The condition is that the threatened libidinal investment must abandon the object and withdraw onto the Ego from whence it had started out. After this libidinal repression, the pain of the loss thus becomes an intrapsychic conflict which is displaced on one hand onto the Ego and on the other onto the Superego: in mourning, the struggle between two adverse parts is internalised in an omnipotent attempt to deny and master separation. In this move, the libido and the Ego play the role of the dead or absent one, and aim to replace the missing function. In the first mother-infant interactions, in the first momentary separations from the environment-mother, this libidinal return goes towards the constitution of the first rudimentary identifications, imitations, the structures of the personality's narcissistic base. Freud calls identification "the original form of emotional tie . . . a substitute for a libidinal object-tie, as it were by means of introjection of the object into the ego," and it can "arise with any new perception of a common quality shared with some other person who is not an object of the sexual instinct" (Freud, 1921), and so it is a complex mechanism which can perform many functions. Besides being a stage in the transformation of desire, after it has been projected onto the other, identification is also a process in which the Ego is constructively modified when the desire and the libidinal investment return to their proper place in the subject. If introjection is always initially correlated to projection, in the movement from inside to outside, and if during this movement the Ego is not modified, when the object is instead taken into the Ego, although in a rudimentary manner, we have a transformation of the introjective mechanism, a remodelling of the Ego itself on the model of the object, which becomes identification, a function which will later be stably acquired. Thus, identification is the possibility of elaboration, the decisive point in life where being replaces having, the base mechanism, always utilised in any of the situations of disengagement in order to effect the displacement towards new investments. We should also remember how for Freud identification is precisely the mechanism behind the forming of the psychic agencies, the Ego Ideal and the Super-ego, and the acquisition of power over the Id and over the Ego's demands.

With psychotic patients, the significant point in therapeutic work on mourning, separation, and identification, so that frustration can be accepted and displacement brought about, seems to be the narcissistic acknowledgement of the painful feelings of loss: that is, it must be effected as an exchange; the patient must renounce direct gratification, the total help of the object, and the analyst must appreciate this and acknowledge the sacrifice. I believe that the decisive factor for change and for psycholog-ical gain by working through the narcissistic transference (from the forma-tion of Ego-structures to learning at school) consists in two fundamental relational transitions: the first is that, as a result of giving up immediate satisfaction, a need for narcissistic gratification is released, which needs to be confirmed and witnessed by an adult. The other, following straight on from this, is the narcissistic investment which the therapist and patient must make together in relation to the new function onto which the libidi-nal investment has been displaced. The example is that of the exit from the initial mother-infant fusion when a relational dynamic is created, thanks to the investment which the mother makes onto certain infantile functions. There needs to be a repeated transition in which the first fusional identifi-cation is superseded. This was based on the fulfilment of two desires, the oral pleasure of the new-born's satisfaction at the breast and the soothing of bodily suffering, and the satisfaction of maternal desire. Primary iden-tification, according to Aulagnier (1975, 1979), is a narcissistic identifica-tion where the loss of the loved object is felt as a lack within the Self and as loss in the other who can also become alienating if the introjection of the lost object into the Ego occupies the whole internal space. In analysis, when we address the narcissistic levels, we are in a phase shortly after this fusion where the slight distinction between the Ego and the other has its beginning; the moment of exit from fusion is when the mother requires the infant to perform a function. Following the fundamental rule is moving out of passivity and fusional dependency, and valuing a function, a narcis-sistic symbol, which becomes a focal point for identification.

Structuring the narcissistic base

In therapeutic work, if we are to structure the narcissistic base and stim-ulate the formation of autoeroticism we must try to maintain a neutral level on which the relationship can as far as possible take the form of an indistinction between subject and object which allows the patient to be nourished by the quality of the emotional exchange, internalising it and making it her own without recognising the presence of the object in this exchange. This quality of the interaction is the precondition for the development of healthy narcissism because it nourishes the pleasure in one's own function while there is still a strong dependence on the object. This is one of the paradoxes of development: the subject must feel that she is herself while she is so abundantly dependent on other. Only in these conditions can she take on their capacities, but only if she does not become conscious of the relationships between what she takes and what belongs to the other. The development of the personality depends on the dilemma by which we need to nourish ourselves on others in order to be ourselves and at the same time need to differentiate ourselves from them. It is a paradox, a psychological contradiction, which, if it emerges in adolescence, can be experienced as insoluble since, like all paradoxes, it can be thought of only indirectly in après-coup or as meta-thinking.

Therefore, it matters how we conceive of the work we have to do: in other words, we must be aware of both the mechanisms of identification and the models of functioning in which we are to intervene, bearing in mind that an important part of the narcissistic disposition resides in the maintenance of a transitional area of undifferentiation between subject and object. In adolescence, for example, this can become the area of ideology or beliefs, the home of all the implicit, silent things which we share – or think we share – with our environment: convictions, expectations, the unsaid, which compose the backcloth on which family ties are woven, as are those with the therapist. It is a highly delicate fabric where we can discover that what we thought had been acquired in our psychological functioning actually depends on its context and that the support of an ideology is fragile, which is why it is desperately defended. We need to be aware that it is not mere opinions or moral values that are being expressed for the sake of discussion or to convey information, but externalisations of narcissism, a search for external support: if this aspect is not understood, its function is nullified, making the anchorage to the object more intolerable than necessary. In the grip of the relational dynamic, the therapist can lose sight of his role as a narcissistic support, in which he should satisfy the needs of dependency without creating a dependency on himself, on his own narcissism. This means transforming the therapy, perceiving it as happening more in a spatial play of fluctuating distances during a single encounter, rather than in an exchange of contents, and considering the externalisation of the emotions as an adjustment of the relational distance we must be able to aim for, a meta-language almost without content, like some outbreaks of rage or seductions. The relationship must be tolerant and narcissistically supportive because it lets the patient choose the distance and thereby become capable of reactivating the processes of internalisation without provoking defensive reactions against the object. Shared subjects, like interests and passions, become a transitional area, an area of exchange and pleasure that is not sexualised or excitatory. The goal is to restore the pleasure of the functioning to the greatest possible degree, while there is the support of an object which evokes the least possible conflict. As therapists we need to understand the structural value of these exchanges, these shared activities, and not dismiss them, thinking that nothing has happened, because nothing has been said on our part as "analysts", thinking that only interpretative speech has therapeutic value.

Using different terms from the Freud of *Mourning and Melancholia*, Winnicott describes a further aspect of the acquisition of the narcissistic bases through the mechanism of identification which he infers from the clinical observation of "antisocial" features. This procedure is effected through an imitative mode which, following Winnicott on "antisocial" features, I would call a "theft", an incorporation which is the converse of an acting-out: i.e. an acting-in. However, in order that one's own affective deficits can be supplied in this way, there needs to be the confrontation with a mind, the analyst's, that is in a similar state to "primary maternal preoccupation" (Winnicott, 1958), a mind which has been able to deconstruct itself. When we are able to deconstruct ourselves for the patient, we can offer him the chance of a particularly accepting holding of his needs, in which he can find the opportunity to confront a sort of mental reset, a reduction in the therapist's narcissism to its vital minimum, as Kohut (1976) suggests in relation to the creative transference. In this way, patients can utilise a free space, an undefended mind, where they can project their "subjectivity" in the fullest sense of holding, of indistinctness from the object. At the same time, it is demonstrated to them that thought, autonomy, and differentiation are being reconstituted, despite the reduction of self-control, both as thinkability and as the vital possibility of thought becoming re-integrated. These countertransferential experiences of testing the possibility of mental survival occur frequently in the therapy of serious pathologies and demonstrate something more than the survival of the object. They seem to me rather to be moments of identification, learning the function of thought; indeed, I find that patients pass with particular sensitivity through these phases, which they have often induced themselves, and with an "imitative" attention of which they are unaware, trying to perceive how the analyst is able to reintegrate herself after such deconstruction in order to regain symbolic levels. According to Winnicott (1988),

in regression in a psycho-therapy the patient (of whatever age) must be able to come eventually to an unawareness of environmental care and of dependence, which means that the therapist is giving a good enough adaptation to need. Here is a state of primary narcissism, which must be achieved at certain moments in the treatment.

(p. 142)

If I call this mode of narcissistic identificatory acquisition a "theft", it is because we know that if it has no way of being achieved in early child-hood, it can translate into real theft, the concrete attempt to supply such deficits later in life. In therapy, the work must be organised in order to "do with" the patient and to share the pleasure only through this sharing, without measuring this pleasure and asking "who it belongs to": that is, the patient should not wonder to whom he owes it and where it comes from. This pleasure in functioning will be all the more nourishing when it is protected by the "unawareness" of the analyst, the new environment-mother, who is authorising the patient to live as herself, without being confronted with the object (Calamandrei, 2012). I shall conclude with a dream which, after some months, Maria tells me near the end of a session, another dream about the devil.

Maria: (*Very disappointed, attaching little importance to the fact, as if she dis-missed it or had made the same mistake countless times.*) I dreamed about the devil again. I didn't like the way it ended, there was no fight. I only remember that at the end, while he was still close to me, I held out my hands (*She puts her hands together, crossing her fingers, palms up, as if forming a barrier in front of her*) in a ges-ture I used to make as a child, to mean "mirror". What I mean is you're a long way from me, that way it didn't bore me and didn't go in, but then I hugged him, to say goodbye, and since he didn't notice, I made the same mirror gesture behind his back, and I trapped him, I defeated him. (*She makes the gesture again, this time reversed, with her fingers crossed, but her palms turned towards herself, as if in an embrace, or an imaginary container*)

Recently Maria has substituted my voice and my internal presence for the many others she used to hear and be disturbed by, confusing mine and theirs, leading her to believe in an impossible attempt at self-produced dependency which prompted her to act out and to behave oddly. This dream seems to indicate the initial acquisition of an autoerotic filtering mechanism which marks out an internal space and a slightly more auton-omous identity less troubled by the invasive presence of the other.

References and further readings

Aulagnier, P. (1975). *The Violence of Interpretation*. Hove: Routledge, 2001.

Aulagnier, P. (1979). *Les destins du plaisir*. Paris: Presses Universitaires de France, 2009.

Bleger, J. (1967). *Symbiosis and Ambiguity*. London: Routledge, 2013.

Calamandrei, S. (2008). Il lavoro interpretativo nelle patologie gravi. In *Rivista di Psicoanalisi*, 54, 4.08, pp. 855–873.

Calamandrei, S. (2012). Perdersi per ritrovarsi: identificazione e transfert narcisistico. In *Rivista di Psicoanalisi*, 58, 3.12, pp. 549–566.

Freud, S. (1915a). Instincts and their Vicissitudes. *Standard Edition*, XIV.

Freud, S. (1915b). Mourning and Melancholia. *Standard Edition*, XIV.

Freud, S. (1921). Group Psychology and the Analysis of the Ego. *Standard Edition*, XXII.

Jeammet, P., and Corcos, M. (2005). *Evolution des problématiques à l'adolescence. L'émergence de la dépendance et ses aménagements*. Doin: Rueil – Malmaison Cedex.

Kohut, H. (1976). Creativeness, charisma, group psychology: Reflections on the self-analysis of freud. In Gedo, J.E., and Pollock, G.H. (Editors), *Freud: The Fusion of Science and Humanism*. Psychol. Issues, IX, 2/3, monograph 34/35 pp. 379–425. New York: International Universities Press, 1976.

Kohut, H. (1996). *The Chicago Institute Lectures: Heinz Kohut*. Edited by P. Toplin and M. Toplin. Hillsdale, NJ: Analytic Press, 1996.

Quinodoz, J.M. (1991). *The Taming of Solitude*. London: Routledge, 2003.

Rinaldi, L. (2003). Dal caos alla significazione. In *Stati caotici della mente*. Milan: Raffaello Cortina.

Sassolas, M. (2011). *Il funzionamento psicotico*. Paper given at the Centro Psicoanalitico in Florence.

Searles, H.F. (1979). *Countertransference and Related Subjects*. New York: International Universities Press, 1999.

Winnicott, D. (1963). The development of the capacity for concern. In *Maturational Processes and the Facilitating Environment*. London: The Hogarth Press, 1965.

Winnicott, D. (1956). Primary maternal preoccupation. In *Through Paediatrics to Psycho-Analysis*. London: The Hogarth Press, 1987.

Winnicott, D. (1988). *On Human Nature*. London: Free Association Books.

Chapter 8

Pain in search of psychical shelter[1]

Sarantis Thanopulos

A short theoretical premise

One of Freud's early intuitions still today remains a fundamental keystone of psychoanalytical thought regarding psychosis:

> In both the instances considered so far, defense against the incompatible idea was effected by separating it from its affect; the idea itself remained in consciousness, even though weakened and isolated. There is, however, a much more energetic and successful kind of defense. Here, the ego rejects the incompatible idea together with its affect and behaves as if the idea had never occurred to the ego at all. But from the moment at which this has been successfully done the subject is in a psychosis, which can only be classified as "hallucinatory confusion".
>
> (. . .) It must be regarded as the expression of pathological disposition of a fairly high degree and it may be described more or less as follows. The ego breaks away itself away from the incompatible idea; but the latter is inseparably connected with a piece of reality, so that, in so far as it achieves this result, it, too, has detached itself wholly or in part from reality.
>
> (Freud, 1894, pp. 58–59)

In this passage, Freud gives a clear definition of the defence mechanism in psychosis, distinguishing it from repression. He uses the verb *verwerfen* (reject, refuse) to describe the expulsive movement of psychical content (consisting of idea and affect) from the ego. In *The Schreber Case*, he returns to the concept, stating that what has been repressed within the self then returns from outside. In *The Case History of the Wolf Man*, after discussing the incident of the hallucination of a cut finger, he identifies three different attitudes in the patient regarding castration: on the one hand, he accepts and fears it, and on the other, denies it, but on a deeper level he wants nothing to do with it; he rejects it. In the second case, Freud puts together, although without explanation, the mechanism of splitting (the coexistence of two defensive mechanisms which express two opposing attitudes regarding castration: repression and denial) and rejection. Following his work, splitting would become explicitly named and defined as a defensive mechanism first in fetishism and perversion, and then in psychosis. The concept of rejection, *verwerfung*, would not, by contrast, ever be taken up again by Freud or by other psychoanalysts until Lacan exhumed it, remodelling it on the legal/grammatical concept of *foreclosure*.[2]

From his perspective, Lacan substantially favours this model: the subject rejects that which from his/her experience is not able to access "primordial symbolization" (entry into a world ordered by the structural power of the word); consequently, "that which is not born as symbolic appears in reality" in the form of a hallucination.

In revisiting Freud's discourse, Lacan gives excessive importance to the signifying power of the word (basing his argumentation on the concept of the linguistic signifier borrowed from De Saussure) and overlooks its subjective pre-signification. Children are not orthopedically structured by verbal language: before being able to use it, they subjectively create their own means of expression and communication starting from bodily gestures. This first means of expression is an original idiom of the demonstration of their spontaneous existence, which they do not communicate intentionally, and which then becomes a preverbal language constructed and shared with the mother in the sphere of reciprocal imitation (Thanopulos, 2009). For verbal language to acquire a subjective significance, children must grasp the word with all the strength of their personal bodily expressivity, to go beyond it according to their own way of being. The poet inside everyone uses words in a unique, unrepeatable style. The common language which structures social relationships is the expression of the fact that all human beings are made of the same individual qualities, while the way of using it according to a personal idiom corresponds to the fact that the individual composition of these qualities is irreducibly original.[3] When the subjective pre-signification of verbal language is struck at the root, words become disembodied and their use becomes purely cognitive: the subject is capable not only of using them, but also doing so in the appropriate manner (respecting the relationship between signified and signifier, which is, it should be remembered, formal), although the speech is impersonal, an anonymous adaptation to the objective conditions of existence.[4] The language is void of desire and emotions, but in a conventional context, this existential falsehood can remain unseen. Nothing is more harmful than such invisibility of one's own being that the subject feels and from which he/she cannot re-emerge without neologism or delirium.

With his concept of *evacuation*, Bion aligns himself with the perspective of rejection to explain the creation of a psychotic idea of reality, but differs from Lacan on two points: (a) he links rejection with projective identification (M. Klein) and with deformation of the perception of reality (bizarre objects) rather than with hallucination; (b) by introducing the concept of *alpha elements* (the transformation of sensorial impressions into dreamlike thoughts during sleep and waking states), he underlines the importance of pre-symbolic signification of experiences over the linguistically significant. Furthermore, Bion follows through on the Freudian concept of splitting when he underlines the division between psychotic and relatively healthy parts of the personality.

Winnicott agrees with the idea that in psychosis, experience is without psychical idea, but, in contrast to Freud, Lacan and Bion, he does not attribute this consequence to a preventive expulsion of unbearable material (idea, sensorial impression, emotion). His argumentation (1964) changes the perspective: that which cannot be represented, psychically elaborated, is not expelled, but creates a void in representational capacity and in subjectivity. *The pain cannot find psychical shelter.*

As I underlined in a previous work (2003), *verwerfung* is not an active psychical mechanism but the result of an impotent passivity:

> *Verwerfung* removes the subject, it impedes it, at the point in which it occurred, from existing. It is not strictly a defence through which the subject rejects an unbearable experience in external reality (eliminating it internally). It describes, to use an expression borrowed from Winnicott (referring to breakdown), "the unthinkable state of affairs that underlies the defence organization".
>
> (p. 217)

What determines this void in the psyche? The mother's inability to reflect the subjective experience of the child as it begins to take shape (Winnicott); a serious lack of maternal "reverie" (Bion); excessive primary violence in interpretation (Aulagnier). The first two views are complementary; the third is compatible with them but requires some clarification.

The mother who is excessively violent in the interpretation of her child's experiences is described by Aulagnier as incapable of adequately reflecting on/dreaming her child's experience because she interprets it according to her own idea of order. In this order, which does not take into account the child's spontaneity or the autonomy of his/her desires and thoughts, two orders converge – the impersonal order of objectifying discourse/knowledge, which the mother controls in her own favour, and the defensive, anxious order with which she seeks to settle a personal crisis of her own. Her interpretation of the child occurs according to an invisible manual of commonly accepted ideas, largely based on objective parameters of growth, whose sole aim is to control the child's free expression, making his/her existence predictable, predefined.

The mother has mad ideas: she fears the child's spontaneity, which might involve her emotionally beyond a destabilizing threshold (which defines the level of her personal vitality), and imposes a way of thinking that, dictated by her anxiety, may have meaning for her but is totally senseless for the child. However, the fear of involvement is not specific to the mother of a psychotic subject. It is more typical of the phallic, intrusive mother who has a central role in determining the psychic suffering present as perversion of desire: *non-desire of desire* (Aulagnier) or *disubjectualisation of desire* (Green). The mother described by Aulagnier influences the child's destiny in a psychotic manner, only if her inaccessibility leads to a radical interruption of the meeting with the child, a sudden chasm which no complaisance of the child towards an intrusive, alienating signification of its own experiences can resolve.

The child loses contact with the mother, and the ground opens up below his/her feet because she is not in a position to respond to the desire the child expresses to her, not even in the terms: "Do as I say, be like I want you to be". The violence is no longer tied to the maternal interpretation but to its absence, which deprives the child of any grasp and throws him/her out of the world. *It is an impersonal violence (the queen of violence) that has no agent, only victims.* A part of the child's subjectivity collapses, and the surviving part tries to give meaning to unthinkable violence which he/she cannot contain, viewing the intrusive mother as a persecutory figure (whom he/she hosts within).[5] The mother being a necessary object, the paranoid anxiety tends to be shifted onto other objects.

1. Escaping: to go where?

Nicola is a 26-year-old maths graduate. He has a brother who is two years younger. Having finished his studies, he returned to the provincial city where he lives with his parents. After some time, he decided to look for work in a northern city. One day, he just set off without any precise plan. On the second day after his arrival, he had a powerful paranoid anxiety attack (he thought crooks were following him), and he went to a police station to ask for protection.

On his return home, he began therapy with me. What follows is a partial account of the first 15 months of our work.

There rapidly emerges a highly ambivalent relationship with his mother who has invested highly idealistic expectations in him. He describes his father as being absent from his life, taken up with his work and incapable of having genuine contact with him.

Nicola dreams a lot and demonstrates a notable level of comprehension which, however, stops all of a sudden, like a path suddenly interrupted. In the third month of our work, he tells me about a dream in which the paranoid experiences in the background of his perception of the world emerge vividly:

> *I'm walking in a shopping mall with a girl I like. She's holding a really large cockroach which controls people, including her. There are some people controlled by the cockroach who are looking for it. They're a sect and I realise that I mustn't get too familiar with the girl. I have to protect myself from the sect.*

He associates the cockroach with a puppy. He then talks about his mother, whom he avoids because he finds her intrusive. When he was small, he always tried to please her, but he felt manipulated. The girl in the dream is a schoolmate. He trusted her because he felt that she was attracted to him. He was also attracted to her but never managed to tell her.

I comment that if the object we desire is manipulated, it is difficult to bring it closer because we are not able to involve it and rather we risk being involved in its manipulation.

He answers:

- I've always feared being manipulated by women.

I wonder if his paranoid experiences are finding containment in the dream space or if I am in fact witnessing the return of an uncontainable anxiety which is about to overflow. The manipulative cockroach, the main symbolic element in the dream, while it may take on a meaning (representing the patient himself as a child manipulated by a mother seduced by her own power over him), remains partly disconnected from the pervasive anxiety which undermines an apparently ordered dream texture.

Two weeks later, Nicola tries to run away again, taking the train to another city. Brought back home, he jumps from the balcony of his house into the courtyard: he falls onto a tree and is unharmed.

After three weeks in a psychiatric clinic, his parents organize for him to be taken into a community. Nicola, however, decides to continue with our work. His parents agree to undergo family therapy with him (carried out by a colleague).

On his return to analysis, Nicola is very upset. One day he tells me about a dream:

> *I'm in the corridor of my high school. There are women shut, like guinea pigs in a lab, in cages all along both sides. They're thin, almost skeletal. I stop to look at B., a colleague at university, who's in the last cage: I'm struck by how disfigured she is from thinness. Then I go into class. An outside voice coming from somewhere unknown orders me to strip in front of a boy and a girl who are at a desk in front of me. I'm lying on a bed, resting. I'm ashamed to obey and decide to resist. A battle with myself.*

B. was a sweet girl, I liked her a lot. We were friends, we sat together at the desks at university and talked about things. Once as we were leaving the classroom, she stopped to talk to me but I hurried out. She followed me but I didn't say a word to her. I was afraid of what it might have led to. She cried a little then turned away. Years later she moved abroad. When I found out, I cried a lot, to my surprise.

- The fear finally dissolved into crying.
- A dormant desire which I thought was no longer there. But it was ready to re-emerge. I didn't say a word to her, nor did I allow her to reach me. As if I'd shut her in a cage.
- In the dream you were lying on a bed. Like here?
- Just like this. Lying down is like becoming dormant: not being ready to catch what's in front of me.
- Dormant in your desire.
- I'd say drugged. The cage also describes my situation: being shut in, trapped in predefined plans. I can't let myself go, show what I am.
- Desire is forced on you, organized from outside.
- It's my mother who organizes, puts my desire in order. She treats me like a small child who has to get undressed to go to bed. It was my mother, but the voice was neutral, it had no particular tone.

I decide to keep certain thoughts to myself until they come into focus, which then happens:

The neutral voice, coming from beyond the mother, represents the psychotic quality of the experience which in this way enters into the dream. The form of a toneless voice, impersonal, difficult to recognise outside of the self as the voice of another subject.

The extreme thinness/anorexia takes on the form of the cage of the female body, of the female body of Nicola as well. The cage holds in the female desire of the woman (B., the mother) as in himself. In the dream, undressing expresses the female desire to let oneself go (and not the masculine one: to show one's penis), but it is dormant (fear of being drugged). The disfigurement of B.'s body reflects Nicola's attack on his own female body to defend himself from seduction/narcosis, but also fear of damaging the woman's body with his desire (complicated by anger). In the disfigurement, however, there returns the psychotic quality of the experience: a loss of self-image, signification of the female body which is heightened in the aporia of a shedding of restraint which is incapable of being reflected in the pair of adolescents exploring the field of sexual difference.

On a transferal level, the bed/couch takes the analysis into the place of the trauma. The analyst waits for him to relax, but the figure of the analyst is confused with that of the patient's mother, who wants to drug him. Be that as it may, the analysis also seems to be the place in which he can resist the order, disobey.

In one of the following sessions, Nicola describes a long, complex dream:

I go to stock up for the war: various foodstuffs to keep at home in case of necessity. At the shop counter, there are two girls: one of them is a masculine girl from high school. I court her. I go back several times to stock up and eventually we agree to meet outside the shop. As we're leaving the shop, the girl turns into an old man: the body becomes gaunt, her colour is dark as if it were going mouldy, rotting, the lips become thin, the hair white. I leave. The next day I go back and the girl starts flirting with me. But, knowing what this girl turns into when she leaves the shop, I decide to create a dividing wall between us, a barrier.

At school, this girl used to sit behind me. I turned round to speak to her and I could look her in the face but the desk divided us. There was vague courting but she was slow, hard, dictatorial: "I hold the truth". We had nothing in common. The eyes of the old man she turned into were sunken, like two black holes. He was blind like my paternal grandfather, who had lost his sight from glaucoma. The girl/old man had a hood on his head which reminded me of my father's hat. He wears it to cover his white hair. And as protection against the cold. The face was similar to my grandfather's. Like my face, actually. Like I'll become as well.

- Do you think it's men's fate to become blind?
- It's a possibility, it's necessary to be aware of it. The dream was a warning that old age, death can arrive suddenly. Following the masculine girl, old age arrives earlier.
- The old man in the dream was a transformation of the girl. Do you think that the girl lives in you?
- No, it's something I'm looking for outside myself. It's old, without any vital energy, something dead, destined to wear out very quickly. A fruit to be picked that's going to rot. The masculine element is something formless, without the desire to live, which perishes quickly. Something that shows itself in the shape of a young girl (firm, strong, full of the desire to live), in fact it's old, already worn out.

This time as well, I hold back some thoughts which I will develop later:

A woman's bond with an idealized paternal figure who substitutes her erotic link with the man has a central position in the space of signification. Nicola, looking for the woman, meets this ideal figure which his mother asks him to incarnate, and he reveals it for what it really is: a narcissistic object unsuitable to real life which when tested by desire proves to be exhausted, irredeemably worn out and dying. This object, which inhabits the maternal space, overlaps the masculine figures of the paternal tradition (the father and grandfather), invalidating them (blinding them, castrating them).

On a transgenerational level, a parental couple takes shape in which the father/real man reaches the matrimonial meeting delegitimized (due to the fragility of his own father figure) and is overdetermined by the father/ideal man who is within the mother, ending up emasculated. However, this hypothesis, which the analyst can pick up on without too much difficulty – relating to the patient's hysterical part, which is capable of dreaming and creating a phantasmatic idea of his own experience – does not offer the chance of an adequate interpretation. The phantasmatic combination of the old man with the girl has a less important psychical function than its delusional use as arbitrary material to bridge the vacuum of signification between the psychotic and non-psychotic parts of the personality.

Two weeks later, Nicola once again approaches the transgenerational dimension of his trauma.

> I feel anxious, controlled by my maternal grandmother. Just before my jump from the balcony, I'd had a dream. *My mother and grandmother next to each other putting bread and pizza into the oven. My grandmother was taller than my mother and together they formed a pyramid, a hierarchy.*
>
> This dream expresses my grandmother's dominant power. She stuffs me with sweet things, homemade pizzas. She has a prickly character, she's stubborn and prudish. A wild goat, a masculine figure. I'm afraid she's going to stick needles under my skin, in my eye, behind my ears, under my nails. I developed similar anxieties towards my mother. Evidently they have a common source.

- What do you think is the common source?
- The absence of my father. My father doesn't give off the strength of these insistent characters. They're solitary, dominant characters, my grandmother more so than my mother. Their shells can sting: they're porcupines covered in quills. They protect themselves against feelings, against emotions that come from outside.
- You can't get close to them, involve them: they close up and become prickly.
- Prickly, awkward, my grandmother more so than my mother.

In the following session, he recounts a dream:

> *My father's on the ledge outside a window of a building, similar to yours,*
> *Doctor, and he's trying to open it to get in, because for some reason he's been*
> *shut out. I'm on a balcony on the building opposite, really worried because*
> *I can see he's unsteadily balanced. After three attempts, he gets distracted*
> *because he's shouting something at me and he falls screaming into the void.*
> *Luckily he falls into the branches of a tree, just as actually happened to me.*
> *And he's saved. I wake up anxious.*

What happens accidentally to my father in the dream is what happened to me when I jumped from the balcony of my home. I remember the fear as I was falling, but I had to escape from *people* who wanted to harm me. Jumping was the only solution: the anxiety that they would harm me was greater than the anxiety of throwing myself off.

- Had you seen the tree?
- Yes but I didn't think I would fall onto it. I didn't want to kill myself but to stop the whirling inside me. To stop the anxiety, I risked dying.
- In the dream you feel anxious for your father.
- I'm worried about him as if it were me falling. I feel guilty because I've distracted him. Like I feel guilty for my actions. I went blindly down a path that leads who-knows-where. The fact that the building which my father falls from is yours makes me think that I abandoned the right path. I could have called you instead of jumping. I should have come into your building, got in touch with you.
- Your father tries to come in through the window and not through the door.
- He's angry with me because it was me who closed the other entrances, for the mistakes made. He has no choice but to try and break in through the window.

Nicola seems to be aware that his impossible escape from the domination of his mother damages his father. What future could his father have within him, if he remains subordinate to the manipulation in which his grandmother has closed his mother (thus becoming a victim herself, prisoner of a fate which has in store for her, in spite of herself, the role of executioner)? This awareness remains fragile as his right to life gets lost in the face of the void which opens under his feet in his attempt to break through the window: a desperate desire, without a way in to the desired object (the mother), which he tries to bring back to life in his analysis.

2. Between the door that won't open and
   the window that closes

Some weeks go by:

> Last night I dreamt that I was on a train, surrounded by women, my ex-
> classmates. I felt desired but I was immobile, mute, held back by a sense of
> shame. Sitting next to me was a girl I don't know. I managed to speak and
> seduce her. I arranged to meet her in the train toilets for a sexual encounter.
> The encounter was a failure because I couldn't keep an erection. The girl was
> frustrated and going back to the compartment, she put me down in front of
> everyone. Then the ticket inspector arrived and asked me if I wanted to fly,
> that the train flew, that it could take off. My female friends encouraged me to
> make the train fly but I stayed in my seat without moving anymore.
>
> I'd be interested to know if I should go to a specialist or continue
> with normal therapy. I don't know how to take the bull by the horns.

- The bull?
- My sexual power. The bull represents the uncertainty which sur-
  rounds my sexual sphere.
- Would trusting in a "specialist" be a way of distancing yourself
  from your erection as something that comes from within yourself?
- It's true that I tend to see it as something mechanical, distant from
  my emotions.
- Something external from yourself, to trust to the erection plumber.
- That means that I separate my erection from myself. Interesting.

A few sessions later, he comes back to the dream in which his father fell.

- My father falls due to a sense of shame. I'm closed to sex.
- Like the window.
- Yes, I don't let myself be penetrated. My father falls because I can't
  come in through that door.
- Wasn't it a window? A window from which one looks out but also a
  door through which one enters. A communication with the outside.
- An outside which is a ledge overlooking the void.
- A communication with the void.

Nicola sees the door/window (the entrance of the man/the looking out
of the woman) in communication with the void. The door is closed, so the
father cannot enter and the mother (grandmother) – and also the patient
who is identified with himself – cannot look out onto life. The patient is
divided between the closed mother and the unsteadily balanced father in
the marriage relationship and within himself (because his feminine part is

closed to him). The fall condenses the fall of the man (fall of the erection) with the fear of the erotic encounter, experienced as a leap in the dark of the closed woman.

In the background there remains the hypothesis of the fall as a leap (Nicola's real leap from the balcony of his home): not the rising (left without paternity) of the man towards the door but the flight from the window, an impossible challenge to the laws of gravity, of a bird-mother.

In the following session he says:

- My father falls into the abyss and I feel abandoned. In the end he's saved but that doesn't save me from loneliness. It was as if I'd closed the windows. Standing, like my father, outside the window unsteadily balanced.
- You're torn between two opposing desires: having a relationship with the woman and at the same time preferring her closed. Thus your father and you are unsteadily balanced.
- My mother's closed to my father, there's no doubt. And also B., the girl at university, was closed to men, that's what I liked about her. My mother is obtuse, introverted, there's no key to unlock her introversion, no combination.
- You're afraid to approach the relationship with the man, to fall into the void, the abyss.
- You're telling me I protect the woman from her desire to enter into a relationship with the man.

I realize that the phantasmatic fabric of his experience is acquiring greater definition and consistency. This allows greater space for the interpretation of his form of creating meaning and leads towards a focus on the identification of the patient with the woman's fear of letting herself go, of dissolving her body in orgasm. Even so, the symbolic texture remains discontinuous, gaping despite the improved consistency of its fabric. The reproposal in a symbolic form in the dream of the concrete act of flying/falling certainly reduces the tearing of psychic space which should have accepted the pain (caused by the collapse of the emotional pillars holding up the meeting with the desired object) but does not eliminate it. The void remains active and threatens the process of recomposition of living flesh in Nicola's experience.

It is highly possible that his erection is threatened by his feminine part's fear of letting go into the overinvolvement, but it is necessary to distinguish between his condition and that of a patient whose symbolical/hysterical texture holds up without profound tearing. In the latter case, the fear of involvement (experienced as loss of the self without finding it again) may lead either to an erection of desire which is entirely based on stimulation and remains superficial or to the perception of one's own penis as something dangerous (a perception which leads to erectile impotence or premature ejaculation). In Nicola, by contrast, this fear of involvement goes well beyond his unconscious identification with his mother's fear of orgasm.[6] The actual possibility of his involvement is largely precluded, and feeling desirous exposes him to the threat of losing his sense of the existence of his body: this also precludes *a priori* the possibility of an erection, the finalization of his desire.

This external understanding which psychoanalytical knowledge offers nevertheless risks not being of any use and even being damaging, since it is fraught with an objective truth which arbitrarily fills the void of a subjective truth, making it worse. The only thing that counts is the loss of meaning which no external reconstruction can repair, since it is by starting from this loss that the subject's torn subjectivity can re-weave its fabric with its own material. This re-weaving, which follows original pre-symbolic paths, can be accepted and reflected in the analytical relationship, but cannot be constructed by it according to the codes of shared symbolization. Following the symbolic discourse together with the patient in the places where it has survived requires the analyst's constant attention, so as not to overstep in a precocious attempt to bridge the space of a discourse which is all still to come, starting from the *ex novo* birth of its roots. The symbolic signification must follow the paths of mental tissue which has stayed alive and stop at its lacunae, avoiding the creation of an incorrect artificial tissue which fills the void of inertia. This would further suppress the excluded life, which spontaneously tends to reappear and expand if it is given the chance and acceptance. Only when new living tissue takes shape and the vascularization of desire has unified the new living tissue with the old can the exploration of new symbolic meanings make possible the expansion of the meaning of existence.

In this initial phase of Nicola's analysis, *the tree that saves* – seen in its symbolic signifier and concreteness – bridges and, at the same time, leaves open the lack of signification as it takes shape in the convergence without meeting of the door which opens and the window which looks out onto life.

Before the erection: smearing the canvas

One day Nicola appears particularly discouraged.

- I can't manage to take off.
- I'm thinking of the ticket inspector who asked you in a dream if you wanted to make the train fly.
- Good point! I said no but I would have liked to. It would be like my dreams coming true with girls. Their invitation to accept, I felt it as an invitation to a sexual encounter. But I'm afraid of flying, I don't feel

sexually adequate. The ticket inspector makes me think of someone who's already had that experience.

- Why should having an erection, making love to a girl, be a legendary feat, making a train fly? It seems like one of Hercules' labours.
- A Herculean feat. Astonish the woman. A superior performance. Making love like an act of total fusion. A rebus: an erection beyond normality. A powerful bull advancing unopposed.
- You and the woman fused into a bull.
- Everything centres on the performance. I don't see sex as something which follows an emotional involvement, but as a bull-like performance to fulfil with the woman. Without communicating with her. I remember a dream in which *an anaemic horse vomited continuously on a metallic, mechanical, robotic thing. The horse was disgusted. It was refusing what it had to keep inside.*
- The vomit is connected to the metallic structure, I think.
- Yes, the metallic structure provokes the vomit. It's something dead. The horse is anorexic, whatever it takes in. It has to expel things that aren't its own, but it can't. Inedible things.
- Of the same material as the metallic structure.
- Yes, dead material which isn't functional to the horse's life. I should get away from the mechanical dimension, but that frightens me because I'm really inside this dimension of the world. I'm like an unreined horse, indomitable, which encounters the mechanical nature of the relationship as an obstacle.
- The horse, the bull force the desire to be unreined, untamed, towards a mechanical dimension.

Silence.

- I sense something but I find it difficult to define.

A few sessions later.

I'm in the bathroom of my home. It's all red and yellow. I see my head as if I were floating above it. On my head there's a lot more space than there should be. There are enormous pimples. I see them from within. Scabs with pieces of brain stuck inside.

The image of *pimples* was disturbing: a malformation, a sort of tumour. You could actually see pieces of brain outside of the head stuck to these scabs. They were on the scalp.

- They weren't part of your brain.
- No, they were outside of my head. Malformations on my skin caused by chemical agents in which parasites were stuck. They

were really delicate pustules. They could be squeezed but they would explode like a geyser. Cerebral matter would come out, together with pus, infected material.

- Where did the cerebral matter come from?
- As if it came from my brain and was infected by contact with the air.
- The matter which came from you met a parasite which came from outside.
- Inside-outside. It's as if my mind was made of parasites. They come from outside but they're already in my mind.
- What do you think of the red and yellow of the bathroom? A strong contrast.
- They pre-empt something disturbing. I might have seen them on the poster for the film *The Great Beauty*. In the film a little girl smears a canvas and covers it with all the colours of the rainbow. At a certain point, the canvas becomes an almost mauvish brown. The same colour which appears in my bathroom.
- What does the little girl smearing make you think of?
- Rubbing things together, contrasting. The girl cries while she's contrasting the colours together. I too would cry if I touched the pustules. In my dream the colours come from my imagination, it's as if they were created by me.
- You feel that thoughts which are not yours have infected your mind. You want to distinguish them from your thoughts, free yourself of them with a gesture that frees something beautiful: the geyser. Anyway they're stuck: they're inside-outside, they've become a skin infection, an infection of what's between the inside and the outside. Breaking this puzzle has the same meaning for you as the freedom of contrasting, jarring the colours on the canvas, giving shape to your thoughts without letting yourself be guided by forms which do not originate within yourself. But you find yourself in the same situation as the girl: freedom has a dose of rage which is part of it, it brings with it crying, the pain of smearing, of dirtying.
- In analysis things come out which are important to me but which others might consider strange, which make me wrinkle my nose, twisted things. Things you can't say. If you say them, you give them shape. You have to repress them.
- If they're things that are taking shape, why call them twisted?
- Could I say things freely, as they come to me, accepting them without judging them?
- How can you judge something while it's taking shape? Expect it to have a shape from the start, to have a shape before it takes it on?

He does not comment on my words. As he is leaving at the end of the session, he unexpectedly says: "Thanks".

The "viper": a frightening shape

After a few weeks, Nicola says to me:

- Today I feel less tense, more open to life. But this puts up a wall of fear in me, it creates a void in me. *I dreamed of a friend of mine who was running in a park. He seemed mad to me.* The movement makes me anxious. Anything that can take on a shape.
- A movement which can give shape to something.
- Anything which doesn't have a shape, which is unresolved makes me anxious. I take a frame and put things inside it. Once, in the third year of high school, the [female] teacher put us in a circle and invited us to talk. My lips started trembling. The idea of the frame started then: things taking shape in front of me in a frame filled with anxiety. With a brush I drew a reality turned against me, my mother telling me that I'm not doing well. Talking in front of others spread in a circle terrifies me. As if I were naked. Struck with anxiety, I tremble.
- Trembling can be the joint result of your wish to run and stay inside the frame at the same time.
- I believe so. I feel a friction inside me.

A month later he recounts a dream:

> *I'm talking to my mother and my maternal grandmother is also there. I criticise my grandmother and then I see that on my mother's back there's a viper with its head between her shoulder blades and its tail attached to her belt. It's as if the viper were part of her outfit.*
> My grandmother loves me in a selfish way, she isn't really interested in my happiness. My mother's sometimes like that: you can feel my grandmother's influence on her.
> Two days earlier, I had another dream: *a girl I really liked was interested in another guy. Paradoxically I managed to get into intimate contact with her, we established a dialogue.* I was struck by this new form of relationship with a woman. The girl in the dream interested me but I gave up any contact with her when she started seeing someone else. In the dream the opposite happens.

- If you accept the presence of a rival, the woman becomes more accessible. The presence of your father next to your mother, a father who doesn't fall off the window ledge, makes the relationship with her more peaceful.

- I've thought about that. But then I had this dream with the viper. It's better to have nothing to do with vipers. I'm afraid of them, they can strike unexpectedly. They're unpredictable.
- It's difficult to face something unexpected, the void you can fall into while we approach what we desire, which turns love or hate into a viper in us or in the other. The viper is something between you and your mother, fear of the unexpected, of the immediate event that can strike, hurt a lot.
- I agree.

I think that on the level of the primary encounter, the viper represents a catastrophic, unpredictable void in his meeting with the desired object, while on a more evolved level, he uses the mental fabric which has survived the collapse to represent a conflict which entails a mortal danger (destructive manipulation or hate).[7] Recognising his father's presence through jealousy, Nicola can criticize his grandmother and her malign influence on the object of his love, his mother, but he gains nothing better than the incumbency of death, which forces him to retreat. Either way, for the first time a terror without representation (an unexpected void) is beginning to take shape, which is not the viper itself, but the catastrophic speed of its unpredictable movement.

After about three weeks, Nicola associates the dream of the viper with the anxiety he always feels. He describes the anxiety as an almost electric dimension, "a lightning bolt" which goes through him. It almost excites him. In one of the following sessions he says:

- Three years ago I got a tattoo on my back: a *dragonfly*. The dragonfly as a symbol of a transformation, a landing. At a recent dinner they asked me to take off my T-shirt to show the tattoo. I did so. They were saying "strip, strip". There were also some girls. I joked to one of them: "You want me to strip to see the dragonfly, not to go to bed with me".

I note that the viper has gradually been associated with the lightning bolt, where the catastrophic movement finds its distressing link with desire (a desire which "burns" instantly), and with the dragonfly, the unbearable lightness, the evanescence of the loved object.

Nicola moves to another city to pursue a Master's degree in journalism. His brother lives in the same city, but they do not share an apartment. He continues his analysis with the same frequency (two sessions a week). The family therapy also continues.

Shortly after his move, he recounts a dream:

I'm speeding really fast on the motorway towards Milan, where my woman is, but I'm driving with skis on my feet. It's hard to control the car and

I realise that going at such a speed, I might miss the exit for Milan. I decide to leave the motorway early. At the exit there's a barrier and a crash happens, but the car has already disappeared and I'm on skis and I'm saved. However, I can't get to Milan.

Once, I came down a ski-slope really fast through other skiers, without causing any damage, but the instructor told me off. I'm thinking of the dream about the viper. A few days ago, I dreamed about a girl who looked like my mother.

- The viper could be related to anxiety linked to freedom, to the unpredictability which destroys the relationship.
- That's true, I don't feel free to do as I want. But freedom doesn't make me anxious.
- Perhaps what makes you anxious is the worry that freedom isn't compatible with the relationship. So you might be tempted to go further, to be free beyond every relationship. A reckless challenge with the risk of going off the road. You can't slip like a viper through the other skiers.

He laughs.

- I've always found freedom and relationships incompatible.

The search for a shape

In a phone call from his father, I discover that Nicola is no longer following the Master's degree, although he is still living in the other city, seeing few friends and spending most of his time alone. In the meantime, he is beginning to have fewer dreams.

After many sessions without dreams, one day he recounts two. In the first dream, *there are shapeshifters. They're beings who possess people, take over their lives and actually kill them.* In the second dream, *he is in a session with me but on the couch there is his brother. Nicola is in a dark corner of the room in silence and he feels very lonely.* His brother, he says, is not afraid of life; he'll be fulfilled in his job.

I have the impression that something of the psychotic abrasion of his experience, which has always threatened the dream fabric of his idea of himself and of the world, is giving way to a potential of mental life which, even if in an elementary, precarious way, is managing to take shape.

I sketch an interpretation:

- Your brother represents the part of you which could fit into social life. But another part of you risks not being recognized in your analysis and remaining in the dark, set aside.

- It's a part of me that's always been isolated.
- In the dream it reappears as a presence that is also an absence. It's an absence that is beginning to be present. We can't ignore this absence and only work with the socializing, performative part.
- I've always given more importance to effectiveness than to substance. I don't trust my things.
- You use things which take shape not from yourself but from outside. So you surrender your place to a shapeshifting monster.
- I'm thinking about a dog. Something that changes shape without being a monster. This dog knocks at the door of a villa. They don't let it in. They feed it from a dish. The dog goes away and turns into a duck. A hunter shoots the duck. The duck turns into a tortoise. A wolf takes the tortoise and carries it to its lair. The tortoise turns into a bat, leaves the lair and turns back into a dog. The dog goes back to the villa and turns into a man. The man knocks at the door and this time they let him in. Inside, the villa is large but bare, gloomy. The man leaves the villa, disappointed.
- When you try to give shape to your experience, to your emotions, there's always someone who shoots at you, attacks you.
- Are you the protagonist of the story?
- I identify with the feeling of sadness which the man has when he leaves the villa.

One day, a few weeks later, Nicola says to me (after about half an hour of silence without any apparent signs of anxiety):

- There's something which has nothing to do with giving shape to an experience: it's being calm without thinking of anything in particular.

I think that his exile in another city is an attempt to create an intermediary space between the impossible escape (wandering in an undefined space with the risk of falling into the void) and the oppressive atmosphere of maternal expectations (the shapeshifting monster). And I feel that the *present absence* of his last dream is becoming the "material" of our relationship.

One day he says to me:

- I live for the pleasure of small things, I listen to music. I love creativity – it's linked to passion. Not to the sheep sleeping in the meadow, as I feel I am now.
- And if you were to put passion into it?
- I'm thinking of a falcon, a falcon flying, dominating the situations from above.

On the couch, the Nicola of intense dreamworld activity has given way to the part of himself which was previously in the dark. This other part – the properly psychotic one which is once more facing life, with countless difficulties – looks at reality in an elementary way, without symbols, intentional instruments.

This perspective appears within me during a session, like the natural landing of my previous disquiet: the tension between the sensation of greater calm in Nicola and the evidence of a reluctance to connect which creates a frame for the absence of dreams.

Nicola starts the session in silence. He seems particularly calm. After about ten minutes, I note a certain tension in the widening of the fingers of his right hand, making them paler. I ask him what he is thinking about.

- I wouldn't know. I'm living without passion and without anxiety. The falcon is still. Passion doesn't lead to anything. Better to deal with practical things.
- It's difficult to deal with practical things without passion.
- That's true. Anyway, I'm not the falcon. Maybe my passion interrupts the anxiety, an alarm. Even if I don't know if it's really anxiety. I'd say worry.
- Which interrupts your passions, things as you'd like to do them.
- The alarm often interrupts the things I like.
- Perhaps the alarm is the contrast between the falcon's movement and the pleasure it gives and the absence of movement of the sheep.

Two weeks later he suddenly announces that his brother is about to graduate.

- I don't think I'll ever become like my brother, I'll never reach his position: it's out of my reach.
- You're afraid that the secluded part of you won't be able to join the part of you that dreams. In the last dream that you recounted.

A long silence.

- Occasionally when I come here, I hear music. Is there someone who plays in the building?
- Yes, there's someone who plays the piano.
- Today he hasn't been playing. I like hearing it. This is a moment when I would have liked to hear it. I'm in a good state of mind.

Final considerations

The void which occurs in the psychotic patient's primary encounter with the mother creates a profound fracture between the part of his/her subjectivity which has collapsed under the pain of the void – which he/she was not capable of accepting – and the part that has survived the collapse, which seeks to contain its impact. The latter part is not in direct contact with the void or with the collapse and withholds the pain only in the muted, weakened forms in which it arrives. In one way, the fracture between the gravely damaged part (psychotic) and the part which has survived (relatively healthy) of his/her subjectivity reproduces the void which has developed between the spontaneous subject and life. Alienated from life, but at the same time from that part of himself which remains laboriously attached to it, Nicola, in his most intimate, intrinsic truth, feels more real, alive through his absence.

He cannot escape from this condition except by starting from that which might spring up spontaneously within him, and which is a long way from having an accomplished configuration. This concerns his experience left without borders and collapsed in on itself at the moment in which, by moving, it was about to take shape. Left in his psyche as potential, it tends to reappear spontaneously and occupy the space which belongs to it, but the recurrence of the absence of borders hangs over it like a mortal threat. Faced with this prospect – the least visible part of his anxiety, hidden beneath its more evolved form, the fear of harming that which he desires – Nicola defends himself by navigating in the safer waters of an "intellectual" relationship – as he himself defines it – with reality, in which the relatively healthy part of his subjectivity takes advantage of a symbolic dream fabric of representation and bridges the gaps with a purely cognitive reliance on language.

I have tried not to follow the inviting prospect of deeply interpreting the complex, rich dream material which Nicola produced for many months. I have limited myself to elaborating some perspectives, keeping them alive, so as to allow the part of his desire which has survived. Within the analysis, this allowed the necessary tension to be maintained between two truths: that of the unconscious phantasy, never capable of converging towards a sufficiently defined form and constantly on the point of sliding into the abyss of non-sense, and that truth awaiting a movement and a space even before a shape – in the knowledge that in the absence of tension, the gap between the two truths would be bridged by delusion or retreat.

If one gives in to the temptation to work too much on the relatively healthy part of the patient, the division between that and the psychotic part becomes accentuated. Words become disembodied, losing their link to the spontaneous movement of the body and its expressivity.[8] The delirium moves into the background, but remains active and silently expands until it re-explodes.

None of my interpretations, considered for what they are, were genuinely good. I used them above all to face the occasional necessity of incomprehension between myself and Nicola,[9] which forced my working comprehension to change perspective, leaving space for the patient's psychical movement to evolve and affect the relationship. Reflecting on this movement, accepting it into my mental and emotive disposition, with the deconstruction of my vision which that entailed, was the real aim of my work of interpretation. In work with psychotic patients, it is in the radical transformation of our way of seeing and experiencing them that they are reflected and manage to exist as whole people.

The important element is that a spontaneous part of the patient's existence, left without an approach to life, on the point of revealing itself and at the same time on the brink of the abyss, can begin moving again without collapsing once again in a definitive, irremediable way. Only the patient holds the key to this return, which is an *ex novo* realization and requires the analyst to recognize it as an Indispensable part of the patient's relationship with life (since it is pure life rising again from death).

The figure of the viper was an important passage in Nicola's analysis. On a more evolved level, still very fragile, this figure was a proto-symbolic element of transition from the purely subjective to the objective (Winnicott). The serpent here was not a symbol of the penis but represented hate and the unexpected as the venom of love.

On a more primitive level, the connection between the figures of the viper (the unexpected), the lightning bolt (the immediate) and the dragonfly (the ephemeral) – which on a more evolved level converge towards a meaning: "the immediate which suddenly sets" – represented above all a repair, though still inadequate, of the mental fabric supporting the symbolic texture and containing the failure of symbolization. What counted was the coming back into play of potential psychical content which had collapsed while about to take shape: thus the viper, in its spontaneous, elemental sense, was psychical movement which threatened the order of the world (the encounter with his mother) and, collapsing, made the world inaccessible. This became clear in the movement of the falcon, the psychical surge which is the spontaneous movement of the body and which seeks to overcome failure but remains suspended, waiting in silence.

One day Nicola said to me:

• I don't see how it's possible to heal with words. I wonder why you believe it is.

I answered:

• I don't believe you can heal with words. You heal with what lies behind the words and you bring it out. However, words can be useful to set in motion what lies behind them.

Notes

1 This chapter has been translated into English by Peter Henderson.
2 *Forclusion* in French.
3 Between subjective use and shared objective use of words, there exists a reciprocal determination (which implies a certain tension) which makes experiences

both expressively and socially communicable. The conflict between these two dimensions is basic to all linguistic deformations (starting from Freudian slips) and finds its most complete expression in the dream phantom.

4 Freud speaks about this at length in *The Unconscious Mind* when he states that in psychotics only conscious ideas are invested (investment of unconscious ideas is lacking).

5 If in the perversion of desire, the subject has to deal with the excessive maternal interpretation which dominates, in the psychotic subject it is the impersonal violence of the maternal void which he/she seeks desperately to contain, giving it the significance of interpretational violence.

6 In fact, this identification represents the attempt by the relatively healthy part of the self to re-take control of the perception of its own body.

7 On a more evolved level, the viper might have something to do with the patient himself (who like a snake raised at her breast can strike the mother in the back) and, at the same time, with the poisonous maternal intrusiveness, connected to its link to the grandmother and its meaning in the relationship with Nicola's father. A reciprocal mortal danger, a land of vipers.

8 The void is always an emptiness of body and spontaneous gesture.

9 Occasionally made explicit by Nicola himself.

References and further readings

Aulagnier, P. (1975). *La violence de l'interpretation*. Paris: Presses Universitaires de France (English edition: *The Violence of Interpretation*, The New Library of Psychoanalysis 2001).

Freud, S. (1894). *The Neuro-Psychoses of Defence. The Standard Edition of the Complete Psychological Works of Sigmund Freud, Volume III (1893–1899)*. Early Psycho-Analytic Publications, 1962.

Green, A. (1993). *Le travail du negatif*. Paris: Éditions de Minuit (English edition: *The Work of the Negative*. London: Free Association Books, 1999).

Thanopulos, S. (2003). *La preclusione della significazione soggettiva nella relazione primaria e la costruzione delirante* (The preclusion of the subjective signification of the primary relationship and the construction of delusion) in *Stati caotici della mente* (Chaotic states of the mind). Edited by L. Rinaldi. Milan: Raffaello Cortina Editore, 2003.

Thanopulos, S. (2009). *Lo spazio dell'interpretazione* (The space of interpretation). Rome: Edizioni Borla, 2009.

Winnicott, D. (1964). *Fear of Breakdown in Psycho-analytic Explorations*. London: Karnac Books, 1989.

Part III

Particularities of thought

Chapter 9

The reversal of thinking

Bion's theory of psychosis

Giuseppe Civitarese

The "reversal of thinking" is the most cogent and concise expression that comes to my mind to indicate what immense contribution Bion made to the understanding of psychosis. His key hypothesis is that with psychosis we are in the presence of an alpha function that is structurally deficient. It must also be said that for Bion the term "psychosis" has more to do with one type of thought than with a specific pathology. Psychotic functioning reflects the conflict between the "truth drive" (Grotstein, 1975), which can be understood as the search for mutual recognition with the other (and respect for reality), and the ability of human beings to self-deceive in order to survive. Only a truth that is sustainable can be accepted, because otherwise it could prove traumatic.

The "reversal of thinking", which is based on the fine mechanism of so-called transformations into hallucinosis (T→H), is not even exclusively a property of seriously ill patients, but also of the psychotic part of each person's mind. There is a difference in degree but not in nature. Bion's concept of the psychotic part of personality is invaluable because it demands that we do without pathological splits, those that determine psychosis, and use instead non-pathological, that is to say, dynamic or dialectical splits. In this case, it requires us to consider that there is a gradient between the normal states of hallucinosis and the most severe manifestations of psychotic disorders, even those on the spectrum of schizophrenia, which is the type of disease in which these processes appear most evident (Grinberg and al., 1975). Transcending this caesura is an essential exercise because it immediately re-humanizes the patient and avoids identifying him with a condition of absolute and impenetrable alienation.

However, before examining the concept of T→H what I have called the fine mechanism of the "reversal of thinking", I would like to present a vignette to show how some of Bion's main concepts, and in particular those of reverie and negative alpha function, can be used in clinical practice. I would also like to point out straight away that the model I shall be outlining can obviously be extended to the "container" represented not by the mind of the individual therapist but by the group of carers.

The earthquake

R. arrives and lies down on the couch. For a while, she remains silent. Then she asks whether I am feeling well ("Erm . . . how are you doing, doctor?"). Her question makes me feel somewhat embarrassed and uneasy. I hesitate a couple of seconds and then answer – "yes, I'm fine". I feel that being silent would not be the right choice. Then, in a tone conveying that I am interested to know why she asked that question, I add: "And you?" (that is, "Why are you asking me the question in this way?"). She replies: "Everybody hates me, and rightfully so". I suddenly realize that, in spite of the apparent politeness of her manner, she is tense, almost angry. And then, just as abruptly, a very vivid scene, similar to a daydream, comes to my mind: I see R. getting up from the couch and assaulting me violently (!). In a fraction of a second I consider that she may have a gun, and with the two of us alone in the room I would not stand a chance: she would quite simply do away with me. A few minutes pass, and then R. says: "Have there been any deaths in Pavia in the past few days?" I ask her, very surprised and alarmed: "Why should there have been?" R. replies: "I don't know, like an earthquake or something". Another few minutes of silence follow. I wonder what kind of relation there can be between her belief that everybody hates her, my reverie and her idea about earthquakes and deaths. I ask her whether she can or wants to tell me something more about what (allegedly) happened in Pavia. After a long silence, she replies: "I don't know, I have nothing more to say on this subject".

Never as in the treatment of psychosis do we experience situations in which Bion's phrase about the analyst and the patient being two frightened and dangerous animals seem so true, or equally the image of the analyst as an officer in battle. What also comes to mind is Ogden's observation (2006, p. 1081, italics added) that it is hardly surprising that analytic patients "fly at us after we have prematurely put into words something which for most of their lives has been unconscious. *What has been unconscious has been so for good reason*". But what had happened here? Why, at least in the virtuality of my reverie, did the patient "throw" herself at me?

The session I am describing was the first one of the week, on a Monday. R. hadn't been up to coming to the previous session. A few days earlier something serious had happened to her family that had affected R. very much: her older brother had nearly lost his life in a car crash. A veritable "earthquake", and indeed, one that was also immediately transferred onto the stage of the treatment. Reflecting on R.'s utterance "Everybody hates me", I hypothesize that R. has gone through a process of unconscious turmoil whereby she has found herself dealing with her attack on her father (whom she deeply hates), and that is here displaced onto her brother and onto me (because of the session she missed; it does not matter that it was *her* decision not to come), as well as with the imaginary retaliation of both.

The aggressive fantasy and the guilt had challenged the patient's ability to transform raw sensory and emotional data into alpha elements (mainly images), an activity that can be considered as the first step in the process of symbolization. However, since this ability – in Bion's word her alpha function – was underdeveloped, the resulting emotional tsunami sparked off a kind of fear even deeper than the threat of retaliation by her father and by me (which would have still provided R. with some form of meaning, however distressing): the terror of non-representation (Botella and Botella, 2001).

R. seems to have experienced all these events as a major threat that had shaken the very foundations of her existence, that is, the intimate core called "sensory floor" by Ogden and meta-Ego by Bleger (Civitarese, 2008) – the symbiotic-psychotic-primitive-undifferentiated part of the personality. Only at a superficial level does the "accident" of the missed session reflect R.'s conflict with her brother/father. In effect, however, it is a wound opened in the body of the setting as concrete-symbolization (an oxymoron), or, better still, as the beginning of a process of symbolization of what was once a pre-Oedipal hole in the being of the subject.

At this stage, R. is not able to think, nor to transform, this set of highly entangled emotions, which remain sheer sensorial proto-emotions, or beta elements: "elements like an unpremeditated blow which is related to, but is not, thought" (Bion, 1977, p. 3). These psychic entities cannot give rise to visual images, pictograms or oneiric thoughts that can be used for dreaming or thinking. They can only be evacuated through acting out, delusion (which, from this standpoint, can be understood as having a self-containing function) or hallucinations (which we could regard, however, as the first step of representation or beta elements). Thought reverts to its primitive concrete quality. There is no longer any distance (or perhaps only an extremely small distance) between words and things. In this respect, to the extent that both events share the features of concrete thought, missing a session and being delusional are equivalent to each other. R. cannot shift from the level of symbolic equation to that of symbolic equivalence. At present, she is able neither to dream nor to be awake, because she cannot create the contact-barrier, in other words, the semi-permeable film made of proto-sensorial and proto-emotional micro-units transformed into alpha elements (which may also be stored in our memory) that separates consciousness from the unconscious. For this reason, in order not to produce any further shocks to R.'s private system of meanings, my approach is to measure my words very carefully – that is to say, to reduce the voltage of interpretation as much as possible.

In such situations, it is essential that the patient's emotions are (to a minimal, sustainable and yet sufficient degree) identified and named by the analyst, who, by adopting the patient's perspective and cautiously commenting on the explicit layer of his narratives, actually sustains and develops his capacity for thought (both thought and feeling). In fact the oscillation band of the emotional unison, that is, the ability to tolerate points of view different from one's own, is very narrow (Ferro, 2010). For example, Green (1983) warns against being silent. In the area of narcissistic disorders, silence can sometimes plunge the analysis into a funereal boredom. It is better to use the setting as a transitional field and to act as a constantly alive, interested and awake object – who, I would add, is passionate, prompt and respectful. Only in this way can the analyst testify to the patient her (the analyst's) vitality through her associative ties or ability to engage in reverie, without for this reason going beyond neutrality and without slipping into intrusive interpretation. Silence would be traumatic, although sometimes you have to tolerate it for a long time. At the same time the best attitude to take is to behave as if there were no limit to the time available and to put aside any kind of therapeutic zeal.

R.'s resort to a psychotic solution to her unconscious predicament suggests that she has not received the "psychic nutrients" that normally enable one to introject the capacity to attribute meaning to one's experience, especially in situations when this is significantly challenged by an overflow of disturbing stimuli. This capacity is the alpha function, and the nutrient factors include being listened to, held in the mind and dreamt; in metapsychological terms it is the dynamics of projective identification/reverie (as well as container/contained). If the mother (*caregiver*) is not receptive to her child's anxieties, these will "bounce back" on the child in an even more virulent form and may generate a "nameless terror" (Bion) or induce a state of "psychic agony" (Winnicott). In such cases, instead of introjecting the maternal thinking function, the child will introject a reversed, negative function (the opposite of thinking-dreaming) characterized by attacks on the link of oneiric thoughts in the process of dreaming and thinking – and, therefore, of giving meaning to his experience. Unlike less severe mental conditions, psychoses (and the psychotic nuclei in the mind) probably result from a relative lack of maternal alpha function, the deficit of primary symbolization Lacan termed "foreclosure".

Such a deficit in a person's ability to learn from experience – in other words, the ability to think/dream – generates a negative process, a downward spiral with obvious, disastrous consequences. Of course, my understanding of the word "dream/dreaming" in this context is informed by the Bionian revolution of psychoanalytic theory, whereby dreaming, in Ogden's words (2009, p. 104), is: "the most free, the most inclusive, and most deeply penetrating form of psychological work of which human beings are capable [. . .] the principal medium through which we achieve human consciousness, psychological growth, and the capacity to create personal, symbolic meaning from our lived experience".

A corollary of this theory is that the dream space, which is equivalent to the space of subjectivity and also of the unconscious as the matrix of every symbolization, is not given at birth, but must be created within the primary relationship with the object. It takes two to make a mind (or to enable a mind to develop again), and one of the two must be able to symbolize, in other words, be able to carry within itself the paternal signifier, the third). As Kojève (1947), an author who inspired both Lacan and Ogden, writes, summing up briefly the Hegelian conception of the nature of subjectivity, it takes at least two people to make one. In fact, in normal conditions we should say at least three, if we rightfully include the "paternal metaphor or function".

The concept of paternal function can mean various things. Already at birth it intervenes in the two-party relationship as an internal presence in the mind of the mother, who has another object of investment in addition to the child. In the same way the analyst is perceived as someone who has his own private life, other patients, his own interests and so on. The third/father as a separating element, as bearer of the Law, of the sense of limit and of reality, appears then in all the inevitable (and necessary – I'm not saying arbitrary) moments of affective disjunction or lack of attunement resulting from the absence of the other; and this is also what happens in the session between patient and analyst. Finally, it is present in the structuring function of the setting, which ensures a vital dialectic of identity and difference, a rhythm of absences and presences, of hate and love. Finally, it is above all the mother's ability to say "no" and to modulate the distance from the baby.

The key aspect that I am trying to highlight with the vignette is a certain use of reverie in the session, and thus how the new experience of the therapeutic relationship can change things. My reverie with R., the fantasy and fear of being murdered, was involved in the process of giving meaning to a nameless terror that R. might have experienced in her early life, and that can be inferred from her deficiency in alpha function reflected by her previous acting out and delusion. The extremely vivid scene suddenly generated in my mind adds the idiosyncratic "texture" of my emotional reaction to the catastrophic scenery of the earthquake described by R., involving death, destruction, ruin, urgency, survivors, anxiety and a general "end-of-the-world" feeling. From within myself I retrieve a kind of somato-psychic integration, whereby I respond "in parallel" through thought processes just as regressive as R.'s dereistic communication. However, R.'s delusions are better understood not when they are interpreted as misperceptions or misjudgements in the broad sense but (potentially) as "hyper-perceptions" that grasp her personal truth about the interpsychic, historical and relational scenario she finds herself in. From this multiple standpoint, the image of the earthquake appears to have several closely intertwined layers of significance. It is simultaneously the foreclosure/ inversion of the alpha function, R.'s brother accident, the gap in (the body of) the session and, finally, a delusion – in other words, a return to the concrete signification of the body. To sum up, an unsustainable emotional flood rooted in R.'s infantile neurosis reveals at the same time her fragile Ego structure.

To put it very briefly, an unsustainable emotional wave that is set off by the impact of an event that has awakened childhood neurosis unmasks a fragile constitution of the Ego and, as soon as the right frame is found, pervades the analytic field and causes it to "fall ill". The more sensorial (hallucinatory) the quality of the analyst's reverie, the higher the degree of thinkability achievable by very early traumas suffered by the patient in non-verbal or pre-reflexive stages of his life. The reverie is the locus where the patient's partially obstructed oneiric area and the (hopefully more accommodating) oneiric space of the analyst overlap – it is where the analysis actually takes place. My reverie about getting killed (so emotionally charged that for a moment I felt genuinely frightened!) is in some respects the fulfillment of my readiness and willingness to dream R.'s undreamt dream. This type of interaction recurs in several mental disorders – not only psychoses, but also psychosomatic illnesses, autistic nuclei, perversions, drug addiction, various kinds of somatization, non-affective states of mind, self-destructive actings and so forth. Thanks to my unexpected reverie, I manage to connect with R. on a deeper level: I get in tune with the bodily quality of her emotions and her terror of getting killed – in other words, with a very archaic state of psychic agony. This is precisely what Bion means by his phrases "becoming the O of the patient" and "allowing the O of the session to evolve": going beyond conscious identification, and transcending a merely rational approach to the comprehension and analysis of the events.

As in more mentalized types of conflict, the traumas ingrained in the inaccessible unconscious cannot be worked through *in effigie*, "talked about" or simply "made known", but *need to be reenacted* on the scene of analysis – in this case, first and foremost in the body of analysis, that is to say, in the non-processual aspects of the setting – where they need to encounter the analyst's capacity for reverie. If an analyst were not willing to play all the necessary roles in this game, he would act as the too intelligent mother described by Bion in *Transformations*, an exact counterpart of the non-receptive mother. I believe that this is the rule in a number of disorders: psychosis, but also psychosomatic diseases, autism shells, perversions, drug addiction, somatization, anaffective states, etc. In my opinion, a post-Bionian theory of the analytic field puts the analyst in the best state to exercise this vital function. Like other psychic productions, such as ideas, memories or sudden and transitory bodily sensations, reverie is a probe that allows us to grasp the unconscious dimension of the analytic field. Reverie is equivalent to that slight surprise that helps us perceive the emergence of the unconscious as something that is not "under" or "behind" – in some storeroom/reservoir/sack/recipient – but *inside* the conscious, as long as we know how to interpret it. Thus, by entering into a state of deep, somatic-psychic attunement we can expand the psychic container (a process that weaves emotional threads into an ever-stronger fabric that can hold contents in suspension).

The terror that unexpectedly pervades the analytic field, seen as the intersection of mutual projective identifications between patient and analyst, becomes the disturbing emotion/thought to be dissolved for the most part through narration. It is an emotion (an agony that belongs to the patient but that enters the field) – perhaps the fear of being annihilated by fantasies relating to the conflictual relationship with the father? – that the patient feels without knowing that he does and for which I manage to provide at least the outline of a set and a script. And this is true even if it is a nightmare, and even if the micro-transformation that takes place is only a shift from an un-dreamt dream to an interrupted dream. To tell R. all this, however, would serve no purpose – either in the immediate future or probably also for a long time. On the contrary, it would probably heighten her experience of persecution.

We now see the sequence of events in external reality that precipitated a crisis, the way in which R. experiences it as a catastrophe in her internal world, and how she brings it into the session and into the transference. The skipped session takes on the meaning of replicating the earthquake that perhaps occurred in distant times in the primary relationship with the mother, and the very recent one that produced the acute psychotic episode in which an Oedipal conflict might be active. It also anticipates the turbulence of the emotional field of the analysis. The psychotic part of the personality comes back in the role of Civil Protection, and delusional thinking begins to flourish again. From the technical point of view it is not so much a matter of interpreting the unconscious dynamics of the interaction but rather of dissolving the emotion that traps us in a shared unconscious fantasy/bastion (W. Baranger and M. Baranger, 1982) or basic assumption, in this case, of attack/escape, that threatens the analytic process.

To repeat: in the real and metaphorical sense, the patient's delusion is a hyper-"perception". It should not be seen as inherently "wrong" but paradoxically as "excessively" apt as a way of describing her internal world. The earthquake is not an absurdity, but an (albeit failed) image/representation to be developed and explored through narrative in order to grasp its truth and be transformed into metaphor, narration, symbolic thought, words – and not only with respect to the patient's inner world, but also as the description of the vicissitudes of the unconscious (proto-) emotional intersubjective field.

In order to get in touch with the patient, it is necessary to "forget", or better, to put between parentheses all knowledge about psychopathology and metapsychology, which often only serve the function of defensively closing the channels of receptivity to the rashes of beta elements.

Or rather, we should have a model that allows us to make correct use of theories (and experience) in the very act of temporarily obscuring them. It is not always possible to contain severely disturbing emotions. In some cases, hospitalizing the patient – which is what then happened with R. – is the equivalent, for Ogden, of an interpretation, or, in his exact words, an interpretive action. At all events, memory, desire and comprehension come back to the analyst in the form of reverie. Once we have effectively interiorized them, as Grotstein wittily points out, even if we try to put them away, they do not forget us.

The analytic technique for severe patients or patients with significant autistic nuclei (but not only for them, because after all the principles of sustainability and of listening to the unconscious signals that come from the field are *always* of key importance) is therefore completely different from the classical Freudian technique. More than reflective (like a mirror), the analyst must be reflexive (in the sense of introducing her own mental functioning as a function or a place in the analytic field). She should work mostly upstream of psychic contents, privileging the development of the ability to think and contain/learn emotions, which thus regain their essential cognitive and motivational value, and not so much thoughts and emotions as contents seen in themselves.

It should, I hope, be clear that this way of thinking about psychosis is based on transcending a whole series of caesuras in binary couples of opposite concepts: understandable/unintelligible; being-able/not-being-able to make a transference (in narcissistic neurosis); analyzable/non-analyzable; health/madness; psychotic parts/non-psychotic parts of the mind; the continuist/discontinuist nature of the different expressions of psychopathology; intrapsychic/interpsychic; past/present; unipersonal/bipersonal (the isolated subject or the couple as elementary unity); conscious/unconscious experience (as separated or as in the extraordinary figure of the Moebius ribbon, seen as processes that capture different aspects of a single psychic entity, or dimensions of the same awareness).

Transformations in hallucinosis

Bion conceived his theory of transformations in hallucinosis in his wonderful 1958 article on hallucination, later reprinted in *Second Thoughts* (1967), and he developed it in subsequent books. Faithful to his method of transcending the caesuras, to his Cartesian principle of systematic doubt (Civitarese, 2008, 2011), Bion wipes out all distinction between perception and action. As we have said, the sense organs can function as if they were muscles, getting rid of aspects of themselves that have been identified as dangerous. They "expel the images into the external world. These hallucinated images are then 'perceived', seen, heard, smelt, felt, as if they were real, and provide instant satisfaction to the omnipotent self. The emotional experience, the reality of the session, is transformed into sense impressions which are then evacuated as hallucinations, yielding pleasure or pain but not meaning" (Symington and Symington, 1996, pp. 115–116).

Initially intended as a replacement mechanism for denial, T→H becomes more and more "physiological" in Bion (as has happened to many psychoanalytic concepts, from repression to projective identification, etc.), and in normal people it stands for the minimum amount of projective activity that forms the background of familiarity necessary to absorb novelty and the difference. Hallucination sets up a para-excitatory screen to oppose the virtual traumaticity of reality (which for the newborn is represented by the object and remains so fantasmatically for the whole of one's life). This screen also works as a frame and as a canvas for drawings and colors that perception spills out. From this point of view hallucination is the zero degree of representation. For Botella and Botella (2001), it accomplishes a process of simplification of the chaos of reality or of "primary abstraction" that precedes the secondary abstraction of logic. Hence there is a very close link between hallucination and memory: a minimal and invisible hallucinatory activity, so to speak, is nothing other than that element of memory that acts as a warp in the texture of perceptions and thus safeguards the identity of the subject.

T→H can run from a minimum compatible with a completely normal (and indeed necessary!) life to situations of severe psychotic imbalance with openly hallucinatory production. The most clinically interesting situations, and in relation to which the concept of T→H is particularly illuminating, are intermediate situations where the subject, despite suffering, but in a way that can be very difficult to intuit, maintains a (superficial) adaptation to reality. He may even seem *too* adapted. This is why Bion uses the term that in psychopathology indicates the presence in a well-preserved individual of hallucinations experienced in a state of lucid consciousness. In pathological but not extreme T→H there are no real hallucinations or real delusions. The accent is not on hallucinations but on hallucinations that subtract meaning: invisible or, if anything, negative.

These are the situations in which there is an excess of concreteness. This impression is given by the patients who – as Italo Calvino would have put it – drown in the sea of objectivity, of things, of factual reality. The analyst can be collusively sucked into this world. In the session he converses in a rational way and seems to be able to explain everything to himself on the basis of the known theories and models of psychoanalysis. Everything seems to be meaningful or "scientific". Everything or almost everything can be explained perfectly. Sometimes the patient may make pedagogical, moralistic or authoritarian demands, which betrays a tendency to assume a position of superiority. Such fantasies embody the rules of transformation into hallucinosis. In this case, hallucinosis serves to deny dependence and to maintain a position of pseudo-self-sufficiency.

References to emotionally significant facts may be spread over a very long period of time, in a way that dilutes the meaning they may have had or dissolves it altogether. It's like enlarging a photograph immeasurably and observing it at close range. Each individual element is still understandable, but you can no longer see the figure. If it's a story, you lose the plot and the general meaning. All the details are precise, but the atmosphere is rather disturbing, albeit in a very subtle way. Things are clearly seen but are suspended in a kind of void, as in a story by Kafka or a novel by Ishiguro. Rarely do true emotions appear to give coherence and vitality to the discourse. Analyst and patient are imprisoned in an effect of reality (Barthes, 1984) – not "real" reality, but a flat reality, a world that has no depth, such as the artificial sets used in films shot in the studio. What "may then appear to the observer as thoughts, visual images, and verbalizations must be regarded by him as debris, remnants or scraps of imitated speech and histrionic synthetic emotion, floating in a space so vast that its confines, temporal as well as spatial, are without definition" (Bion, 1970, pp. 12–13).

Paradoxically, then, these patients testify to having suffered from an excess of reality, either internal or external. They were repeatedly beset by waves of violent and uncontainable emotions that harmed their alpha function. As a consequence they suffer from an impaired ability to symbolize the real ("O"). More evident in some than in others, as defenses T→H show this fullness (or, better, this flood of beta elements) that has marked their lives traumatically by reversing the sign and converting it into a void of emotions. This means that upstream of all this there has been "an intense catastrophic emotional explosion O" (*ibid*, p. 14), that is, the patient has suffered a traumatic experience of lack of psychic containment. Beta elements were unable to find good forms that would give them a meaningful configuration and therefore could not be transformed into psychic elements. It is the disaster of living through a state of anguish that, if it not assuaged, increases in intensity until it becomes "nameless terror" (Bion, 1962). Now, if each of us has a psychotic part of our personality, this means that we all may have suffered at least from microtraumas. These must have been episodes in which the container "exploded" (or the object "disappeared"). So T→H are not exclusive to people with real psychological disorders, because in actual fact what they do is ensure the stability of the psyche in these situations, and indeed they lend our perceptions the indispensable background of familiarity and predictability. Of course, it is a matter of measure.

But let us look in more detail at how this process unfolds. (I begin by saying that I do not claim to be saying what Bion really said, but that I read him in a personal way.)

If reality gets too violent, the (beta) screen thickens. Invisible and normal hallucination can go as far as to become actual hallucination. But what meaning do we give to these hallucinations? The reader may remember *All the Mornings of the World*, a beautiful film by Alain Courneau (1991) with Gerard Depardieu in the role of Marais, a young musician student of Monsieur de Sainte Colombe. When he plays the viola and the memory of his dead wife becomes unbearable, the Master hallucinates her. One cannot really understand the meaning of hallucinosis and hallucination except within the framework of the relationship with the object. Freud writes that the child hallucinates the mother when she is absent for too long. But it is also true that through hallucination he searches for the real object, and uses memory to find it again – and not in order to do without it completely, as one might think. Paradoxically hallucination does not distance us from reality; it moves towards the object (reality) and expresses our urgent need to return to it.

Thought is not born, as Freud maintains, because the child discovers that hallucinatory satisfaction is illusory and because, driven by frustration, it automatically turns to reality.[1] No, it is born if the object responds to the frustration of the child, if it can cure fever or the thirst for hallucination. Similarly, when Bion writes that thought is born of the non-thing, of the absence of the object, here too we must conceive of this absence only as a first moment: the no-thing has the structure of an essential rhythm, which goes something like this: no-thing-no-thing-no, that is, presence/absence, *fort/da*, on/off and so on. It is not pure absence, which would be nothing, *nought-ness*, that makes thought blossom, but a happy rhythm of absence/presence with which the object modulates and makes the frustration tolerable.

But what happens after the initial catastrophe, when this basic lack of thought has already occurred? I believe that due to a defect that has become internal, such fragility and intolerance to frustration will remain, as well as such a marked difficulty in transforming it that the individual may easily find himself re-experiencing the same catastrophic experiences, once again thinking "upside down", and each time the symptom is the intensification of the transformations into hallucinosis, the burning sense of thirst. As one can see, the initial disaster will be repeated. Therefore, I do not see the transformation into hallucinosis so much as a defense against the relationship but rather as an emergency measure and as a spasmodic request for relationship. This request is, however, difficult to satisfy precisely because of the shortcomings of the alpha function that has to deal with it and because of the hyperbolic state of need that generates it. Therefore, it is not necessarily a case of the object going away and now being missing (this may have happened in the initial trauma), but it is the need, which has become too intense, literally in-containable, that every time makes it explode/disappear and reveals its dramatic inadequacy.

We need to be careful, though. It is not that at the same time the subject does not withdraw from the object for fear of being betrayed again, because he could not learn to "use" it; this is quite understandable. Rather, he has not yet met it or has not met someone who (ideally) is also capable of containing this fear; thus the fever continues. It is of course even possible that his need is too great and inexhaustible, or that reality continues to prove traumatic. At all events, I would not place defense against the relationship within hallucinosis or hallucination. Or one could say that it is true that hallucination provides the gratification of a temporary solution – hallucination is indeed a defensive barrier against the greatest danger of all, the absolute loss of representation (C. Botella and S. Botella, 2001) – but in order to go *towards* the object and not to exclude it. Avoidance behaviors can coexist with transformations into hallucinosis, but I would not see them as determined by these and therefore completely coincident. In other words, it is not the "no" of hallucination, of the evacuated beta element, that hinders the relationship; however, what is an obstacle to the relationship is when the "thing", that is, the object, is provoked and thus "misses the appointment" (like when one trapeze artist fails to catch the other).

But what does it mean when we say that the object "disappears" or "explodes"? To explain this point Bion imagines that the senses can function as muscles that evacuate perceptions in infinite space. Spatial dispersion also implies temporal dispersion (think of a word written on a balloon that inflates infinitely . . .): it takes a very long time to relate two elements that are at a vast distance from each other. I believe that this is how Bion's notion of an "attack on links" can be understood. But the beta elements thus expelled are different from beta elements as material impressions, proto-emotions and proto-sensations that could not be processed; they are saturated, they carry with them "traces of Ego and Super-Ego" and they constitute so-called "bizarre objects"; they have, however, been partially transformed, like undigested pieces of food that are then vomited. Beta elements that were vomited are impregnated with psychic moods.

The mechanism of T→H is triggered when envy and frustration reinforce each other in an infernal vicious circle (which Bion calls "hyperbole"). A certain threshold is exceeded, and the mind, instead of digesting the real, spews it out. To repeat: the hyper- or neo-reality that is thus generated can be sustained by states of hallucinosis or by real hallucinations. We can imagine these hallucinatory productions as projections, in the cinematographic sense, of internal images – as the citizens of Gotham City do when, anxious about the threat from the Joker, they project the symbol of the bat into the sky to call upon Batman for help, or as many outstretched arms to grasp and hold the container-object from which salvation is expected. Depending on the perspective, it is as if the exploded container violently sucked up the subject's raw psychic contents that are still raw subject or as if they desperately tried to remain hooked to the container. (It is clear that in describing phenomena that cannot be seen, we can only use metaphors that, depending on the point of view, may seem to varying degrees rough or refined.)

If the object does not respond or if the need is too urgent, the result is a sky covered with infinite projections. Naturally, these images can give the impression of having reconstituted a container. Indeed this is the case, and what is more it is one that draws on the repertoire of mnestic traces of fairly successful past encounters with the object – alpha images already stored in memory. But it works at a minimum level: basically it filters only the smallest elements of novelty. But reality is never static, and we need it to feed on, just as we need food. The fact is that with T→H the subject meets reality not with preconceptions but with predeterminations. This, however, *is* the "reversal of thinking", the realm of anti-thought. If the two alternatives are shock and freezing, and then if nothing new can be assumed, nor too can anything be known.

To sum up, in pathological situations, after the catastrophe the patient lives in a kind of wasteland, devoid of life and in hate. Thinking about pain is intolerable to her. That would be tantamount to annihilating herself. Then she finds herself projecting her proto-emotions into emptiness as undigested facts or elements. Outside, however, she no longer finds a container to accept them. By exploding, the container has become infinite, like the gigantic face of the mother that the child vainly tries to touch in Bergman's *Persona* (1966). Emotions are now scattered across sidereal space. They are in fact registered but no longer suffered, because they no longer have any meaning. But without emotions, without the subject's truth about herself – in fact for Bion emotion always has to do with a relationship, and is therefore always the expression in various combinations of the bonds of love (L), hatred (H) or knowledge (K) with the object – she becomes impoverished and sick.

Losing emotions is like bleeding to death in one's own tissues as a result of a surgical shock (Bion, 1970). It means having to give up vital preconceptions and the realizations that might correspond to them, and having to resort to "hallucination" because of its value of immediate satisfaction. But hallucinatory satisfaction is illusory, because it staunches the wound but does not close it. Frustration grows, and the patient interprets it projectively as the effect of the analyst's rivalry and envy. The patient experiences him as someone who wants to steal her ability to satisfy herself in an omnipotent and immediate way. Reality then becomes even more persecutory and feeds fanaticism and hatred. It gets more and more difficult to contain them. The more unlimited the three-dimensional space (at the origin) of the container (of the object) becomes – and for this reason cancels itself out – the more the mental space of the subject narrows and flattens out.

A salient feature of Bion's model of "attacks on links", "bizarre objects" and transformations in hallucinosis is that despite the "absence" of the object, it is always a question of processes inserted within an intersubjective frame. The object *seems* absent, because it has become infinite and cannot be seen, but precisely for this reason it is all the more looming and threatening. In a dream one of my patients saw himself at Godzilla's feet but at first did not realize it because the monster was immense and towering over him: the scene could be taken for a less abstract illustration of the same process. The sense of threat is so intolerable that you focus on only one detail in the scene. To sum up: *in Bion, the understanding of psychosis, of the reversal of thinking, is based on a radically social theory of the subject.* The affective and cognitive quality of the therapist's mind becomes the main therapeutic instrument and implies on his part – as well as on the part of the group, when the "therapist" is a team – a clear assumption of responsibility, not only towards the patient but also towards one's own internal world and unconscious functioning.

Note

1 Green (1995) warns against falsehoods and simplifications of drive theory, commenting however that *Freud starts from the point of view that the child will autonomously find his own path towards hallucinatory satisfaction.* An endogenous thrust that follows mechanistic principles produces the psychic transformations that construct the subject. Freud adopts *an eminently unipersonal vertex,* and is aware of it. He knows he is employing a useful convention, a "fiction". Nonetheless, his choice implies specific consequences on the level of theory and technique. Bion traces the same path but based on a model that emphasizes the interaction between mother and child and for this reason puts at the center of everything the theme of digesting emotions. Without the help of the object, that is, without its capacity for reverie and without a mature and complete alpha function, no transformation from beta to alpha is guaranteed. The functional reorganizations that take place at the key junctions of the railway traffic conveyed along the nervous pathways are, due alone to their anatomy, necessary but not sufficient; they must continue along the *psychic* pathways of the mind of the Other. The mother does not only give milk, "she nourishes him also psychically, she daydreams feelings and 'mental' states about the child. And so she enables the child to reintroject his own projections that are now changed through her" (*Id.,* 1998, p. 656).

References

Baranger, W., and Baranger, M. (1982). The analytic situation as a dynamic field. *International Journal of Psycho-Analysis* 89: 795–826.

Barthes, R. (1984). *The Rustle of Language.* Berkeley and Los Angeles: University of California Press, 1986.

Bergman, I. (1966) (Director). *Persona.* Sweden.

Bion, W.R. (1962). *Learning from Experience.* London: Tavistock.

Bion, W.R. (1967). *Second Thoughts: Selected Papers on Psycho-Analysis.* London: William Heinemann Medical Books.

Bion, W.R. (1970). *Attention and Interpretation.* London: Tavistock.

Bion, W.R. (1977). *Two Papers: The Grid and Caesura.* London: Routledge, 2018.

Botella, C., and Botella, S. (2001). *The Work of Psychic Figurability: Mental States without Representation.* London: Routledge, 2004.

Civitarese, G. (2008). 'Caesura' as Bion discourse on method. *International Journal of Psychoanalysis* 89: 1123–1143.

Civitarese, G. (2011). *The Violence of Emotions: Bion and Post-Bionian Psychoanalysis*. London: Routledge, 2013.

Courneau, A. (1991) (Director). *All the Mornings of the World*. France.

Ferro, A. (2010). *Torments of the Soul: Psychoanalytic Transformations in Dreaming and Narration*. London: Routledge, 2015.

Green, A. (1983). The dead mother. In *On Private Madness*. London: The Hogarth Press, 1986, pp. 142–173.

Green, A. (1995). *Propedeutica. Metapsicologia rivisitata*. Roma: Borla, 2001.

Green, A. (1998). The primordial mind and the work of the negative. *International Journal of Psycho-Analysis* 79: 649–665.

Grinberg and al. (1975). *Introduction to the Work of Bion*. Lanham: Jason Aronson, 1977.

Grotstein, J.S. (2004). The seventh servant. *Int J Psycho-Anal* 85: 1081–1101.

Kojève, A. (1947). *Introduction to the Reading of Hegel, 1947–1969*. New York: Basic Books.

Ogden, T.H. (2004). On holding and containing, being and dreaming. *International Journal of Psycho-Analysis* 85: 1349–1364.

Ogden, T.H. (2006). On teaching psychoanalysis. *International Journal of Psycho-Analysis* 87: 1069–1085.

Ogden, T.H. (2009). *Rediscovering Psychoanalysis: Thinking and Dreaming, Learning and Forgetting*. London: Routledge.

Symington, J., and Symington, N. (1996). *The Clinical Thought of Wilfred Bion*. London: Routledge, 2002.

Chapter 10

Dream, psychosis and separation anxieties[1]

Luigi Rinaldi

The dreams of an analysand in the time immediately before and after periods of analytical vacations have given me the opportunity to reflect on the relationship between dream and psychosis and in particular on the vexata questio of the presence, quality and function of dreams in psychotic states.

What emerges from my clinical experience, considered in the light of a careful analysis of the literature, is that when the psychotic process is not in an acute phase and has not invaded the entire psychic structure, dreaming is possible. Dreams, in these cases, do not have an exclusively evacuative function, as is often reported (Bion, 1958; Grinberg, 1967), and can function, like the dreams of non-psychotic people, as the via regia in the exploration of the unconscious.

In psychotic states, a partial or total failure of dream work is often found, which can be connected to a deficit in symbol formation and to concrete thinking, and therefore it does not lead to the fulfilment of repressed desires and to the protection of sleep from assaults of drives or of external reality. However, the dream preserves its function of representation of the Self and of its attempts to integrate current and past emotional experiences, including those stored in non-verbal memory. For this reason, dream regression can indeed illustrate a deficit in integration between the body and the psyche, and the transference experiences can be represented in sensory and physical terms. In these cases, it is a question of representations that derive from the reactivation, carried out by the psychosis, of that pictographic register (Aulagnier, 1975) which mirrors the oldest experiences related to the primary relationship and describes how this "primal process" can be a kind of preform of subsequent phantasms of fragmentation, annihilation and loss of ego boundaries.

Starting from Freud

The analogy between dream and psychotic states of various kinds is very old. Freud (1900, 1915) gave a metapsychological explanation, considering them both to be regressive experiences, characterized by the prevalence of primary thought processes, by the lack of the notion of time, by the absence of contradiction and by the hallucinatory realization of the repressed desire. In the case of the dream, the closure of perceptual afferents and the preclusion of motor efferents, which occur during sleep, allow the exciting of the unconscious memory to transport the preconscious verbal thought, by a retrograde pathway, to the perceptive system, giving rise to dream hallucinations. In the cases of non dream hallucinations and of psychotic thought, the regressive experience is due to an excess of excitement, the related unconscious representations of which cannot be held back from bursting in upon the scene, because of the weakness, momentary or chronic, of the ego structures (lability of ego boundaries).

Along the same lines as his work regarding dream productions, Freud thus opened the way for the interpretation of delirium and psychotic productions, and encouraged the search for the meaning and signifi-cance of these manifestations. Sixteen years after *The Interpretation of Dreams* (Freud, 1900), in *A Metapsychological Supplement to the Theory of Dreams* (Freud, 1915), he continued to declare dream and hallucina-tion to be identical, except for a few small details. For this reason he always paid more attention to the analogies rather than to the differ-ences between dreams and psychotic phenomena, starting from the theme of the continuity and the alternation between dream material and psychotic contents.

I remember, for example, that in the case of President Schreber, Freud (1911) noted that the onset of the second psychotic episode was predicted by a dream in which the representation came to him that it would have been really nice "to be a woman who is submitting to coitus". And later, as a confirmation that the patient was struggling with the same mate-rial that would become part of his psychosis, Schreber communicated, in his delirium, that he had been transformed into a woman and had been impregnated by divine rays.

But also in his subsequent work, Freud continued to be interested in the relationship between dream and psychosis. Already in 1894, with regard to the neuropsychosis of defence, he had begun to conceive of the exist-ence of an unrepressed unconscious, proposing the theory of repudiation (Verwerfung), taken up and developed by Lacan (1966) using the term "foreclosure" to indicate that what is rejected in psychosis is not a percep-tual datum, but a "signifier", which in this way is expelled from the sym-bolic order. Finally, in *Constructions in Analysis* (Freud, 1937) and *Splitting of the Ego in the Process of Defence* (Freud, 1938a), he correlated the fixity of the delusional formation to a kernel of historical truth contained in it. At the same time, it became fundamental to carry out the task of promoting the integration into the psychic reality of the subject of that which had escaped representative symbolization and yet tended to re-emerge in the form of dreams, somatic disturbances or repeated actions.

After Freud: a brief look at the literature

These Freudian intuitions have been amply confirmed by later generations of psychoanalysts. For example, Arieti (1963) observed that the appearance in a dream of content very similar to delusional material can mean that such a "patient no longer tries to deal with his conflicts in an openly psychotic way, but in that psychotic way which is physiologic and usable by every human being: the dream-world" (Quinodoz, 2001: 60). Along the same lines we find Schulz and Kilgalen (1969) and Blechner (1983). The latter speaks of "reallocation of madness" when, in patients who improve because of analysis, the content of hallucinations and delusions can begin to appear in dreams, while conscious psychotic experiences diminish or disappear.

On the other hand, in the area of the differences between dreams and psychotic phenomena and with regard to the specificity of dreams in psychotic patients, an obvious first distinction must be made, keeping in mind the various phases of the psychotic process and the extent of its invasion of the individual's psyche. In *An Outline of Psychoanalysis*, describing the splitting of the ego in psychosis, Freud (1938b) speaks of a psychotic patient in whom the split, healthier part of the ego functioned in dreaming. The situation changes if the psychotic process has invaded most of the psyche. In these cases a concept that is very present in the literature concerns the function that is mainly of "evacuation" (Bion, 1958; Grinberg, 1967; Green, 1986; Segal, 1991), attributed to the dreams of psychotics. These dreams are not thought to express the fulfilment of a desire, and their purpose is not seen to be the elaboration of drive derivatives, but rather the relief for the psychic apparatus from painful stimuli, especially from the persecutory part, which the patient wishes to get rid of, instead of representing it. This function of "psychotic dreams" is considered to be the reason for their bizarre nature, that is, the fact that they are characterized by concretization rather than by condensation, to the point of being confused with reality. These dreams do not carry out the function of elaborating and symbolizing the latent thoughts of the dream, but rather that of getting rid of the psychic content. They are not primarily needed for communication, but for acting out, and they do not function as symbolic communication, but rather as symbolic equations (Segal, 1991), or beta elements that are expelled (Bion, 1958). "The aim is twofold: one, to split off and get rid of certain psychic contents, and two, to affect the object" (Segal, 1991, 50). And this can happen both with the dream in itself and through its recounting, devised to arouse certain feelings and emotions in the analyst and then perform a projective identification (Ibid.).

It is necessary to add, however, as a partial correction of what has just been said, that the careful analysis of these so-called psychotic dreams can be, in any case, very useful: it shows us the fabric and the mechanisms of construction of psychotic thought, and shows how these dreams, like, on the other hand, all dreams, represent the silent metabolism of the Self, and how they become the bulletins of its condition, of its developmental process, of the meaning attributed to its relations (first of all, with the analyst), etc. It is easy to understand, therefore, how the attentive reading of these dreams, not so much of their latent content, as of the dreamer's experience, can be particularly profitable. It can reveal a fragile and fragmented ego that asks to be recognized and supported, or that presents to us its attempts to enter into or emerge from psychosis (De Masi, 2006), to reformulate traumatic experiences (Ferenczi, 1931). In less favourable cases, we can see the failures of the normal function of the dream, which lead to awakening, nightmare, the expulsion of the psychic content and a related confusion of the boundaries between internal world and external world.

Inability to produce a good dream and psychotic potentiality

In three important articles on the dream and the dream experience, Masud Khan (1962, 1972, and 1976) introduced the concepts of the "good dream", of "dream space" and of "dreaming experience".

By "good dream" he meant "a dream which incorporates through successful dream-work an unconscious desire and can thus enable sleep to be maintained on the one hand and can be available for psychic experiences to the ego when the person wakes up" (Khan, 1962, 35).

In order for this type of dream to be produced, a series of requirements were seen to be necessary, including:

- "Ego's narcissistic capacity to derive satisfaction from dream-world in lieu of either the pure narcissism of sleep or the concrete satisfaction of reality. This implies a capacity in the ego to tolerate frustration and accept symbolic satisfactions.
- A capacity in the ego for symbolization and dream-work, in which sufficient counter-cathexis against primary process is sustained for dream to become an experience of intra-psychic communication" (Ibid., 34).

Khan also pointed out that, as Freud had observed in chapter 7 of *The Interpretation of Dreams*, "wish-fulfilment in dreams is only possible if the mnemic images of previous satisfaction of needs are available for cathexis". Khan continues, "We can elaborate on this to say where in a person's experience of infant care such satisfactions have not been either reliable or consistent or have been inadequate, the capacity to use these 'mnemic images of satisfaction' for mobilization of dream-wish must by definition be lacking or distorted (Winnicott, 1945a)" (Ibid., 40).

In such circumstances, in order to compensate for the deficiency of these first experiences of satisfaction, there could be in later life – as happens in certain psychotic illnesses – the abuse of the dream to build a magical, omnipotent dream-world, which has the function of denying dependence on real external objects which are necessary for satisfaction (Ibid.).

In these cases, moreover, for the reasons that we have indicated earlier, "the capacity to use the dream-mechanisms and the dream itself as a psychic experience", which "is the result of adequate environmental provisions", is missing, and that capacity is dependent on "the availability of certain ego-functions to be able to use that symbolic discourse which is the essence of dream formation" (Khan, 1972, 311). What is missing is what Khan defines as "the dream-space", that psychic zone "in which the dream actualizes", which must be kept distinct from the process of dreaming, which articulates impulses and unconscious conflicts.

In the compulsion of certain patients to dream and recount their dreams theatrically in analysis we find, for example, a special type of passage to action that screens the absence of the dream-space. This absence does not allow the personalization of the dream experience and of all that this implies for the experience of the self and object relations.

In a subsequent article in 1976 Khan stated that the "dreaming experience" is different from the dream text (in which it is possible that no trace will be found), and is a paradoxical form of subjective self-experience that expands and completes the experience of self, making use of the functioning of the primary process and fulfilling integration tasks that far exceed the capacity of conscious mental activity.

Putting together Khan's three concepts,[2] we could say, ultimately, that a good dream is such if it brings together in a narratively coherent experience aspects of one's self that were previously split, denied or even simply repressed.

I believe that in this way the healing mechanism of dreams can be hypothesized. I remember in this regard that Winnicott (1947) talked about "healing dreams", regarding some personal dreams, considered important not so much for the interpretation given to them as for the simple fact of having dreamed and remembered them. And the same can be said of the "reparative dreams" Eissler wrote about (1953) regarding one of his patients, citing an analogous concept of Freud's, according to which ordinary reality bursts into the dreams of a psychotic, just as drive material bursts into the dream of a non psychotic, thus helping the subject to become aware of it.

From what has been said, it can be deduced that it is possible to hypothesize a parallelism between the inability to dream and psychotic potentiality. Both presuppose the missing or insufficient internalization of the primary maternal functions of care, holding and rêverie towards the infant. Regarding the dream, following Khan, we can say that the lack of internalization of this function impedes the establishment of the dream-space, a metaphor of the maternal body, in whose arms the dreamer regressively takes refuge. In addition, the lack of rêverie in the mother (so that she does not comprehend and therefore fails to give meaning and adequate response to the need underlying the child's crying) leads to a poor formation of representations of thing, of mnemic traces left by previous experiences of satisfaction. Consequently, since "The first wishing seems to have been a hallucinatory cathecting of the memory of satisfaction" (Freud, 1900, 598), the individual will not be able to count on a sufficient repertoire of mnemic images of satisfaction that will allow him or her the mobilization of the dream-wish.

At the same time, this lack of satisfaction sets the premises for a potential psychotic development: the child does not accumulate those experiences of pleasure that anchor the infantile libido on the erogenous zones and the relationship with the other. In this way, the development is not favoured of security, which is necessary in order to be able to tolerate the absence of the primary object, and to meet those structuring experiences of separation that lead to the representation of the absent object and its replacement through symbolic construction.

The symbolic deficit will lead to a psychic functioning based on affect-sensation, of the drive discharge sort, rather than that of cathexis, of anchoring oneself to those mnemic traces that constitute the first self-erotic nuclei, early signs of the cathexes and of the later identifications that will give rise to the ego. This lack of cathexis throws a heavy burden on the future process, which should lead, from the stage of non-integration of the fragmentary coenaesthetic sensory experiences (tactile, olfactory, etc.) of the functioning of the self in relation to the environment, to the subsequent stage of primary integration of these experiences. In this way, there is an undermining of the platform for development of the first nuclei of the ego, and of the possibility of its satisfactory structuring, in terms of the coherence, continuity, integration and solidity of its boundaries.

Ultimately we could say that psychoanalytic research has made it clear that an inadequate primary maternal accompaniment, which does not manage to establish itself as an internalized lost object, having a containing and meaningful differentiating function (para-excitatory function in Freudian language, formation of the alpha function in Bion, etc.), does not succeed in endowing the infant with the representative and symbolic patrimony necessary for the mobilization of the dream-wish and thus the possibility to benefit from dream work in order to give a deep and vital meaning to his or her sensations and emotions. Deficient symbolic development will give rise to a basic mental functioning that will always remain tributary to the external reality of the object – or, which is the same thing, to its total rejection – and will be characterized by primary defensive modalities that cancel desire, transforming it into extreme need. This is the way that the foundations of the various forms of psychopathology are laid, and their gravity is directly proportional to the extent of the deficit of symbolic construction, to the point that, in the most serious cases, content which has not been symbolized bursts into consciousness, in the form of delusions or hallucinations, or, alternatively, in the form of an inability to control impulses and, therefore, of a tendency to act out.

Dream life as a generative theatre of meaning

This beautiful metaphor by Meltzer (1984) is a lucid description of Bion's thought (1962) on the relationship among symbolic construction, ability to dream and learning from experience. For Bion, the central concern of psychoanalysis is the dynamic container-contained interaction: between the thoughts and feelings derived from the lived emotional experience (the contained) and the ability to dream and think those thoughts (the container). This ability to dream is primarily provided by the maternal rêverie, which is capable of accepting, that is, carrying out the unconscious psychological work of "dreaming" the emotional experience that the child projects onto the mother, because he or she is unable to elaborate it alone. Identification with the maternal containment capacity allows the child in turn to learn to dream his or her own emotional experience. The dream becomes for Bion the attempt to generate meaning, starting from the perception of one's own emotional experience, and thus it is the pre-supposition for learning from experience. It is a particular and basic form of symbolic function, a first step of thought.

The dream has a metabolic and creative function, thanks to the ability of the primary process to break down and recompose the elements at play in the internal world of the subject. For a person to dream, however, it is necessary to possess an alpha function, capable of transforming sensory impressions into (alpha) elements, suitable for being used in unconscious thought while awake or in dream thoughts, and to differentiate the conscious from the unconscious, in this way allowing ordered thought to occur. If the alpha function fails, the patient cannot dream and therefore cannot sleep, as in the case of the psychotic person: raw sensory impressions (beta elements), not treated by the alpha function and not suitable for unconscious thought while awake or for dream thought, can be evacuated only by means of projective identification through acting out.

In other words, following Bion, we can hypothesize the existence of "an apparatus for thinking thoughts and dreaming dreams" that allows us to remember by dreaming, instead of repeating by acting out. When the anguish is so great that it has destructuring effects, as happens in cases of acute psychotic illness, it is this apparatus that is affected. The extent of the damage determines the characteristics of the psychotic thought and psychotic dreams, which, when they exist, oscillate from being predominantly of an evacuative and non-communicative type – discharging outside or inside the dreamer unmetabolized raw material – to becoming a more mixed or more frankly elaborative type (Grinberg, 1967), the more the dreamer is acquiring integrative and reparatory abilities, and is able to take care of himself or herself.

Dreams and images of the body

What struck me most in my analysand's dreams, which I will discuss shortly, was the frequency in them of often terrifying body images to represent the Self and its attempts to elaborate current emotional experiences, which awakened old memories and primordial anguish, probably due to early traumatic experiences, stored, for the most part, in non-verbal memory.

The quality of these images and the corresponding experiences, which were primitive and distressing, connected to the disappearance of walls, of himself, to a necrotic body, etc., seemed to be the only possibility for the dreamer to represent the dramatic nature of his anxieties – of fragmentation, annihilation, loss of ego boundaries – elicited by the analytical separations. By confining and limiting this type of anguish to the analytic situation and to the dream space, he relived, in a tamed form, and therefore with the potential to be elaborated, what, in the other separation experiences that had permeated his life (family, scholastic and professional), had been undergone in a highly dramatic manner, and had led to temporary breaks with reality. The drama was so great because, après coup (Nachträglichkeit), the oldest anxieties were awakened, those experienced in the primary relationship, when it was the body that was talking.

I am referring to that period in which the infans is little more than a bundle of inexpressible and sometimes lacerating sensations, which can cause, in the presence of a deficit of maternal rêverie, a lack of integration of mind and body. This lack of integration manifests itself phenomenally, in the course of development, as a sort of potential psyche-soma dissociation, deriving from the fact that the lack of maternal containment can provoke distrust that the somatic datum can be communicated, accepted and given meaning (the mother who cannot tell, for example, whether the child is crying because of hunger or because he or she is wet or wants to be held in her arms), that is to say, mentalized, and therefore potentially made manageable by mental abilities. It follows that the psyche, which for Winnicott in the newborn and the young child is nothing but "the imaginative elaboration of somatic parts, feelings, and functions" (Winnicott, 1949, 224), cannot become "well lodged in his body" (Winnicott, 1950, 207), and consequently the child will never be able to feel at one with his or her body. The vulnerability to processes of mind-body splitting derives from this lack of integration. Feelings both pleasant and painful, rather than tending to representation and therefore to vectorization towards emotion and symbolic thought (transformation of beta elements into alpha, according to the language of Bion), so that they can be catalogued and pursued according to the pleasure principle and the reality principle, are discharged on the body, tend to be ends unto themselves, do not leave lasting traces and tend to eliminate, so to speak, that dash that unites the psyche to the soma. The soma tends to incorporate the psyche. The result is a psychic functioning characterized by the predominance of the sensation-affect, by the continuous search for excitation and drive discharge (as we will see in my analysand), while intellectual productions, not sufficiently rooted in a valid libidinal-emotional investment of the Self and of the world, are often split, and do not succeed in influencing emotional development and the ability to have mature relationships.

This potential dissociation becomes actual when the subsequent encounters with the external reality in the course of development (for example, in our case, the essential absence of the father during the developmental process of the child, with intervals of castrating attitudes)[3] do not succeed in remedying the deficits in the primary relationship.

In other words, to cite Aulagnier (1975), there is movement from psychotic potential to a phase of decompensation when the external reality communicates to the subject the mirror image of the pictogram of rejection, that pictographic representation that he or she has of himself/herself, which is reactivated when, "since the relationship with the other is impossible, the I has only its own body to allow it to have the sign 'relation' in its alphabets, an indispensable sign for the organization of the primary and the secondary" (De Mijolla-Mellor, 27).

Before moving on to Giacomo's dreams, I must add that, when I set about writing this paper, and I looked through the literature on dreams and the mind-body relationship, I was struck in particular by the following contributions:

1   E. Jones (1948), who, in his classic work on the theory of symbolism, demonstrates that all symbols refer to the body or parts of it, to immediate relatives or to the phenomena of birth, love and death.
2   Armando Ferrari (1992) and Riccardo Lombardi (2006), who, in developing Bion's approach, place the body in the role of the principal object of the psyche (original concrete object), and consider dream activity to be an exemplification of the functioning of the network of contact between the body and the mind. The transformation of the somatic trace of Affekt in Vorstellung (representation) is connoted as a phase of passage that opens the way to self-awareness and is the prelude to mentalization and thought. From this point of view, they repropose the Freudian intuitions which set the autoerotic investment of one's own body as the foundation of the later organization of a primary

narcissism, which is the prelude to the object relation, and they attribute value to the relationship that the subject maintains with himself or herself. It is a "vertical", intrapsychic relationship, the scaffolding of which consists of what happens inter-subjectively. I would add, from my point of view, that the good functioning of this relationship with one's bodily Self is an expression of the true Self, and gives rise to an incarnated language, to a word that is fuller, precisely because it sinks its roots into the sensory, emotional and affective tissue.

3   J. B. Pontalis, who in his "Between the dream as object and the dream-text" in *Frontiers in Psychoanalysis* (1981) talks about the dream as "displaced maternal body" (pp. 26–27). It was this way for Freud, who "committed incest with the body of his dreams, penetrated their secret and wrote the book that made him conqueror and possessor of the terra incognita" (p. 27); but every dream, as an object in analysis, refers to the maternal body, the secret of which one wants to penetrate, or, on the contrary, the secret of which one can prohibit oneself from knowing.

Finally, Pontalis cites the following passage, taken from *The Hands of the Living God*, by Marion Milner (1969), which is illuminating, in my opinion, in understanding what can confer on the psychic its weight of reality, differentiating that reality from compulsive fantasizing, fantasying in Winnicott (1971), that psychic pseudo-reality that results, instead, from the maniacal negation of internal reality: "surely it is one's own inner body awareness that takes over the role of the external mother; not just in the sense that one learns to do for oneself the external acts of bodily care that one's mother once did, but in this sense of fashioning a kind of psychic sphere or new womb out of one's own body image, as being the only safe place to inhabit and from which to put out feelers to the world" (op.cit., p. 273).

Giacomo's dreams

I will now move on to the dreams of my analysand, clarifying that these are the dreams of a manic patient produced in the time periods surrounding analytical vacations.

Because of my obligation of discretion, I will mention what is strictly essential to the associations and as little as possible of the case history of my analysand.

These are dreams that took place quite some time after the beginning of the analysis. Previously in their place the sessions had been mainly occupied by the story of his addictions to the internet, food, smoking (up to 60 cigarettes per day), alcohol, coffee, etc. and by idealization towards the analysis, to the point that, in order not to lose the supposed omnipotent protection of the analyst, he had to resort to a continual subtle self-celebration of the efforts and the progress that he said he had achieved, thanks to the analysis, in the struggle against his addictions.

I had developed the idea that from a certain period onward food, tobacco, etc. had become for Giacomo objects that were "neoneeds" (McDougall, 2003), able to alleviate an unbearable psychic tension, caused by the lack of self-healing introjections. He had to resort, therefore, to the activation of his own sensoriality in a self-referential way (Gaddini, 1982) in order to avoid the intolerable experience of emptiness.

The absence of dreams for this first long period seems to support the Freudian intuition that under the influence of primitive mechanisms such as rejection, splitting and denial, what has escaped representative symbolization can manifest itself through compulsive acting out or through a destiny that repeats itself or in the form of somatic disorders or hallucinations. In short, the more severe the compulsive acting out or psychosomatic disorder, or the more frequent the hallucinatory disorders, the less the patient dreams.

The dreams I will now discuss are situated along this continuum and were produced, I repeat, when the acting out and addictive behaviours had almost completely disappeared.

I will present these dreams in a schematic way, for the sole purpose of highlighting their main characteristics.

1st and 2nd dreams. In a session ten days before the beginning of the summer holidays, Giacomo recounted: "I dreamed of a house, which in the dream was as if it were my house, in which the living room was missing: there were only a bedroom, a kitchen and a bathroom".

His comment: "the living room is where one sits, one speaks. I cannot find a space between you and me where I am with you. . . . You remember the dream in which I had become a little ant with thin legs (it was a dream that he had told the last day before the previous Easter holidays). It's the same as always . . . when you are not there, there is the spectre of disappearance, of death, of the terror of not seeing you again, as if in my inner world I did not have reassuring objects that have taught me the game of peekaboo".[4] And another time he had said: "I cannot do analysis for fear of being abandoned. I live in the phantasm of abandonment. I'm a flood victim . . . I'll tell you about a typical session: I come here and I'm angry because you have not been there for a week. And so the first quarter of an hour goes by, the last quarter of an hour goes by because I'm angry at the end of the session, what's left for me? 10–15 minutes of session!"[5]

We can see that the holidays were experienced by Giacomo as a traumatic abandonment on the part of the analyst, who deprived him, in this way, of the possibility of being able to fulfil the needs that do not concern mere survival: the rooms that make up the house – bedroom, kitchen and bathroom – allow him only to carry out bodily functions – sleeping, eating, evacuation – the living room is missing, where one sits, one speaks.

The living room is the place of the relationship with oneself and with the other: one gets comfortable, sitting on a sofa, and speaks. The absence of the living room indicates first of all the loss of the word, of the incarnated word, that which, sinking its roots in the sensory, emotional and affective tissue, gives rise to the symbolic exchange, ensuring, at one and the same time, contact with oneself and with others.

His lack of success in finding a space between himself and the analyst indicates that, at certain levels, there was no differentiation between the two. Hence there was the mutilation caused by the absence of the analyst and the complaisance always shown by Giacomo towards me (but also towards his privileged interlocutors), his imitative defenses that led him to talk like his interlocutor, to "be the analyst", in order to avoid suffering from his absence.

When he had dreamed about the little ant, he had said: "And yet I have arms and legs", as if to distance himself, as we had commented, from the content of the dream, which revealed that the separation from the analyst, who was enormously idealized and seen as an unavoidable support, was experienced as the mutilation of everything that made him a human being: the loss of a body with which perhaps he had never fully identified, because it had never been sufficiently invested, psychicized, and thus it became separable from the psyche.

The industriousness of the ants, which seem to run or flee continually, dramatically describes his flight of ideas, his maniacal keeping busy to compensate for the state of impotence, his state of inconsistency, which he perceived when he felt abandoned, and could not support himself with the exoskeleton supplied to him by those around him.

Then he went back in this session to his being a procrastinator, and said that his timing had never coincided with that of the Other, ever since birth. "Once my mother told me that her waters had already broken and she, ever the perfect one, interrupted the delivery because that day my father's sister was dying. She did not want to let the two dates coincide and made me stay 48 hours in bad waters, and as gynaecologists say, a delivery must never see the sunrise or the sunset twice!"

The analyst's timing also did not coincide with his, since the analyst decides the holidays, and this reminded him, or rather, I would say, made him relive the mortal danger that he ran when his mother, without taking into account the needs of the unborn child, wanted to decide when to give birth. With respect to this memory, even if we consider it to be a screen memory, we should say, in agreement with Freud (1899), that it is a patchwork that contains, in any case, the essence of what marked his childhood, that is, the non-coincidence of his timing with that of his mother. Many other memories, such as the one, for example, that his first words pronounced in childhood had been "drink and pee", confirmed to him the lack of investment on the part of his mother: he had had to wait until he was able to speak and express his needs clearly to ensure that these could be understood and fulfilled.

In fact, from his stories and from the transference experiences, it was possible to hypothesize that during his childhood there had been a serious deficit in the mother's function of rêverie, both because of a certain iciness of her personality (even now, Giacomo often jokingly calls her mammoth) and because she was absorbed by another son born immediately after Giacomo and by a severe mourning process, so much so that it caused the emergence of the complex of the dead mother, mentioned by Green (1985). When the mother "has become abruptly detached from her infant", says Green, this "carries in its wake, besides the loss of love, the loss of meaning, for the baby disposes of no explication to account for what has happened. Of course, being at the centre of the maternal universe, it is clear that he interprets this deception as the consequence of his drives towards the object" (Ibid., 1982, 150). The terror of his own drives, held to be responsible for the "dead mother", led him to the impossibility of negotiating his desires and needs for fear of coming into conflict with his interlocutor. For this reason, probably, he was not able to find a space between himself and his mother and now between himself and me. On the other hand we know that, if the quality of early mothering does not allow the child to develop the ability to organize a potential field capable of creating a transitional space and a transitional object, the first symbol capable of mitigating and compensating for maternal absence, the child is unable to confront those structuring experiences of separation that allow a libidinal-emotional and representative knowledge of the world. Instead, there will be the prevalence of an "autistic-contiguous" and "sensation-dominant" modality of having experience (Ogden, 1989), which functions as a powerful attracting agent. In these cases, in order to recover feelings of pleasure and to defend oneself from separation anxieties, experienced as mutilating and destructuring, the child is forced to adhere to the object and is condemned to a magically self-sufficient basic mental organization founded on primitive mechanisms that tend to "make concretely its own (to 'assimilate' into the self) what otherwise would be recognizable objectively" (Gaddini, 1980, 113).

3rd dream. "Monday of the last week before the summer holidays. I had a dream in the last few days, a nightmare! I am witnessing a scene in which a person goes into progressive necrosis due to respiratory problems and I wonder why he does not die".

His associations: "In the morning I always wake up with emotions of death. Two things come to mind: Tausk dead by suicide and the relationship between the mind and the body. . . . I won't go to the dietician, I know what he would tell me, it would be a despoliation of the ego".

We can see, in my opinion, that separation causes the intertwining of two movements: one on the intersubjective level, the other on the intrapsychic level. On the intersubjective level, that of transference, the missed sessions are equivalent to the lack of oxygenation of the blood that leads to necrosis. We see here the concrete representation of the setting as the depositary of the psychotic part of the personality, that is, of the undifferentiated and unresolved part of the primitive symbiotic bonds (Bleger, 1967). I remember Winnicott's famous words that "for the neurotic, the couch and warmth and comfort can be symbolical of the mother's love; for the psychotic it would be more true to say that these things are the analyst's physical expression of love. The couch is the analyst's lap or womb, and warmth is the live heat of the analyst's body" (Winnicott, 1947, 199).

The associations with his emotions of death, Tausk dead by suicide and the relationship between the mind and the body indicate that he, too, could commit suicide if he lost the protection of his analyst, as happened to Tausk, when Freud refused to continue treating him.

The temporal sequence of these associations (Tausk dead by suicide and the relationship between the mind and the body) helps to demonstrate, interestingly, that the intersubjective level represents the scaffolding of the intrapsychic level: the termination of the connection with the analyst, in anticipation of the summer holidays, also causes the disappearance of the connection, that dash that connects the mind to the body. This can happen because mind and body, psyche and soma, quite probably, had not been inseparably connected to one another: his psyche had not been able to become "well lodged in his body", in the absence of that "imaginative elaboration of somatic parts, feelings, and functions" which the psyche of the newborn and child consists of, according to Winnicott (1949), and which, originally, is nothing more than the maternal rêverie.

I mean to say that the failed introjection of the containment function carried out by the "maternal psyche" leads to an enormous tragic idealization towards his preferred interlocutor, the analyst, experienced as his indispensable support and as omnipotent, and therefore imagined as not having any need for himself. This makes him experience the imposed separation (at the end of the session, and holidays) as a completely gratuitous perfidy: taking away his oxygen. The homicidal rage thus unleashed, by the law of retaliation, is turned against himself, destroying the perceptual apparatus, the sensory apparatus, etc. (the person in progressive necrosis) that tie him to a reality about which he would not like to know anything and by which he feels "despoiled".

In other words, to cite Marion Milner: it is a body in necrosis that occupies the role once occupied by the mother, and left by her in inheritance; how can this body replace the role of the Mother? How can it take care of itself?

In a concrete and condensed way we see, therefore, that the dream describes and communicates the operations and means used in order to enter into the psychotic state. We also see that the dream can have a predictive value as well: warning in the face of traumatic abandonments that could trigger a psychotic crisis (De Masi, 2006).

4th dream. On his return from the summer holidays he began by saying: "I don't know if it's a question of negative transference but I did a series of things that I should not have done (the reference was to a real estate investment that he regretted). But why didn't you tell me that I should not have done them?"

Analyst: "So many times you yourself had told me that I was not your real estate consultant, why was it necessary for me to give you my opinion?"

"Because I wanted to get you out of the setting, I'm not like the other patients, your silence is annihilating for me.

I'll tell you the dream I had this summer, accompanying my daughter to . . . At a certain point while I was in the hotel room the wall disappeared, then my bed with me in it and later my daughter disappeared in the next room".

Once again the analytical holidays were resurrecting dramatic experiences of loss, annihilation and loss of ego boundaries. This dream seems to me to be an analogon of the body in necrosis; it describes the progressive disappearance of the house of the ego, including a loved one: his daughter!

This dream, through its associations (to be found in what Giacomo said before telling the dream), also informs us of his compulsive acting out and masochistic rage ("see what trouble I have got into because you were not there"), aimed at making me feel guilty and at filling the emptiness caused by my absence.

The images of the dream, however, seem to me to tell a lot more; they strike me particularly, stimulating my countertransference and the theoretical background that accompanies it. They make me think in particular of an article by Carla De Toffoli and the work of Piera Aulagnier. I remember an article by De Toffoli in which she noted, astutely, that while it is often and opportunely quoted, from *The Ego and the Id* (Freud, 1922), that the ego is first and foremost a bodily ego, it is much less often cited that in the same work Freud based the continuing existence of the ego on its network of loving relationships: "To the ego, therefore, living means the same as being loved" (Freud, 1922, 58) (De Toffoli, 2001, 469). I think, therefore, that the images of the dream – and I am thinking also at this point about the person in progressive necrosis in the last dream before the holidays – thanks to dream regression, refer to the continuing existence of the embryos of the ego in the network of loving relationships. These images recount what words cannot say, because there were no words at the time to which reference is being made, which perhaps one can attempt to describe only by resorting to a pictographic register (Aulagnier, 1975). I think it is possible to hypothesize that these images represent the pictogram of rejection and the desire for self-annihilation that is coextensive with it. These are pictograms that reflect the encounter of the "primal" psychic process with an external reality, which did not give rise to a hoped-for experience of fusion and to those repeated experiences of pleasure and desire that give rise to the autoerotic investment in the body and to the subsequent sense of being and of a self settled in the body.[6] Or, to cite Winnicott, what better illustration can be given of "primitive agonies"? Of the fear that the unity of the Self will collapse? Of the procession of catastrophic sensations deriving from dream regression, extended to the point where the object is indistinguishable from the Self, so that the disappearance of that object (the analyst and his other figures of reference – he was alone in a hotel room) coincides with his own disappearance?

The images of this dream seem to me the best possible illustration of the anxieties from which his clinging behaviours derived, his complaisance (for fear of destroying the object), his hunger for contact, through the internet or by activating his own sensoriality in a self-referential way, by overeating. It is possible to understand even better "the despoliation of the ego" that the dietician could have caused him: expressing ourselves with the dream images of the first dream, we could say that his house would also have been deprived of the kitchen, not only of the living room.

5th dream. "The following Monday: I was on the bed, a double bed. I hear the sound of a wooden person who is knocking into something. I wake up, I'm terrified. It is a face without a mouth, with maple veining. Then I go back to sleep, I think: all right, it's my psychotic nucleus".

Comment: "this wooden character is my psychotic nucleus that makes trouble. . . . The problem is exuberance, and this causes addiction, it is a being high on cocaine in a natural way. . . . I am high on mania and so I relish the fantasy of finding a beautiful woman via the internet, doing a lot of things . . . while I feel battered by you when you urge me to think".

In the next session, in a sort of rumination, he adds: "in the dream I had of the wooden man, I think he is a phantasm of mine from my childhood who has grown older. I had seen a film, the green man, for a while I had to sleep hand in hand with my sister. Working on this wooden part also means being more able to listen to others . . . it comes to mind that the head of this wooden man is the same as that of a painting by De Chirico, Metaphysics, and also as my head in a photo with my sister which dates back to that time. She was in a white dress for her First Communion and I also demanded to be dressed in white".

Analyst: "Was the green man a materialization of your being green with envy of your sister?"

Giacomo: "Yes, the mannequin is me, the freezing of those emotions".

Here, too, we can see that the function of the dream of containing and elaborating anxiety fails in part ("I am terrified"), but the annihilating experience of the previous session seems partly mitigated, thanks to the resumption of the analysis. Having found the analyst again after the holidays restored to him that bit of basic trust in the relationship, which allowed him access to the introjected interpretative word ("it's my psychotic nucleus") and the trust in his ability to succeed in functioning in an integrated way. This is a trust that can be glimpsed in the next session from his associations with the man who is green with envy and his insight of what makes him similar to a mannequin: the freezing of those emotions.

It seems to me that it is possible to see the activation in Giacomo of the "psycho-analytic function of personality" (Bion, 1962, 89) which, as Ogden points out (2005, 103), is based on the vision of experience contemporaneously from the points of view of the conscious mind and of the unconscious mind, a vision that typically occurs in the experience of dreaming. The annihilating experience of the previous dream disappeared one week after the resumption, and was mitigated, thanks to a greater emotional closeness, which had been created in the analysis room, due to the effect that his latest dreams had had on me (the person in necrosis and the disappearance of the walls . . . of the daughter). It seems to me that these dreams had been used by my analysand to expel into my mind not only distressing dream contents but also his abilities to contain the anxiety and elaborate them. The dreams seemed to have the meaning of an extreme attempt to convince me that he really was not able to tolerate separations. These dreams partly achieved their goal; that is, they had seemed exceptionally eloquent to me and had touched me more than any other previous communication of his. I have the impression that my tone of voice had changed in these sessions, evidence of the change in my way of considering his emotional experience.

At the same time, we can see a change also in Giacomo: he became a mannequin, a puppet. This was an attempt at reorganization, which may appear incongruous: the mannequin that must freeze emotions.

However, in recognizing his non-human status as a puppet (my psychotic nucleus) he became aware of it ("I'm high on mania"), and this was a good omen for the "emotionalization" of the self, which it seemed to me he was able to accomplish, starting from the experience of resonance that was created in the analytic relationship.

After some time I thought of this last dream as "a dream that turns over a page" (Quinodoz, 2001) because it was indicative of the return into the ego of what had been denied and split off (the face without a mouth with maple veining, my psychotic nucleus). Whereas the perception of these split parts on the one hand generates anxiety because of the threat to the cohesion of the ego (I am terrified), on the other, it can signal the increased identification of the patient with the analyst's capacity to contain.

The fact is that such distressing dreams were no longer as frequent in this analytical journey.

Here is one, for example, of a very different quality, related to a more advanced phase of the analysis.

Monday session: "The police calls me and tells me that I have to bring them my identity documents".

He associated this with a football match he had been watching. At a certain point he had to go towards a different part of the field, where, as it were, another game was being played: some young men were throwing smoke bombs onto the field with the risk that the match would be annulled just as Giacomo's team was winning the match and championship.

Compared to the previous dreams, we see a completely changed scenario: his existence is no longer dramatically at stake, and therefore there is no longer any clinging to the pictographic representations of bodily things, which are the first representations that psychic activity produces of itself (Aulagnier, 1975). The scenario is more evolved: there is a minimum of narrative structure, words appear, there are other characters with a clear symbolic content (the police), the associations refer to a conflict that is probably of a narcissistic nature and the dream is also able to carry out fully, unlike previous dreams, its function of protecting sleep.

The problems we encountered were less archaic: the doubt about his existence became the doubt about his identity – the police who wanted to know who he really was – and about the narcissistic problems connected to it. I believe the young men who were throwing smoke bombs onto the field because their team was not winning represented the omnipotent and infantile narcissistic part of Giacomo, which did not tolerate well the dependence on the analyst, and the procession of envy, jealousy and abandonment anxieties (the dream was told on Monday).

I said to Giacomo: "do you remember the dream that you had of thinking of yourself as a mannequin that must freeze emotions? It seems to me that we are seeing their unfreezing, the appearance of emotions that were very strong at certain periods in your life and which are reactivated by the current situation. There are young men who want to be the only protagonists of the match, they do not tolerate that there is, for example, a referee who whistles for the beginning or end of the match (like the analyst), and they throw smoke bombs onto the field, so as not to allow the players to 'achieve the result', that is, so as not to allow the analyst to make his interpretations and yourself to listen to them".

In this context the police (his internal judge) seemed to have some doubts about his real intentions and asked for the documents to check his age, his profession, etc. and try to understand why he went to that part of the stadium where the smoke bombs were being thrown: to fight the young men or to join them?

Final considerations

The dreams that I have discussed are related to a phase of Giacomo's analysis in which his acting out, his pathological addictions and other expressions of the psychotic part of his personality were greatly diminished.

This first fact is a confirmation of what is reported in the literature on the relationship between the ability to dream and these psychopathological manifestations: the dream is basically an expression of the non-psychotic part of the personality, and has a protective role towards the dreamer.

Even the so-called evacuative dreams, as we could consider at least in part those that I have recounted (except for the last one), in order to have the possibility of being produced, need for the dreamer to have incorporated a breast-container, capable, at least, of "containing" his projective identifications within the screen of the dream. Although in these cases there may be little evidence of elaborative transformation of the projective identifications deriving from the relationship that internal objects have among themselves, with the self, and with sensory experience, the containment in the dream screen prevents their violent expulsion to the outside and the resulting explosion of symptoms.

If one adds to this first result the fact that the deficit in dream work present in these dreams can be compensated for by the further containment and elaboration provided by the analytical couple, one can conclude by reaffirming the value of the via regia also for this type of dream. The work of the analysis, in these cases, provides a gestational support to the dream images that are insufficiently processed by the dream work (due to the insufficiency of the alpha function, of the requirements that allow a good dream) and continues its work of symbolic construction and conferring of meaning to sensory and emotional experience.

The emotional impact caused by listening to a dream (both in the person who has dreamed it and hears his or her own recounting of it, and in the analyst) is such as to cause a series of associations that act like a picklock in opening doors blocked by repression, and at times even by foreclosure, and allow access to dissociated and split emotional truths, buried in implicit, somatic memory. In this way, a series of memories can be reactivated, setting off a process of emotional recovery of past experiences and their possible integration with current experiences lived in the transference.

We have seen, for example, that the missing living room in the first dream referred to the lack of analytic dialogue, because of the summer holidays, and to the dream of the little ant, dreamed in similar circumstances. The current event, the separation from the analyst, was a trauma, the regressive pressure of which made it true, après coup, that what happened in early times – when Hilflosigkeit (helplessness) and the lack of encounter between the timing of the mother and that of the son were dominant – was not distinguishable from what was happening at the current time: the analyst who did not care about him, about his timing, and went off on holiday. We see the same mechanism in action also in the other dreams:

the associations to the intense sensory and somatic experience present in the dream refer to the painful memory of the dreamer's developmental traumas, so much so as to assume, potentially, that "traumatolytic function" introduced by Ferenczi (1931) and taken up again by Martín-Cabré (2011), who described it as a process "whereby traumatic experiences were dissolved and undone".

The intense sensory and somatic experience present in Giacomo's dreams (the body in necrosis, the head made of wood, the little ant, the sudden disappearance of himself and of his daughter, etc.) refers to the traumatic experiences of the primary relationship, to a body which, because it was not recognized by the dialogue with the mother and not accepted by the maternal rêverie, even now seems not to belong to him, and not to recognize signals (this can be seen in his somewhat awkward way of moving and his eating disorders). These dream images, rather than being phantasmatic productions, probably refer to more archaic productions, and seem to be an effect of the laws that regulate the activity of representation of the beginnings. In fact, they seem very close to those representations of bodily things (pictograms) that originate the psychic metabolization of the need states of the body. I believe that it is possible to hypothesize that dreaming of bodily things, and providing a picture of them to the analyst, expresses "the hope of encountering the psychic process in which [the patient] is immobilized, frozen and apparently out of reach" (De Mijolla-Mellor, 1998, 121, see Moscato, 2013). In this way, the analyst is offered a possibility of representation and consequent symbolic construction that in the patient's childhood was missing on the part of the maternal rêverie.

These dreams, more than trying to inform the analyst about the unconscious discourse (often foreclosed rather than repressed), try to act out on him. On these occasions, the analyst finds himself or herself in the situation of a mother who listens to her child's screams and signals of despair and must look for their meaning, translating it into gestures and words, and in this way taking on the role of the child's apparatus for thinking.

I believe that interpretation, in these cases, can only aim at making thinkable and shareable a concrete image that is the result of the encounter in external reality with something – traumatic separations, unbearable void – which, through dream regression, can send to the dreamer the mirror image of the pictographic representation that he or she has of himself or herself, that is to say, of those primal representations of the infans that do not know exteriority.

If one succeeds in making these images of bodily things thinkable and shareable, one can succeed in disanchoring them from the somatic memory and inserting them into a process of phantasmatic activity that avails itself of an expanded mental container, including the analyst's mental apparatus and its capacity to tolerate anguish.

If this happens, the patient will be helped to move onward from a tyrannically auto-sensory functioning, which requires excitations and continuous stimulations, to the possibility of a libidinal-emotional cathexis of the Self and of the world. It is a cathexis that comes about through a preliminary renarcissization of the Self, which involves a more harmonious mind-body relationship, and allows the patient to tolerate those structuring experiences of separation that lead to the representation of the absent object and to its replacement through symbolic construction.

Notes

1 This chapter has been translated into English by Molly Rogers.
2 An interesting elaboration of the concepts of Khan, of Pontalis (1977) and of M. Milner on the experience of dreaming and the dream text can be found in the book by L. Russo (2013), *Esperienze*.
3 Among the many episodes recounted by my analysand that testify to the lack of the role of the accompanying father during childhood and adolescence, when he could have modulated sometimes unbearable affects and emotions, facilitating, among other things, the passage from emotion to speech, there is the memory of a three-hour car trip, made with his father. They did not exchange a word, and upon arrival, his father said to him: "Well done, you have been able to be silent for the whole trip".
   This was one of the many missed opportunities on the part of the father to teach his son to think and tell about himself, that which according to Ricoeur (1983) helps to form "the narrative identity", the achievement of that degree of coherence and continuity of the Self that makes us feel that we are authors of our story, rather than impotent spectators of a story that concerns us.
4 I want to emphasize that the language used by Giacomo does not derive, as some might imagine, from his professional membership in the psychological world (his profession is completely different), but rather from his culture and imitative mechanisms, which I will mention later.
5 Note, among other things, the amplification: in the experience of Giacomo the usual time interval between one session and another has become a week, whereas our encounters were three times a week.
6 Following the thought of Aulagnier (1975), this first time period, this first experience, carries out an inducing role if the later encounters with external reality do not succeed in curing this first injury: if "In its turn, the primary has sought in vain in the outside-self for signs that might allow it to find in the locus of the Other the cause of a state of pleasure that one may link to one's desire and, what is more, signs that would deny one's fantasies of rejection, which would help one to recognise that the world and the other's body are also loci in which pleasure is possible, in which desire may be fulfilled"; and finally if "the I encounters in the space in which it must come about, in the statements that must establish it and which will constitute it, *the order of having to be*, whereas *whenever it becomes*, in each image of itself that it tends to cathect, it comes up against the prohibition of being that form, that image, that moment, as soon as they are presented as *its* choice" (Aulagnier, 1975, English edition 2001, 226). The occurrence of these three conditions provokes the psychotic response and delirium with which the ego defends its possibility to exist.
   The story of Giacomo seems to confirm the existence of these conditions.

References

Arieti, S. (1963). The psychotherapy of schizophrenia in theory and practice. *Psychiatric Research Report* 17: 13–29.

Aulagnier, P. (1975). *The Violence of Interpretation: From Pictogram to Statement.* Trans by A. Sheridan. Hove and East Sussex: Brunner-Routledge, 2001.

Bion, W.R. (1958). The hallucination. In *Second Thoughts* (Selected Papers on psychoanalysis). London: William Heinemann Medical Books.

Bion, W.R. (1962). *Learning from Experience.* London: William Heinemann Medical Books.

Blechner, M. (1983). Changes in the dreams of borderline patients. *Contemporary Psychoanalysis* 19: 485–498.

Bleger, J. (1967). Psychoanalysis of the psychoanalitic frame. *International Journal of Psychoanalysis* 48: 511–519.

De Masi, F. (2006). *Vulnerabilità alla psicosi.* Milano, Cortina.

De Mijolla-Mellor, S. (1998). *Penser la psychose. Une lecture de l'oeuvre de Piera Aulagnier.* Paris: Dunod.

De Toffoli, C. (2001). Psicosoma. Il sapere del corpo nel lavoro psicoanalitico. *Rivista di Psicoanalisi* 47: 465–486.

Eissler, K.R. (1953). The effect of the structure of the Ego on psychoanalytic technique. *Journal American Psychoanalitic Association* 1953: 104–143.

Ferenczi, S. (1931). On the revision of the interpretation of dreams. In *Notes and Fragments: Final Contributions to the Problem and Methods of Psychoanalysis.* London: The Hogarth Press, 1955.

Ferrari, A.B. (1992). *From the Eclipse of the Body to the Dawn of Thought.* London: Free Association Books, 2004.

Freud, S. (1894). The neuro-psychoses of defence. *Standard Edition* 3.

Freud, S. (1899). Screen memories. *Standard Edition* 3.

Freud, S. (1900). The interpretation of dreams. *Standard Edition* 4–5.

Freud, S. (1911). Psychoanalytic notes on an autobiographical account of a case of paranoia (dementia paranoides). *Standard Edition,* 12.

Freud, S. (1915). A metapsychological supplement to the theory of dreams. *Standard Edition,* 14: 217–235.

Freud, S. (1922). The ego and the ID. *Standard Edition* 19.

Freud, S. (1937). Constructions in analysis. *Standard Edition* 23.

Freud, S. (1938a). Splitting of the ego in the process of defense. *Standard Edition,* 23.

Freud, S. (1938b). An outline of psycho-analysis. *Standard Edition* 23: 139–208.

Gaddini, E. (1980). Notes on the mind-body question. In *A Psychoanalytic Theory of Infantile Experience: Conceptual and Clinical Reflections.* London: Routledge, 2005.

Gaddini, E. (1982). Early defensive fantasies and the psychoanalytical process. *International Journal of Psycho-analysis* 63: 379–388.

Green, A. (1985). The dead mother. In *Life Narcissism, Death Narcissism.* London: Free Association Books, 2001.

Green, A. (1986). *On Private Madness.* London: The Hogarth Press.

Grinberg, L., Apter, A., Bellagamba, H., Berenstein, I., De Cereijido, F., Garfinkel, G., Faigon, D., De Failla, I.S., Liendo, E.C. and Sapochnik, L. (1967). Función del soñar y classificatión clinica de los sueños en el proceso analitico. In Grinberg, L. (Editor), (1981). *Psicoanalisis. Aspectos teoricos y clinicos.* Paidos: Barcelona-Buenos Aires.

Khan, M.M.R. (1962). Dream psychology and the evolution of the psychoanalytic situation. In *The Privacy of the Self*. London: The Hogarth Press, 1974.

Khan, M.M.R. (1972). The use and abuse of dream in psychic experience. In *The Privacy of the Self*. London: The Hogarth Press, 1974.

Khan, M.M.R. (1976). Beyond the dreaming experience. In *Hidden Selves*. London: The Hogarth Press and the Institute of Psycho-Analysis, 1983.

Jones, E. (1948). *Papers on psychoanalysis*. London, Baillière: Tindall & Cox Ltd.

Lacan, J. (1966). *Ecrits. The first complete edition in English*. New York: W.W. Norton and Company, 2006.

Lombardi, R. (2006). Catalizzando il dialogo tra il corpo e la mente. *Rivista di Psicoanaisi* 52 (3): 743–766.

Martín-Cabré, L.J. (2011). Responce. *International Journal of Psycho-Analysis* 92: 272–274.

Mc Dougall, J. (2003). L'economia psichica della dipendenza: una soluzione psicosomatica al dolore psichico. In Rinaldi, L. (Editor). (2003) *Stati caotici della mente: psicosi, borderline, disturbi psicosomatici, dipendenze*. Milano: Cortina.

Meltzer, D. (1984). *Dream-Life*. London: The Roland Harris Educational Trust.

Milner, M. (1969). *The Hands of the Living God. An Account of a Psychoanalytic Treatment*. London: The Hogarth Press and the Institute of Psychoanalysis.

Moscato, F. (2013). Significati del sogno nell'analisi degli stati limite. Presentazione o rappresentazione della pulsione di morte? *Rivista di Psicoanalisi* 59 (1): 49–68.

Ogden, T.H. (1989). *The Primitive Edge of Experience*. Northvale, NJ and London: Jason Aronson Inc.

Ogden, T.H. (2005). *The Art of Psychoanalysis. Dreaming Undreamed Dreams and Interrupted Cries*. Northvale, NJ and London: Jason Aronson Inc.

Pontalis, J.B. (1977). *Frontiers in Psychoanalysis: Between the Dream and Psychic Pain*. London: The Hogarth Press, 1981.

Quinodoz, J.M. (2001). *Dreams That Turn Over a Page: Paradoxical Dreams in Psychoanalysis*. London: The New Library of Psychoanalysis, Published in association with the Institute of Psychoanalysis, 2002.

Ricoeur, P. (1983). *Temps et Récit*. Paris: Editions du Seuil.

Rinaldi, L. (2003) (a cura di). *Stati caotici della mente: psicosi, borderline, disturbi psicosomatici, dipendenze*. Milano: Cortina.

Russo, L. (2013). *Esperienze. Corpo, visione, parola nel lavoro psicoanalitico*. Roma: Borla.

Schulz, C.G., and Kilgalen, R.K. (1969). *Case Studies in Schizophrenia*. New York: Basic Books.

Segal, H. (1991). *Dream, Phantasy and Art*. London: The New Library of Psychoanalysis, Published in association with the Institute of Psychoanalysis.

Winnicott, D.W. (1945). Primitive emotional development. In *Through Paediatrics to Psycho-Analysis*. London: Tavistock, 1958.

Winnicott, D.W. (1947). Hate in the countertransference. In *Through Paediatrics to Psycho-Analysis*. London: Tavistock, 1958.

Winnicott, D.W. (1949). Mind and its relation to the psycho-soma. In *Through Paediatrics to Psycho-Analysis*. London: Tavistock, 1958.

Winnicott, D.W. (1950). Aggression in relation to emotional development. In *Through Paediatrics to Psycho-Analysis*. London: Tavistock, 1958.

Winnicott, D.W. (1971). *Playing and Reality*. London: Tavistock, 1958.

Chapter 11

Note on psychotic activity in pathological organizations

Paul Williams

A 60 year old man diagnosed with a hebephrenic schizophrenia says to his analyst:

> *It's still a very difficult problem. I'm always in situations of pressure. I've lost my job and see threats all round me. I can't rely on bits of work here and there. I've become terrified of going out because I'm convinced I'll freeze. I should resign from everything.*

A 25 year old man with a severe personality disorder says:

> *I thought I was going see my dad this weekend but my step mother rang to say it wasn't convenient. I know my dad got her to say that. I don't want to be on my own but they don't want me. I'm a nuisance, a pest. Thoughts come in like a barrage. There is no hope anything will change. I should die.*

A 31 year old woman who was sexually abused over several years as a child reports:

> *I had a dream. I can't remember anything much except there was a cata-strophic scene, a terrorist attack, in which bodies were strewn everywhere. I try to tell someone who laughs at me and says I'm overreacting.*

A 62 year old female patient reports a 'Robber' who steals all good experiences away whenever she has something she wants.

A woman in her 20s says:

> *I liked talking to you last time, then on my way home a voice in my head told me nobody wants me. I am on three dating agencies and no-one has contacted me, no-one writes. It's hopeless. It's true: nobody does want me. It has always been that way.*

These statements, and other similar statements familiar to psychiatrists and psychoanalysts, indicate the presence of extreme anxiety which destabilizes the capacity to think and feel and disconnects the individuals from others. They are not formal auditory hallucinations that cripple the individual's functioning, but rather chronic, interfering 'voices' or 'presences' that control, usurp and destabilise ego functioning, constraining the personality and rendering psychological growth or change difficult, perhaps impossible. This ideation, I suggest, lies at the heart of pathological organization activity.

Pathological organizations

Pathological organizations are defensive structures fuelled ultimately by the individual's primitive aggression that deploy omnipotent thought purporting to prevent the ego from succumbing to anxieties (felt as dread) and from the notion that the individual will disintegrate and die. Their 'instruction' to the ego is to avoid any emotional pain associated with object need. They use emotional coercion, as though such pains are fatal. Change or growth is viewed as catastrophic, so thinking about internal and external reality becomes extremely difficult. Pathological organizations are not coterminous with superego activity: their presence involves *invasiveness*; neither guidance nor benign control of the ego is provided, but rather absolute tyranny over it on pain of death (Williams, 2010). This hold over the ego is maintained to the degree that the ego remains identified with the ideas, images and part-object representations used by the pathological organization.

Pathological organizations are considered to arise in response to traumatically disrupted dependency states in childhood in order to provide a delusional belief in a state of psychic equilibrium, one that is inherently precarious as it is derived from dissociation from experiences of human need. *Dictats* from the organization supplant ego functioning in order to supply pathological forms of containment acting *in loco parentis*. Attempts by the ego of the individual to develop in healthy ways are viewed as portents of ruin – repetitions of the prior traumatic experiences – and are prevented at all cost.

The degree of narcissistic disturbance in the individual has a crucial bearing, in my experience, on the intensity and function of the sadism employed by the pathological organization to restrict or immobilize the ego. The extent of the ego's submission to a dominant, narcissistic, psychotic part-object affects the severity and outcome of pathological organization activity. If a patient is narcissistic and disconnected from normal dependency states and associated anxieties, and idealizes and identifies with a narcissistic part-object, pressure to identify with the pathological organization's commands is greater, attacks on links to objects are more ruthlessly destroyed and the destruction of non-psychotic thinking is longer lasting. Control over the subject by the organization is maintained by threats of annihilation or else perverse seductions by the narcissistic part-object upon which the patient has become dependent (cf. Williams, 2004, 2010). The threats are premised on the need to avoid an even greater threat – repetition of traumatic loss of a needed object. Narcissistic patients in the grip of such a pathological organization may be experienced as cold, psychopathic or cynical and held in thrall. The pathological organization activity that controls such individuals occurs 'outside' normal parameters of paranoid-schizoid/depressive position thinking or normal lines of development. These patients experience psychotic anxieties and can exhibit paranoid thinking, but the pathological organization activity needs to be distinguished from paranoia in terms of its origin, although the two conditions can interact.

Where the presence of severe narcissism is less evident, for example, in certain borderline or depressed patients, and the relationship between the subject and internal part-objects appears to be more openly conflicted (giving rise, for example, to more strident expressions of object hatred and sadomasochism) the role and function of sadism directed towards the ego may be seen to take on a more openly declamatory, seductive, mocking form of bullying and enticement, as opposed to the chilling threats of annihilation emanating from its more severely narcissistic version. The aim appears to be the same – to control the ego – but in more borderline and depressive conditions the ego can appear to be at the mercy of an attacking part-object figure whilst, tantalisingly, being permitted more latitude compared with the absoluteness of incorporative identification in severe narcissism. Patients located at or near the narcissistic end of the pathological spectrum find analytic treatment extremely difficult to bear, whereas patients located towards a declamatory, openly conflicted sadomasochism find analysis difficult to bear but can show greater tolerance of transference pressures and affect storms. Generalization isn't advisable as the picture is mixed, sadism being apparent in both situations: what is described here reflects tendencies rather than strict classifications.

Object relations theory argues that we develop to the extent that we internalize good objects: we are not so much driven in pursuit of pleasure as in need of relatedness. The more integrated and whole our internal objects are, the less likely we are to succumb to emotional, psychological or mental illness: yet internal objects are, as we know, often far from whole or integrated. The term 'object' is found in Freud (cf. Freud, 1905, 1915) but not in the sense used by subsequent object relations theorists. It is distinctive in and central to the work of Klein on forms of identification (cf. Klein, 1997, p. 49) and takes what might be thought of as a pure form in the work of Fairbairn, for whom an internal object denotes a psychopathological structure in contrast to relations with real, external people that are satisfying and non-pathological to the extent that they do not give rise to internal objects. The establishment of internal objects is the result of disappointment, a universal psychological occurrence, producing active psychic structures with a dynamism of their own interacting in the unconscious (Fairbairn, 1952), and these include an agency homologous to the pathological organization originally referred to by Fairbairn as an 'internal saboteur'.

Building on Klein's work on projective identification and schizoid mechanisms (Klein, 1946), Wilfred Bion, in his paper on the differentiation of psychotic and non-psychotic personalities, depicted organised, minute splitting of parts of the personality associated with internal and external reality. These parts are expelled using extreme forms of projective identification: engulfment of their objects and the surviving ego can lead to an existence that is predominantly hallucinatory, characterised by a preponderance of destructive thoughts, dread of annihilation and impairment of processes of introjection and regression. In Bion's view, contact with reality is never entirely lost by these patients, and the clinical objective is to find the neurotic personality concealed by psychotic activity (Bion, 1957). He also referred to an 'ego destructive superego' as an internalised psychotic figure that attacks links between objects and between emotion and reason in an extreme attempt to avoid emotional pain by destroying mental functioning. Linked to this is his concept of an 'obstructive object', a term denoting a projective identification refusing object, originally the mother, seen as a precursor to the instigation of pathological splitting and projective identification (1959, 1962). Herbert Rosenfeld investigated clinically in considerable detail splitting and excessive projective identification activities that break down the sense of self through confusion between what is 'good' and what is 'bad' (1950). He identified how extreme, persistent projective activity in narcissism can give rise to grandiosity and self idealization as a defence against destructiveness towards the needed object and to an idealization of the expelled 'badness' leading to submission to a pathological narcissistic organization (ibid., 1964, 1971, 2004). Meltzer, like Rosenfeld, described a phantasized 'narcissistic gang' in the mind – a type of 'internal Mafia' (a phrase also used by Rosenfeld) – that demanded allegiance using sadism and seduction (Meltzer, 1968). O'Shaughnessy (1981, 1992) also provided detailed accounts of narcissistic defensive organizations that illustrate subjugation of the neurotic personality and a rigid imperative to avoid emotional contact. A number of other analysts have developed these lines of thinking.

Pathological organizations attempt to control the subject by subduing the ego to a psychotic imperative. The impact of a pathological organization is confusingly kaleidoscopic as it is propelled into action by omniscient and omnipotent ideation, including magical thinking, to confound the non-psychotic mind. Less discussed in the literature on pathological organizations is the perversely constructed *in loco parentis* role used to authorize the confounding activity. Distortion, perverse logic, sadistic aggression and seduction are used in coercive, ruthless ways against the weakened ego to indoctrinate it, the aim being to forestall phantasized, imminent traumatic separation. Affect is whipped into psychotic dread to generate aversive responses and to promote dependence upon psychotic thinking. In addition to whipping up of dread, the ego's fears are met by pseudo-explanation, lies and distortion of reality operating in the guise of containment: heightened affect and external reality may often appear as conflated. A frequent experience in analysis is for the patient to feel the onset of sudden dread if and when she or he feels understood by the analyst. Perception of the analyst may shift rapidly from a needed, benign object to a powerful, irrational adversary. These negative therapeutic reactions involve a sudden 'hijacking' of neurotic anxieties that are distorted into psychotic dread, distracting the patient and preventing emergence of the need to depend upon a trustworthy object. Realistic object-relating may have become so misconstrued as to feel unmanageable, rendering the patient despairing. Directives for evasive action are frequently issued according to primitive, binary forms of thinking related to the principle of fight or flight. Experiences of grief and loss of the object are equated with death of the subject and are to be avoided: mourning is demeaned as a portent of self-destruction. A perilous irony is that the organization's task, ostensibly to keep the patient alive, can persist through advocacy of strategies of self-destruction and even suicide: death does not appear to exist whilst the threat of it exists everywhere.

One feature of pathological organization activity that can be difficult to recognize is its quasi-autonomous functioning. The psychotic system operates, in this author's view, in parallel to non-psychotic thinking, monitoring it and opposing it. This can create confusion that runs deeper than may be apparent in verbal presentation or behaviour. For example, a patient might voice mixed feelings regarding something the analyst has said: mixed feelings are the prerogative of a non-psychotic mind. If the pathological organization is ascendant no mixed feelings or doubts are tolerated, only certainties issuing from unmediated aggressive and sexual phantasies. What might appear to be 'mixed feelings' can often be attempted co-operation by a non-psychotic mind opposed by and under the sway of antipathy from a psychotic personality. The two opposing systems of thought functioning simultaneously generate chronic psychological confusion and can paralyze the ego: knowing which system is prevailing at which moment can be difficult, requiring careful attention to the countertransference. The implications for the way we talk to patients in these states of mind are significant. If we assume in the earlier example that we have available a mind that can think, feel and reason, albeit in a conflicted way ('mixed feelings'), we may mistake for conflict the radical, structural disconnect born of psychotic ideation that eliminates links to objects, internal and external, and asserts itself as a superior dependable resource. If we appeal to the patient's higher order thinking to resolve the dilemma, instead of facing up to the intimidation taking place to immobilize thinking, impasse or compliance may follow. To deal with intimidation requires registration within the analyst of both psychotic and non-psychotic communications of the patient. The types of patients described in this paper rarely if ever see themselves as unitary personalities with a recognizable, coherent sense of self. They report feeling alienated, persecuted, possessed, superhuman, worthless, numbed, suicidal, may be addicted to grandiosity, sexual phantasy or risk-filled activity, and rarely do they convey the experience of being whole persons or in possession of a dependable capacity to think. They often enter analysis through *force majeur* when life becomes crushingly difficult, sometimes after many previous treatments, or else they may feel it is impossible to go on due to fear of what they might do to themselves. Even then subjugation and allegiance to the edicts of the psychotic organization can remain firm. Only through a gradual unmasking of the forms of coercion exerted over the patient's non-psychotic mind and a capacity to face these with the analyst can the meaning of the patient's illness become clear. Attempts to integrate psychotic thinking into more healthy ways of thinking are likely to fail, in my experience, and can provoke heightened psychotic attacks. Analytic work with such patients requires the analyst to make an imaginative link between the patient's communication of neurotic anxieties and the distorting activity of their psychotic overlords and to 'dream' these links, including with the patient (Ogden, 2007), a triangulating activity, the aim of which is to differentiate human fears from their magnified, psychotic counterparts. This is a countertransference task of considerable complexity requiring openness in the analyst to the experience of neurotic and psychotic anxieties. Impasses and terminations of treatments of patients controlled by pathological organizations may frequently be the result of a collapse of this triangulating perspective due to the ascendancy of psychotic ideation to a degree that both parties become embroiled in the patient's primitive dyadic struggle. In the following vignettes, ways of talking with patients suffering domination by pathological organizations, and who *know* they suffer this way, are illustrated and discussed for their technical implications.

Clinical example I

Mr A.

What follows is part of a session with a patient who experiences a severe pathological narcissistic organization. The man has been in treatment for 13 years, for 10 of these years five times weekly on the couch (he sat in a chair for a period at the outset) and for the last three years four times weekly on the couch due to his analyst having moved further away from the patient's home, which has made travelling more difficult. Mr A might have received a diagnosis of borderline personality disorder had he presented initially to out-patient psychiatry, and there may have been truth in this imaginary diagnosis as his ego functioning appeared to be driven by anger and indignation which frequently disrupted the treatment. It took five or six years before Mr A was able to begin to talk about himself. Prior to this I witnessed continuous outrage, vindictiveness and self-hate. He denounced banks, corporations, rich people, poor people, immigrants, his parents, neighbours, anyone who offended him, including himself. He appeared to be grandiose and all-knowing, a superior being who held the failings of humanity in contempt, showing pitiless derision for the limitations of others, particularly his analyst. He read a good deal to stimulate his intellect, only major authors, was interested in Freud, scrutinized psychoanalysis as a conceptual system but viewed analytic treatment, particularly as practised by me, as marred by feeble-mindedness or else arrogance. My patient saw himself as a genius or demi-God of infinite skills and capacities, and on occasion as a stupid, witless fool.

He was the fourth of six children born into a chaotic, middle class Catholic family with a depressed, withdrawn housewife mother and charismatic father, the headmaster of a liberal private school. The father seems to have treated the family home as a commune or open house providing solace, play, education and entertainment to children less fortunate than his own, and the patient described strange children rampaging around the house, often bullying each other in an atmosphere of excitement and competitive ill-will – a routine of chaos, the patient said, construed by the father as creative and counter-culturally life-enhancing. My patient felt as a child like a performing dog trying to emulate the tricks of larger dogs. He did not feel close to his mother despite longing for her and found his unavailable father grand, remote and tantalising. When the patient was 7 his father suffered two serious strokes in short succession and after a brief period of hospitalisation died. The family did not discuss the matter; he was neither told what had happened nor comforted and from then on was baffled about his father's whereabouts. Isolated in the crowded home, he retreated into a private inner world bolstered by a sense of superiority, contempt and a belief that he was in complete control of the world in which he lived, including his ineffective, depressed mother. He told me that after the death of his father he never relied upon human beings again whilst at the same time 'taking charge' of his mother, by which he meant studying her moods in order to find ways of extracting some attention from her. He relied mainly on a phantasy world of adventure stories, particularly about soldiers, armies, military exploits and battles. He began collecting militaria of the Third Reich and idealized its leaders. The family foundered, his depressed mother became unable to cope and five of the six children were sent away to boarding school. The patient was one

of them and for the ensuing years until the age of 18 was bullied merci-
lessly. On the basis of 'if you can't beat 'em, join 'em' he took on his bullies'
ways, vowing to outwit them. He told me that from the age of 6, although
it might have been earlier, a voice in his head had guided his actions. It
announces what he should do to impress or ingratiate himself with others,
only to tell him that when he speaks people hate him and are laughing at
him because what he said was stupid. When he retreated into isolation the
voice issued condemnation of his inability to socialise, condemning him
to a lifetime of humiliation if he didn't change his ways. As an adult he
worked in irregular, mostly undemanding jobs as he never felt competent,
whilst believing that no job is good enough for him. In his 20s he met a
retiring, patient young woman whom he later married, and the marriage
has continued reasonably despite his difficulties.

Mr A's pathological organization reacted with violence when he tried to
talk to me: he was obliged to succumb to its viewpoint and yell at me and
himself. Such events had the quality of sudden, all-out war, the outcome
in him being icy silence with occasional sarcasm and contempt. From the
outset the analyst was berated at full tilt with accusations designed to
inflict disdain and shame, the end result always hostile silence. After 18
months of yelling and silence, which I could not change (all attempts to
break the silences reactivated the yelling), I said to him that his behaviour
was making us both sick and analytic work impossible. If he was unable
to control these tirades we may need to think about stopping the analysis.
Alternatively if, when he felt compelled to yell at me, he could manage to
stay quiet and wait until he had something he wanted to say, we would be
able to continue. If he could not prevent himself from screaming in the session, he could leave the session and return the next day, and we could try
again. I appreciate that this is an unusual way of working, in effect asking
the patient to not say what comes into his mind, but he accepted it with,
to my surprise, what appeared to be a certain amount of relief, and things
began to improve a little in that he became slightly more able to talk without a tirade. The icy contempt persisted, but on only two occasions has he
needed to leave sessions when screaming was unstoppable. The curb on
screaming allowed for more awareness of the complexity in his responses:
it became more possible for him to question why he was angry when he
became angry in contrast to an immediate succumbing to the whipping up
of indignation to prevent discussion of his anger. A capacity to distinguish
between a complaint and tyranny began to emerge: a space, albeit small,
in which his difficulties might be observed and, occasionally, talked about
began to develop in proportion to his capacity to not instantly defer when
under siege from the pathological organization. The following vignette
is not from the beginning of the analysis but from a session several years
in when he had become more able to talk to me about his needs and feelings and to be aware of his experience of repeated, violent opposition to

needs, desires and feelings. The session was on a Tuesday, the second of the week.

Mr A: Hallo.

A: Hallo.

　　　pause 2–3 mins

Mr A: (the tone is flat) I don't know what's going on today. I'm not sure I'll be able to talk. It's telling me I've got nothing to say, you must be bored with listening to this year after year. I am tired of the way I do this and have done it for so long. Nothing has changed. (the tone becomes increasingly agitated) I'm so stupid.

A: Something's happened: it seems you knew before the session how I feel about you and that the explanation for your difficulties is so obvious as to not be worth discussing – you're stupid.

Mr A: I AM stupid (angry). You are not seeing the point. (*pause*) I think it must be something to do with the last session. I felt better after we talked then very sad. The weekend was difficult. It made sense when we talked that I felt hopeless about my mother not being able to take in anything I said to her. It was terrible. It was like I was always alone, looking for her but she was never there. My father was never available either. I remember trying so hard to talk to her and her looking blank or swatting me away like I was a pest and I kept trying, following her around for years like she was a robot. I felt sad in the afternoon yesterday and last night had a horrible dream. I was in a house like the one we lived in when I was young. The phone rang and it was a man from a company that employs me from time to time. I couldn't understand it but he was saying something about his company having gone bust and I wouldn't get paid: the contract between us was useless now and I shouldn't go back. In the dream I panicked: I thought we'd be homeless. I woke up terrified and checked with Jane (his wife) but she said everything was alright, it was just a bad dream. I couldn't work out if it was happening, even after I talked to her, and had to ring him this morning.

　　　pause

　　　It's saying you don't want to hear this, how many times have I said all this before . . . but these things ARE terrifying. If I lost my job we could lose everything.

　　　pause

　　　I should stop this analysis and save the money. I've been doing it for too long. Jane has to work hard . . . we never get to enjoy the money we earn or have time together (the tone becomes coldly contemptuous) Isn't it reasonable to want to stop having therapy after such a long time?

A: I think things are meant to spiral out of control inside you and
        between us as feelings of alarm, being misunderstood and self-
        hatred are whipped up. This familiar story of catastrophe is one
        you and I are meant to believe completely right now, I suspect
        because you and I aren't meant to think about the most impor-
        tant thing you have told me today – that you felt better yester-
        day and then very sad. You felt compassion for a small boy lost
        and in distress, unable to talk to his mother, a boy in need of help
        and understanding, only then your sad feelings switch and he/
        you are stupid and useless, I am angry with you because you are
        apparently boring and your true feelings get lost.

Mr A: (angry) Things ARE terrible. You are not responding to my point.
        Work is difficult and it's not just in this country. What IS wrong
        about wanting to stop!? I can't go on like this for years. We'll have
        nothing!! Can't you see?

A: I think that boy in you, we might call it your deepest needs, has
        to be murdered *because* you need and want help from me. If you
        need me, you have someone, something you could lose and this
        makes you frightened, understandably. You are not meant to take
        this risk so you have to cut me out, cut you out and cut everyone
        else out. Quit and retreat. Then you'll be safe on your own, the
        story goes.

Mr A: I know this. (shrieks briefly but then speaks in a more disjointed,
        despairing way than this transcript depicts) I can't STAND it!
        I can't do it. It's hopeless, I am sick of it. You're not listening to
        ME. Who do you think you are anyway? You force your point
        of view on me and I get ignored . . . you call yourself an analyst?
        I really think I should stop.
            (He becomes upset and tearful in addition to enraged and then
        falls silent for 10 mins, I think in part complying with our agree-
        ment that he does not succumb to yelling. I sense he is trying to stay
        in the present, whilst also feeling contemptuous, under pressure to
        remain disconnected and yet struggling with something upsetting.)
            I spoke to Jane. She said that whilst things were difficult the
        chances of me losing my job and things going disastrously wrong
        were probably very small. Her job is secure. I don't know what to
        believe.

A: It is difficult to know what to believe.
            short pause

Mr A: Oh, it's hopeless. Today is hopeless. When you don't speak to me
        it makes it hopeless and it makes me furious. For God's sake! Why
        I should put up with this?

A: You wanted more of a reply, so what I said is meant to signify a
        refusal to reply or perhaps evidence that I am incapable of replying,

like a depressed, unavailable mother. You tried to reach me to stop feeling isolated, it feels momentarily better, then you feel suddenly anxious as though it's going nowhere because you're made to feel I'm not replying, maybe like the way you felt so often with your mother. Fury erupts as though I've abandoned you.
> *pause*

Mr A: I can see that. It feels like it was with my mother. It doesn't feel like that when it happens. It feels real.

This vignette illustrates, I think, the essential intentions of Mr A's pathological organization. He is obliged to disconnect and withdraw into a narcissistic world under the weight of ruthless commands, above all when he experiences a need for human understanding and help – a situation that was much worse at the outset of his analysis, restricting him largely to screaming and silence. His rage towards me and others does not contain hope for change in him or his objects: it is secondary to an imperative to destroy links to objects, and rage is the means of achieving it. As he has become more able to distinguish this isolating activity from more legitimate needs and concerns he has become able to begin to talk a little about a terror of being seen as a criminal if he complains openly – that he will destroy forever fragile links to objects that keep him alive and be abandoned. The neurotic origins of his anxiety about ruination at his own hand have begun to be thought about, alongside internal storms whipped up by the pathological organization designed to prevent this.

Clinical example 2

Mr B, a case I supervise and who is in analysis on the couch four times weekly, appears at least on the surface to be a more overtly psychotic individual. The first of two children to a manic-depressive father and a depressed, confused mother, neither of whom seemed malignant in their intentions, he grew up overwhelmed by their psychological troubles, becoming eccentric, self-preoccupied and eventually exhibiting psychotic symptoms. He tried to kill himself by overdose in his 20s and was admitted to hospital for an extended period during which time he received psychiatric and psychotherapeutic help. Fragile on discharge, he came into analysis and after several months of extreme anxiety and confusion began to settle tentatively into the routine. Hospital staff had been worried about his suicidality, but his hospital consultant felt confident that provided he was not left alone for too long, that he received psychiatric out-patient care and that he was offered the analytic understanding he needed, he was unlikely to kill himself. Mr B is a gifted writer whose work had for years been impaired by his illness, violent self-deprecation having immobilized him. What follows is a brief excerpt from a session early on in the analysis that illustrates high levels of anxiety and self-loathing. The breaks between spoken phrases are powerful, confusing disruptions; he had a way of halting after each statement and then had to summon up the will to speak again:

Mr B: There is so much . . . I don't know where to start . . . the thing is . . . it's all come to a head . . . come to nothing . . . I've been feeling . . . (upset) . . . it's all too much . . . (starts to sob) . . . I can't stand being with Julie (girlfriend) . . . (looks to one side, shouts in the direction of the floor) STOP IT YOU STUPID FUCKING IDIOT, JUST FUCKING STOP IT . . . STUPID FUCKER.

(highly agitated)

A: You are very upset and it is difficult to talk to me. You did tell me you were going to tell her how hard it was living together.

Mr B: (Looks to one side again, shouts) Get OFF me! . . . FUCK OFF! . . . I told her . . . I told her . . . about the time I felt happy . . . with Carol . . . and nothing before or since has ever been like that . . . Julie told me she had never been happy in her life . . . I told her I was sorry . . . I went to my parents' house . . . you see I have nothing . . . had to go back to them . . . she leaves, I want her to come back . . . this is difficult . . . (shouts 'I am a pathetic fuck!! Fuck Off!!') . . . she goes away . . . I want her back . . . everything is fucked up . . . so fucked up . . . nothing is ever going to work . . . (mumbles what sounds like 'fucking bastard') . . . I stayed in my brother's room . . . there wasn't another room . . . Carol's painting was there . . . I went up close . . . even when it is dark the light shines on the surface of the painting . . . I went up close . . . saw her signature . . . I saw the date . . . 10 years ago . . . (cries) . . . 10 years . . . I've done nothing . . . nothing . . . I have no imagination . . . people produce things . . . I produce nothing . . . (looks aside) FUCK OFF YOU STUPID FUCKER LEAVE ME ALONE . . . FUCK OFF!!

A: You are upset and feeling very mixed up about Julie, Carol, your parents, but I think something tyrannical is close by, something with no compassion for the pain you're in.

Mr B: I know it's there . . . I know what you mean . . .
        pause

Mr B: The thing is I don't want to be alone . . . I hate being alone . . . (sobbing) . . . (snarls) FUCKING IDIOT!

The way Mr B talks, despite the intrusive verbal violence and sadomasochism, is more connected to an object than is the inner experience of Mr A. Mr B is visibly upset as well as angry, his feelings about his losses and suffering are more palpable and he can express them somewhat more openly. The schizophrenic-like psychotic asides, which abated over a period of about two years, seem to be linked to an intrusive internal figure that infuriates him by its maddening interference. Its aim is to force him to withdraw, but its authority is not as great as the tyrannical figure that has invoked cold-hearted, inhuman detachment by Mr A. Mr B is depressed, hate-filled and profoundly disappointed by what has happened to him. His predominantly sadomasochistic pathological organization seems to serve the purpose, amongst other things, of sparing objects the impact of his hatred in order to prevent isolation. Mr A's pathological organization, by contrast, actively promoted isolation, manufacturing hope of an intensely delusional kind. Mr B spares his objects out of fear of losing himself to a narcissistic world; his tendency is towards idealization, falseness and masochism.

Here is a further brief vignette from a session three years after the start of the analysis:

Mr B: I've been annoyed all day. I can't remember anything. My memory is shot to pieces, I hate this. I'm getting worse. I feel I'm slipping into a depression. Nothing makes sense anymore. I feel lost. Not remembering things is really getting me down.
pause

Mr B: Last Thursday was a disaster. When it came to it, I couldn't write a single word. It was like I had never written anything before. I forgot everything I'd been thinking about. Someone I knew said I've been distracted for weeks. I feel like walking away from everything. I can't stand this anymore. No matter how much I try something like this happens: thinking about a plot, preparing, drafting things is all supposed to increase your ability to do the bloody thing right.

A: Not if something in you is hell bent on destroying your potential and your achievements.

Mr B: I don't want to destroy everything.

A: Of course you don't, but something in you is trying to. What's happening, do you think?

Mr B: No matter what I do, it gets thwarted, everything turns bad, and then I feel like walking away.
long pause
Maybe my thinking it was going good sealed the deal.

A: You mean sealed the deal that you must never succeed, that everything that's growing in you must be halted, killed?

Mr B: (angry) It's so fucking frustrating. Terrible. I don't have any thoughts that make sense, I can't string a sentence together, I can't understand any fucking thing.
long pause
I was listening to a piece of music yesterday that moved me: quite a simple piece and I began to write down an idea and it felt

good and all of a sudden everything went blank. It was an idea that should have been quite straightforward to develop but it disappeared like it was stolen.

A: As you begin to enjoy experiencing something it feels like you lose it, it's taken away, but what's actually happening, I think, is that you mustn't take any pleasure from anything. Especially if the pleasure is sensual.

long pause

Mr B: It's never been any other way. Dad wanted to know what the eventual plan was, how everything would work out but there was no plan, nothing made sense, it was all in his mind. I was trying to follow something that made no sense. It was never going to work, trying to get to where it was he thought I should be. I don't know what I'm supposed to do. Nothing makes sense.

A: Your writing makes sense to you. What doesn't make sense to you is how it gets destroyed.

Mr B: I hate the way things get contaminated. My mother always had this double meaning thing going on. She would think sex was appalling, disgusting, she tried to tell my brother something about it one night, about not getting involved with girls and sex when my brother, who was only a teenager, was just starting to go out. She was giving my brother the message there was something disgusting about girls and about him. I saw red. I can't act on my own behalf. I couldn't stand up to her when she was like this with me, but for some reason I reacted against her when she did it to my brother. I'm not proud of the fact that I grabbed her and put her up against the wall and warned her to never say any such things again – I wish I could remember what she actually said. And she never did. I put my fist through the door that night. I'm not proud of that either.

pause

I hated my mother. So many fucking things, how my father was, his madness, my mother's constant hard to understand double meanings in everything. How everything is hard to work out. I hate it.

These two vignettes of Mr B seem to indicate that his withdrawal is an attempt to control aggression towards his mother and father in order to not destroy them – his worst phantasy. His rage was not of the pitiless kind evident in Mr A but a more object-related hatred with some indications of grief deriving from a wish that his father would change his impossible behaviour and his mother would show more love. His rage towards his father was tempered by Mr B's knowledge that, whilst his father drove him crazy with his self-preoccupied demands, he was not overtly cruel.

The torment the father inflicted consisted of intrusive idealization of his son and of ideas he imposed on him. Mr B felt misrecognized, frustrated, enraged and eventually despairing of any solution. Apparent in his confusion is significantly compromised sexual feelings towards both parents along with intense anger towards his mother, whom he felt to be alternately seductive and rejecting. Mr A, it must be said, needed to spare his objects (from his 'criminal' self and the acts of revenge he imagined would follow), but he did this by eradicating all human contact: little or no evidence of a sexual life has emerged to date in the analysis of Mr A.

Conclusion

The purpose of discussing these two patients is to illustrate some of the activities of internal pathological organizations, in these cases along two different lines according to different underlying psychopathologies. In addition, it has been important to find ways in which these activities could be talked about and differentiated from the patients' non-psychotic anxieties. Mr A, in the grip of a highly narcissistic organization in which annihilation of the need for an object is paramount and driven by omnipotent terror of isolation and the consequences of paranoid, narcissistic rage, gave little evidence of contact with good internal objects, and this had left him exposed to the full force of a perverse, psychotic narcissistic organization. Mr A's sadism appears to be a secondary activity, a means by which he phantasizes a reduction in his anxiety through the elimination of object contact and emotion. Triangulating the experience of such a person whose thinking has been usurped is not easy. The patient needs to become aware that he is in the grip of something tyrannical. It is then useful to talk in terms of *both* his non-psychotic needs and the attempts to obliterate them by referring to the objectives of the pathological organization's seeming activity outside the patient's conscious control. A 'phenomenologically oriented' interpretive curiosity on the analyst's part at the start, directed carefully to the non-psychotic personality of the patient in order to make links between events – the patient's attempts to express need and the violent psychotic opposition to this – inflamed the pathological organization far less than direct interpretations of the patient's fears of his hatred that carried high emotional valency and which were promptly distorted by the pathological organization into psychotic condemnation of the patient (by me). In attempting to create a triangular perspective in which the patient's non-psychotic mind might identify with this curiosity and impartiality, even for a short time, this patient became increasingly aware, crucially often with feeling, of the scale of the absurdity and irrationality of the pathological organization's virulent attacks. Latterly, it has become more possible for him to feel his fears of rejection, his narcissistic rage towards his analyst and the depressive collapse that he imagines will occur if he admits his true feelings of need and loss. In the process, his intimidated responses to the intensity of the pathological organization's condemnations have reduced, which I take to be due to increased psychic investment in object-related reality. Directing emotional truth towards his analyst has the effect of draining off some of the fuel needed by the pathological organization. The earlier request to Mr A to stop screaming was based on similar thinking: rather than make an interpretation that might be quickly confused with the pathological organization's authoritarianism, I put a request to the non-psychotic mind of a respected equal to consider the conditions needed to make analysis possible; the screaming removed those conditions. Directing ordinary language to his non-psychotic mind seemed to arouse interest and enough concern in him to agree to this, even though he found it difficult. At no time then or since has he issued a rebuke against me for asking him to do this, although his rage has become more evident in different ways, which I take to be significant as rebukes are a lifelong speciality. It is likely that triangulation of the problem permitted sufficient identification between non-psychotic minds to think about a legitimate problem to do with an inability to think and feel, and this allowed him to give a (relatively) non-threatening experiment a chance. Gradually I have been able to learn that Mr A has hallucinated a criminal past and has felt forever on the verge of being exposed by the authorities for having killed someone, to his everlasting condemnation, humiliation and shame. Fighting off the threat of exposure by destroying his humanity and that of others became for him a *raison d'etre*. The extent of Mr A's self-murder and submission to a psychotic part-object has become available for analytic work after many years of painstaking effort to differentiate his non-psychotic thinking from the aims of the pathological organization.

Mr B suffers an essentially depressive condition with some narcissistic features in which unresolved hate of needed and loved objects has given rise to sadistic controls over his objects and withdrawal from others and his own needs but without the degree of annihilation of object contact and emotion exhibited by Mr A. Instead, his vociferous sadomasochism permitted a greater affective range, centred around outspoken blame and self-blame. His underlying fears seem to be associated with the destruction of fragile, confusing and hated internal objects. As his fears have been addressed, particularly in the context of his masochistic tendencies, so tolerance of his aggression has grown, his depression is less pronounced and his writing has resumed. He has become aware of the way in which his sexual development has been impeded by his failure to deal with his profound aggressive feelings. At one point Mr B conveyed that his disruptive speech patterns (which have receded, as can be seen from the second vignette) resembled his fear of sex: to speak full, meaningful sentences would be 'too exciting'. A compelling irony is that Mr B presented initially in a much more disorganized and psychotic manner than Mr A, who seemed more controlled, self-contained and outwardly in charge of his life. The reality is that Mr A has succumbed to psychotic thought much more than Mr B, a fact that could have become clear only once the nature of the object-relating crisis and corresponding pathological organization activity had emerged.

It is suggested in this paper that the main task for the analyst with such patients is to render communication intelligible by differentiating, in the transference and countertransference, the non-psychotic appeals of the patient unable to speak for him or herself from the systematic, psychotic distortions created to misrepresent these appeals as potential catastrophes. This is a demanding task, particularly with severe narcissistic disturbance given pressure upon the ego to identify with the pathological organization's psychotic views. Where more depressive or emotionally elaborated sadomasochistic behaviour is evident the transference and countertransference task is somewhat less obstructed. It is also suggested that it can be of help technically for the analyst to acquire within him- or herself as fully as possible an understanding of both of the patient's ways of communicating, psychotic and non-psychotic, and to introduce this understanding to the patient's non-psychotic mind in a spirit of curiosity and concern. By triangulating experiences of the healthy side of the patient, the patient who feels mad or is with someone mad and the impact on the relationship with the analyst of these different, frequently oscillating positions, a psychological space may be opened up to permit joint investigation of the patient's polarized experiences and give access to true expressions of feelings. Over time, it can become possible for the patient to see increasingly the nature of the investment she or he has made in a delusional view of relationships and emotions and to pursue the painful process of disengaging from the pseudo-protection offered by the pathological organization.

References

Bion, W.R. (1957). Differentiation of the psychotic from the non-psychotic personalities. *International Journal of Psychoanalysis* 38: 266–275.

Bion, W.R. (1959). Attacks on linking. *International Journal of Psychoanalysis* 40: 308–315.

Bion, W.R. (1962). The psycho-analytic study of thinking. *International Journal of Psychoanalysis* 43: 306–310.

Fairbairn, W.R.D. (1952). *Psychoanalytic Studies of the Personality*. London: Tavistock.

Freud, S. (1905). Three essays on the theory of sexuality. *S.E.* 7.

Freud, S. (1915). Observations on transference-love: Technique of psycho-analysis. *S.E.* 12.

Klein, M. (1946). Notes on some schizoid mechanisms. *International Journal of Psychoanalysis* 27: 99–110.

Klein, M. (1997). *Envy and Gratitude and Other Works 1946–63*. London: Vintage.

Meltzer, D. (1968). Terror, persecution, dread – A dissection of paranoid anxieties. *International Journal of Psychoanalysis* 49: 396–400.

Ogden, T.H. (2007). On talking-as-dreaming. *International Journal of Psychoanalysis* 88: 575–589.

O'Shaughnessy, E. (1981). A clinical study of a defensive organization. *International Journal of Psychoanalysis* 62: 359–369.

O'Shaughnessy, E. (1992). Enclaves and excursions. *International Journal of Psychoanalysis* 73: 603–611.

Rosenfeld, H. (1950). Note on the psychopathology of confusional states in chronic schizop . . . *International Journal of Psychoanalysis* 31: 132–137.

Rosenfeld, H. (1964). On the psychopathology of narcissism: A clinical approach. *International Journal of Psychoanalysis* 45: 332–337.

Rosenfeld, H. (1971). A clinical approach to the psycho-analytical theory of the life and death instincts: An investigation into the aggressive aspects of narcissism. *International Journal of Psychoanalysis* 52: 169–178.

Rosenfeld, H. (1987). *Impasse and Interpretation: Therapeutic and Anti-Therapeutic Factors in the Psychoanalytic Treatment of Psychotic, Borderline, and Neurotic Patients* (The New Library of Psychoanalysis). London: Taylor & Francis, 2004.

Searles, H. (1986). *My Work with Borderline Patients*. New York: Jason Aronson.

Williams, P. (2004). Incorporation of an invasive object. *International Journal of Psychoanalysis* 85: 1333–1348.

Williams, P. (2010). *Invasive Objects: Minds Under Siege*. New York: Routledge.

Part IV

Flexible integration between psychoanalysis and pharmacology

Chapter 12

The current state of psychodynamic treatment of psychosis

Ira Steinman

There is nothing new under the sun.

– Ecclesiastes

When my good friend and colleague Riccardo asked me to write a chapter in his book on the subject of whether or not there is anything different in the way I currently treat psychotic people, I was a little perplexed. For my answer would simply be "Not really." In fact over the last more than 40 years of treating severely disturbed patients my approach hasn't changed much at all. Perhaps the field of the psychodynamic psychotherapy and psychoanalysis of schizophrenia and other psychoses has changed a great deal, but I have not changed much at all in my approach. I tend to inquire into the nature of severe distortions of reality and inquire as to how the patient developed hallucinations, delusions and bizarre phenomena of thought and action. I also look to the origin in the patient's mind of other persona, usually stuck in some early painful and traumatic series of events.

As far as I am concerned a psychodynamic psychotherapy, making use of the concepts of unconscious motivation, resistance to change, transference and counter-transference phenomena and the benefit of interpretation of these occurrences, is crucial in the psychotherapeutic treatment of schizophrenia and other psychoses. In addition, just as there is meaning to dreams, there is symbolic meaning to the patient of his or her hallucinations and delusions, almost as if they are self told fantasies and fairy tales; it is our job to help the patient understand his or her own metaphor and symbolism that have taken on the concretized form of psychotic delusions and hallucinations.

I'm sure this is what we all do, those of us who aspire to a psychodynamic psychotherapy of schizophrenia and other forms of psychosis. I'm sure that we all try to ferret out the initial origin of all self states, disturbing ideas of reference, painful hallucinations and delusions. Or at least that is what we all should try to do.

All too often however I find that disturbed people are treated with an amalgam of more and more medication, with less and less of an attempt at elucidating how these various states began. Unfortunately, contemporary psychiatry views nearly all psychosis as an expression of brain diseases.

It's not that current practitioners of psychiatry have evil intentions in the treatment of psychosis. It's not that practitioners are unempathetic to the severely disturbed patients they see. It is much more the case that the field of psychiatry for the last 45 years or so has thought that schizophrenia is a brain disease with an organic and biological basis, hence it needs treatment with antipsychotic medication. Under the barrage of Big Pharma advertising and the academic psychiatric establishment having bought into the notion that there is nothing psychological in a psychotic person's delusions or hallucinations, worldwide psychiatry has capitulated to the biologic and genetic origin school of thought, of schizophrenia being a brain disease.

This is a simplistic view, in fact. A closer look at the origins of psychotic thinking in people who end up becoming schizophrenic, or psychotic in some other fashion, reveals that these people are very upset. With anxiety, with intense terror, with withdrawal from the world comes a cascade of thoughts and swirling neurochemicals that worsen the situation. Of course, antipsychotic medication can be helpful to quell intense anxiety, but finding out the origin of disturbed beliefs is an all-important task of practitioners with an analytic or psychodynamic bent. Sometimes medication is helpful for that, but, generally, not as a lifetime treatment.

All too often medication, meant to help someone look at psychodynamic issues that have played a major part in the development of psychosis, becomes a treatment for life. Of course, I use antipsychotic medication if necessary but generally for a short period of time. This use can be during a period of crisis, of intense anxiety or psychotic decompensation into delusional beliefs, altered personalities, hallucinations, bizarre thoughts and feelings. There are many cases that exemplify the type of work that I do; suffice it to say that a large percentage of my psychotic patients respond to psychodynamic exploration, often titrating down and stopping antipsychotic medication.

Several years ago colleagues and I held a meeting on the traumatic origin of psychosis in Santa Monica. Now not every case of psychosis appears to have this kind of intense traumatic origin, but quite a number of them do. Certainly, over the years of practice, I have had quite a number who easily fit into that way of looking at psychosis.

As length permits let me highlight several recent cases that demonstrate how painful external, hence internal, events led to dissociation or withdrawal into a world of psychotic thought. Even though these patients had come to me from a psychiatric hospital setting, psychotic thinking and symptoms ceased once the origin of psychosis had been understood by the patient and me and worked through in the usual psychodynamic psychotherapeutic fashion.

Amanda was an attractive woman in her 40s who had recently moved to the San Francisco bay area. She had been involved in energy work since coming here six months earlier and had become increasingly pressured, agitated, sleepless and both fearful and paranoid. In an increasingly desperate and agitated state, she overdosed, requiring hospitalization for the better part of a month. During this hospitalization, she was extremely paranoid and fearful of being attacked sexually by other patients and ward personnel. She was medicated with antipsychotic medication while on the unit and diagnosed as Psychosis not otherwise specified.

She had been a reasonably high functioning person, had gone through a difficult marriage ending in divorce a number of years earlier and had now remarried five years previously. The hospital staff was uncertain as to how someone who had previously been so well functioning had become so markedly disturbed. Aware of my interest in the dynamic psychotherapy of severely disturbed people, the staff referred this patient to me, knowing that I would do my best to try to help her understand the origin of her suicidal thoughts, suicidal action and markedly deteriorated paranoid psychosis.

After four weeks in the hospital Amanda came in with her husband for the first session. She was distraught, plaintive, wan and tremendously fearful. She spoke in a hoarse near whisper. As I took a history it became apparent that she had gone through a period of increasing sleeplessness for more than a month prior to her hospitalization, often sleeping as little as an hour per night. It doesn't take much to set off someone who was already on the edge, so it seemed to me quite likely that the lack of sleep played a tremendous part in her clinical deterioration.

I asked her what she was doing; she told me "energy work." By energy work she meant she worked with someone on various energies in her body, not necessarily psychologically. She believed that she had, during her energy work, gotten in touch with a previous therapist who died a number of years earlier. In fact, when she made a suicide attempt, it was in part to rejoin the previous therapist, whom she had cared for and from whom she felt a great deal of caring. But Amanda still did not know why she had tried to kill herself.

She was a diligent person and would spend the days between the energy sessions working as hard as she could to deal with various feelings in her body; the upshot was that she had become increasingly distraught. During the first session she told me in a halting voice that she knows that her mother tried to strangle her the day she was born. I asked her how she knows this, and she said that she just knows, that it's a certainty that her mother had tried to kill her. I asked about the relationship with her mother; was her knowledge that her mother tried to strangle her an indication of how her mother was with her or a metaphor for some negative interactions with her mother?

This was a surprising question for her. She said she had a happy childhood, but the possibility that there might be some symbolic meaning having to do with the interaction between her and her mother caught the attention of both Amanda and her husband. Shortly thereafter, during the first session, I said something along the lines of hallucinations and delusions, even the fear that Amanda had on the psychiatry ward that she would be sexually attacked by staff members or other patients, might have some meaning within the context of her life. By the end of the session, both Amanda and her husband had the feeling that there might be some way to explore and understand her rapid decompensation, by making sense of her own feelings, paranoia and hallucinations.

The psychotherapeutic process is such a powerful one that it doesn't even require that the patient know me, or whom I am. Certainly, it doesn't require that she know my name. Something happened during that first session, for when Amanda came in for her next session. the next day, by herself and without her husband, she brought me a letter. It was a message from her previous dead therapist, a message she had gotten that morning.

It was also a message to Dr. Ian, not to Dr. Ira. Now I'm not sure if the name Ian was the responsibility of Amanda or her imagined communication with her previous long dead therapist. But having the bent, the attitude, that I do, I, of course, believe it all came from Amanda.

"Let me read you this letter." For it was a letter that contains a great deal of what would become crucial to explore in an extremely successful therapy over the next few months.

Here's the letter that held so much material, material beamed to the patient from her dead previous therapist. We, of course, understand that all of this was a vehicle for Amanda to present to me and to herself the basic outlines of her previously unacknowledged past.

"Dr. Ian,

For the past six months I have been uncovering dissociated traumas from my early childhood. My body's memories were too prevalent to ignore. These body memories coupled with working with Dr. Norman (in spirit form) have helped me identify the specific, trauma.

Number one. My mother choked me on the day of my birth. She was filled with psychotic energy, which I took on and apparently still have. The target has become conscious. I would like more than anything to release the scary psychotic energy that I have never had any awareness of in the past.

Number two. I was raped by a man named Mr. Q., he picked me up at my family home once per week for 3 1/2 years. My mother arranged it. He kept me in his car against my will. I was in the backseat. There was another woman (aged 40) in the front. He leapt from the back to the front seat and yelped some horrible scary sounds. Each time I had to endure a full hour and a half of him penetrating every orifice. I have and more. Each session would last for 1 1/2 hours. I never told anyone. I didn't know how to care for myself. I was 13 1/2 to 15.

Then my mother divorced and took me to an apartment where I was left alone, day and night, when she was not working or going to school. She had sex with her lover to the extent that I heard and saw everything. They seemed to enjoy having me witness this. Most of this was dissociated as well. I was devastated by the lack of boundaries and re-triggered at all times, regarding my rape.

Number three. I was lost in the mall when I was to be finding new school clothes. My brother took off and my mother ran after him. I was five years old. A man found me and gave me candy. He then asked if he could help me. I said yes and he took me and sodomized me in the men's public bathroom. This is why I was so terrified to be in a coed hospital.

Number four. A neighborhood boy molested and sodomized me outside of my family house. He was 10 and I was six years old. It was devastating to me physically and emotionally given all I had gone through.

Please help me Dr. Ian. I believe that I am a very quick student and look forward to working with you.

Best,"

Amanda had laid out the bare bones of much of her difficulties. Something had transpired between us during the first session, allowing her to feel safe enough to tell me what she had figured out in the guise of her dead previous therapist talking to her. It didn't matter that she called me Dr. Ian. To her, whether I was Dr. Ira or Dr. Ian, there was safety and hope on her part that her suicide attempt and subsequent psychotic behavior might be understandable, as I had outlined in the first session. In fact, she even says that the previous sexual abuses at the hands of a neighbor and an older boy had led to her looking so psychotic, when she was in a coed hospital fearful of the men on the unit.

Consequently, Amanda not only felt safe enough to give me this message from her spirit world, but her spirit therapist, long dead, and I would work in concert, helping Amanda reintegrate from her psychosis. Clearly, something was changing in Amanda. She had identified that traumas from the past were critical in her becoming psychotic.

In addition, it is easy to see how her hard working and extremely intense attempt to make sense of phenomena going on within herself over the previous six months had led to her state of a month of sleeplessness and a worsening psychotic picture, culminating in her suicide attempt in an effort to see her previous therapist, long dead. Amanda even makes sense of the terror of being attacked sexually by male staff and male patients on the previous psychiatry unit from which she had just come.

Following the cues I had been given, I decided to follow the message of her previous deceased therapist. There was likely something in her intuition that she had been severely traumatized. So, I began to ask questions like, "Did anything bad happen to you when you were growing up?"

As is so often the case, Amanda told me that she had had a happy childhood until the time of her parents' divorce.

I persisted. "I'm trying to make sense of all this material that you've written down here. How do we make sense of what you just wrote me about trauma that repeatedly happened when you were young? Especially, if you tell me that you had a happy childhood?"

"I don't know" was Amanda's response.

I believe in playing it as it lays, in dealing with the current situation and trying to make sense of it within the context of the patient's life. Most probably, early childhood and subsequent experiences needed to be explored to see if there were any recognizable patterns. In Amanda's case, we had to look for some source of dissociated memories and states. We had to look at her belief in a happy childhood and make sense of it in conjunction with the message from the long dead previous psychiatrist that there was a long history of trauma and abuse.

This had apparently never been tried before. She had seen a number of other therapists over the years, and most of them tried to deal with the current crises of divorce, a difficult marriage and painful ongoing circumstances without much attention being paid to early life. Now part of this may have been due to Amanda saying that she had had a normal, perfectly happy childhood. But one should always keep one's eyes and therapeutic ears open for the possibility that a "happy childhood" was, in fact, anything but a happy one.

And so it was with Amanda. Within 10 days of this kind of inquiring approach in two to three times per week psychotherapy, Amanda, on her own, discontinued her antipsychotic medication. Gradually she began to uncover her history, which was replete with painful memories and images of emotional, physical and sexual assaults going back to her earliest days. With the exception of several occasions of a day or two of the low dose use of antipsychotics when she was chaotic and suicidal, Amanda has remained off antipsychotics as she has recovered and reintegrated the most painful, sad and traumatic history.

Needless to say, her long dead previous therapist would have been delighted by her new found sanity and integration. By the way, she no longer believes she is communicating with him, even though the message she delivered from him when she believed she was getting messages from him was so helpful. Now, Amanda realizes that all of this material, paranoia, delusions and messages from beyond came from herself.

Here is another case vignette demonstrating the usefulness of a psychodynamic approach in someone suffering from several years of a far-flung paranoid delusional system.

Alfred is a 40-year-old contractor who has been suffering from paranoid ideation and delusions for more than 2 1/2 years. He had become so certain of the far-flung and wide reaching effects of the conspiracy that was directed against him that he was certain it had followed him from city to city, mustering hundreds of people, who were all surveilling him and noticing his every move. When he came to San Francisco to be closer to his family, they were so alarmed at the extent of his disorganization and paranoid thinking that they took him to a psychiatry emergency room, where he was hospitalized and diagnosed as suffering from paranoid schizophrenia. There he was placed on antipsychotic medication.

After leaving the hospital, he was brought to my office by his family. He was an isolated, lonely fellow, who had a past history of smoking marijuana in the city in which he worked. As with all patients, I took a history and tried to see if there was anything in his background that might have accounted for the difficulties from which he was suffering. In addition, I told him that smoking marijuana could play a large part in his beliefs and recommended that he stop it immediately.

Alfred had been on a job; the client was very slow in paying him. In frustration, normally mild-mannered, Alfred had poured paint on some family artifacts of his client. Shortly thereafter, the client paid the bill, and Alfred began to suffer paranoid delusions.

The delusions centered around the client who had been slow to pay his bill, the client whose family artifact Alfred had destroyed. Quickly the delusional system became more and more elaborate as Alfred was certain that the client had hired numerous people to keep him under constant watch, for he was certain that his every move was noted. He became quite certain that his activities were being entered into a giant database dedicated to him and his movements.

He began to see dead animals at job sites. When he saw dead rats on his toolbox he quickly jumped to the conclusion that the client was saying that he was a rat. He was further convinced that the previous client knew that he had destroyed the family artifact and was gradually going to get him or drive him crazy.

No reality testing seemed to make the slightest difference to Alfred. His family had tried it; the doctors in the hospital had tried it; I tried it. He was convinced that hundreds of people were devoted to monitoring his every gesture and move. Passersby in the street said things that indicated he was under constant surveillance; television shows said things that indicated the extent of the plot; cars followed his path, from jobsite to jobsite and from city to city, cars that entered information about him into the database that had been set up to monitor him.

Alfred was very reluctant to stay on antipsychotic medication and stopped it; his symptoms remained the same. I encouraged him to again try some antipsychotics and gradually was able to build them up to a tolerable level for a matter of three months. During that time, he and I had some talks about his family in what was essentially a once per week psychotherapy. I was wondering if, in the history, there would be something that might indicate a psychological thread that would help us make sense of his delusional behavior and thinking.

Alfred was the youngest of four children in an immigrant Catholic family. The father ran the family with an iron fist. When Alfred was a teenager he and his father had many fistfights, with his father always trying to retain and exert control. If Alfred would try to stand up to his father, his father would punch him; if Alfred fought back, his father would hit him harder. When he finished high school, Alfred moved away. The parents divorced years before Alfred's psychotic decompensation. He had girlfriends, but no one serious during these last few years.

I tried to make sense of things with Alfred. Could Alfred standing up to the client have been similar to trying to stand up to his father? Just as his father would hit him back even harder, was Alfred secretly fearing that the client, whom he had wronged by destroying an artifact, would get even with him? Was the imagined surveillance because of what Alfred himself had done to the client? Even though Alfred could follow my line of questioning, he remained certain that there was in fact a giant plot to monitor him.

Initially, when I asked Alfred how certain he was that he was correct, he said he was 100% correct. Gradually, over the next three months, his certainty declined to 98%, to 60%, to 40%, to 2%. Over these few months, his medication was titrated down as he sat with the notion that what he thought came from outside of himself actually came from him.

He began to develop an observational capacity about his delusions. Alfred had a period of time and gradually diminishing amounts of antipsychotic medication to mull over some of these delusional distortions. He had a chance to think that what he had previously perceived as 100% correct might actually have been his just jumping to conclusions, based upon some fears and apprehension rooted in his childhood interaction with his father, an interaction that was repeated in his dealings with his client. After three months, Alfred was off antipsychotics, was able to return home and understood that what he had previously thought was coming from outside of himself in the form of a far-flung conspiracy against him was actually rooted in his own fear and apprehension.

Was the interpretation about the relationship of the delusional beliefs to his childhood attempts to stand up to his father and his subsequent fear of his father's attacks exact or inexact? I'm perfectly happy with it being an inexact interpretation, one that gave Alfred an outline and a roadmap for understanding that his paranoid ideation was the result of his own thinking, based on his earlier experiences.

In the same vein, could my urging him to stop smoking marijuana have played a part in his relatively quick recovery from such a paranoid psychotic picture? I wouldn't be surprised at all. In fact, I have found that marijuana use is often associated with psychotic thinking; this should be discussed with patients and not just accepted as perfectly natural within the culture.

So what have we learned here? Nothing new. Yet again, we can see how a dynamic psychotherapy of psychosis has yielded not just understanding, but healing – giving up long-lasting belief systems – and curing of previously intractable psychotic appearing phenomena. We have seen again that an inquiring exploration of the meaning to the patient of his or her hallucinations, delusions and strange thoughts leads to an understanding of the origin of these psychotic distortions of reality. With such an approach, these two patients have returned to a life of relationships and function.

How was such a treatment done? It was done via the usual empathic psychodynamic exploration of past events, of transference and counter-transference phenomena and of affective states that occurred around the time of the development of symptoms. It was the usual psychodynamic psychotherapy, with the understanding that terrible, traumatic events may indeed have happened, and that intense phenomena may occur during psychotherapy.

Three things are most important. First is the understanding that there is psychological meaning to the patient of his or her delusions or hallucinations; we have but to explore it in a fashion that allows the patient to integrate the information and to develop an observing self.

Second, and equally important, is the necessity for arriving at what Harry Guntrip called "the lost heart of the self." Sitting there with a person in this vulnerable state allows inchoate feelings to rise to the surface. Trust gradually develops, and soon the underpinnings of a delusional, hallucinatory or other psychotic orientation become clear.

Third, it is crucial that the therapist understand that it is possible to peel the onion and get to the origin of the most bizarre and extreme psychotic phenomena. It certainly helps if one has had the experience of previously helping patients heal from schizophrenic and paranoid delusions, via the use of a psychodynamic psychotherapy.

Often, clinicians attempt to treat patients such as either Amanda or Alfred with long-term use of antipsychotic medication, thereby blunting affect and never allowing the patient to fully explore the emotional and psychological underpinnings of psychotic distortions. The field of psychiatry has turned toward viewing psychotic patients as suffering from brain disease, hence it prescribes medication in a far too facile and cookbook fashion. All too often, it is possible to use medications sparingly, often stopping them as the gains of the psychodynamic psychotherapy lead to the exploration and understanding of previously bizarre seeming phenomena.

This was done with Amanda in the usual way, making sense of different psychotic experiences, and paying attention to terrible traumatic events that led to fragmentation and eventual psychosis. With Alfred, it was necessary to be much more direct and confrontative, urging the cessation of marijuana use and questioning the far-flung nature of his paranoid delusional beliefs. Here too, a psychodynamic understanding led to healing and the resolution of the previously debilitating delusional state.

How much have things changed in my practice with psychotic patients over the last 40 years? Not very much. If anything, I'm even more convinced than I was earlier of the benefits of psychodynamic exploration in the treatment of psychotic patients.

Even back in the early 70s, I found myself looking at various self states and inquiring into how they developed. From a similar four decades long practice perspective, I question people's delusional beliefs over time and tell them that I understand that they believe them, but that to me it makes more sense to try to ferret out how such notions began. Such an approach worked very nicely with Alfred.

As practitioners, we have the option of treating very disturbed psychotic patients with the usual amalgam of supportive psychotherapy and ancillary services, such as day care and repeated hospitalization, coupled with the excessive use of antipsychotic medication. Such an approach often leaves patients in the throes of the psychotic distortions with which they came in, continuing to fear their hallucinations and delusions and continuing to fear those out there who appear to orchestrate giant conspiracies against them. Such an approach often leaves patients consigned to excessive antipsychotic medication, with their lipid and glucose side effects, for life.

I prefer the option of a psychodynamic psychotherapy, with the judicious use of antipsychotic medication, in an attempt to help patients understand the origin of their psychotic symptoms and the meaning to them of their hallucinations and delusions. Such an approach often leads to the cessation of antipsychotic medication and healing and curing of previously unfathomable psychotic dilemmas.

To my mind, the proper approach to a psychotic patient is to attempt to understand the meaning to him or her of psychotic phenomena. This can be coupled with either a short course of antipsychotic medication or the titration downward of antipsychotic medication, as the patient gains control of previously frightening and poorly understood psychological processes. What was previously seen as coming from the outside, as something in the form of voices or delusions, as something over which one had no control, becomes fathomable and understandable during the course of a psychodynamic psychotherapy of psychosis.

Most importantly, psychotic occurrences become under one's own control, as one realizes that hallucinations and delusions emanate from previously unconscious material within the self. Such a psychodynamic approach runs counter to the general run-of-the-mill excessive prescription of antipsychotics, but gives the patient a chance to make sense of his or her psychosis and achieve lasting healing and sometimes become cured.

Such was the fortunate outcome with Amanda and Alfred.

Chapter 13

Psychoanalysis and prescription drugs in the treatment of psychotic disorders

Giuseppe Martini

A review of the literature[1]

The relationship between psychoanalysis and psychopharmacological treatment cannot be considered an idyllic one, in particular with regard to the past. Even in the "golden years" of the meeting between psychoanalysis and psychiatry (post-World War II to DSM 3 in the USA and until the late 80s, early 90s in Europe and Italy) there was, in fact, a certain diffidence towards drugs on the part of psychoanalysts. This meant that pharmacological treatment was sometimes avoided, while on other occasions (the attitude that still in part persists to this day) its use was viewed as a sign of the defeat of the dynamic approach, or, worse still, of the technical inadequacy of the analyst.

We will consider the models of mental disorder underlying these positions later, but it is perhaps necessary to point out two important critical issues, which are generally implicit and not openly declared. The first regards the responsibility of psychoanalysis in taking on a position of predominance within the psychiatric community, which was decidedly lacking in autocriticism. An undesired result was the favoring of the move towards biology we have seen in recent decades with the passage – as expressed some years ago by a renowned North American practitioner – "from psychiatry without brain to psychiatry without mind". The other critical issue is that the fundamental need for medication in major psychotic disorders was ignored, leading, in an extreme case, to the well-known lawsuit several years ago of a patient against Chestnut Lodge Hospital, for not having adopted a suitable treatment (Melega and Fioritti, 1991).

It is necessary, however, to point out that even in those years there was no shortage of refined and constructive psychoanalytical reflections, although they may appear dated today. A systematic text that generated attentive discussion (e.g. S. Malitz, 1963–64; P. Goolker, 1964) was Mortimer Ostow's book *Drugs in Psychoanalysis and Psychotherapy*, which dates back to 1962. The author is firmly in favor of the use of drugs during psychoanalysis, highlighting their ability to re-compact the fragmented ego, thus making analysis possible for patients who, without medication, would be too seriously ill to face the analyst's couch.

Other affirmations seem decidedly daring and rather bizarre, as his colleagues of the day noted (S. Malitz, 1963–64). These include the attempt to explain extrapyramidal side effects in energetic terms, or the proposal of a scale of ego libido, showing degrees from zero for melancholia to ten for schizophrenia and delusional mania. However, Ostow's reflections on the value of drugs in diminishing suicidal danger, in avoiding hospitalization and in reducing the repetition of psychotic episodes are still valid and worthy of endorsement, as well as being expressions of good sense and balance.

Although the relation between drug treatment and analysis is not a particularly recurrent theme in psychoanalytical or psychiatric journals, there have also been important contributions in recent years relating to this issue.

Some of these are in line with Ostow's work, which in a certain sense they continue, like Mintz and Belnap, who propose the foundation of a discipline they call *psychodynamic psychopharmacology*. This "explicitly acknowledges and addresses the central role of meaning and interpersonal factors in psychopharmacologic treatment" (2006, p. 581), considering the patient "not a passive battleground between the doctor and the disease", but rather an important ally or adversary, and it proposes that the primary objective should be "learning, rather than symptom elimination" (p. 592). They move from the position of asking the reasons, which are not exclusively biological, for resistance to treatment, which they subdivide in *Resistance to Medication*, where there are unconscious factors working to maintain important intrapsychic defenses, and *Resistance from Medications*, which refers instead to a countertherapeutic use of drugs, used to avoid a process of psychological development, or even like a fetish. They also take into consideration the position of the doctor's countertranference in the administration of the drugs, which is also considered a potential source of pharmacological resistance, as we shall later see in more detail. Rubin (2001) in turn refers to cultural differences between doctors and the patient, and finally to the personality of the prescriber, among which narcissistic factors take on particular importance. These can lead the doctor to see in a lack of compliance a position of hostility and envy, which interferes with a more correct and functional interpretation in terms of relational dynamics. Rickles (2006), basing his work on the theories of Winnicott and Kernberg, describes the mechanisms by which the drug modifies the construction of subjective experience, identifying changes inherent in (1) the increase or decrease of defensive splitting and dissociation, (2) the modulation of *Integrative Repression* and (3) the modification of the matrix of the mind. In conclusion, psychiatric drugs, like psychoanalysis and like other pharmacological treatments, work by modifying the representations of the Self and of internal objects.

At the beginning of the 70s Zetzel (1970) and many other authors reported that the disappearance of anxiety and of pharmacologically induced depression could interfere negatively with analysis. On the contrary, today it seems more appropriate to note how patients in analysis who are on medication, rather than being prey to emotional flattening and dehumanizing experiences, can find themselves with enhanced insight and a greater ability to remember their dreams. Greater participation in the analytical experience is also reported (Rickles, 2006, p. 726).

We must therefore recognize a growing interest on the part of psychoanalysts and dynamically oriented psychiatrists in the psychodynamic aspects of pharmacological prescription. These are viewed as being able to overcome the impasses and failures of pharmacological treatment that a reductionist model in the biological sense, with no interest in relational dynamics, can have. More recently these studies have also been prompted by the observation that in recent decades psychiatrists have been increasingly lacking in a psychodynamic baggage with the consequent reduction in consultation time to the few minutes necessary for the exploration of symptoms and the DSM 5 diagnosis. Psychodynamic psychopharmacology, originally proposed by Mintz, has thus become a discipline with its own academic relevance and authority. The author has returned to the question (Mallo and Mintz, 2013), proposing residency programs to provide individual supervision for pharmacotherapy (p. 27) and the methodology of Balint groups (p. 28).

To sum up the most significant aspects of dynamic psychopharmacology, we can list the following:

- *transference and countertransference* dynamics: activation of parental transferences, regression and fears of dependency, aggressive countertransference or overprotective countertransference, both resulting in overmedication, polypharmacy as a function of countertransference anxiety (Alfonso, 2009), issues relating to power and control, therapist rescue fantasies, medication as distancing mechanism (Rubin, 2001), unprocessed countertransference as a cause of treatment resistance (Mallo and Mintz, 2013);
- *treatment adherence*: psychodynamic determinants of nonadherence (feeling infantilized, coerced or manipulated, failure of empathy), connection between childhood trauma and nonadherence, correlation between noncompliance and dismissing attachment (Alfonso, 2009);
- conscious and unconscious factors relating to *ambivalence* regarding doctors, medications and illness (Mallo and Mintz, 2013);
- *therapeutic alliance*: warmth, concern, involving the patient as a partner, discussion of anticipated side effects (Mallo and Mintz, 2013); and
- *placebo and nocebo* responses, relating to the psychological significance of the pill used, the treatment relationship and the sociocultural environment (Wing Li, 2010).

In conclusion, "a psychodynamic approach to pharmacotherapy can enhance initial diagnostic assessment and treatment plans, and help manage treatment resistance or nonresponsiveness" (Silvio and Condemarin, 2011, p. 38). The pill can also be understood as a transitional object and consequently "Just as Winnicott remarked 'there is no such thing as a baby', there is no such thing as medication. Medication is always prescribed within an interpersonal and sociocultural context" (Wing Li, 2010, p. 667).

It should also be noted that in all these works, the main focus is on pharmacological treatment per se and on showing the importance of the psychodynamic sensitivity of the psychiatrist in prescribing medication.

An exception is the work of Lebovitz (2004), which takes up the questions posed by Ostow more directly and focuses on the advantages and disadvantages of combined treatment (psychopharmaceuticals plus psychoanalysis). The author discusses this with explicit reference to affective disorders, starting from an assertion of Anna Freud's, who in 1968 had expressed the legitimacy and advisability of a combined treatment in cases of psychosis, excluding its use, however, in cases of neurosis. Along the same lines, Lipton (1983, *quoted by* Lebovitz) reports the ability of drugs to aid the progression of the analytical process, rather than interfering with it, and Kandel (1998 *quoted by* Lebovitz) suggests an effect that is not only additive, but also synergistic. Lebovitz, in turn, concludes his work with an open question as to which patients benefit from a split treatment and which from a unified treatment.

Returning to this line of thought, the theme I wish to consider deals specifically with the problems of integration between the pharmacological treatment and psychoanalysis in psychotic states. In these situations there is almost unanimous need for pharmacological treatment, but psychiatrists (and above all analysts!) should not forget Grotstein's warning (2003); this sees in analysis the only possibility to antagonize the sense of dehumanization that these patients experience.

Questions of method: the drug between symptom as symbol and symptom as sign

Before tackling specific questions of method, let us allow ourselves a general reflection on the relation between drugs and psychoanalysis, inherent in which there is a contradiction *at the point of departure* that can lead to integration *at the point of arrival* only if this contradiction is not ignored. I am referring to the fact that psychotherapy in general, and to a greater extent psychoanalysis, deals with the *symbolic value* of that same symptom that psychiatric semiotics instead considers the *sign* of a mental disorder. It therefore follows that alongside the transformative-elaborative aspect of the former there is the "reductive" aim of the latter (in the sense of reducing the entity of the symptom and if possible making it disappear). There are, therefore, the premises for a contradictory procedure that is not tempered by the fact that the treatments can be delivered by different therapists. The model of mental disorder to which therapists implicitly refer, as well as their ideas regarding the mind-body problem, can exacerbate or reduce this initial contradiction. Many authors position the different mental disorders along a continuum where psychosocial factors progressively decline in importance while the biological factors increase. In this case there is the risk that the conflict between the two positions worsens, and in practice undeserved importance may be given first to one, then to the other, resulting in constant competition between the psychoanalytical and pharmacological treatments. My personal choice is rather a model in which there is a parallel development of the biological, psychological and social dynamics. It follows that the possible and frequent reciprocal interferences do not exclude the basic incommensurability of the observational (and operative) levels. This implies that a psychoanalytical interpretation of schizophrenia is just as legitimate as a biological interpretation of a depressive reaction or of an adjustment disorder. At this point, the contradiction is perhaps of less consequence.[2]

Paul Ricoeur (2001) defines translation as a theoretically impossible operation, while at the same time noting both how this has never in practice stopped translation from taking place, and the fact that it can be done well or badly. We could take the same position with regard to the relation between the symptom as sign and the symptom as symbol. By this I mean that administering drugs and psychoanalysis together may be "theoretically impossible", but this has always been done, it will continue to be done and it can be done either well or badly. We otherwise lay ourselves open to a charge of reductionism, which is significantly more serious, whether of a biological or a psychological nature. The complex nature of our intervention only mirrors the more universal character of the "contradiction" that is inherent in the constitution of the human organism. This "contradiction", which we can reformulate as the contradiction between mind and body, can only result from our instruments of observation. It fades when we consider that knowledge of man is always subordinate to a multiplicity of methods, to fragmentation of the human being and lastly to incompletion (Jaspers, 1959).

The discussion turns progressively towards the operational level, with a shift from theory to method. A further point to consider, perhaps at the limit between the two, regards the different experiences of the drug (from the position of the analyst, the psychiatrist and the patient) in different psychotic conditions.

The discussion is not without importance. Where the psychosis is primarily indicated by narcissistic grandiosity, the drug is seen as the bad object *par excellence*, provoking an intolerable deflation. This aspect, which is dynamically important even for the most collaborative of patients, must be added to the consideration that in particularly critical forms, the psychiatrist will often act in an impositional and authoritarian manner,[3] increasing the experience described earlier with "factors of reality" (e.g. the compulsory treatment!). This can result in sensations such as resentment and betrayal, which survive in the patient at the end of a manic episode. The patient, once stabilized, is able to perceive a discontinuity in the Self between the past and the present. In contrast, however, the memory of the imposition, to which he/she was subjected, possesses its own continuity, and the "violence" suffered is transferred *in toto* to the present Self.

However, such a vivid and reactualized perception of previous interpersonal tensions between the patient and the therapist is not characteristic of schizophrenic disorders, even when their onset has been particularly acute and dramatic. In this case the conflict, at times violent, with the psychiatrist-psychopharmacologist, but also possibly with the analyst, is linked to the denial of illness and/or the persecutory/poisoning dimension of drugs. This gives hope that once these elements diminish the counterposition can be progressively converted into alliance. This alliance can perhaps enjoy a certain duration, although it is clearly exposed to the risk of a new re-acutization and the persistence of the denial of the illness, which is significantly more resistant than the persecutory dimension.

Adhesion to pharmacological therapy is usually less problematic in the case of acute psychotic episodes. In fact, the anxiety here is so great that the patient is often well disposed towards the medication, thanks to the sense of alleviation it provides. It is more complicated in the case of personality disorders with transitory psychotic episodes. In these cases the drug is again loaded with an ambivalence of the type good object/bad object. Its resolution in one sense or the other is often dependent on the modality of the administration (and, yet again, on the weight of the aggressive countertransference of the therapist).

There are complications of a different nature in severe depression, which are greater still when it includes melancholic features. In these disorders, acceptance of the therapy is often tantamount to the incorporation of a punitive and controlling object, with the activation of a masochistic position that certainly benefits neither the pharmacological therapy nor the analyst.

In all of these situations (some of which we will return to later), the drug interacts very differently with the psychoanalytic therapy, considering, however, that personality factors and the modality of the relationship are of utmost importance, quite apart from the diagnosis.

Last but not least, we need to remember that some patients are more prepared to accept a biological vision of their disorder, while others are better disposed towards a dynamic vision.

Returning to the question posed by Lebovitz (2004), as well as distinguishing between split and unified treatment, it is necessary to consider a further distinction with regard to the split treatment. In fact, a psychoanalytical and pharmacological treatment can be administered by more than one therapist without there being a particular problem with regard to coherence, or it can involve a collaboration, in some cases close, in others less so, preferably guaranteed by substantial agreement on the base model (e.g. psychodynamic). For the first situation we will speak of *combined treatment*, which can run the risk of falling into eclecticism. This position is not concerned about avoiding the possible conflict between psychotherapeutic and pharmacological intervention (sadly, not infrequent in academic contexts).

In the second case, more appropriately defined as *integrated treatment*, it is necessary to consider different possible levels of integration. In some cases the contact between therapists is limited (for example, to just a few phone calls), but the therapy program has a basic coherence. This modality is frequent in the analytic environment, and in private practice in general. It is not necessarily disadvantageous compared to an intensive integrated treatment, and can even present significant strengths, in particular in the treatment of so called neurotic and depressive disorders, consisting of "respect" for the therapeutic environment and its autonomy. In the institutional field and with specific reference to psychotic disorders, however, close coordination is common, with frequent briefings between the components of the therapeutic team. In this way changes of any nature or modifications of a particular setting are discussed and evaluated in the light of the interventions already in act. As is to be expected, the spaces of autonomy are reduced both for the individual therapist and for the patient, who is involved in a "network" of interventions: psychotherapy, psychiatric interviews, pharmacological consultations, possible hospitalizations, residential treatments and rehabilitative care. There are advantages (particularly in the area of more severe psychosis), but also possible disadvantages.

Unfortunately, integrated intervention is always at the end and never at the beginning. It is not, therefore, enough to be firm believers, nor to establish models of intervention that are consistent with each other, to guarantee success.

After all, the primary guarantor of the integration of the interventions is in fact the patient, with our ability and skill coming only in second place. This means that it depends on him/her, for reasons that sometimes remain obscure, to perceive (and benefit from!) the coherence between the different experiences. This coherence may crack for him/her in the face of slight and inevitable emotional dissonance between the professionals, while at other times it will stand up to technical orientations that are radically different.

Looking now more specifically at the alternative between *split* and *unified* treatment, we need to consider how this links to a series of complex questions that range from "analytic purity" to the non-medical training of the analysts. In general I believe that the greatest benefit of the unified treatment is the avoidance of a situation of *transference splitting*. In this case the negative or persecutory transference (given that the context is psychosis) can systematically be moved elsewhere (from the psychiatrist's consulting room to the analyst's, and vice versa), in stable or shifting forms, without resolution. The price of this benefit is, however, high: it complicates the transference dynamics with "factors of reality" (i.e. the drug and certainly its side effects), sometimes to the point of making them unmanageable. In any case, these dynamics risk creating an excessive distance from a symbolic level. If we bear in mind the different mental disorders outlined earlier, we can perhaps state that the benefits outweigh the risks in the case of schizophrenia and delusional disorders. Thanks to the unified treatment it is, in fact, possible in these cases to limit the projection of feelings of persecution, which are at that moment absent, and thus to build a more solid working alliance. I believe that for similar reasons Feinsilver (1996) argued that access to the treatments must start separately (as unification is initially untenable) and that it is desirable to unify them only later. It is important to bear in mind the oscillating nature of schizophrenia and of eventual new acute episodes that can easily put the linearity of the process at risk. In contrast, in the case of bipolar disorders, and particularly of type 1 (with evident manic phases), the risks outweigh the benefits for the reasons given earlier. In this case there is also the added risk that at certain moments the therapist works more intensely at the pharmacological level, abandoning, so to speak, the setting of analysis, or assuming psychoeducational positions that are too invasive and therefore of difficult elaboration in dynamic terms.

It would not be inappropriate to argue that there is a moment of particular fragility in the relationship when the analyst feels the need to introduce a drug into the setting or to send the patient to a colleague for that purpose. This can easily activate fantasies of severity, exacerbation or expulsion, but it can also transform the emotional investment in the analytic relationship. This can then swing from a (healthy) reshaping of omnipotent expectation to a denegratory disqualification. The body-mind problem thus becomes an assumption to share within the consulting room, in more emotional than theoretical terms. The analyst must implicitly or explicitly transmit to the patient what the psychopharmacologist (if this is another person) must reinforce. I am referring to the idea (a) that psychic processes are inscribed in bodily ones (from which they are separate in a gnoseological, but not ontological, sense) and (b) that the *gradient of freedom*[4] of the former depends on the equilibrium of the latter (an equilibrium that involves not relationships or psychic forces, but chemical mediators and agents). The consonance relating to this is unquestionably relevant because the patient experiences the drug as a "safe base" from which to increase his/her freedom to work in analysis and to access the transformations desired. To communicate this in an easily transmissible and comprehensible manner we can compare the construction of a house to that of our interior psychic space. We cannot build a house on quicksand or on land that is susceptible to landslides. Only when the ground is stable and the foundations have been laid can we build the house, divide it into rooms and finally furnish it. If, moreover, we stop at the level of the cement foundations (the drugs), instead of finding ourselves halfway through the construction work, we will only have contributed to the "cementification" and destruction of the landscape (the disappearance of the "positive" symptoms and the persistence of the "negative" ones).

Emotional, relational and transference transformations following the use of medication

If there is no doubt about the function of the drug in provoking transformations in the biological substrate, intended to facilitate psychic transformations, also the transformation it causes in the patient-psychiatrist or patient-analyst relationship is certainly relevant from a psychoanalytical point of view. This is then destined to reflect in the more complex "network" of the eventual institutional setting.

In particular the oedipal, schizoparanoid and depressive characteristics of the analytic relationship will be either easily strengthened or else unmasked by the use of the drug. In other cases similar dynamics can be "distanced" from the analytic setting and attracted into the psychiatric setting. If, for example, the administration of drugs favors the oedipal cathexis of the psychiatrist, this could pull in its wake oedipal dynamics that were previously more easily associated with the figure of the analyst.

The introduction of the drug, however it comes about, whether within the session or outside of it, is an important enactment. Its incidence in the process of analysis is difficult to predetermine, as is the case with almost all enactments, but it must, however, be managed.

But how does the analyst react to this encroachment of territory by medication? Although psychoanalysis is atoning for a certain historic diffidence with regard to drugs, it is not rare to find a "hypercorrection" of this attitude. This results in an attitude towards medication that is excessively trusting. In these cases the drug can be mistakenly attributed with the ability to affect the symptoms and the complex relationships that are closely interconnected with the psychodynamic level. If, for example, a patient should decide in a totally incongruous manner to interrupt an analytic relationship because an acute manic episode is in progress, the drug certainly has a good chance of success. If, on the other hand, what is in play is the exacerbation of borderline affectivity, its role will be secondary. The patient can thus be sent to the psychiatrist accompanied by a sort of "hyper trust" that makes his/her intervention ambiguous. Above all, this implicit delegation can have an insidious effect on the analytic relationship, which is thus burdened by an excess of desire, namely, that the transformation capable of reactivating the analysis should take place elsewhere.

In terms of joint treatment, obviously where there is not a problem of delegation, the analyst will face difficulties due to the excessively important position the drug assumes within the analysis. The reactive "solution" can be a persistent inattention towards pharmacological aspects. These are treated as little as possible during the session, and possibly in a marginal manner. This solution of course limits excessive and inappropriate interference of the drug on the analysis, but it gives rise to the dual inconvenience (one analytic, the other pharmacological) of excluding it from the transference dynamics and of not then re-evaluating it (in terms of dosage and consideration of the molecule) with the necessary frequency and rapidity. There is no denying that the analyst always needs to adopt (certainly not only through interpretation) a modulation of the transference impact of the drug. It is equally clear that this operation can be made particularly complicated by certain patients, especially those for whom taking the medication is seen as a challenge and an attack with regard to the analysis. If the attack often goes hand in hand with an excessive trust in the drug, the challenge can more subtly translate into pushing the therapist to show how the analysis can do without the drug.

In line with this, the analyst can also perceive a position of defeat, a sort of surrender to biology, which can be bolstered by the scientific and social competition between the theories. This happens above all when there is a biological and psychological conception of the psychosis in play. Assigning a patient to a pharmacological treatment, especially when colleagues view this possibility with diffidence, can trigger the conscious and preconscious sensation of betrayal of "analytic purity".

Whatever the setting, the drug can be seen as a transitional object that modifies the therapeutic relationship significantly in terms of distance and ties. It is a "third" object, which is positioned between the patient and the analyst, and as such it can have a distancing function. This function can limit the process of projective identification or the perception of an omnipotence of the intra- and inter-psychic, putting back into question the issue of limit. At the same time the drug brings out the asymbolic level of the soma, which is moreover liable to significant change. It is thus possible to see a transformation that is both humoral (of a thymic nature) and cognitive (there is a release in the "pressure" of the ideas of reference and of the delusion), which does not pass through words and symbolic exchange, but is inscribed in the *Körper*. And yet, it needs to be immediately related and rewritten in the *Leib*, meaning it is given significance, resymbolized and reconfigured in the hermeneutic sense. The tranformations of physicality and of the neurochemical framework need first and foremost to be seen in relation not to the repressed unconscious[5], but to the somatic unconscious.[6]

This means that the drug is a transitional object with a dual modality. This is most immediately evident (a) in that, as a powerful mediator of transference, as mentioned earlier, it remodulates the oedipal and preoedipal aspects and above all reconfigures the aggressive dynamic. From this point of view it serves sometimes as a good but omnipotent object, sometimes as a poisonous object, sometimes as a phallic object, activating sadomasochistic fantasies. These are evidently dynamics that belong to the repressed unconscious, and as such they require the analyst to decide whether to interpret them or convey the sense implicitly through the channels of transference-countertransference.

The drug is, however, also a transitional object, as a mediator between the representational and unrepresentable levels of the unconscious (b). This mediation no longer occurs within the dynamics relating to the transference, but rather it regards the relationship in its entirety, and involves the transformation of beta elements, which are closely linked to the body, into alpha elements. These are situated, by their nature, in that terrain that is originally "mute" where the drive to exercise its initial function of representation operates (Freud, 1915). The drug can act by reducing the anxiety of the incomprehensible, intervening on its biological bases. But it can also favor the operation, which in itself remains the competence of the analysis, of "giving a name" to the anxiety, deconstructing it into its components, as an alternative to the attribution of a sense that is conferred by the delusion and by the psychotic insight. This does not mean interpreting, or worse still "explaining", the delusion. Rather, it means re-establishing the thinking apparatus; that is, the formal structure within which representation can take place, or better still, within which the representation, no longer "off limits", can finally interact with the unrepresentable.[7]

Learning from experience (and from failure)

The complexity of the integration between pharmacological and psychoanalytic treatment, and the extreme variability from situation to situation, makes it difficult to find good examples. It is possible, however, to differentiate between the possible settings, broadly proposing a tripartition between the unified setting, the differentiated setting and, finally, the uncoded setting. I include among the latter those treatments, usual in an institutional setting, where the frequency and duration of the meetings are not defined; their value is at the same time psychiatric and psychotherapeutic, and the "action" (e.g. in terms of rehabilitative and group activity) accompanies or takes precedence over the "talking therapies".

A brief discussion of some clinical situations, which will be illustrated in relation to the types of settings adopted, may thus be useful.

Bipolar disorder and the risks of the unified setting

The patient, affected by a bipolar 1 disorder, arrives with an urgent request for pharmacological treatment. He expresses at the same time a positive attitude with regard to analysis, together with numerous resistances that are resolved only after several sessions that aim at establishing the drug therapy. This makes the choice of a unified treatment the "natural" one. In the first three years of analysis depressive type dynamics are prevalent. Sergio takes a mood stabilizer regularly, which is then suspended by mutual agreement given the constant improvement. In the fourth year, however, for the first time since beginning analysis, he presents a manic episode. It does not appear particularly serious, but it is enough to persuade me, pressured also by family members, to organize (by means of a telephone call to colleagues during a session) a brief period of hospitalization. To all appearances, this proves decidedly favorable, with discharge less than a week from admission and his immediate return to his busy professional life.

After a period in which the patient's attitude is of gratitude and there is an idealization of the experience in hospital, there is a phase of closing off and of somber and dysphoric mood (a sort of mixed state) that results in violent outbursts against both the analysis and the analyst.

Initially the rebukes refer to the fact that it was me who had suggested and organized the admission to hospital, and that I had not noticed his disorder in time. (In actual fact, several weeks beforehand I had prescribed medication that he had refused to take.) He also accuses me of not giving him adequate information about his illness, of agreeing to be contacted by his family and of meeting his wife (in his presence). This then leads to his blaming me for not dealing with his relationship with the bipolar disorder and with his sick Self in the analysis. He attributes the responsibility for this to me alone, expressing strong feelings of abandonment. This results in an outpouring of accusatory rage.

It is useless trying to point out to him that the problems with the analysis stem instead from my not being able to touch sufficiently deeply and in an appropriately "felt" way his frequent swings from a sense of abandonment and disappointment to the experience of persecution. We had so often seen this in action "from the outside" with reference to his colleagues. Now we finally had the opportunity to see it in a way that was more direct and affecting for both of us in the context of our relationship. It is no use repeating to him that from this point of view the critical episode could be an important opportunity for us to take advantage of, and that it seemed decidedly inappropriate to end the analysis before dealing with this and at least in part elaborating this negative transference. Sergio decides to abandon the analysis and cannot be convinced to change his mind. He later renews contact by email, and he softens in his position, even expressing gratitude, though he refrains from meeting again.

It is probable that the patient could not accept the fact that the analysis did not "protect" him from the emergence of a new manic episode. In some way the dysphoria that was not present during the critical episode (characterized rather by euphoria) emerged later and played out above all at the transference level. The analyst is experienced in retrospect both as having been unable to predict (despite the repeated prescriptions and the disregarded recommendations to take them) and as the controller who organized the hospitalization.

In the case of mood disorders, the patient perceives the discontinuity with the Self in a violent manner. Pharmacological treatment in conditions of crisis, and to a greater extent the prescription of hospitalization, can therefore be experienced as the intrusion of a factor of non-metabolizable reality into the analytic setting, which is however interwoven with predominantly symbolic relationships. The analytic and psychiatric functions themselves, even though present in the same person, are perceived as violently split. In this way the one negates and nullifies the other, in exactly the same way that the depressive Self and the manic Self cancel each other out.

Another situation that presents the elements of discontinuity, and where the unified setting is at risk, is the treatment of severe hysteria and hysterical psychosis. In these cases, however, the risk is determined not by humoral alternation but by dissociative mechanisms. As there is an active use of interpretation against psychoanalysis (Bollas, 1999), so there is also an active manipulation of the pharmacological treatment. The result is a continuous and confusing exchange of investments between the drug and the analysis, which suggests caution when separating the treatments.[8]

Acute psychosis, schizophrenia and the benefits of the unified setting

In contrast to the diagnoses indicated earlier, in the case of schizophrenic disorders the unified setting presents the greatest benefits. This is fundamentally due to the possibility of favoring a perception of mind-body integration and of reducing disappearance and annihilation anxieties. This can also benefit from the "concrete" dimension of the relationship, which can make use of the drug object. Paradoxically, the schizophrenic patient can perceive its symbolic value more than other patients, perhaps precisely because his/her mode of symbolization is closely linked to a constant interchange and equivalence. Naturally, while this promotes the perception of the drug as a nutritious object, it also means it can easily be perceived as a persecutory and threatening object. However, these oscillations between bad object and good object can make the analysis fertile territory for transformation, indicating that it is appropriate to continue to combine the psychoanalytic and pharmacological treatments. When, after long periods of difficulty, the analytic relationship with the schizophrenic has finally stabilized, he/she will easily perceive that the dynamics of the analytic relationship, especially those confronting nameless anxiety and the unrepresentable unconscious, develop also thanks to the drug that is offered as nourishment for the mind. It is precisely when the drug loses its original meaning (which is often that of a threatening, poisonous and controlling object) that it can acquire a restorative value not only in relational terms, but also with regard to the thinking apparatus, thus favoring the emergence of representation, also in dreams.[9]

The unified treatment can develop much more easily during a continuous analytic treatment following an acute psychotic episode.

Giovanna is fifty years old when I take her on in analysis after a period of hospitalization. This is linked to a *bouffée delirante*, reactive to an accident involving her son. The accident was serious, but the prognosis was good.

The event reactivated, however, the memory of a similar but fatal accident that had involved her first husband thirty years before. The prevalence of depressive elements would seem to indicate a diagnosis of a "major depressive episode with mood-incongruent psychotic features" (which was the diagnosis on her discharge from hospital). However, the rapid resolution of the delusional phase and the presence of confusional elements (lasting three weeks) suggest a "brief psychotic disorder". This is followed by a prolonged depressive period with marked apathy and abulia. The patient is treated in analysis for a total of four years, with concomitant pharmacological treatment for the first two.[10] At the end of this period she makes an excellent recovery, both in terms of her relational capacity and her reacquisition of the ability to work. An illustration of her relational capacity is that she is able to deal with the serious illness of a very close friend. The positive transference that has accompanied the analytic relationship from the beginning has also developed towards the drug, which has at the same time strengthened the positive transference. This has perhaps occurred thanks to the (fortuitous?) total absence of side effects. In these cases the drug object takes on the value of a "gift" within the relationship, which is not devoid of erotic aspects, although these tend to be sublimated. In these situations the reassuring aspect of the transitional object raises if anything the problem of separation from the drugs, which represents an important evolutionary stage. In fact, postponing the separation from the drugs can increase the risk of dependence, and it must therefore be envisioned as an essential watershed in the concluding phases of the analysis, in order to prevent the transitional object from becoming an object of dependence.

Separate settings: the analyst as pharmacological consultant

The situation of separate settings is probably the one that receives the most credit within the psychoanalytic community, and it is perhaps still the most frequently adopted. It is moreover unavoidable, theoretical options aside, when the analyst does not have medical training. As far as separate settings are concerned, however, there are various possibilities that range, for example, from an extremely "discrete" intervention by the consultant pharmacologist to one that is inevitably "massive".

When the pharmacologist is also an analyst – and there are many reasons to support this – it is to a certain extent advisable to "forget" this analytical role, so as to avoid the risk of being too "invasive".

Giorgio is a seventeen-year-old teenager who is referred to the mental health service by an analyst who at the same time also sends him to another colleague to start analysis four times a week.[11] He presents a symptomatology characterized by anxiety, depersonalization, perplexity and disorganized delusion. This meets the criteria of "schizophrenic disorder", with the exception of the temporal criteria since the symptomatology is resolved rapidly, within two months, thus indicating a "schizophreniform disorder". My role as a psychiatrist in the public health service is initially quite active, with frequent periodic interviews and regular contact with the family. Once the acute episode has been resolved and a good analytical process has been established, I decide to move progressively into the background (with occasional short meetings, initially once a month, then bi-monthly and finally every six months). Pharmacological treatment is interrupted at the end of the second year of the analysis, while the analysis continues for a further four years. In this case, given the intensive analytic treatment, the good working alliance and the absence of new psychotic episodes, it seems inappropriate to encourage the activation of collateral transference. In my role as a psychiatrist, I must rather accept the mourning of a relationship that, though short, is deep and meaningful, as is inevitably the case at the moment of the psychotic crisis. I try, therefore, to limit my role to the diagnostic and symptomatic evaluation on which changes to the pharmacological therapy depend (in this case, a progressive reduction from 7.5 mg of olanzapine to suspension of treatment). The patient's inevitable fantasies regarding the psychiatrist and the pharmacological setting are also delegated to the analysis. Unless they create conflicts related to drug therapy (as in the case in question), it is not advisable that they are addressed by the psychiatrist–analyst, nor that they are brought to his/her attention.

In contrast, in other situations, a more complex intervention may be necessary (in the institutional field this is called "patient management"). This involves the psychiatric management of repeated crises and of family conflicts. It also involves intervening with regard to rehabilitation.

Carlo is sent to me by his analyst, who is starting therapy with him four times a week[12] following hospitalization abroad due to an acute psychotic episode. From the beginning the picture is clearly very complex and difficult to diagnose. There are composite personality traits (narcissistic, histrionic, paranoid and even schizoid), conduct disorders, substance abuse and frequent brief acute psychotic episodes accompanied by more persistent mood disorders, especially of a dysphoric and manic nature. This would seem to indicate a diagnosis of "personality disorder" of cluster B and a syndromic diagnosis that is initially identified as "schizophreniform episode", but this diagnosis is then corrected as "mood disorder" with frequent "manic episodes with psychotic symptoms". With such a configuration I am evidently required to intervene in a complex way. I am also called upon to construct a relationship that, as is normal in an institutional setting, also presents significant aspects of control that cannot fail to be in conflict with the attempt to build a therapeutic alliance.

In particular, with Carlo I have to undertake the complex task of modulation of the drug therapy, with frequent changes in medication and dosage (risperidone, sodium valproate, quetiapine) in a situation of variable compliance. I am also involved in mediating with the family, as part of a rehabilitation program developed within a Day Hospital, and called on to discuss the frequent hospitalizations with hospital colleagues. The last of these, which I initiated and managed under emergency conditions, required the presence of law enforcement agencies. The relationship will start to suffer as a result of this episode, leading to its conclusion (though not in an openly conflictual form). It will subsequently be possible to program the conclusion of the analysis. Moreover, Carlo continues his journey towards independence, strengthening his ability to relate to the outside world, also by means of these challenging and provocative behaviors, which are sometimes exacerbated (but not determined) by episodes of manic excitement. The result is a progressive abandoning of "psychotic" solutions and a more fruitful confrontation with his emotions of anger, hatred and aggression.

In this case the psychiatrist, who although extremely involved is still much more detached than the analyst in terms of the emotional experience with the patient, is invested with significant collateral transference. This may mitigate aggressive transference within the analytic relationship through projective mechanisms towards the psychiatrist that are not entirely inappropriate. While on the one hand these mechanisms can favor operations of separation (the sufficiently good analyst and the sufficiently bad psychiatrist), on the other hand they allow the analytic setting to be relatively relieved of the burden and hindrance of reality events (hospitalizations, rejection of drug therapy, management of conflicts with parents) that would risk determining an implosion. Thus a dual protective function of the setting is established. On the one hand, this is entrusted to the drug, where continuous calibration of the dosage ensures that the sedation necessary to reduce behavioral disorders is not excessive. On the other hand, it is entrusted to the figure of the psychiatrist, who takes on a paternal-normative role, which, if this were so strong within the analytic setting, would upset the balance between the analyst as a person and the analyst as object of unconscious fantasies and symbolic investments.

Uncodified setting: there is method, despite everything!

We will now touch on the work of an analyst, who is also a psychiatrist, outside the analytic setting. This is a very frequent occurrence in institutional work, but also not unusual in private practice. This can refer, for example, to those patients who arrive with a request for psychiatric counseling but are unable to access analysis, which would be the preferred treatment, due to resistance or economic hardship. In these cases the work of the psychiatrist–psychoanalyst involves developing a clear picture of the situation by means of a psychodynamic diagnosis and subsequently through analytic listening. This will have a significant effect on the prescription of drugs. For the first operation, the analyst will benefit in only a very limited way from the current diagnostic manuals, DSM 5 or ICD 10. It is commonly known that these give priority to the symptomatic aspect, while neglecting the dimensional side. Unfortunately they ignore the complexity and variety of the psychotic world (which was well defined by European psychopathology in the last century). In contrast, the diagnostic evaluation of the analyst is comprehensive and based on a psychoanalytic psychopathology that derives from the connection between the clinical theory of psychoanalysis and general psychopathology (K. Jaspers) and phenomenology (L. Binswanger, K. Bin, W. Blankenburg, B. Callieri, etc.).

Gabriele, aged fifty, arrives in my consulting room after a two-month hospitalization in a psychiatric ward[13] and then in a private clinic. The hospitalization was carried out under emergency conditions following the escalation of a psychotic condition that had persisted for more than two years, characterized by ideas of persecution and auditory hallucinations. (He reported that the neighbors, disturbed by his noises, sent him sarcastic comments through the walls and, a few days before admission, they had said to each other "we have to liquidate him!"). At the time of the first interview the symptoms have decreased in intensity, but criticism is partial, and, above all, the patient complains of marked sedation and extrapyramidal side effects. In reality, beyond the symptomatic picture, he shows a distinctly introverted personality with schizoid traits and a lack of openness towards social relationships. Nevertheless, he has been married for nearly ten years, although his wife has distanced herself from him since the hospitalization period (and they will soon separate). Rather than a "schizoaffective disorder", the picture seems to be what classical psychopathology defined as *Sensitive Beziehungswahn* (Kretsmecher, 1918). This is a form of delusion with characteristics of persistence and a tendency to repetition, brought on by particularly intense or problematic interpersonal relationships that arises in extremely introverted and sensitive personalities. For these individuals involvement with others requires an unusual emotional commitment. Despite his pronounced introversion and schizoid traits, Gabriele immediately establishes a strongly empathetic relationship with me, progressively developing full awareness of his ideas of reference. These will occasionally reappear, in a very weak form; when this occurs they are immediately criticized in an appropriate manner. Together with these ideas there emerge dysperceptive phenomena of a compulsive character described as "loud thoughts that develop in spite of myself inside my head". Since for economic reasons the patient is unable to undertake either analytical or psychotherapeutic treatment, the relationship work has developed through meetings that take place approximately once every three months. Over this time the pharmacological therapy is modified (with a switch from haloperidol to paliperidone) in order to reduce side effects, and the dosage is later reduced (6 to 3 mg of paliperidone). Above all, however, analytic listening is activated, which undoubtedly represents the most important part of the work. At a strictly pharmacological level, in fact, after the first meetings, only marginal corrections are necessary (the addition of a serotonergic drug for short periods to better contain the obsessive symptomatology). The work is thus organized to support Gabriele (with occasional interpretations) and enable him to navigate his way better in the context of a new and lasting relationship with a woman with personality characteristics similar to his. I work in particular to create a *holding* environment perceived by the patient as a constant point of reference, despite the sporadic nature of our meetings. The function of the drug thus emerges quite explicitly as facilitating the construction of such an environment, within which it is then of limited significance.

Returning to the method . . .

In light of the preceding considerations, some possible lines of development emerge for the study of the relationship between analytic and pharmacological treatment of psychotic conditions:

a   We must proceed, in agreement with the neuroscience, with the development of a model that can combine the theoretical incommensurability of the mind and the brain with the clinical need for treatments based on a conception of *the human being as a whole* (Jaspers, 1959) and of his/her profound and constitutive interaction with the environment.[14] Those contributions that improve our conception of the unrepressed unconscious can contribute significantly to the construction of this model.

b   We need to continue to reflect on the problem of integrating treatment, bearing in mind that it does not come about as a result of a simple theoretical option, but requires continuous effort with no guarantee of success. *Integration comes at the end, not at the beginning.* We must also be aware that opting for integration does not mean opting for ecumenism. Rather, eclecticism, "mindless" psychiatry and "brainless" psychiatry are three positions that are absolutely incompatible with the foundations of psychoanalysis.

c   A "diagnostic" evaluation, carried out in the light of psychoanalytic psychopathology, can provide the first reliable indications, which will then be completed with more specific considerations regarding the relational dimension and transference relating to the individual case.

d   From an operative viewpoint, the pharmacological treatment can clash with the analytic treatment. This sometimes happens in macroscopic form, e.g. where it is provided by a biological psychiatrist, who may be openly hostile to psychoanalysis. But our attention must turn to the less obvious implicit conflicts. Above all we must be careful to understand the reciprocity between the transformation of the underlying neurochemical structure that occurs during the analysis, and the psychic transformations that occur during the pharmacological treatment.

e   Ultimately, the drug can be considered the factor that, by enabling a somatic transformation, promotes a greater gradient of freedom of the psyche. This greater freedom, deriving from the corrections made at the level of neurochemical mediators, can result in the greater transformative potential of the psyche itself. At the same time we need to be aware of how the drug promotes transformation at the level of the "somatic unconscious". It intervenes at the beginning of the path that leads from instinctual representative (*Triebrepräsentanz*) to the representation of things and from here to the representation of words. In this way it plays an essential role in the modulation (neurochemical and non-symbolic) of the circle between the representable and unrepresentable. This same circle will be further modulated, this time symbolically, through the analytic work. The pharmacological therapy and the analytic work, technically so far apart, necessarily rejoin with a view to transforming the *body I have – a dumb body* – into *the body that I am – a hermeneutic body*.

Notes

1 This chapter has been translated into English by Christine Tracey.
2 For a more extended discussion, see Martini, 1998.
3 This mode of action is often inappropriately strengthened by aggressive countertransference factors that manic patients are particularly adept at eliciting.
4 I will return to this idea in the conclusion.
5 As we have seen in these cases the risk is that of finding a somewhat paradoxical explanation for the drug's action; for example, like that of Ostow regarding drives.
6 For Jaspers the true unconscious is fundamentally linked to somato-biological processes and can never become conscious. This unconscious is ultimately not experienced (Jaspers, 1959). Although far removed from, and in contrast with, Freud's repressed unconscious, this position is consonant with Bion's "thoughts without a thinker" (1967) and with his reference to those psychotic patients who experience pain but do not suffer with it (Bion, 1967).
7 See Martini, 2005.
8 For a clinical discussion of this see Martini, 2011, pp. 217–219.
9 For a description of a schizophrenic patient in analysis who was treated with a progressively reduced drug dose, and for whom these reflections are relevant, see Martini, 2011, pp. 157–160.
10 An antidepressant (venlafaxine) administered in a non-continuous manner and an atypical antipsychotic (olanzapine, starting from a dosage of 10 mg). The olanzapine was given both as a mood stabilizer and to prevent new psychotic episodes.
11 The analysis is described in Lombardi and Pola, 2010.
12 The work with this patient is described in Lombardi, 2007.
13 In Italy: SPDC, Servizio Psichiatrico di Diagnosi e Cura (Psychiatric Diagnosis and Treatment Service). This consists of fifteen-bed wards in General Hospitals.
14 It is useful here to remember Jaspers' affirmation (1959) that the misunderstanding that damages psychiatry is due to the fact that it ignores the nature of its subject, which is represented by man as person. For the philosopher man, in his totality, is beyond any possible objectivization.

References and further readings

Alfonso, C.A. (2009). Dynamic psychopharmacology and treatment adherence. *J Amer Acad Psychoanal* 37 (2): 269–285.

American Psychiatric Association. (2013). *Diagnostic and Statistical Manual of Mental Disorders* (5th ed.). Arlington, VA: American Psychiatric Association.

Binswanger, L. (1965). *Wahn*. Pfullingen: Verlag Günther Neske.

Bion, W.R. (1967). *Second Thoughts (Selected Paper of Psychoanalysis)*. London: William Heinemann Medical Books.

Bollas, C. (1999). *Hysteria*. Oxford: Routledge.

Feinsilver, D.B. (1996). Therapist as "mentsh" and the integrated treatment of schizophrenia. *Conference hold in Rome*, June 1996.

Freud, A. (1968). *cit. in* Lebovitz, 2004.

Freud, S. (1915). *Papers on Metapsychology* (Standard ed., Vol. 14). London: The Hogart Press, 1978.

Goolker, P. (1964). Drugs in psychoanalysis and psychotherapy: By Mortimer Ostow. *Psychoanalytic Quarterly* 33: 285–286.

Grotstein, J.S. (2003). Towards the concept of 'rehabilitative psychoanalytic psychotherapy' in the treatment of schizophrenia. In Grispini, A. (Editor), *Preventive Strategies for Schizophrenic Disorders*. Roma: Fioriti.

Jaspers, K. (1959). *Allgemeine Psychopathologie*. Berlin: Springer-Verlag.

Kandel, E.R. (1998). *cit. in* Lebovitz, 2004.

Kretsmecher, E. (1918). *Der sensitive Beziehungswahn*. Berlin: Springer.

Lebovitz, P.S. (2004). Integrating psychoanalysis and psychopharmacology: A review of the literature of combined treatment for affective disorders. *The Journal of the American Academy of Psychoanalysis and Dynamic Psychiatry* 32: 585–596.

Lipton, M. (1983). *cit. in* Lebovitz, 2004.

Lombardi, R. (2007). Shame in relation to the body, sex, and death: A clinical exploration of the psychotic levels of shame. *Psychoanalytic Dialogues* 17: 385–399.

Lombardi, R., and Pola, M. (2010). The body, adolescence, and psychosis. *International Journal of Psychoanalysis* 91: 1419–1444.

Malitz, S. (1963–64). Drugs in psychoanalysis and psychotherapy: By Mortimer Ostow. *Psychoanalytic Review* 50D: 159–161.

Mallo, C.J., and Mintz, D.L. (2013). Teaching all the evidence bases: Reintegrating psychodynamic aspects of prescribing into psychopharmacology training. *Psychodynamic Psychiatry* 41 (1): 13–37.

Martini, G. (1998). *Ermeneutica e Narrazione. Un percorso tra Psichiatria e Psicoanalisi*. Torino: Bollati Boringhieri.

Martini, G. (2005). *La sfida dell'irrappresentabile. La prospettiva ermeneutica nella psicoanalisi clinica*. Milano: Franco Angeli.

Martini, G. (2011). *La psicosi e la rappresentazione*. Roma: Borla.

Melega, V., and Fioritti, A. (1991). Fondamenti di psichiatria. Considerazioni su psicoanalisi e biologia. In margine al caso "Osheroff vs. Chestnut Lodge". *Psicoterapia e Scienze Umane* XXV (3): 127–136.

Mintz, D., and Belnap, B. (2006). A view from riggs: Treatment resistance and patient authority. III. What is psychodinamic psychopharmacology? An approach to pharmacologic treatment resistance. *The Journal of the American Academy of Psychoanalysis and Dynamic Psychiatry* 34: 581–601.

Ostow, M. (1962). *Drugs in Psychoanalysis and Psychotherapy*. New York: Basic Books.

Rickles, W.H. (2006). Listening to prozac, with the third ear: A psychoanalytic theory of psychopharmacology. *The Journal of the American Academy of Psychoanalysis and Dynamic Psychiatry* 34: 709–733.

Ricoeur, P. (2001). *La traduzione. Una sfida etica*. Brescia: Morcelliana.

Rubin, J. (2001). Countertransference factors in the psychology of psychopharmacology. *The Journal of the American Academy of Psychoanalysis and Dynamic Psychiatry* 29: 565–574.

Silvio, J.R., and Condemarin, R. (2011). Psychodinamic psychiatrists and psychopharmacology. *The Journal of the American Academy of Psychoanalysis and Dynamic Psychiatry* 39 (1): 27–39.

Wing Li, T.C. (2010). Psychodynamics aspects of psychopharmacology. *The Journal of the American Academy of Psychoanalysis and Dynamic Psychiatry* 38 (4): 655–674.

Zetzel, E.R. (1970). *cit. in* Rickels, 2006.

Index